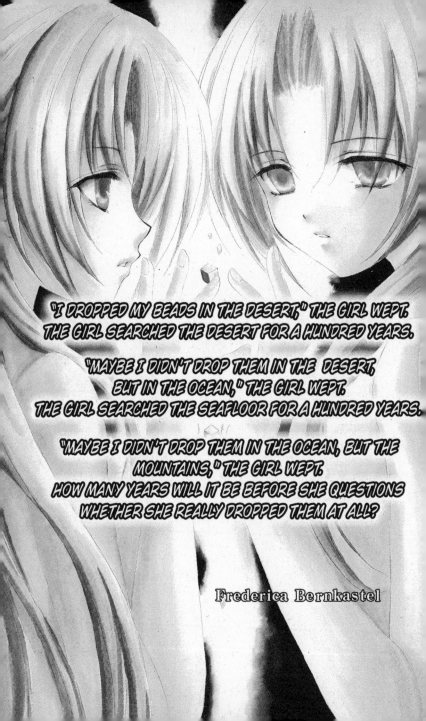

"I DROPPED MY BEADS IN THE DESERT," THE GIRL WEPT.
THE GIRL SEARCHED THE DESERT FOR A HUNDRED YEARS.

"MAYBE I DIDN'T DROP THEM IN THE DESERT,
BUT IN THE OCEAN," THE GIRL WEPT.
THE GIRL SEARCHED THE SEAFLOOR FOR A HUNDRED YEARS.

"MAYBE I DIDN'T DROP THEM IN THE OCEAN, BUT THE
MOUNTAINS," THE GIRL WEPT.
HOW MANY YEARS WILL IT BE BEFORE SHE QUESTIONS
WHETHER SHE REALLY DROPPED THEM AT ALL?

Frederica Bernkastel

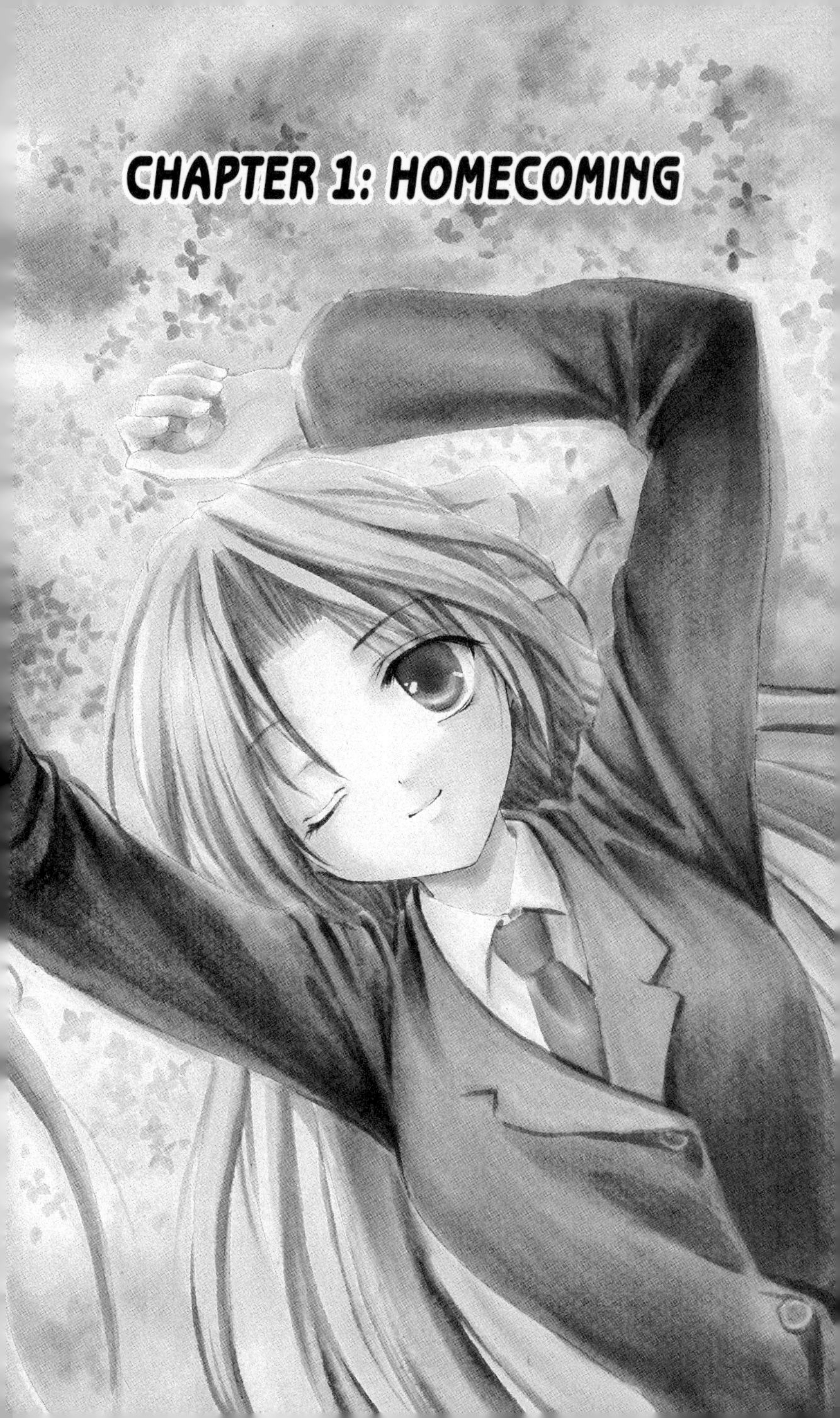
CHAPTER 1: HOMECOMING

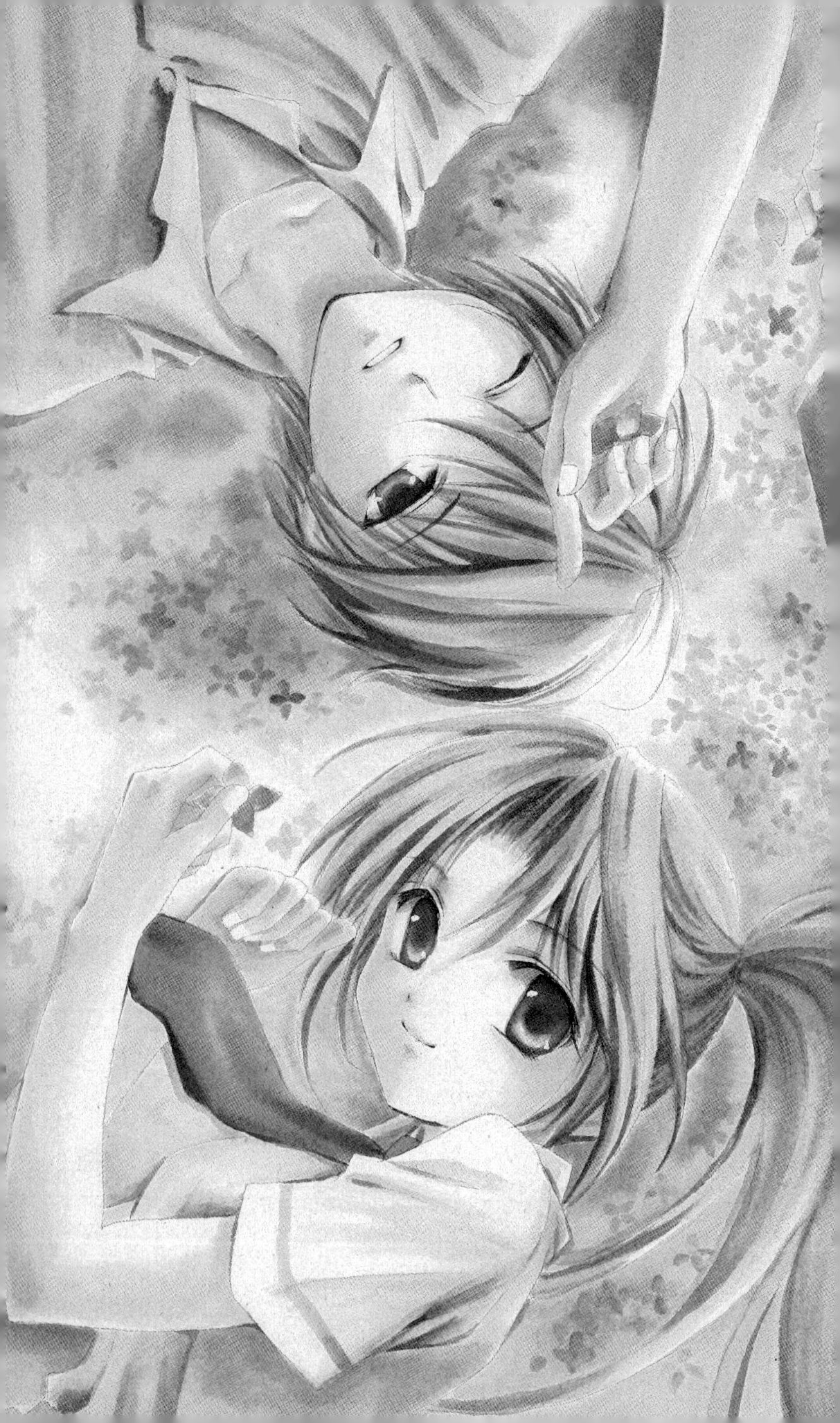

Higurashi
WHEN THEY CRY
EYE OPENING ARC

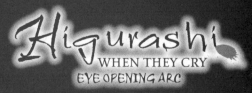

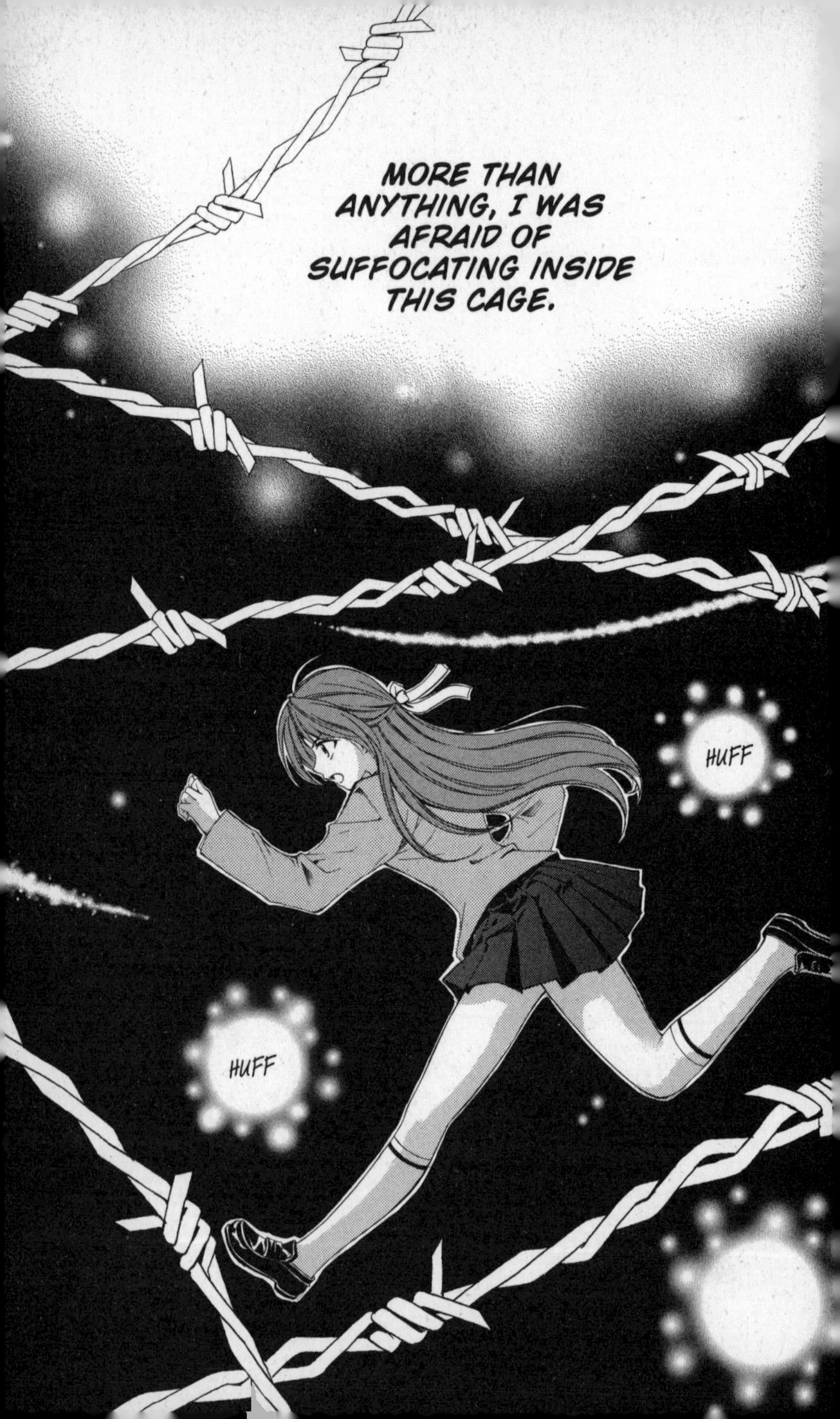
MORE THAN ANYTHING, I WAS AFRAID OF SUFFOCATING INSIDE THIS CAGE.
HUFF
HUFF

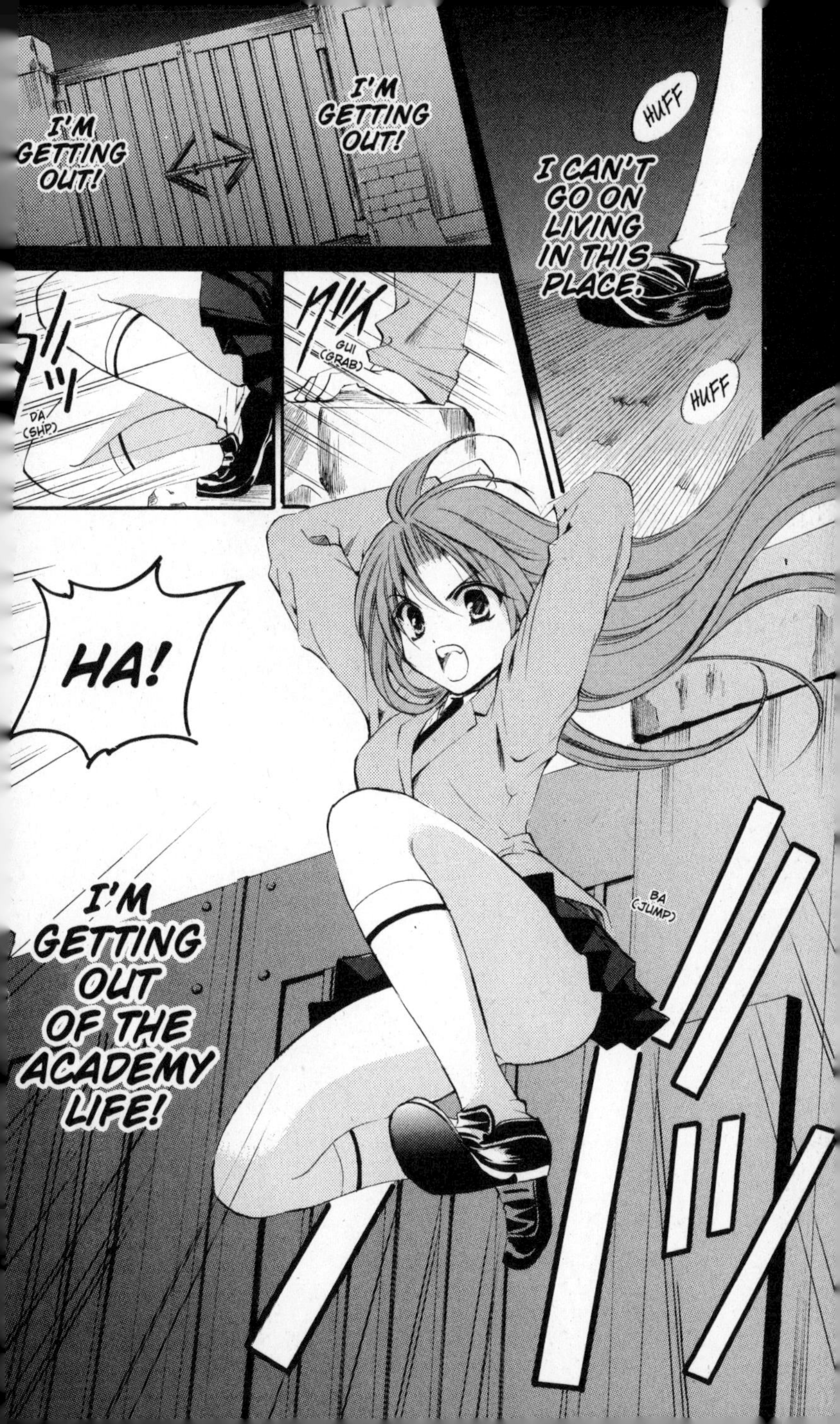
HUFF
I CAN'T GO ON LIVING IN THIS PLACE.
HUFF
I'M GETTING OUT!
I'M GETTING OUT!
GUI (GRAB)
DA (SHP)
HA!
BA (JUMP)
I'M GETTING OUT OF THE ACADEMY LIFE!

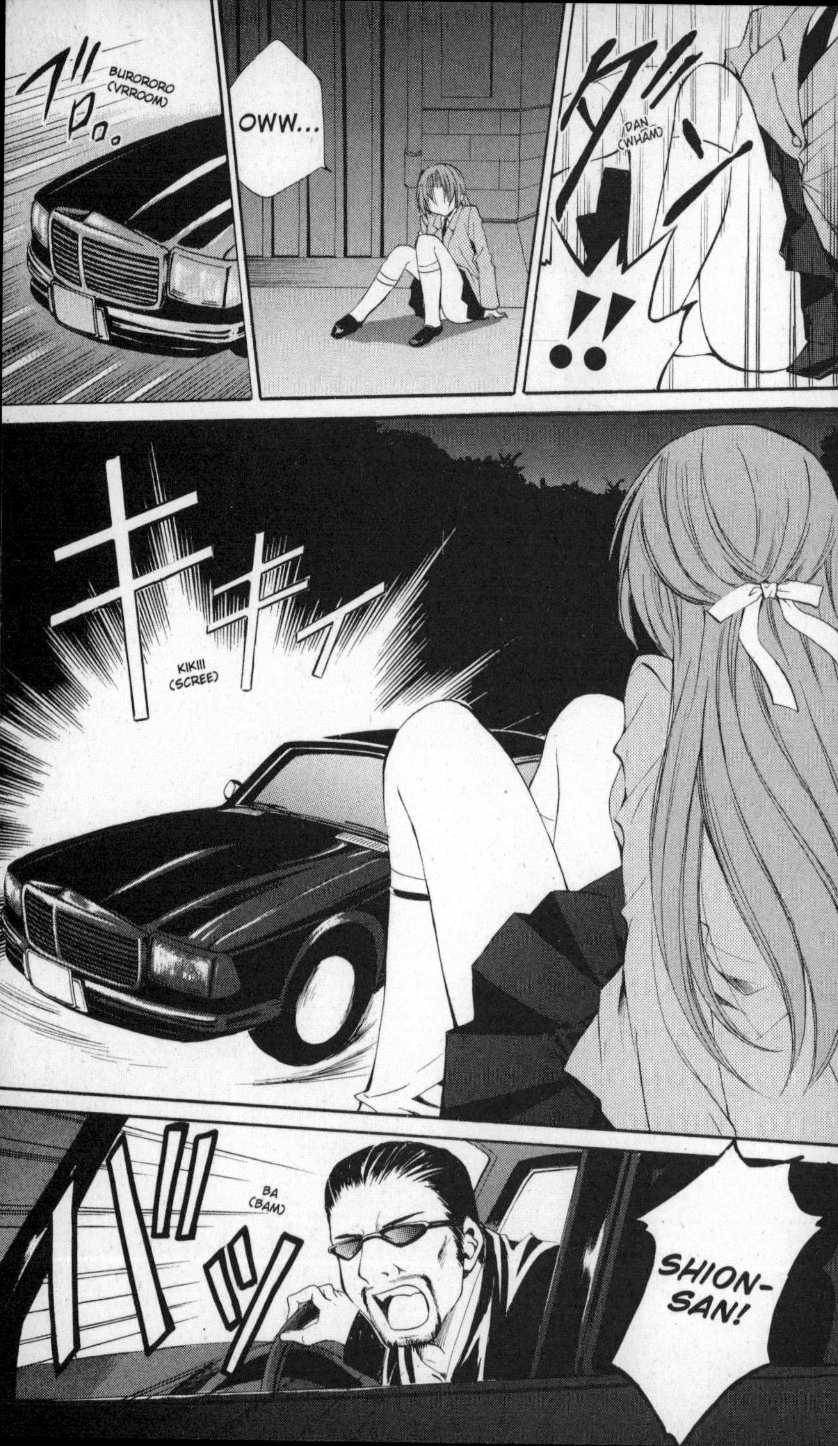
DAN (WHAM)
!!
OWW...
BURORORO (VRROOM)
KIKIII (SCREE)
SHION-SAN!
BA (BAM)

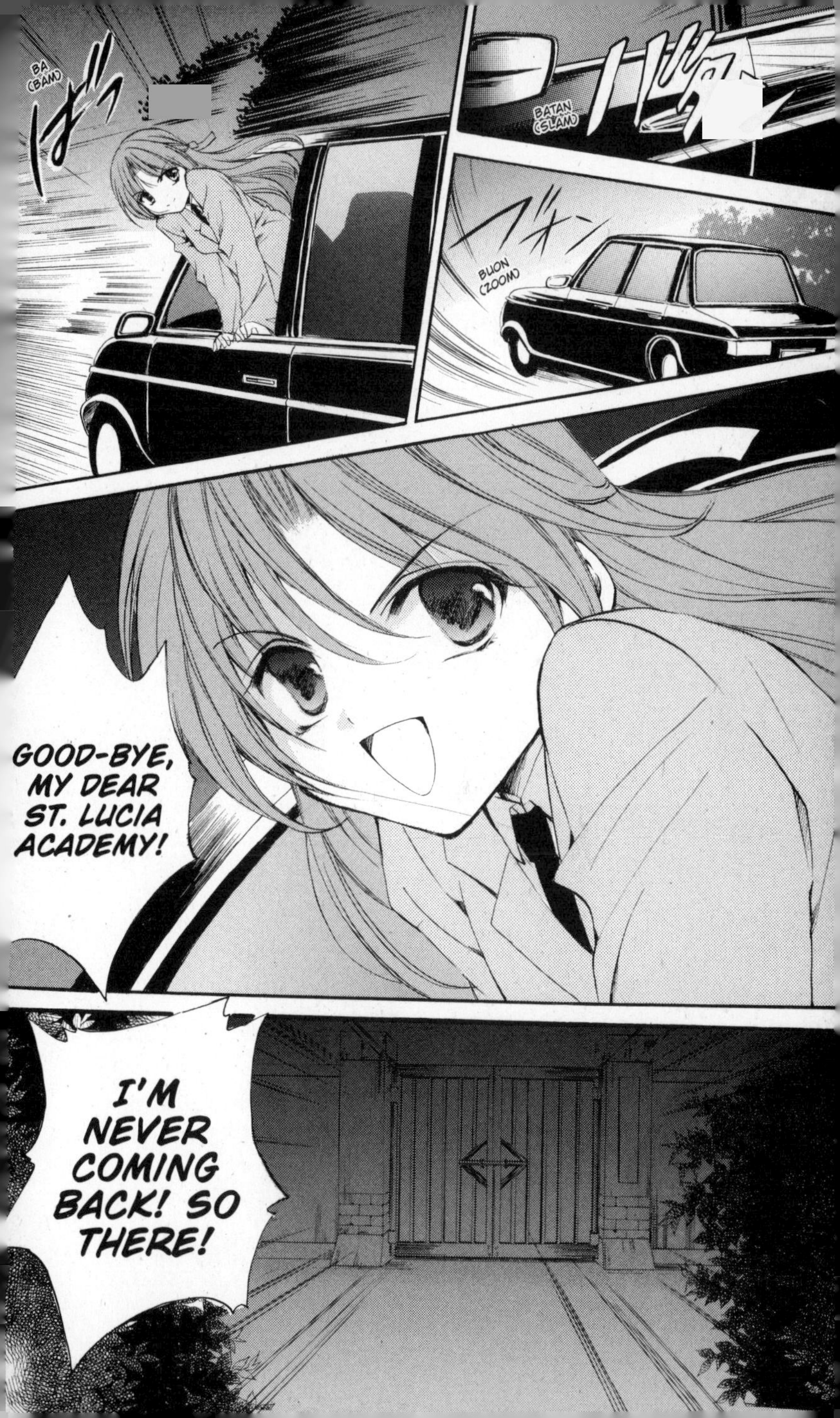
BATAN (SLAM)
BUON (ZOOM)
BA (BAM)
GOOD-BYE, MY DEAR ST. LUCIA ACADEMY!
I'M NEVER COMING BACK! SO THERE!

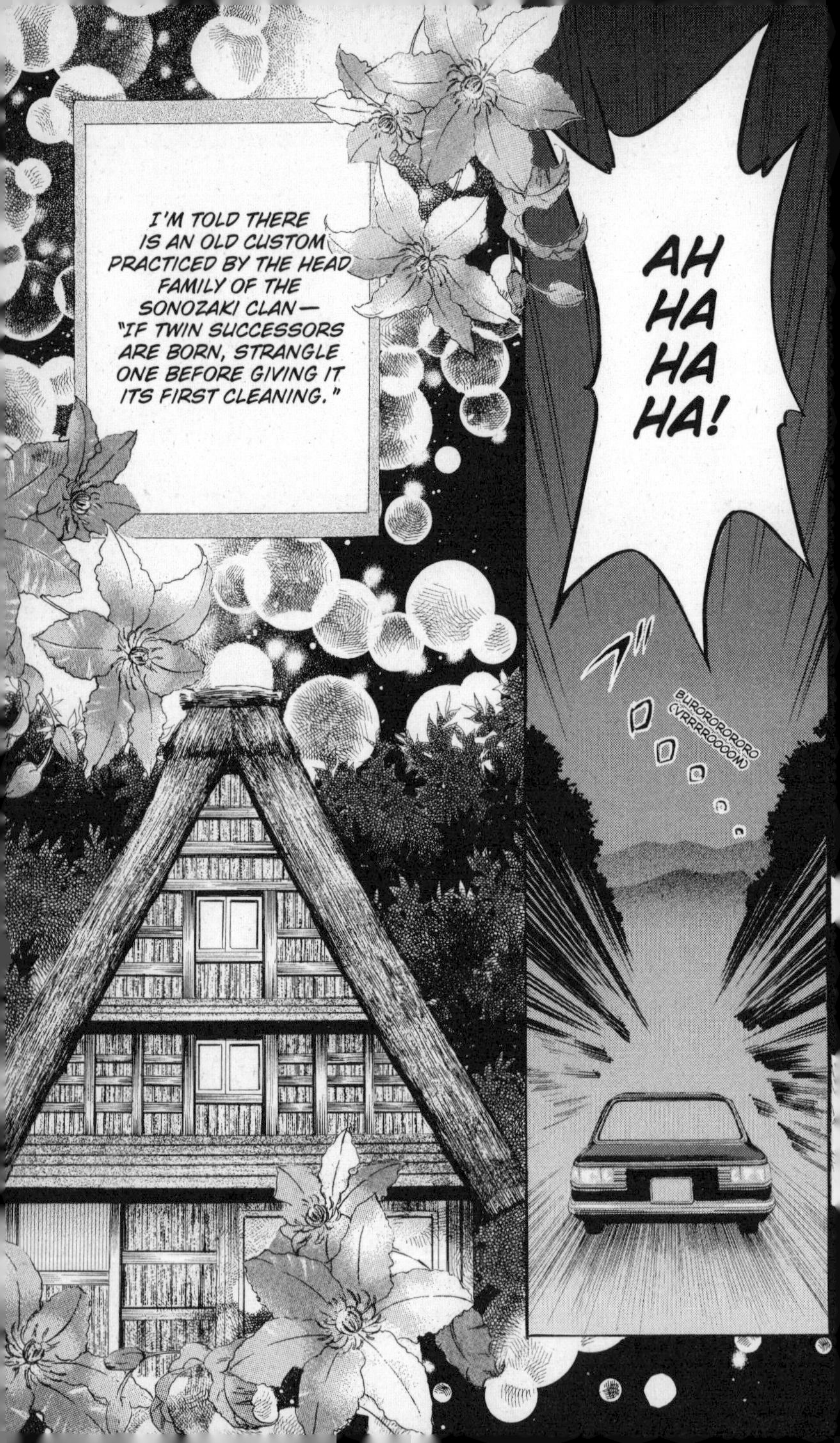
AH HA HA HA!
BURORORORORO (VRRRROOOOM)
I'M TOLD THERE IS AN OLD CUSTOM PRACTICED BY THE HEAD FAMILY OF THE SONOZAKI CLAN— "IF TWIN SUCCESSORS ARE BORN, STRANGLE ONE BEFORE GIVING IT ITS FIRST CLEANING."

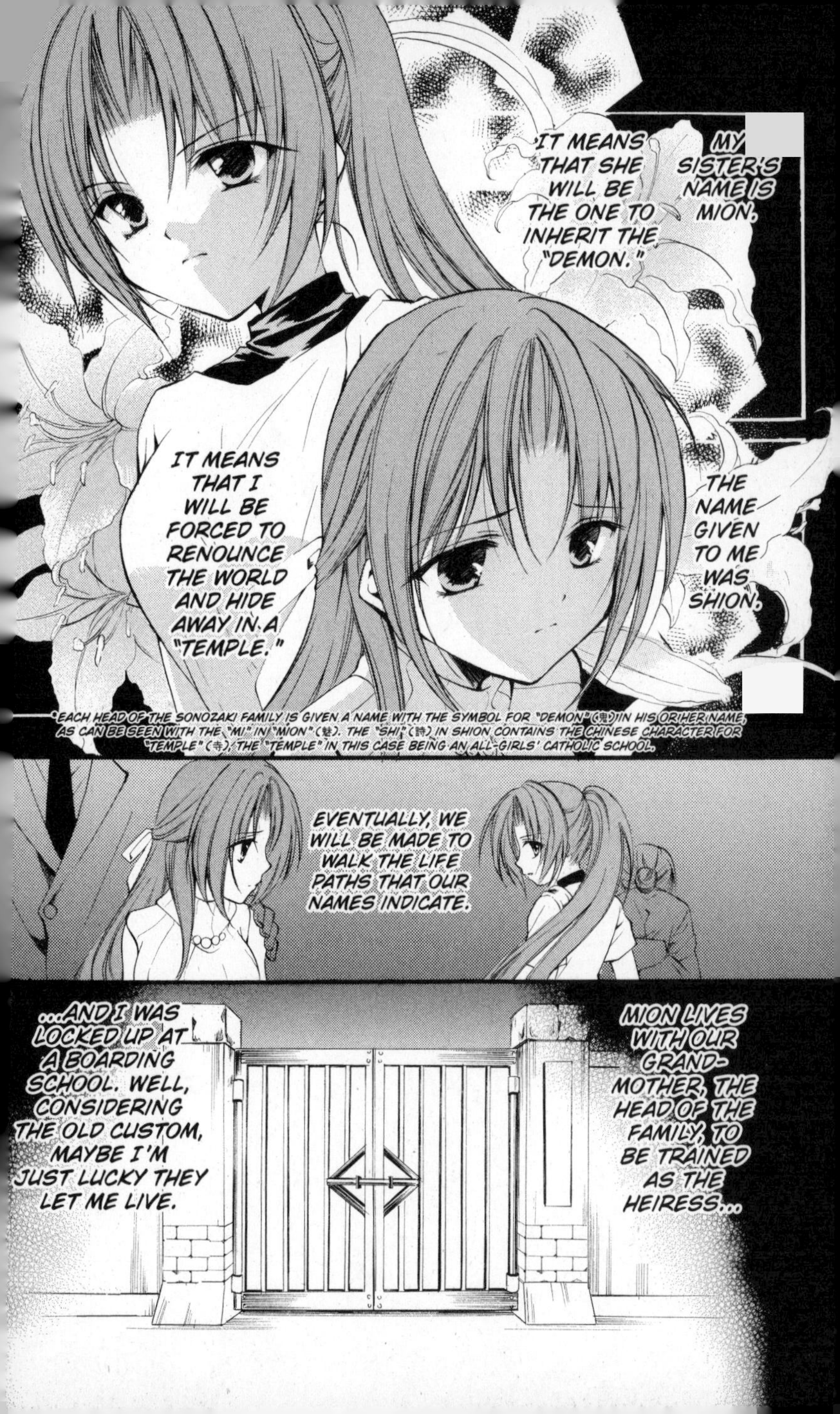
MY SISTER'S NAME IS MION.
IT MEANS THAT SHE WILL BE THE ONE TO INHERIT THE "DEMON."
THE NAME GIVEN TO ME WAS SHION.
IT MEANS THAT I WILL BE FORCED TO RENOUNCE THE WORLD AND HIDE AWAY IN A "TEMPLE."
*EACH HEAD OF THE SONOZAKI FAMILY IS GIVEN A NAME WITH THE SYMBOL FOR "DEMON" (鬼) IN HIS OR HER NAME, AS CAN BE SEEN WITH THE "MI" IN "MION" (魅). THE "SHI" (詩) IN SHION CONTAINS THE CHINESE CHARACTER FOR "TEMPLE" (寺), THE "TEMPLE" IN THIS CASE BEING AN ALL-GIRLS' CATHOLIC SCHOOL.
EVENTUALLY, WE WILL BE MADE TO WALK THE LIFE PATHS THAT OUR NAMES INDICATE.
MION LIVES WITH OUR GRAND-MOTHER, THE HEAD OF THE FAMILY, TO BE TRAINED AS THE HEIRESS...
...AND I WAS LOCKED UP AT A BOARDING SCHOOL. WELL, CONSIDERING THE OLD CUSTOM, MAYBE I'M JUST LUCKY THEY LET ME LIVE.

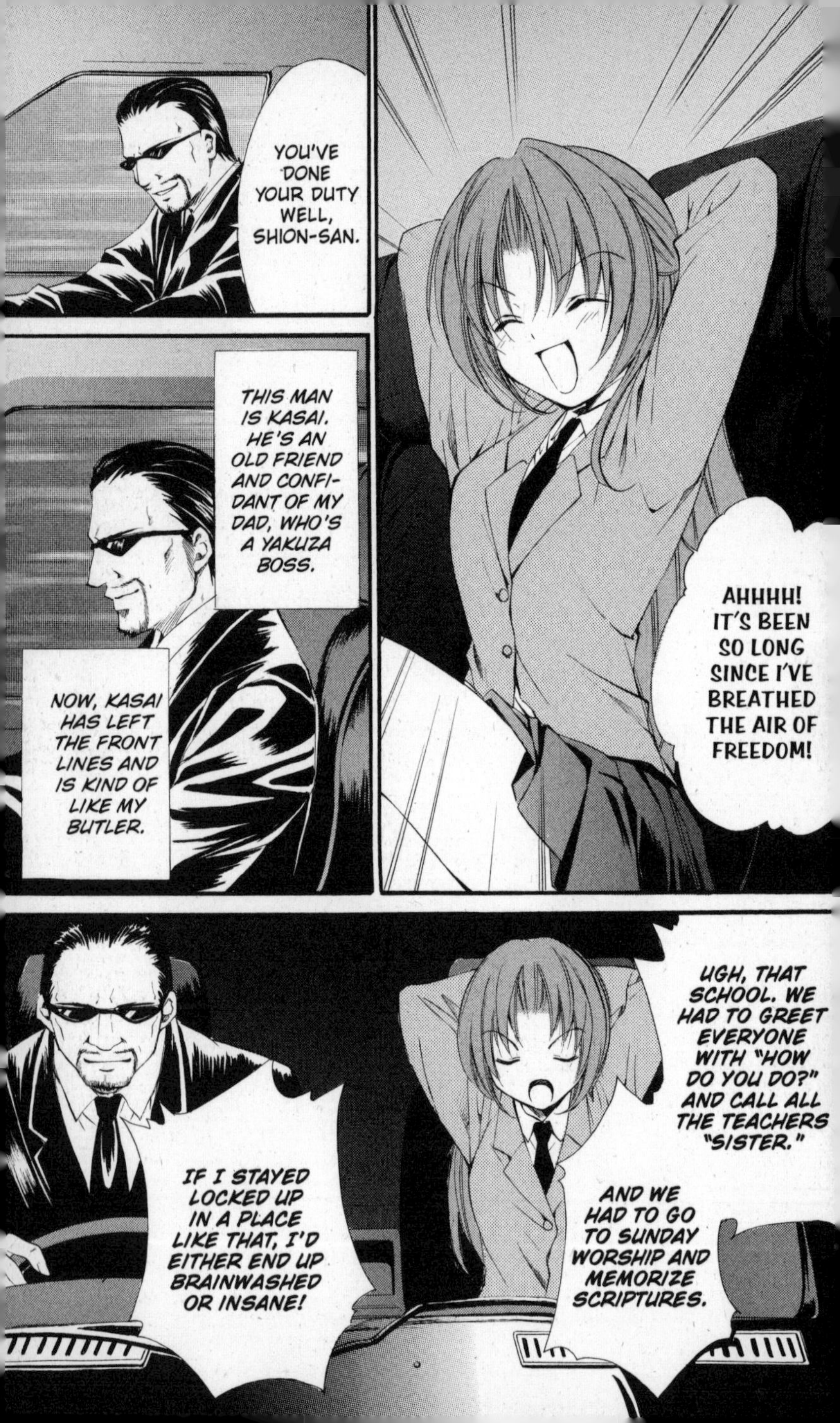
AHHHH! IT'S BEEN SO LONG SINCE I'VE BREATHED THE AIR OF FREEDOM!
YOU'VE DONE YOUR DUTY WELL, SHION-SAN.
THIS MAN IS KASAI. HE'S AN OLD FRIEND AND CONFI-DANT OF MY DAD, WHO'S A YAKUZA BOSS.
NOW, KASAI HAS LEFT THE FRONT LINES AND IS KIND OF LIKE MY BUTLER.
UGH, THAT SCHOOL. WE HAD TO GREET EVERYONE WITH "HOW DO YOU DO?" AND CALL ALL THE TEACHERS "SISTER."
AND WE HAD TO GO TO SUNDAY WORSHIP AND MEMORIZE SCRIPTURES.
IF I STAYED LOCKED UP IN A PLACE LIKE THAT, I'D EITHER END UP BRAINWASHED OR INSANE!

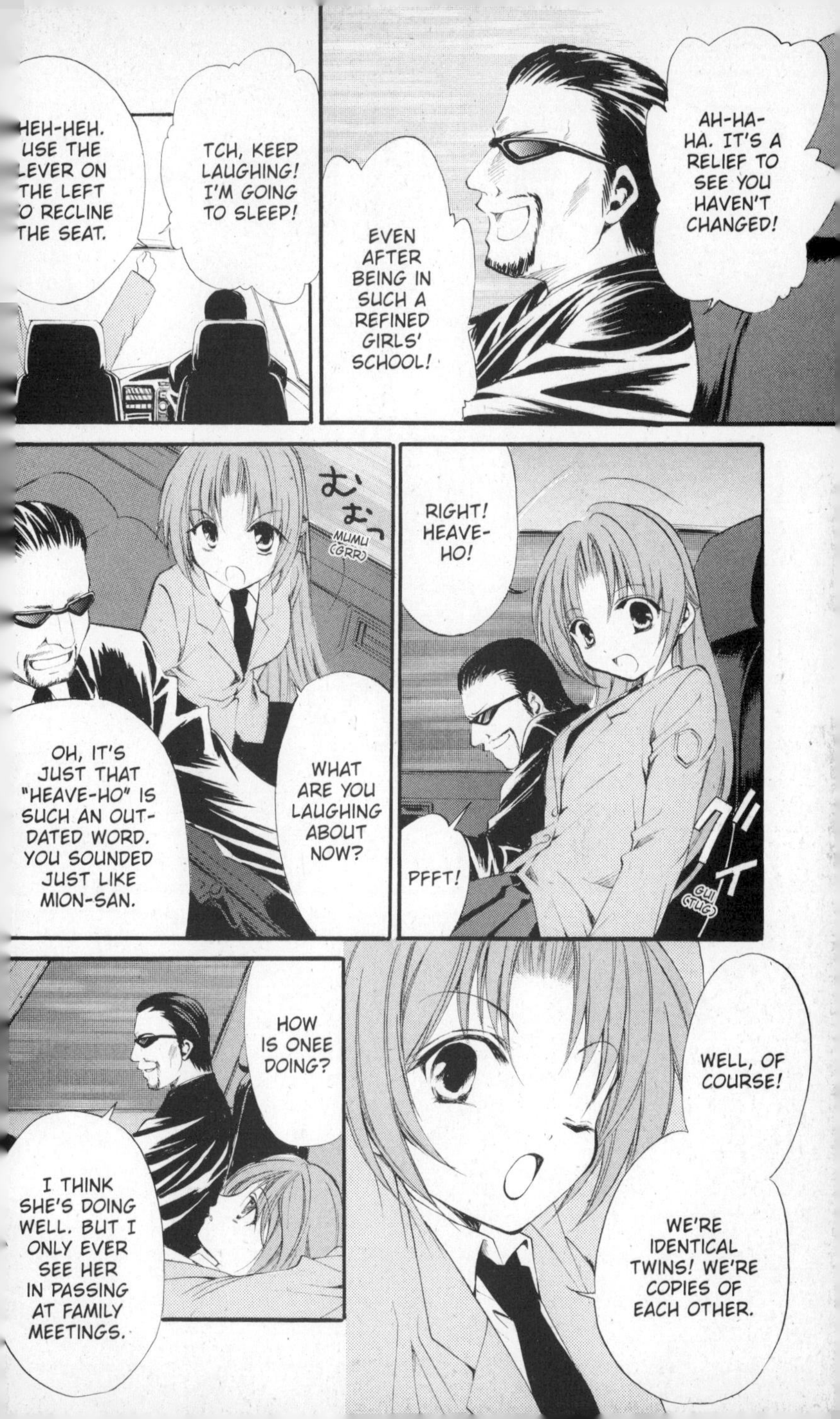
AH-HA-HA. IT'S A RELIEF TO SEE YOU HAVEN'T CHANGED!
EVEN AFTER BEING IN SUCH A REFINED GIRLS' SCHOOL!
TCH, KEEP LAUGHING! I'M GOING TO SLEEP!
HEH-HEH. USE THE LEVER ON THE LEFT TO RECLINE THE SEAT.
RIGHT! HEAVE-HO!
グイ
GUI (TUG)
PFFT!
むむっ
MUMU (GRR)
WHAT ARE YOU LAUGHING ABOUT NOW?
OH, IT'S JUST THAT "HEAVE-HO" IS SUCH AN OUT-DATED WORD. YOU SOUNDED JUST LIKE MION-SAN.
WELL, OF COURSE!
WE'RE IDENTICAL TWINS! WE'RE COPIES OF EACH OTHER.
HOW IS ONEE DOING?
I THINK SHE'S DOING WELL. BUT I ONLY EVER SEE HER IN PASSING AT FAMILY MEETINGS.

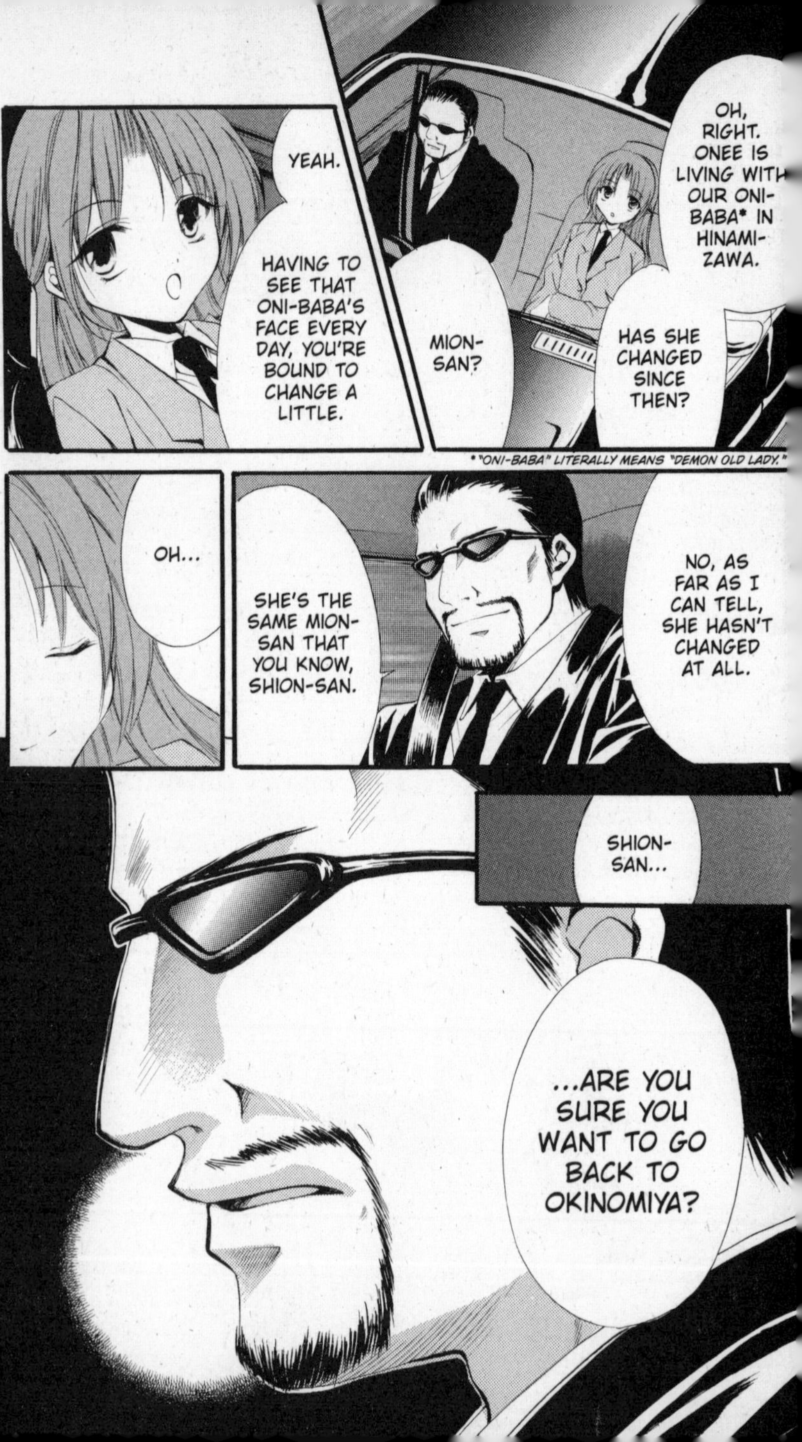
OH, RIGHT. ONEE IS LIVING WITH OUR ONI-BABA* IN HINAMI-ZAWA.
HAS SHE CHANGED SINCE THEN?
MION-SAN?
YEAH.
HAVING TO SEE THAT ONI-BABA'S FACE EVERY DAY, YOU'RE BOUND TO CHANGE A LITTLE.
NO, AS FAR AS I CAN TELL, SHE HASN'T CHANGED AT ALL.
SHE'S THE SAME MION-SAN THAT YOU KNOW, SHION-SAN.
OH...
SHION-SAN...
...ARE YOU SURE YOU WANT TO GO BACK TO OKINOMIYA?

* "ONI-BABA" LITERALLY MEANS "DEMON OLD LADY."

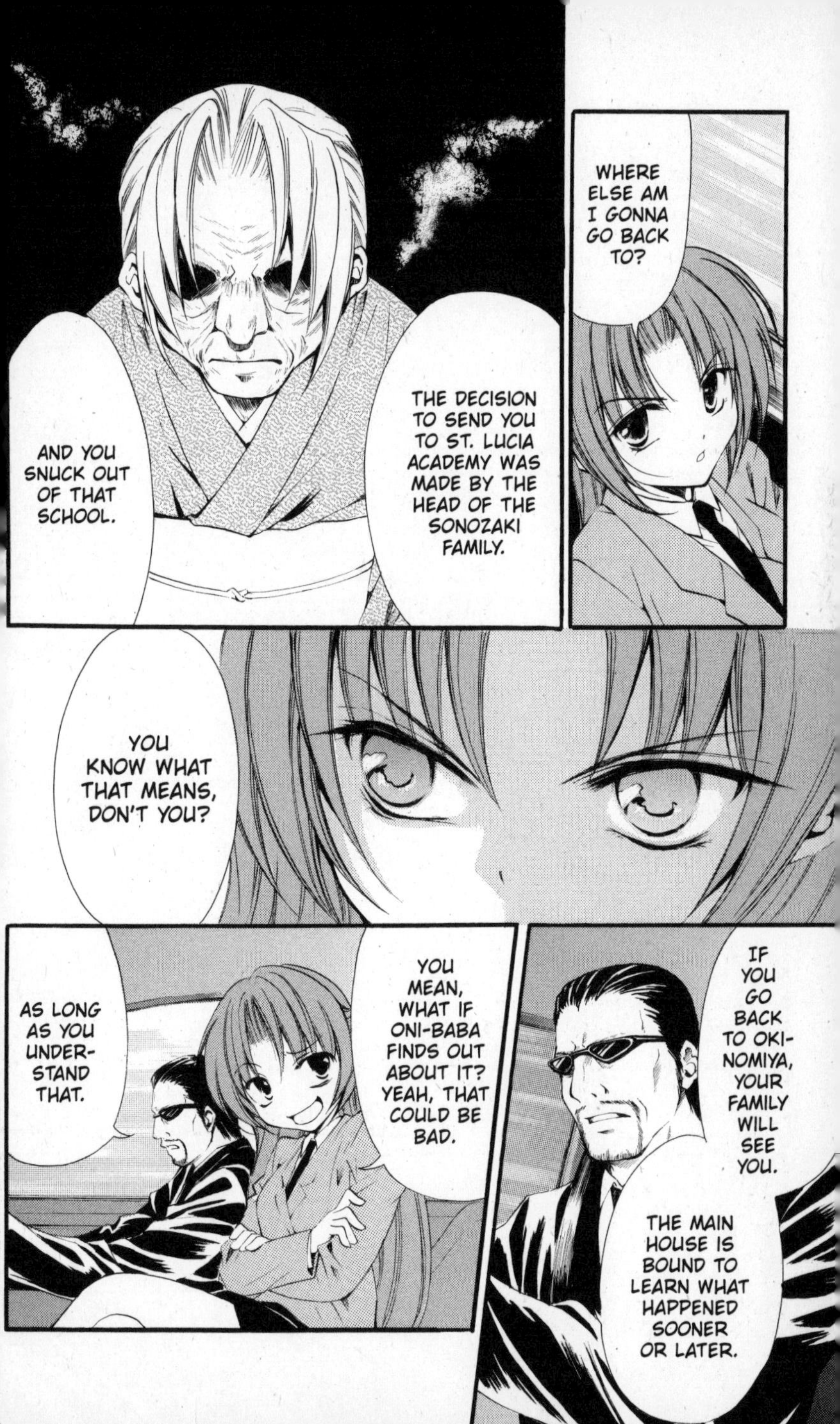
WHERE ELSE AM I GONNA GO BACK TO?
THE DECISION TO SEND YOU TO ST. LUCIA ACADEMY WAS MADE BY THE HEAD OF THE SONOZAKI FAMILY.
AND YOU SNUCK OUT OF THAT SCHOOL.
YOU KNOW WHAT THAT MEANS, DON'T YOU?
IF YOU GO BACK TO OKI-NOMIYA, YOUR FAMILY WILL SEE YOU.
THE MAIN HOUSE IS BOUND TO LEARN WHAT HAPPENED SOONER OR LATER.
YOU MEAN, WHAT IF ONI-BABA FINDS OUT ABOUT IT? YEAH, THAT COULD BE BAD.
AS LONG AS YOU UNDER-STAND THAT.

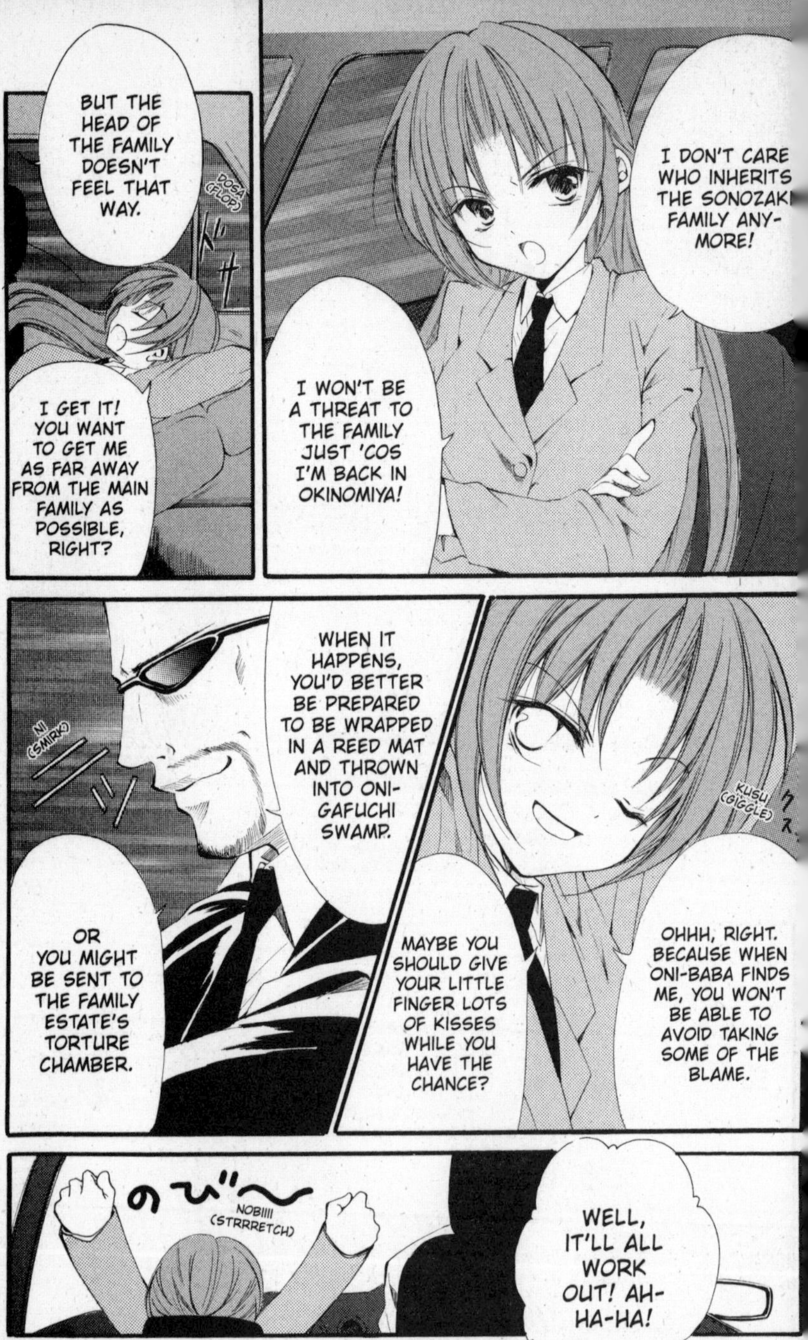
I DON'T CARE WHO INHERITS THE SONOZAKI FAMILY ANY-MORE!
I WON'T BE A THREAT TO THE FAMILY JUST 'COS I'M BACK IN OKINOMIYA!
BUT THE HEAD OF THE FAMILY DOESN'T FEEL THAT WAY.
DOSA (FLOP)
ドサ
I GET IT! YOU WANT TO GET ME AS FAR AWAY FROM THE MAIN FAMILY AS POSSIBLE, RIGHT?
KUSU (GIGGLE)
OHHH, RIGHT. BECAUSE WHEN ONI-BABA FINDS ME, YOU WON'T BE ABLE TO AVOID TAKING SOME OF THE BLAME.
MAYBE YOU SHOULD GIVE YOUR LITTLE FINGER LOTS OF KISSES WHILE YOU HAVE THE CHANCE?
WHEN IT HAPPENS, YOU'D BETTER BE PREPARED TO BE WRAPPED IN A REED MAT AND THROWN INTO ONI-GAFUCHI SWAMP.
NI (SMIRK)
OR YOU MIGHT BE SENT TO THE FAMILY ESTATE'S TORTURE CHAMBER.
WELL, IT'LL ALL WORK OUT! AH-HA-HA!
のび〜
NOBIIII (STRRRETCH)

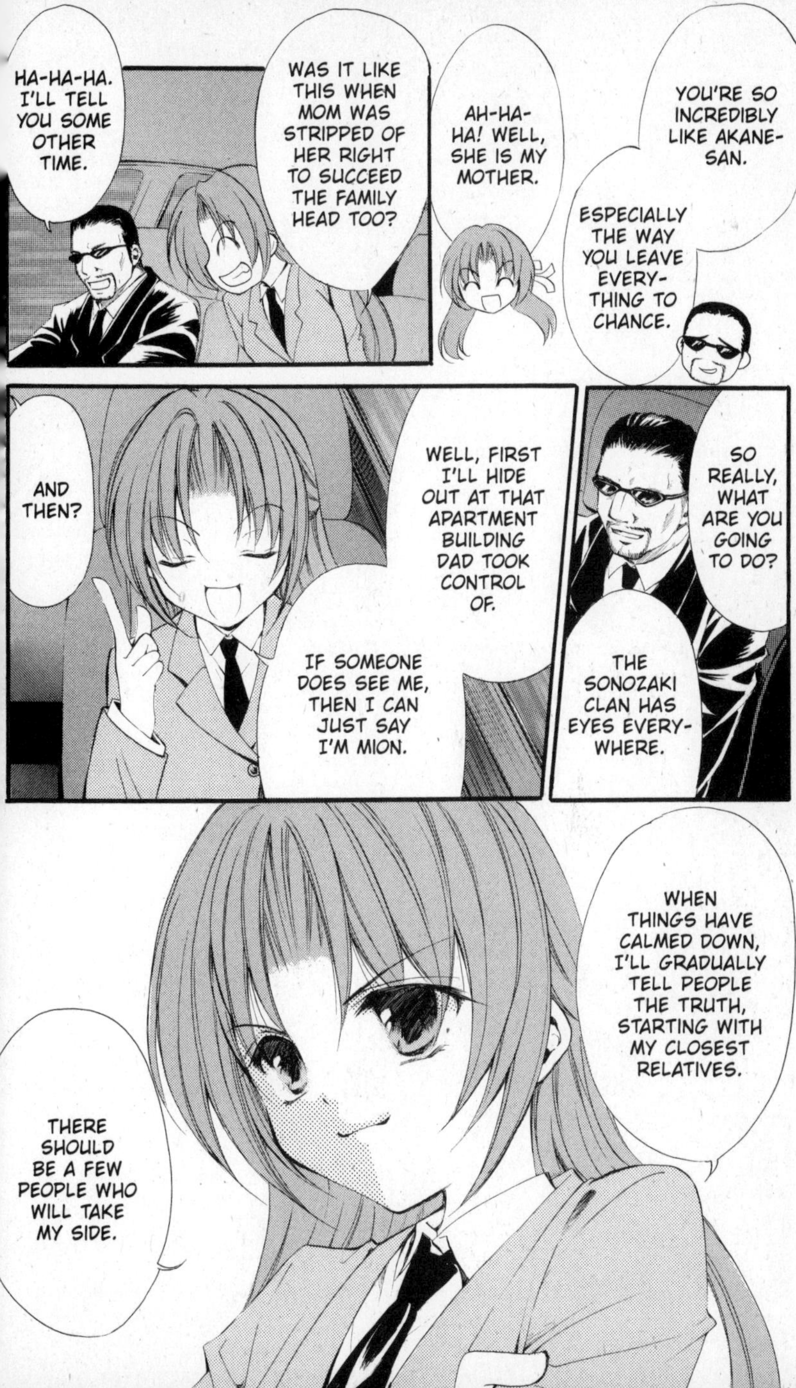
YOU'RE SO INCREDIBLY LIKE AKANE-SAN.
ESPECIALLY THE WAY YOU LEAVE EVERYTHING TO CHANCE.
AH-HA-HA! WELL, SHE IS MY MOTHER.
WAS IT LIKE THIS WHEN MOM WAS STRIPPED OF HER RIGHT TO SUCCEED THE FAMILY HEAD TOO?
HA-HA-HA. I'LL TELL YOU SOME OTHER TIME.
SO REALLY, WHAT ARE YOU GOING TO DO?
THE SONOZAKI CLAN HAS EYES EVERYWHERE.
WELL, FIRST I'LL HIDE OUT AT THAT APARTMENT BUILDING DAD TOOK CONTROL OF.
IF SOMEONE DOES SEE ME, THEN I CAN JUST SAY I'M MION.
AND THEN?
WHEN THINGS HAVE CALMED DOWN, I'LL GRADUALLY TELL PEOPLE THE TRUTH, STARTING WITH MY CLOSEST RELATIVES.
THERE SHOULD BE A FEW PEOPLE WHO WILL TAKE MY SIDE.

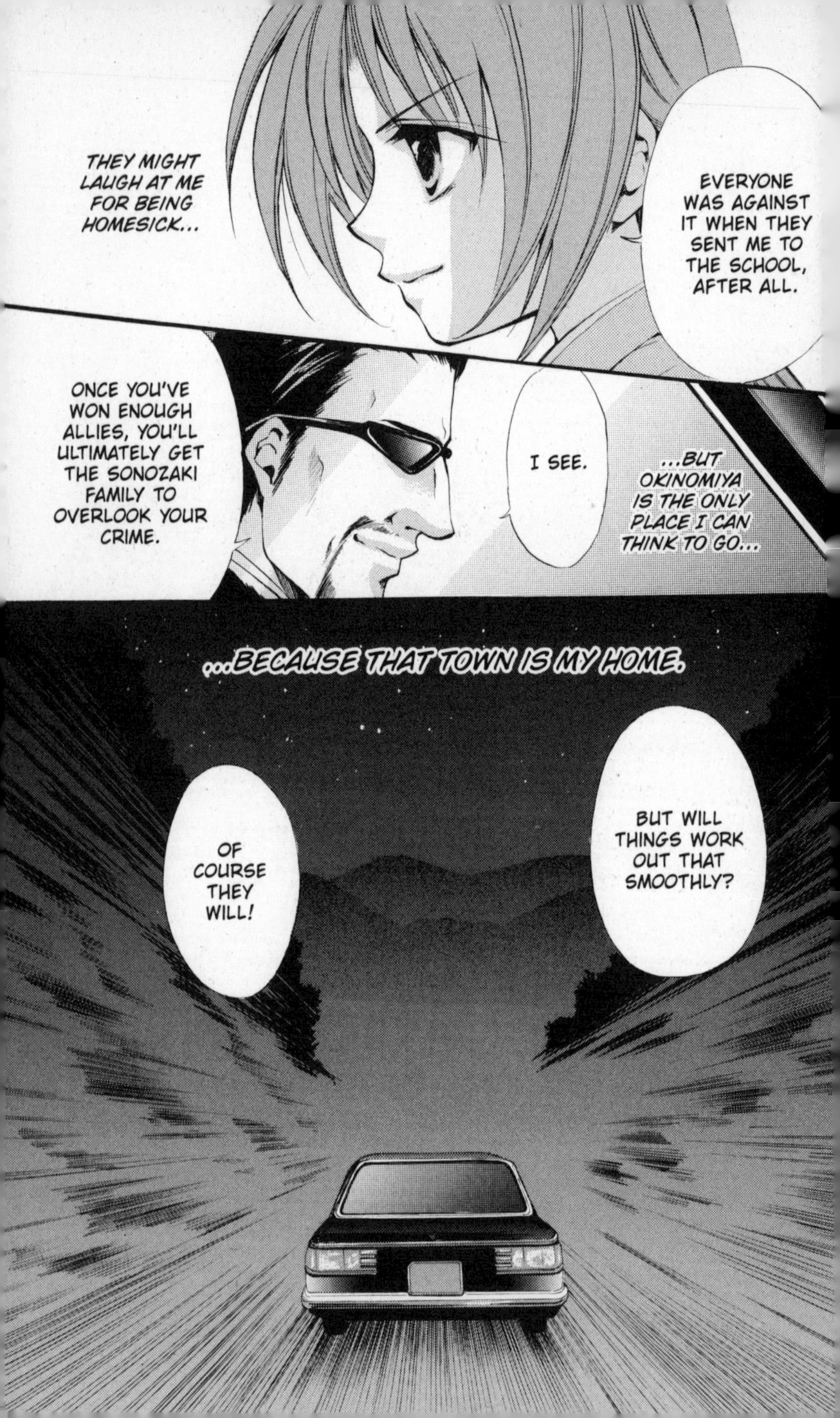
EVERYONE WAS AGAINST IT WHEN THEY SENT ME TO THE SCHOOL, AFTER ALL.
THEY MIGHT LAUGH AT ME FOR BEING HOMESICK...
...BUT OKINOMIYA IS THE ONLY PLACE I CAN THINK TO GO...
I SEE.
ONCE YOU'VE WON ENOUGH ALLIES, YOU'LL ULTIMATELY GET THE SONOZAKI FAMILY TO OVERLOOK YOUR CRIME.
...BECAUSE THAT TOWN IS MY HOME.
BUT WILL THINGS WORK OUT THAT SMOOTHLY?
OF COURSE THEY WILL!

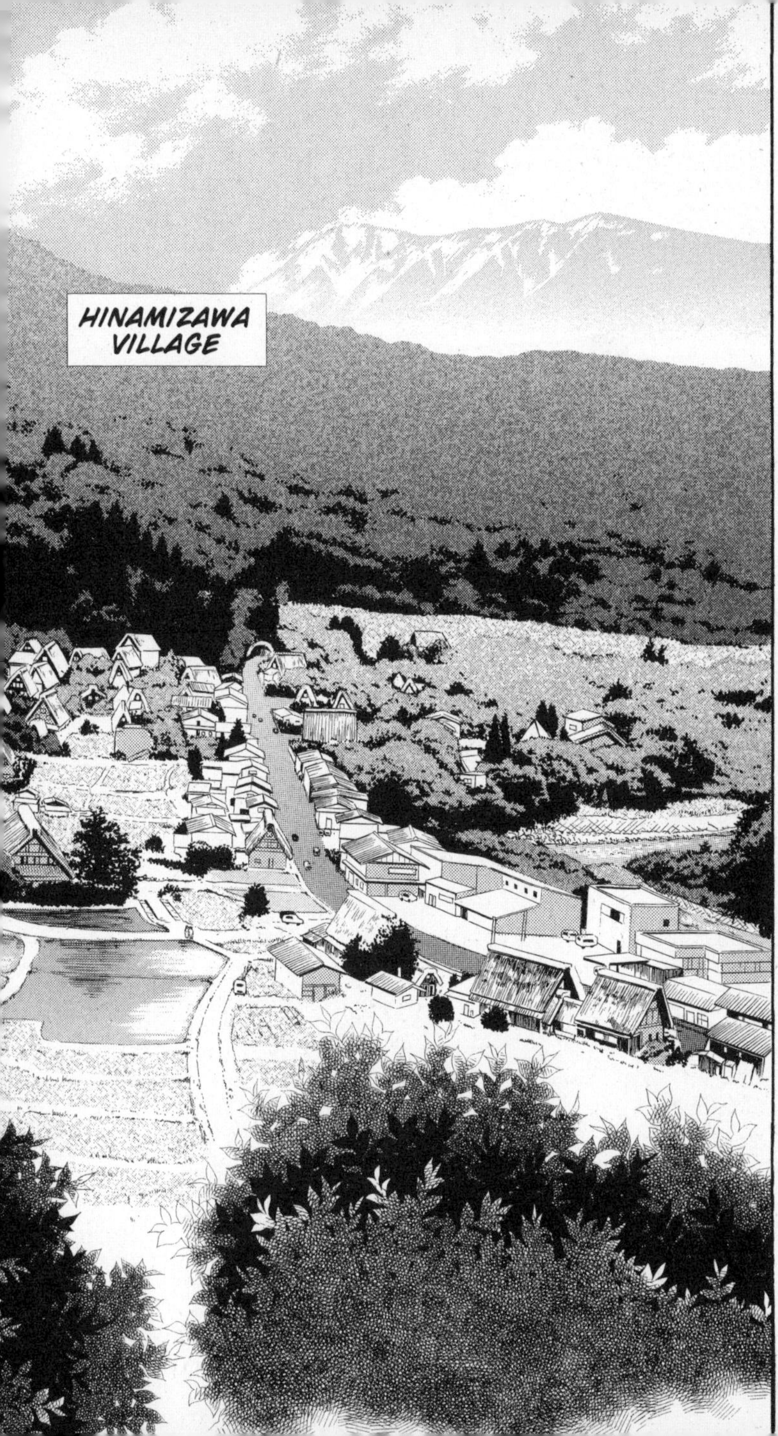
HINAMIZAWA VILLAGE

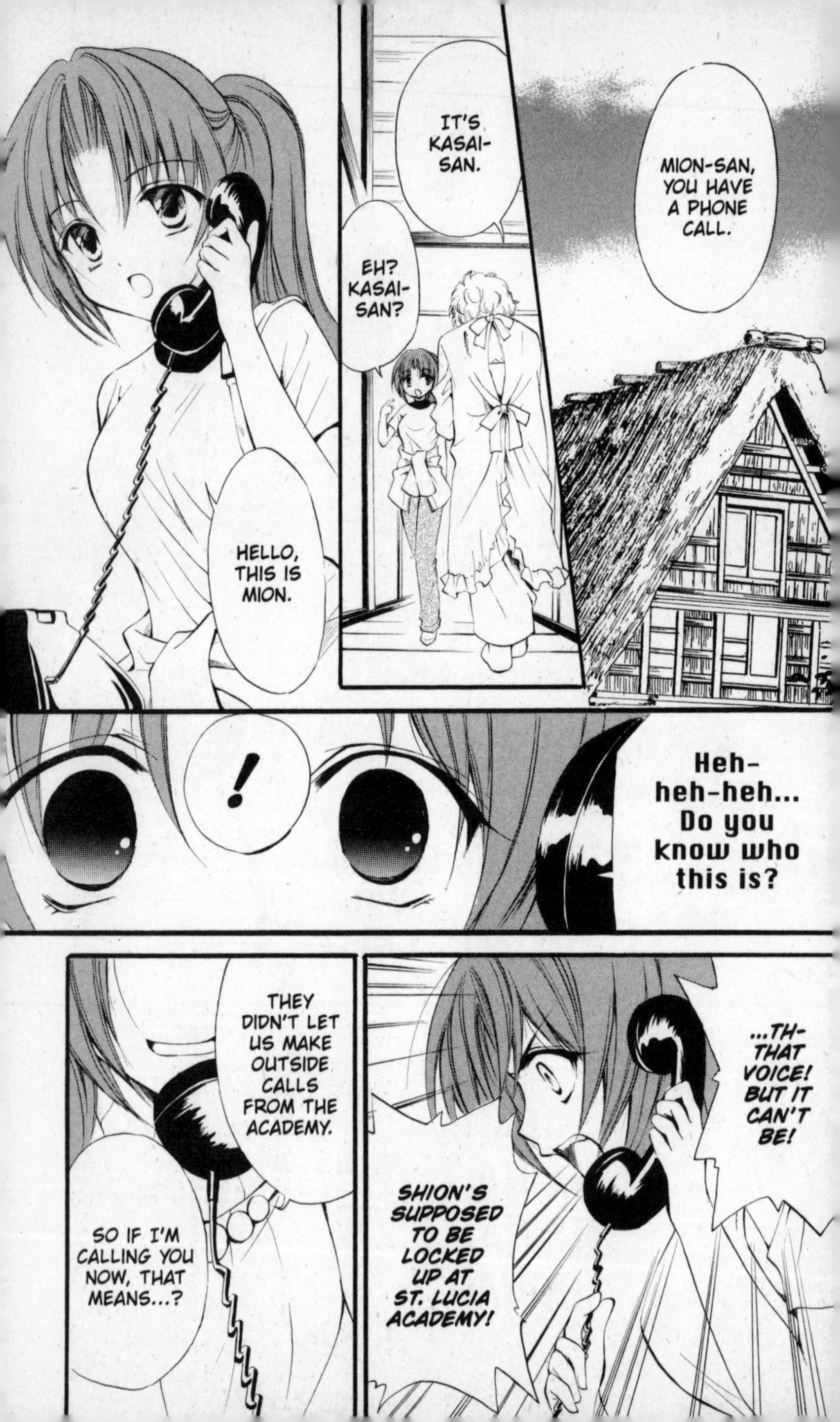
MION-SAN, YOU HAVE A PHONE CALL.
IT'S KASAI-SAN.
EH? KASAI-SAN?
HELLO, THIS IS MION.
Heh-heh-heh... Do you know who this is?
!
...TH-THAT VOICE! BUT IT CAN'T BE!
SHION'S SUPPOSED TO BE LOCKED UP AT ST. LUCIA ACADEMY!
THEY DIDN'T LET US MAKE OUTSIDE CALLS FROM THE ACADEMY.
SO IF I'M CALLING YOU NOW, THAT MEANS...?

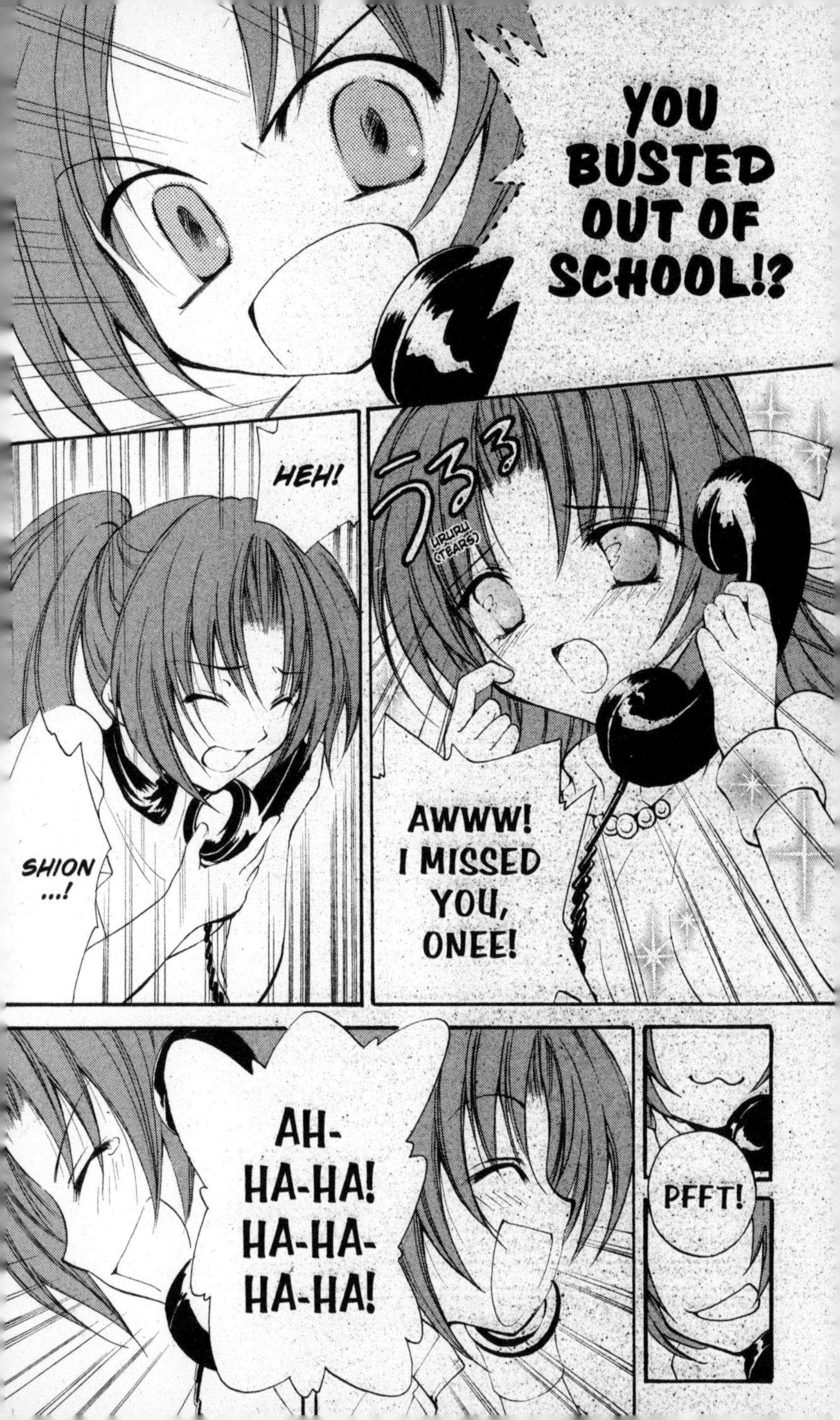
YOU BUSTED OUT OF SCHOOL!?
うるる
URURU (TEARS)
AWWW! I MISSED YOU, ONEE!
HEH!
SHION ...!
PFFT!
AH-HA-HA! HA-HA-HA-HA!

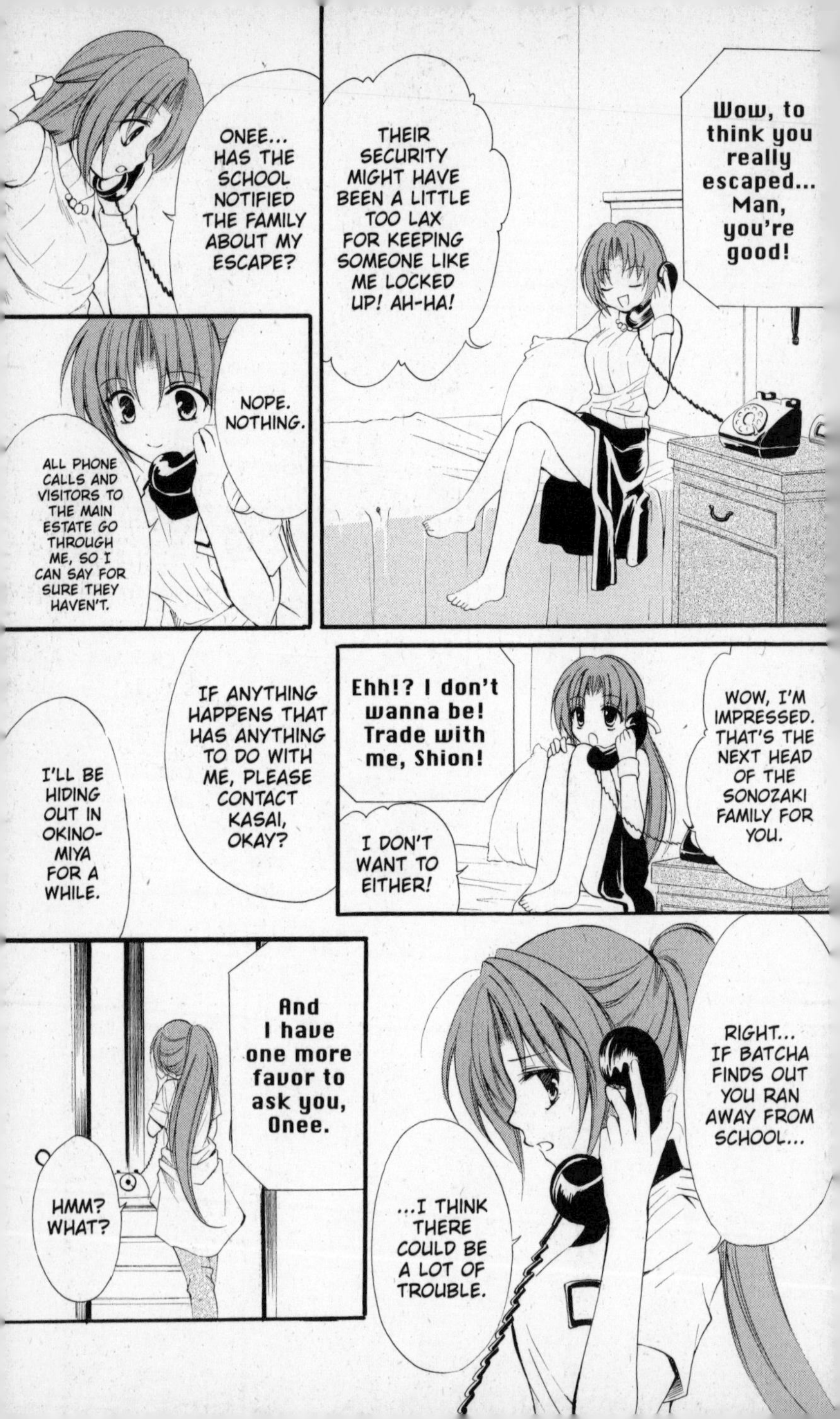
Wow, to think you really escaped... Man, you're good!
THEIR SECURITY MIGHT HAVE BEEN A LITTLE TOO LAX FOR KEEPING SOMEONE LIKE ME LOCKED UP! AH-HA!
ONEE... HAS THE SCHOOL NOTIFIED THE FAMILY ABOUT MY ESCAPE?
NOPE. NOTHING.
ALL PHONE CALLS AND VISITORS TO THE MAIN ESTATE GO THROUGH ME, SO I CAN SAY FOR SURE THEY HAVEN'T.
WOW, I'M IMPRESSED. THAT'S THE NEXT HEAD OF THE SONOZAKI FAMILY FOR YOU.
Ehh!? I don't wanna be! Trade with me, Shion!
I DON'T WANT TO EITHER!
IF ANYTHING HAPPENS THAT HAS ANYTHING TO DO WITH ME, PLEASE CONTACT KASAI, OKAY?
I'LL BE HIDING OUT IN OKINO-MIYA FOR A WHILE.
RIGHT... IF BATCHA FINDS OUT YOU RAN AWAY FROM SCHOOL...
...I THINK THERE COULD BE A LOT OF TROUBLE.
And I have one more favor to ask you, Onee.
HMM? WHAT?

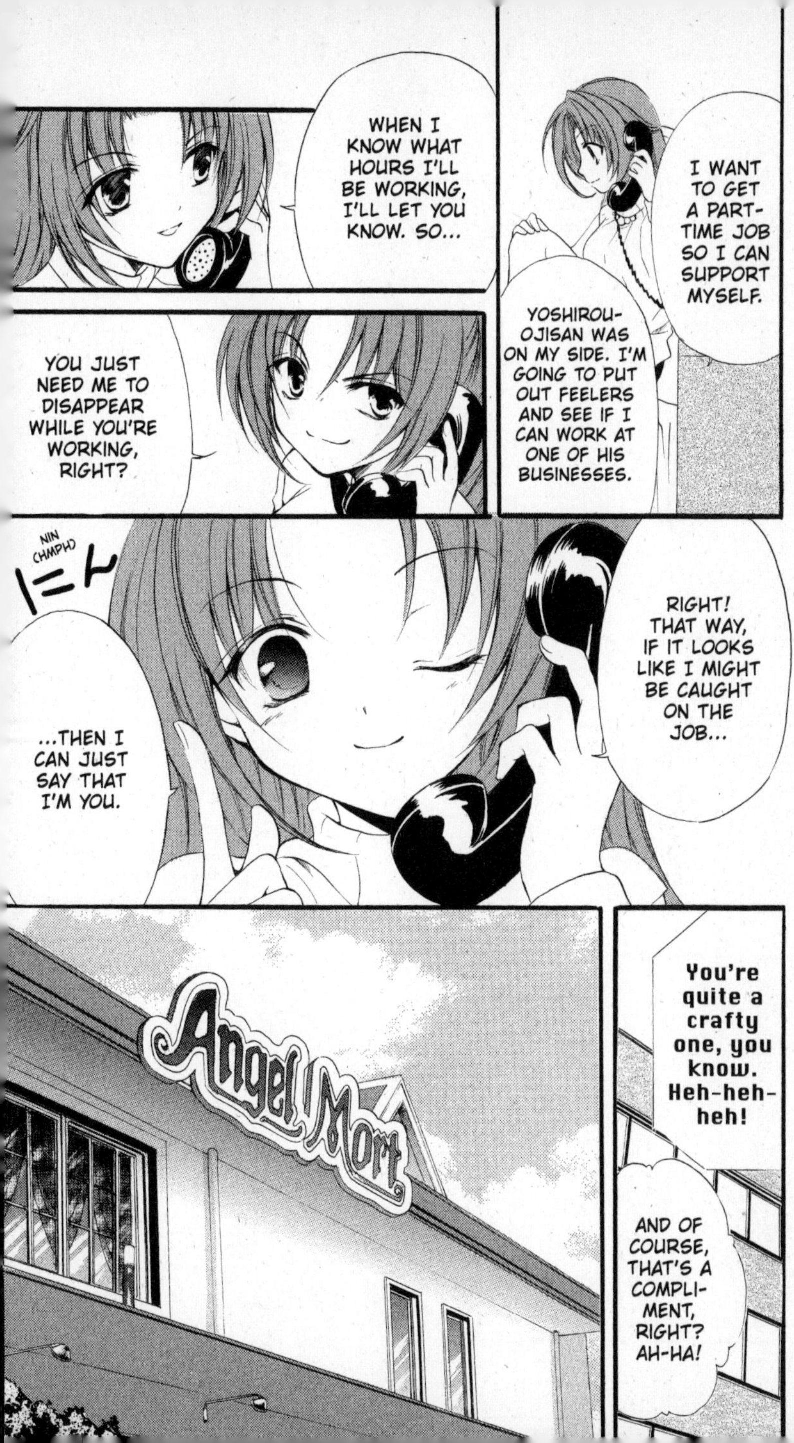
I WANT TO GET A PART-TIME JOB SO I CAN SUPPORT MYSELF.
YOSHIROU-OJISAN WAS ON MY SIDE. I'M GOING TO PUT OUT FEELERS AND SEE IF I CAN WORK AT ONE OF HIS BUSINESSES.
WHEN I KNOW WHAT HOURS I'LL BE WORKING, I'LL LET YOU KNOW. SO...
YOU JUST NEED ME TO DISAPPEAR WHILE YOU'RE WORKING, RIGHT?
RIGHT! THAT WAY, IF IT LOOKS LIKE I MIGHT BE CAUGHT ON THE JOB...
NIN (HMPH)
...THEN I CAN JUST SAY THAT I'M YOU.
You're quite a crafty one, you know. Heh-heh-heh!
AND OF COURSE, THAT'S A COMPLIMENT, RIGHT? AH-HA!
Angel Mort

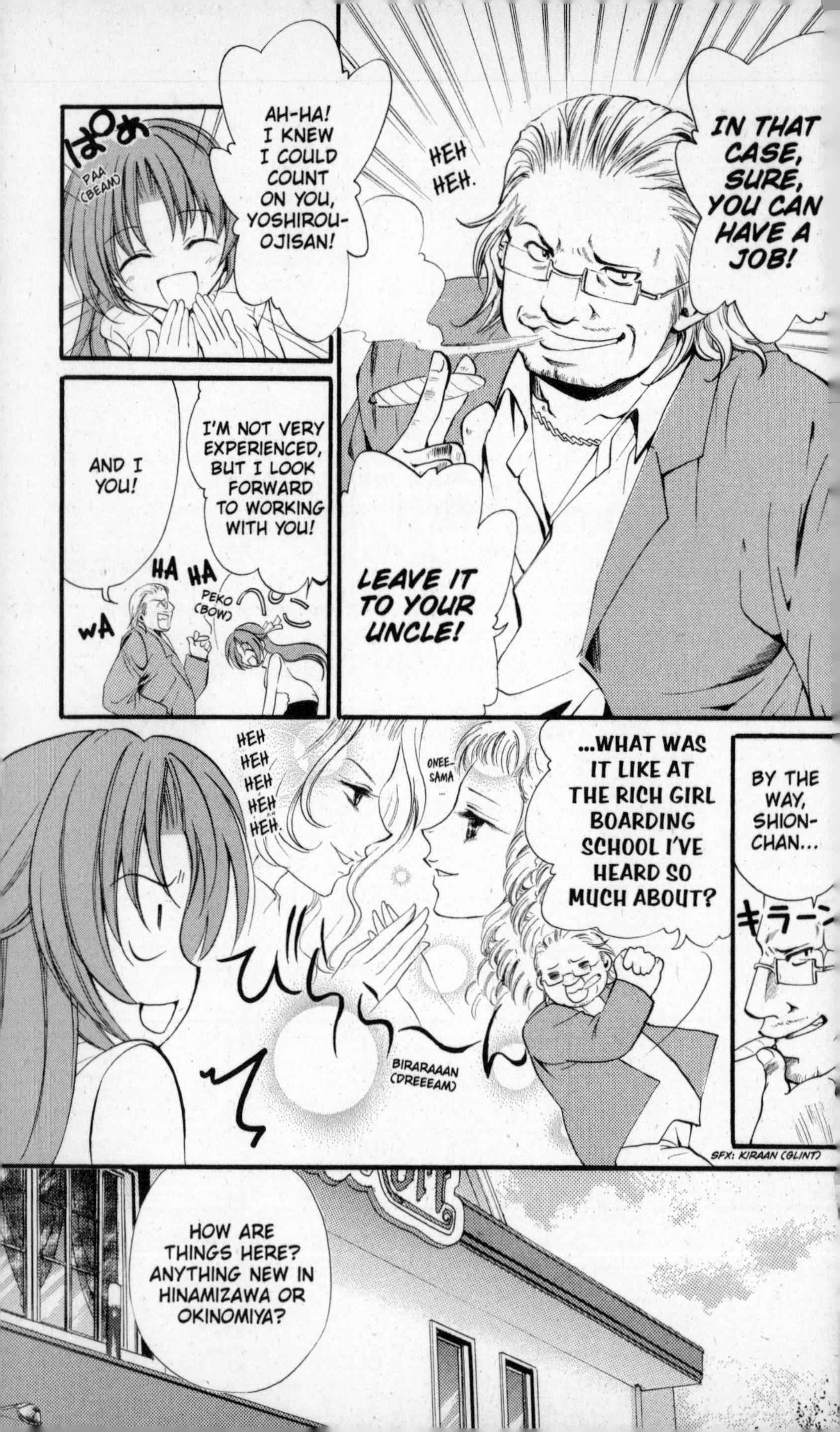
IN THAT CASE, SURE, YOU CAN HAVE A JOB!
HEH HEH.
LEAVE IT TO YOUR UNCLE!
ぱぁ
PAA (BEAM)
AH-HA! I KNEW I COULD COUNT ON YOU, YOSHIROU-OJISAN!
I'M NOT VERY EXPERIENCED, BUT I LOOK FORWARD TO WORKING WITH YOU!
AND I YOU!
HA HA
WA
PEKO (BOW)
BY THE WAY, SHION-CHAN...
キラーン
SFX: KIRAAN (GLINT)
...WHAT WAS IT LIKE AT THE RICH GIRL BOARDING SCHOOL I'VE HEARD SO MUCH ABOUT?
ONEE-SAMA...
HEH HEH HEH HEH HEH.
BIRARAAAN (DREEEAM)
HOW ARE THINGS HERE? ANYTHING NEW IN HINAMIZAWA OR OKINOMIYA?

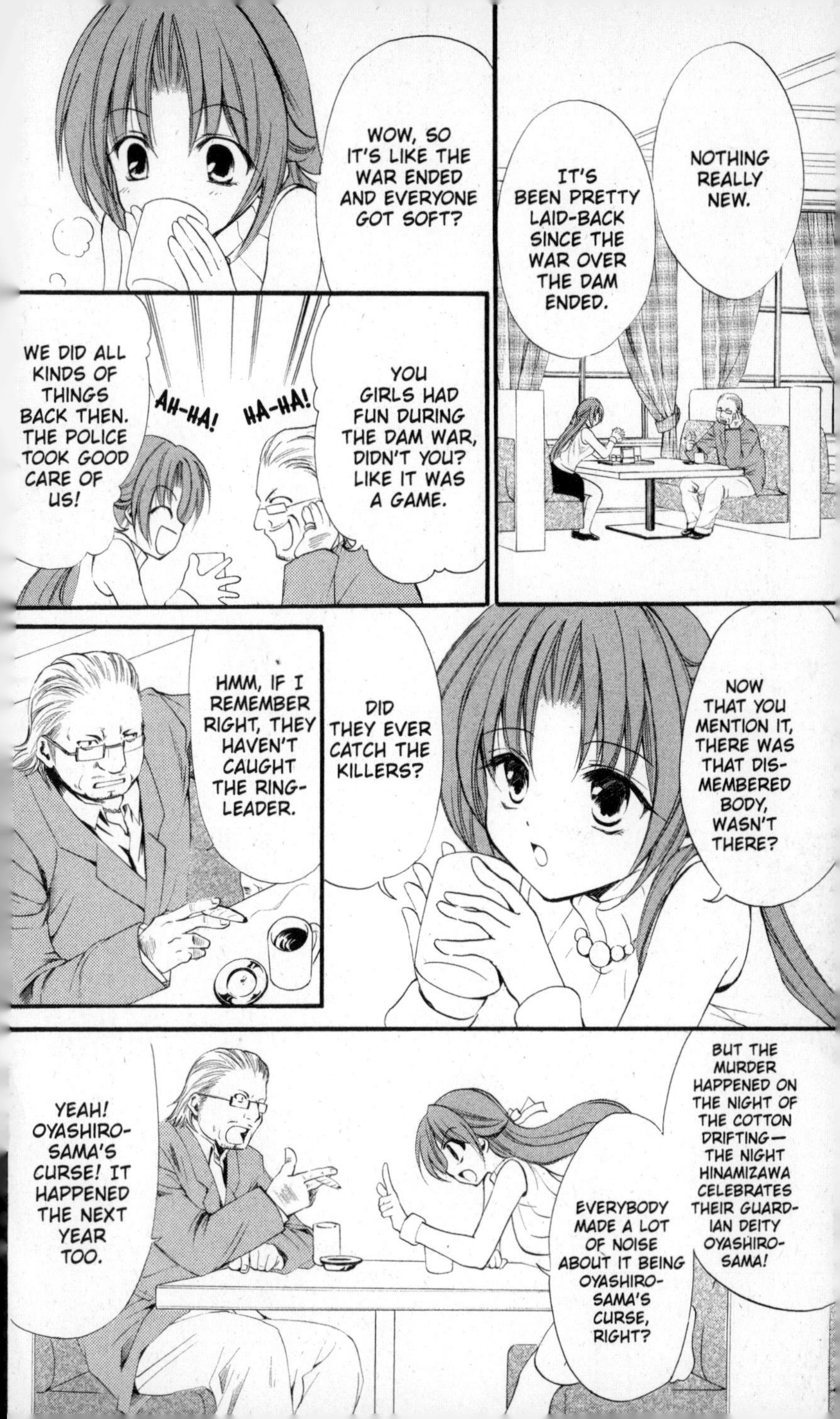
NOTHING REALLY NEW.
IT'S BEEN PRETTY LAID-BACK SINCE THE WAR OVER THE DAM ENDED.
WOW, SO IT'S LIKE THE WAR ENDED AND EVERYONE GOT SOFT?
YOU GIRLS HAD FUN DURING THE DAM WAR, DIDN'T YOU? LIKE IT WAS A GAME.
HA-HA!
AH-HA!
WE DID ALL KINDS OF THINGS BACK THEN. THE POLICE TOOK GOOD CARE OF US!
NOW THAT YOU MENTION IT, THERE WAS THAT DIS-MEMBERED BODY, WASN'T THERE?
DID THEY EVER CATCH THE KILLERS?
HMM, IF I REMEMBER RIGHT, THEY HAVEN'T CAUGHT THE RING-LEADER.
BUT THE MURDER HAPPENED ON THE NIGHT OF THE COTTON DRIFTING— THE NIGHT HINAMIZAWA CELEBRATES THEIR GUARD-IAN DEITY OYASHIRO-SAMA!
EVERYBODY MADE A LOT OF NOISE ABOUT IT BEING OYASHIRO-SAMA'S CURSE, RIGHT?
YEAH! OYASHIRO-SAMA'S CURSE! IT HAPPENED THE NEXT YEAR TOO.

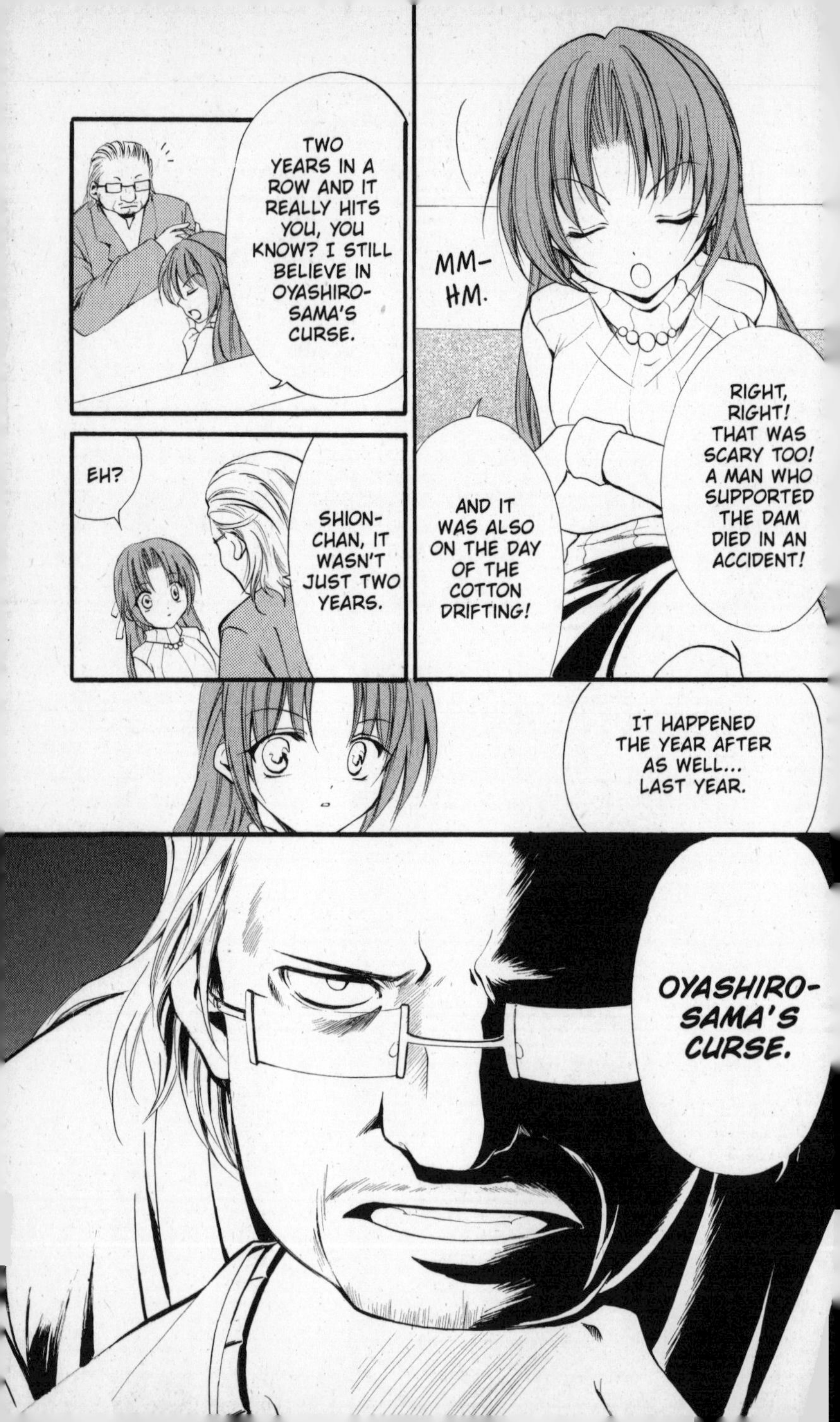
MM-HM.
RIGHT, RIGHT! THAT WAS SCARY TOO! A MAN WHO SUPPORTED THE DAM DIED IN AN ACCIDENT!
AND IT WAS ALSO ON THE DAY OF THE COTTON DRIFTING!
TWO YEARS IN A ROW AND IT REALLY HITS YOU, YOU KNOW? I STILL BELIEVE IN OYASHIRO-SAMA'S CURSE.
SHION-CHAN, IT WASN'T JUST TWO YEARS.
EH?
IT HAPPENED THE YEAR AFTER AS WELL... LAST YEAR.
OYASHIRO-SAMA'S CURSE.

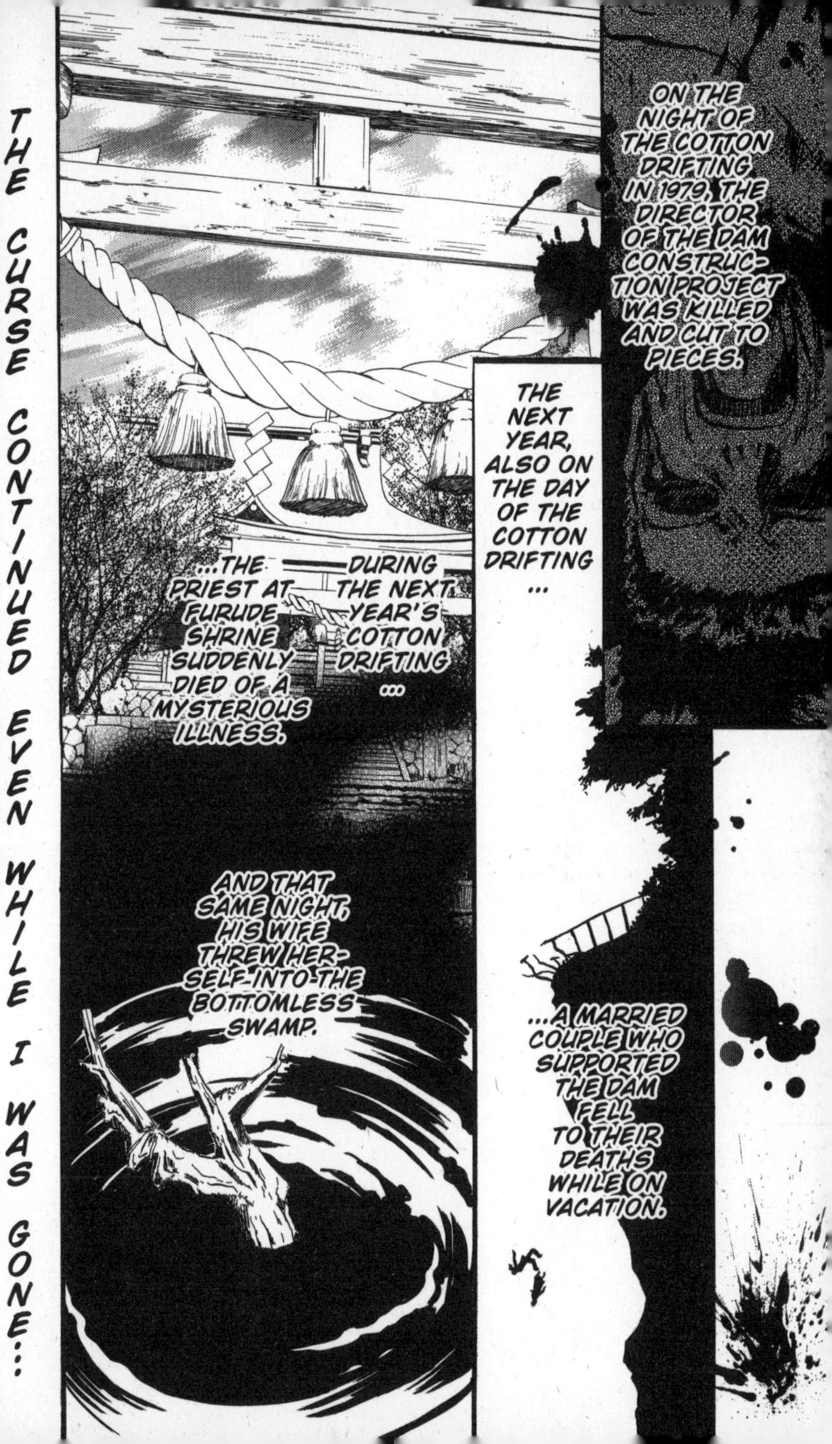

ON THE NIGHT OF THE COTTON DRIFTING IN 1979, THE DIRECTOR OF THE DAM CONSTRUCTION PROJECT WAS KILLED AND CUT TO PIECES.
THE NEXT YEAR, ALSO ON THE DAY OF THE COTTON DRIFTING ...
...A MARRIED COUPLE WHO SUPPORTED THE DAM FELL TO THEIR DEATHS WHILE ON VACATION.
DURING THE NEXT YEAR'S COTTON DRIFTING ...
...THE PRIEST AT FURUDE SHRINE SUDDENLY DIED OF A MYSTERIOUS ILLNESS.
AND THAT SAME NIGHT, HIS WIFE THREW HERSELF INTO THE BOTTOMLESS SWAMP.
THE CURSE CONTINUED EVEN WHILE I WAS GONE...

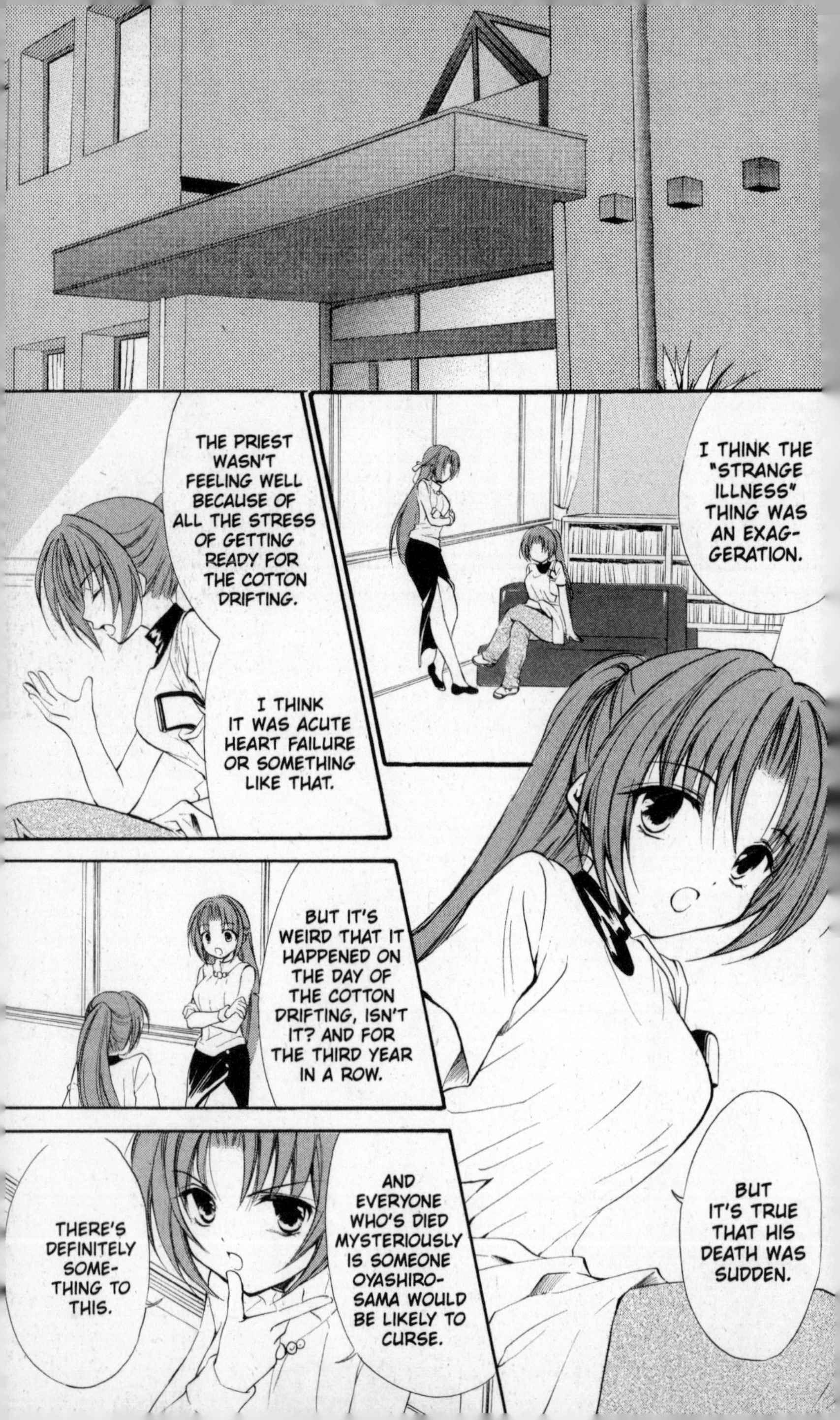
I THINK THE "STRANGE ILLNESS" THING WAS AN EXAG-GERATION.
THE PRIEST WASN'T FEELING WELL BECAUSE OF ALL THE STRESS OF GETTING READY FOR THE COTTON DRIFTING.
I THINK IT WAS ACUTE HEART FAILURE OR SOMETHING LIKE THAT.
BUT IT'S TRUE THAT HIS DEATH WAS SUDDEN.
BUT IT'S WEIRD THAT IT HAPPENED ON THE DAY OF THE COTTON DRIFTING, ISN'T IT? AND FOR THE THIRD YEAR IN A ROW.
AND EVERYONE WHO'S DIED MYSTERIOUSLY IS SOMEONE OYASHIRO-SAMA WOULD BE LIKELY TO CURSE.
THERE'S DEFINITELY SOME-THING TO THIS.

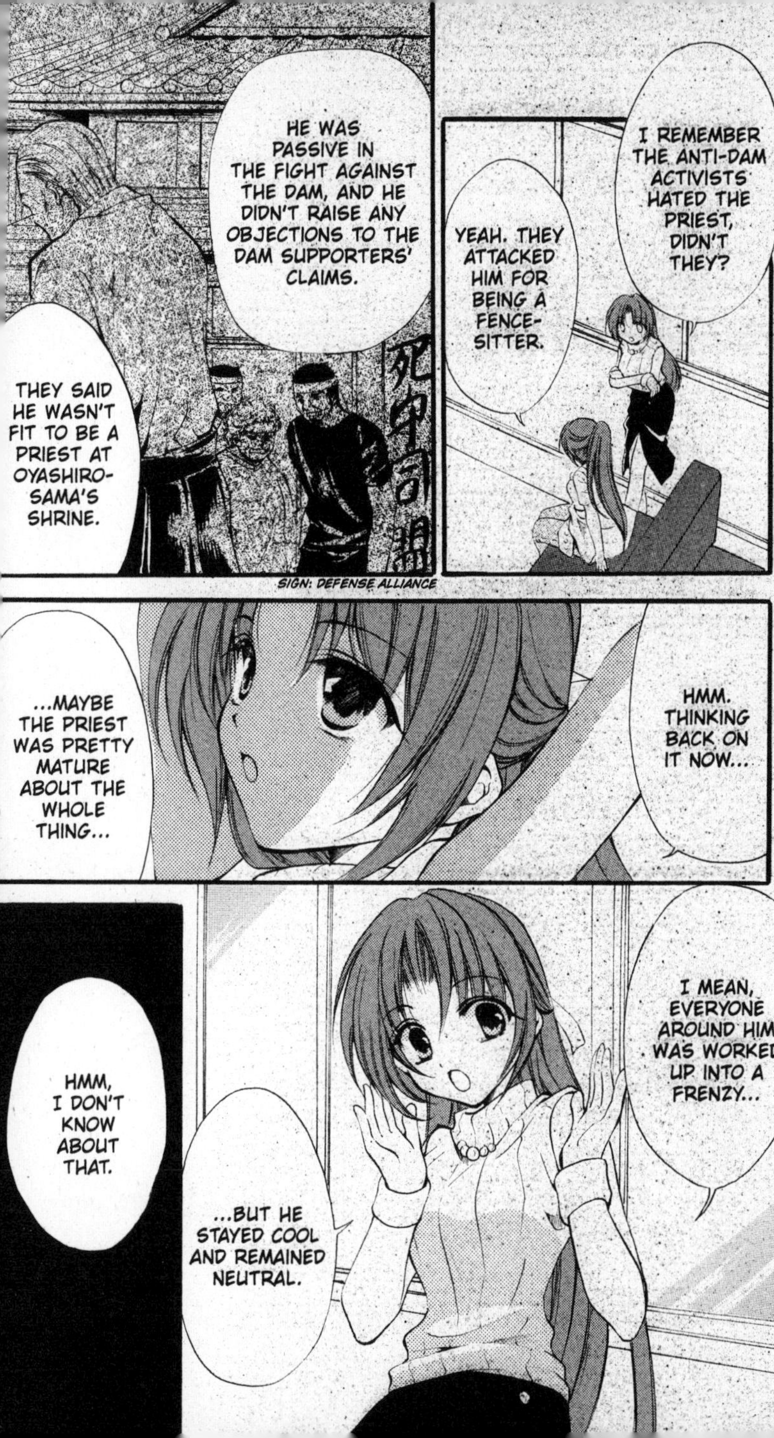
I REMEMBER THE ANTI-DAM ACTIVISTS HATED THE PRIEST, DIDN'T THEY?
YEAH. THEY ATTACKED HIM FOR BEING A FENCE-SITTER.
HE WAS PASSIVE IN THE FIGHT AGAINST THE DAM, AND HE DIDN'T RAISE ANY OBJECTIONS TO THE DAM SUPPORTERS' CLAIMS.
THEY SAID HE WASN'T FIT TO BE A PRIEST AT OYASHIRO-SAMA'S SHRINE.
死守同盟
SIGN: DEFENSE ALLIANCE
HMM. THINKING BACK ON IT NOW...
...MAYBE THE PRIEST WAS PRETTY MATURE ABOUT THE WHOLE THING...
I MEAN, EVERYONE AROUND HIM WAS WORKED UP INTO A FRENZY...
...BUT HE STAYED COOL AND REMAINED NEUTRAL.
HMM, I DON'T KNOW ABOUT THAT.

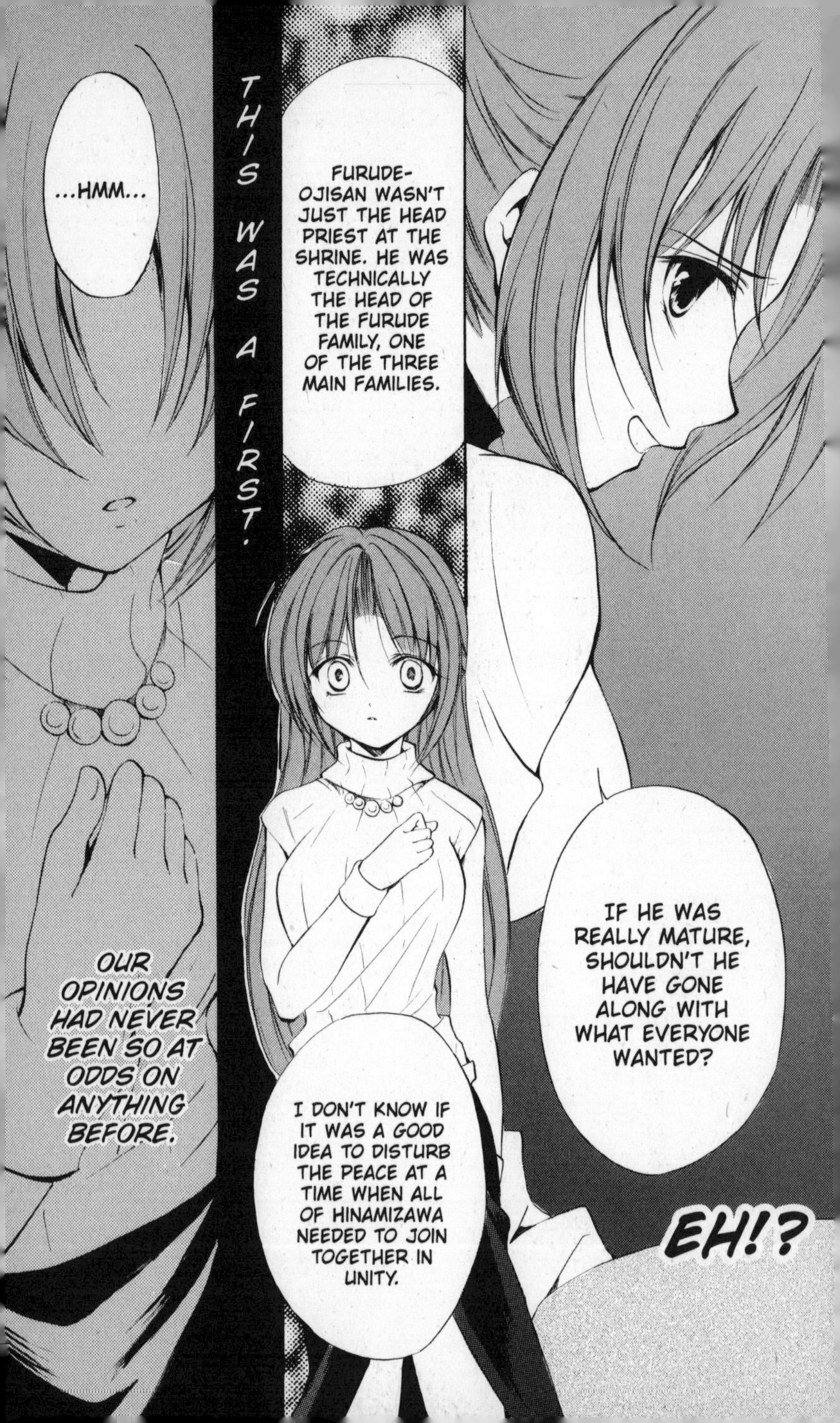
IF HE WAS REALLY MATURE, SHOULDN'T HE HAVE GONE ALONG WITH WHAT EVERYONE WANTED?
EH!?
FURUDE-OJISAN WASN'T JUST THE HEAD PRIEST AT THE SHRINE. HE WAS TECHNICALLY THE HEAD OF THE FURUDE FAMILY, ONE OF THE THREE MAIN FAMILIES.
I DON'T KNOW IF IT WAS A GOOD IDEA TO DISTURB THE PEACE AT A TIME WHEN ALL OF HINAMIZAWA NEEDED TO JOIN TOGETHER IN UNITY.
THIS WAS A FIRST.
...HMM...
OUR OPINIONS HAD NEVER BEEN SO AT ODDS ON ANYTHING BEFORE.

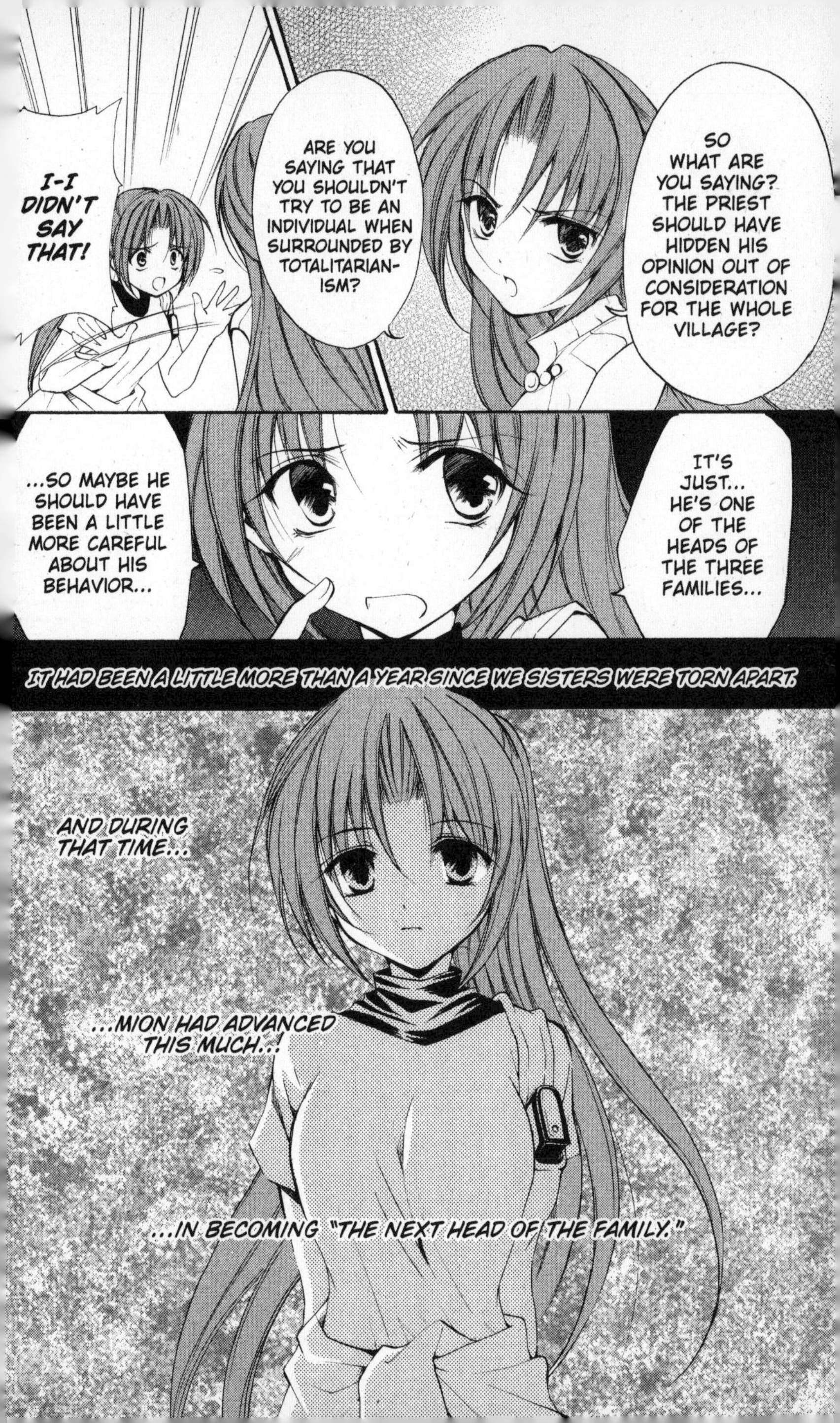
SO WHAT ARE YOU SAYING? THE PRIEST SHOULD HAVE HIDDEN HIS OPINION OUT OF CONSIDERATION FOR THE WHOLE VILLAGE?
ARE YOU SAYING THAT YOU SHOULDN'T TRY TO BE AN INDIVIDUAL WHEN SURROUNDED BY TOTALITARIAN-ISM?
I-I DIDN'T SAY THAT!
IT'S JUST... HE'S ONE OF THE HEADS OF THE THREE FAMILIES...
...SO MAYBE HE SHOULD HAVE BEEN A LITTLE MORE CAREFUL ABOUT HIS BEHAVIOR...
IT HAD BEEN A LITTLE MORE THAN A YEAR SINCE WE SISTERS WERE TORN APART.
AND DURING THAT TIME...
...MION HAD ADVANCED THIS MUCH..!
...IN BECOMING "THE NEXT HEAD OF THE FAMILY."

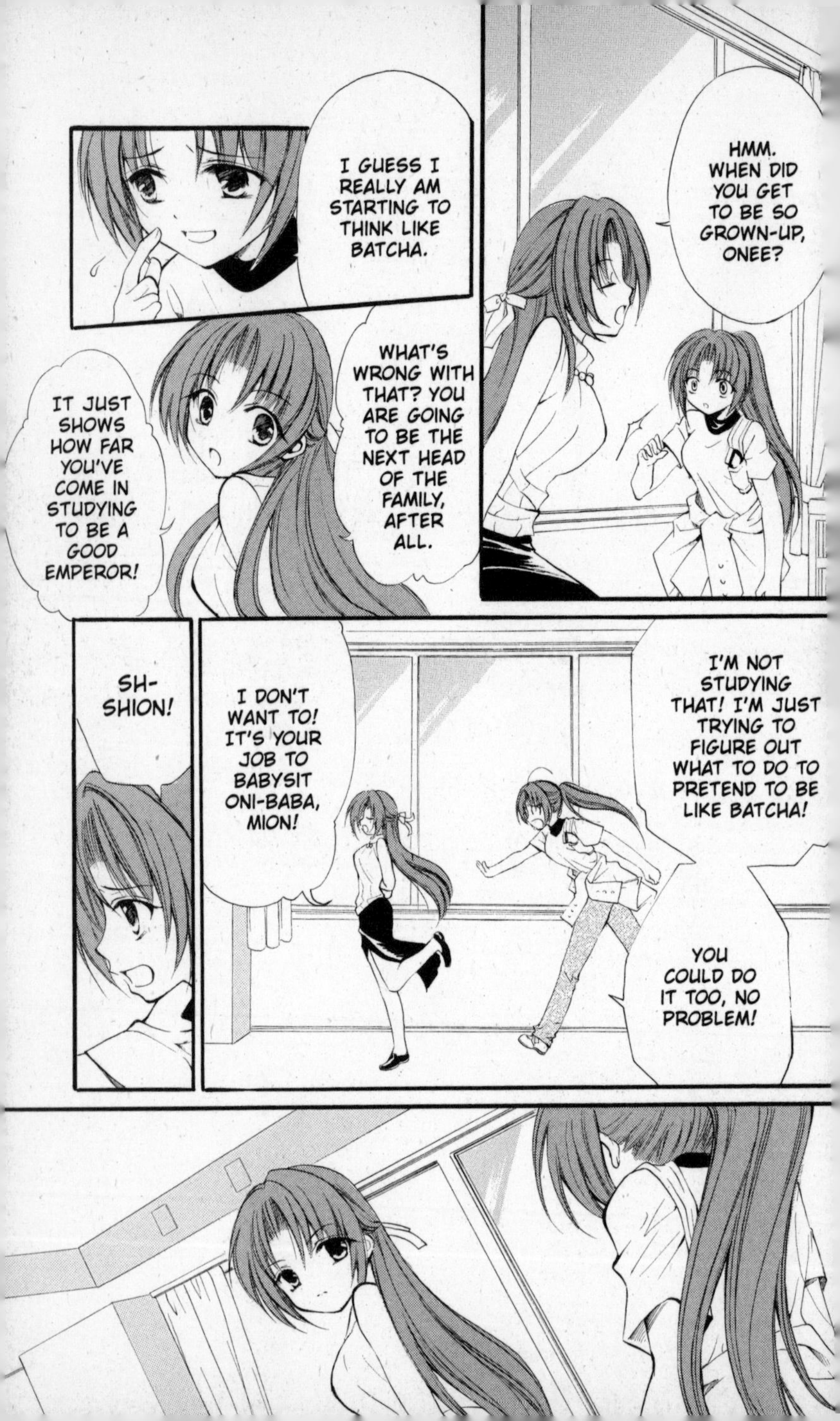
HMM. WHEN DID YOU GET TO BE SO GROWN-UP, ONEE?
I GUESS I REALLY AM STARTING TO THINK LIKE BATCHA.
WHAT'S WRONG WITH THAT? YOU ARE GOING TO BE THE NEXT HEAD OF THE FAMILY, AFTER ALL.
IT JUST SHOWS HOW FAR YOU'VE COME IN STUDYING TO BE A GOOD EMPEROR!
I'M NOT STUDYING THAT! I'M JUST TRYING TO FIGURE OUT WHAT TO DO TO PRETEND TO BE LIKE BATCHA!
YOU COULD DO IT TOO, NO PROBLEM!
I DON'T WANT TO! IT'S YOUR JOB TO BABYSIT ONI-BABA, MION!
SH-SHION!

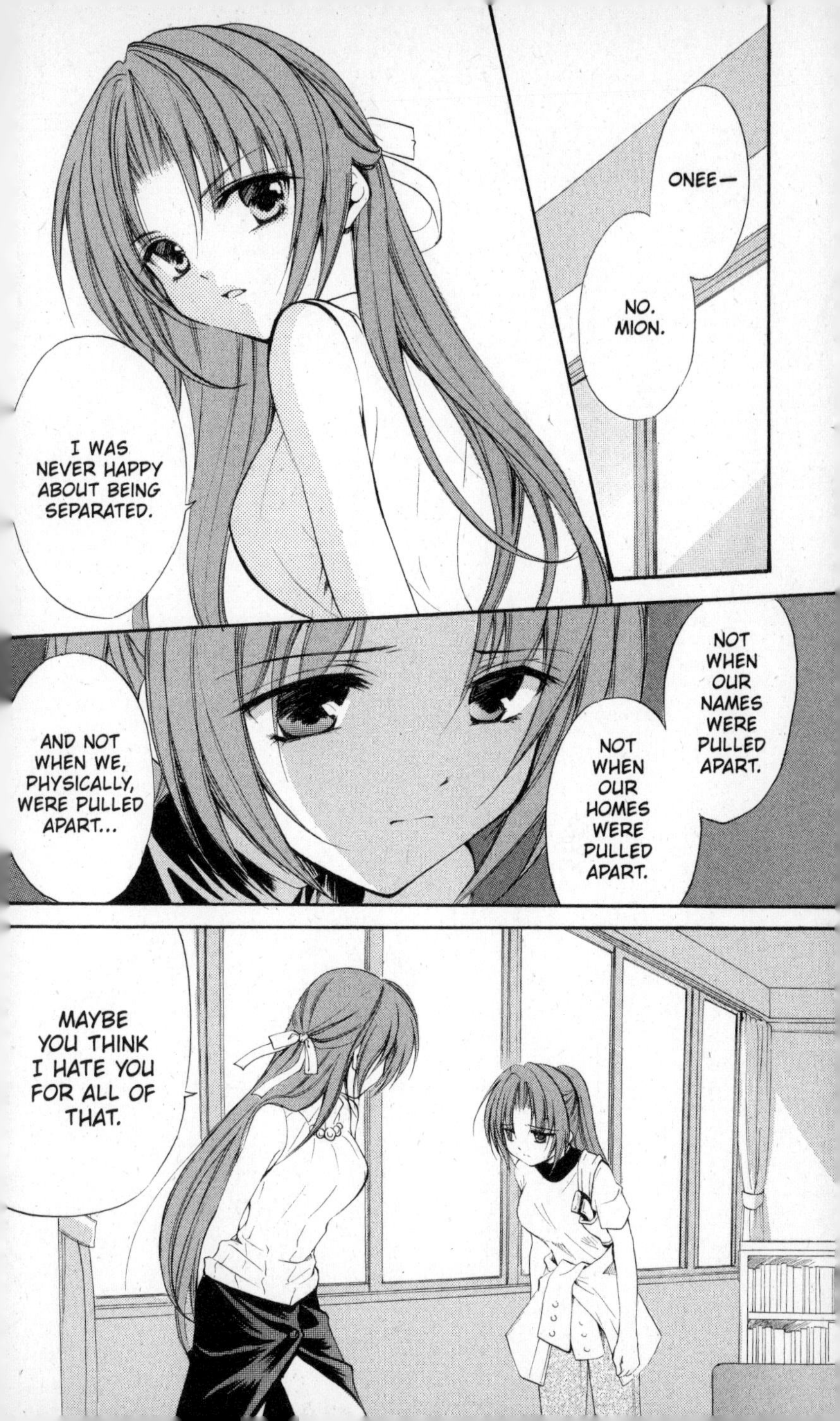
ONEE—
NO. MION.
I WAS NEVER HAPPY ABOUT BEING SEPARATED.
NOT WHEN OUR NAMES WERE PULLED APART.
NOT WHEN OUR HOMES WERE PULLED APART.
AND NOT WHEN WE, PHYSICALLY, WERE PULLED APART...
MAYBE YOU THINK I HATE YOU FOR ALL OF THAT.

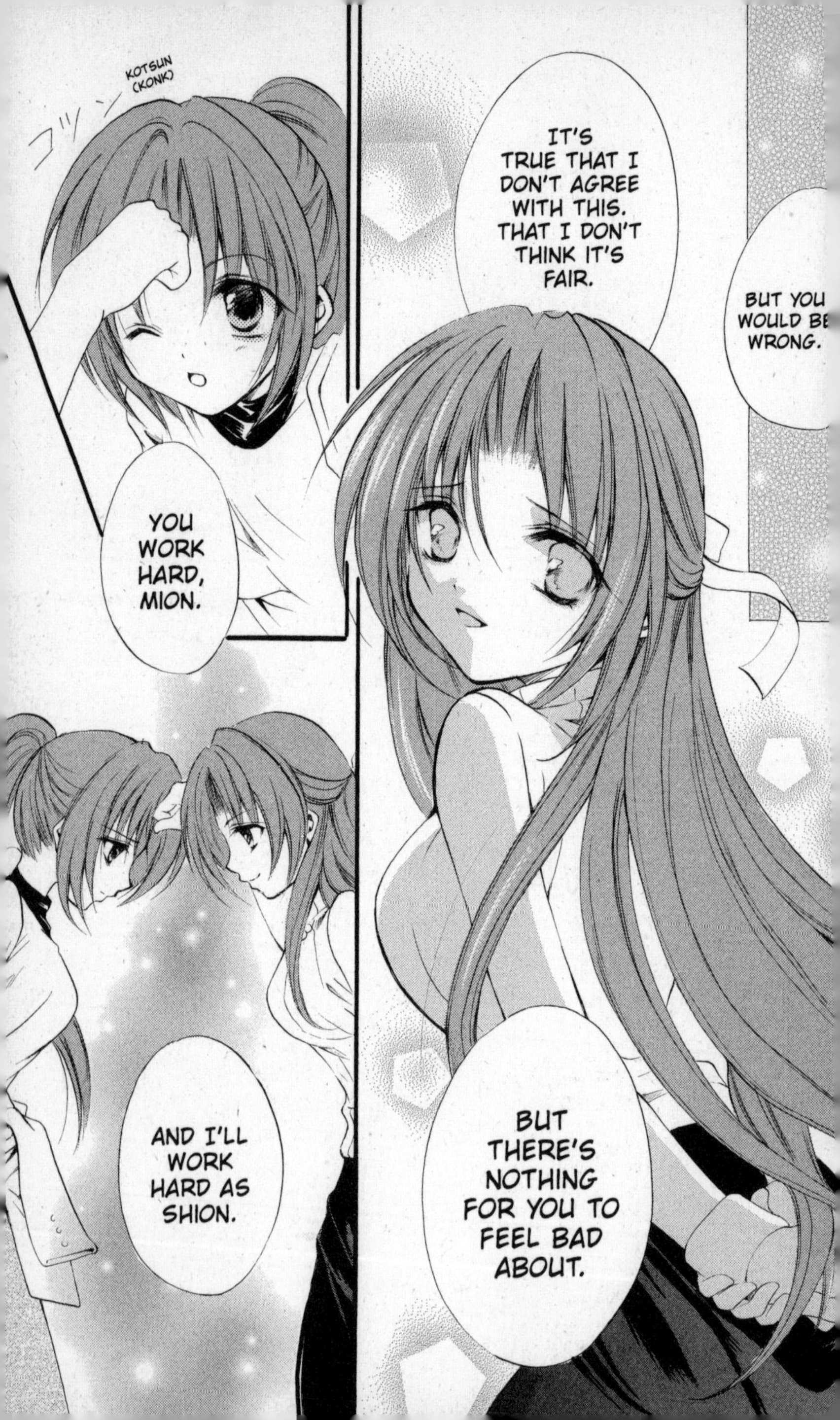
BUT YOU WOULD BE WRONG.
IT'S TRUE THAT I DON'T AGREE WITH THIS. THAT I DON'T THINK IT'S FAIR.
BUT THERE'S NOTHING FOR YOU TO FEEL BAD ABOUT.
KOTSUN (KONK)
YOU WORK HARD, MION.
AND I'LL WORK HARD AS SHION.

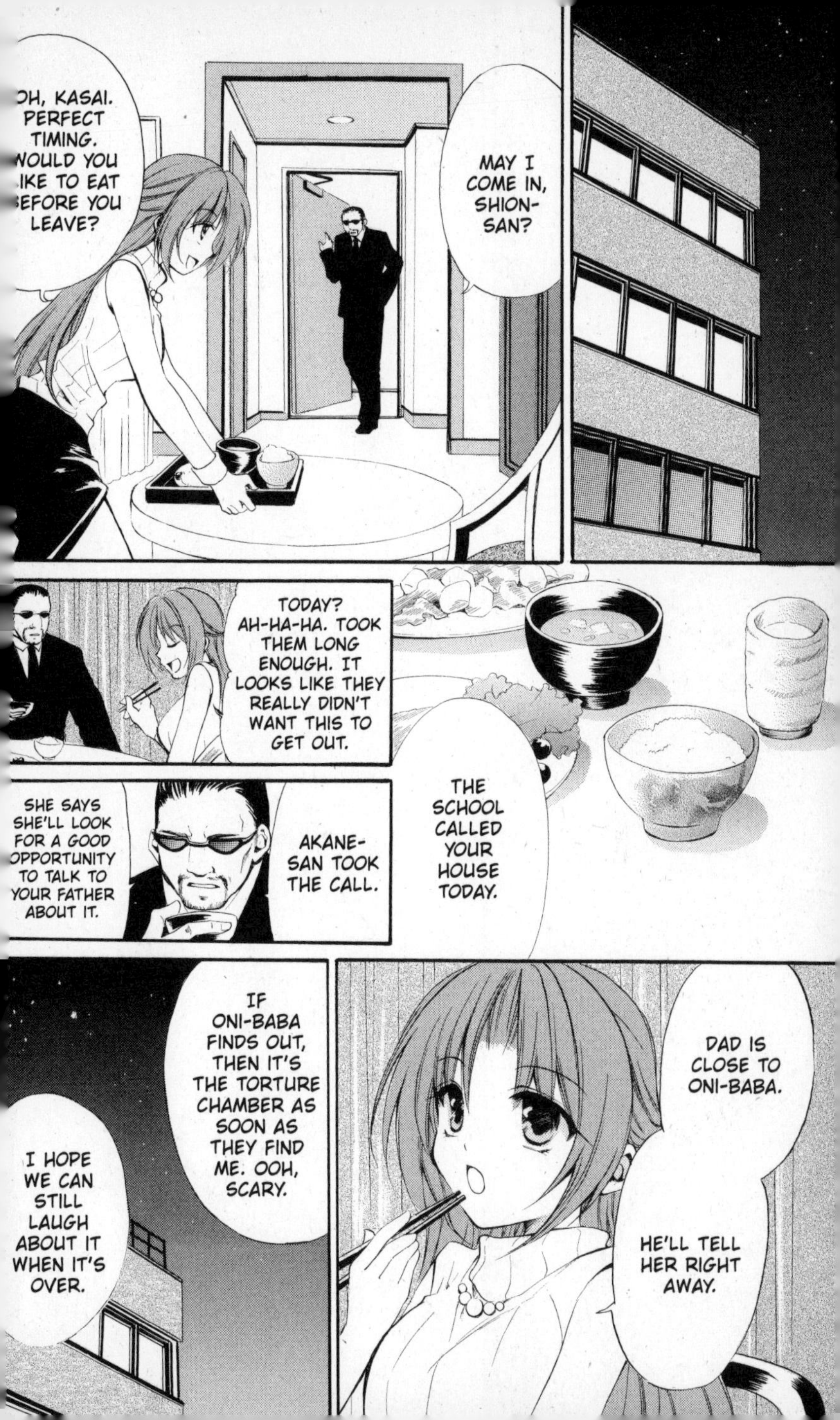
MAY I COME IN, SHION-SAN?
OH, KASAI. PERFECT TIMING. WOULD YOU LIKE TO EAT BEFORE YOU LEAVE?
THE SCHOOL CALLED YOUR HOUSE TODAY.
TODAY? AH-HA-HA. TOOK THEM LONG ENOUGH. IT LOOKS LIKE THEY REALLY DIDN'T WANT THIS TO GET OUT.
AKANE-SAN TOOK THE CALL.
SHE SAYS SHE'LL LOOK FOR A GOOD OPPORTUNITY TO TALK TO YOUR FATHER ABOUT IT.
DAD IS CLOSE TO ONI-BABA.
HE'LL TELL HER RIGHT AWAY.
IF ONI-BABA FINDS OUT, THEN IT'S THE TORTURE CHAMBER AS SOON AS THEY FIND ME. OOH, SCARY.
I HOPE WE CAN STILL LAUGH ABOUT IT WHEN IT'S OVER.

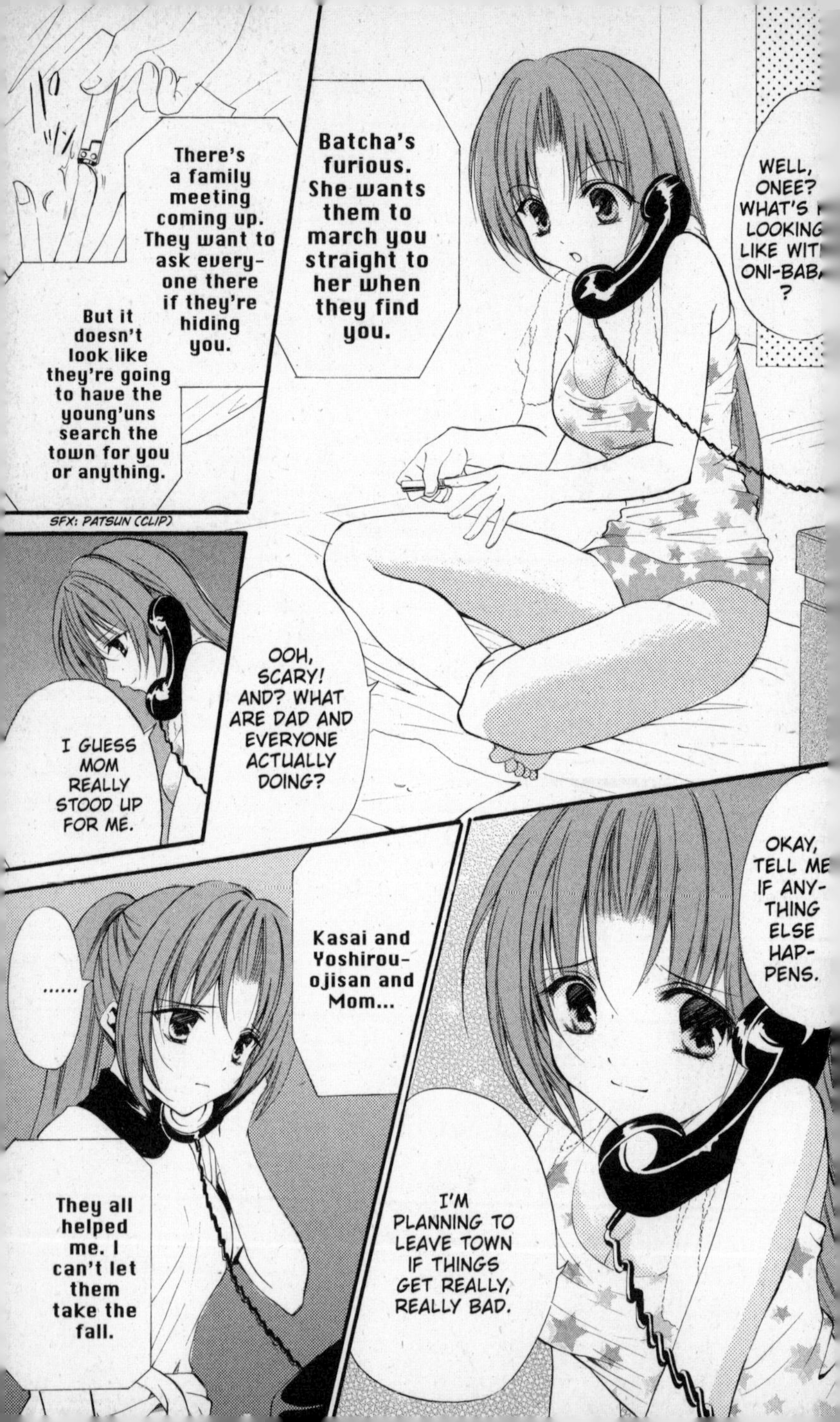
WELL, ONEE? WHAT'S LOOKING LIKE WIT ONI-BAB ?
Batcha's furious. She wants them to march you straight to her when they find you.
There's a family meeting coming up. They want to ask every-one there if they're hiding you.
But it doesn't look like they're going to have the young'uns search the town for you or anything.
SFX: PATSUN (CLIP)
I GUESS MOM REALLY STOOD UP FOR ME.
OOH, SCARY! AND? WHAT ARE DAD AND EVERYONE ACTUALLY DOING?
OKAY, TELL ME IF ANY-THING ELSE HAP-PENS.
I'M PLANNING TO LEAVE TOWN IF THINGS GET REALLY, REALLY BAD.
Kasai and Yoshirou-ojisan and Mom...
......
They all helped me. I can't let them take the fall.

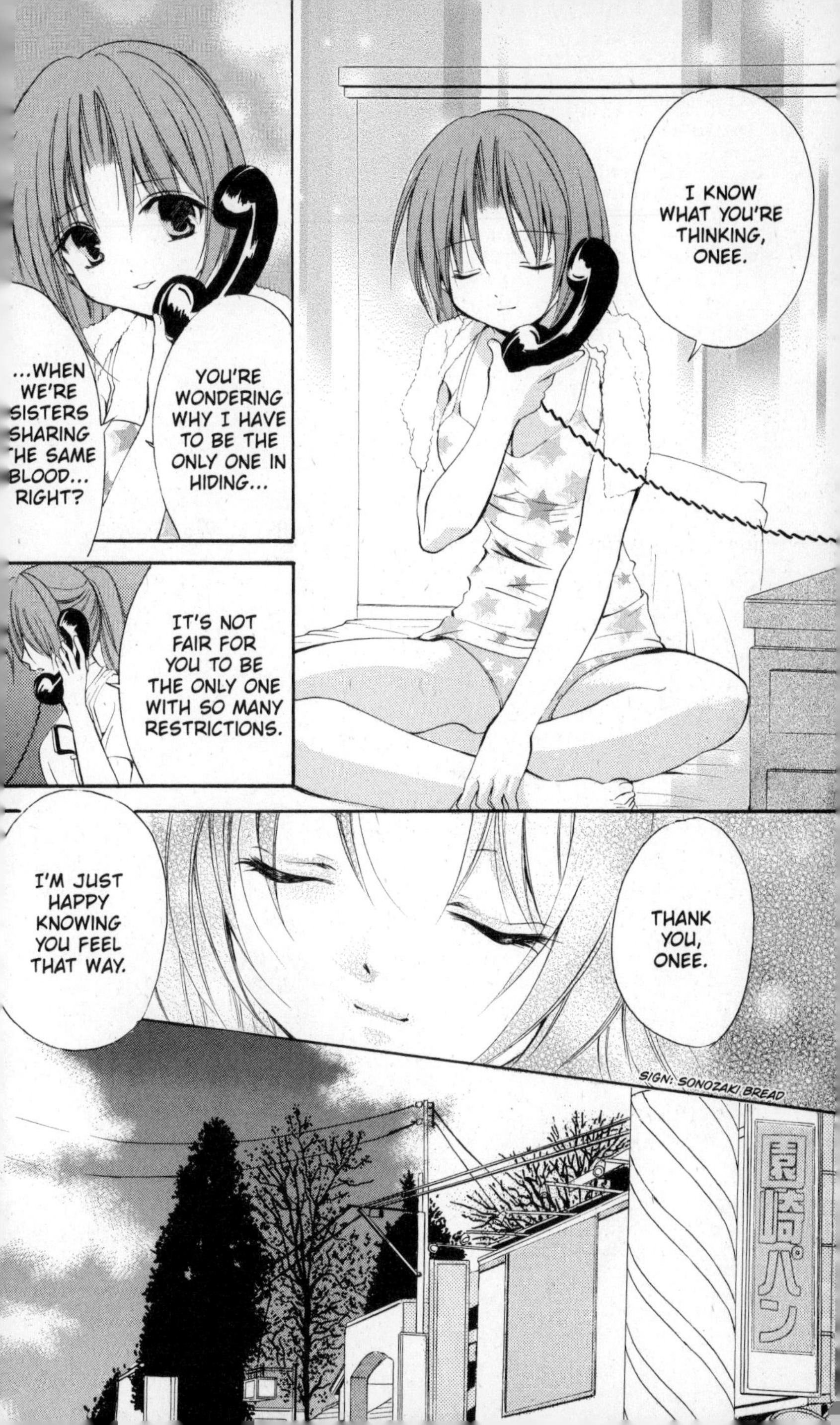
I KNOW WHAT YOU'RE THINKING, ONEE.
YOU'RE WONDERING WHY I HAVE TO BE THE ONLY ONE IN HIDING...
...WHEN WE'RE SISTERS SHARING THE SAME BLOOD... RIGHT?
IT'S NOT FAIR FOR YOU TO BE THE ONLY ONE WITH SO MANY RESTRICTIONS.
THANK YOU, ONEE.
I'M JUST HAPPY KNOWING YOU FEEL THAT WAY.
SIGN: SONOZAKI BREAD
園崎パン

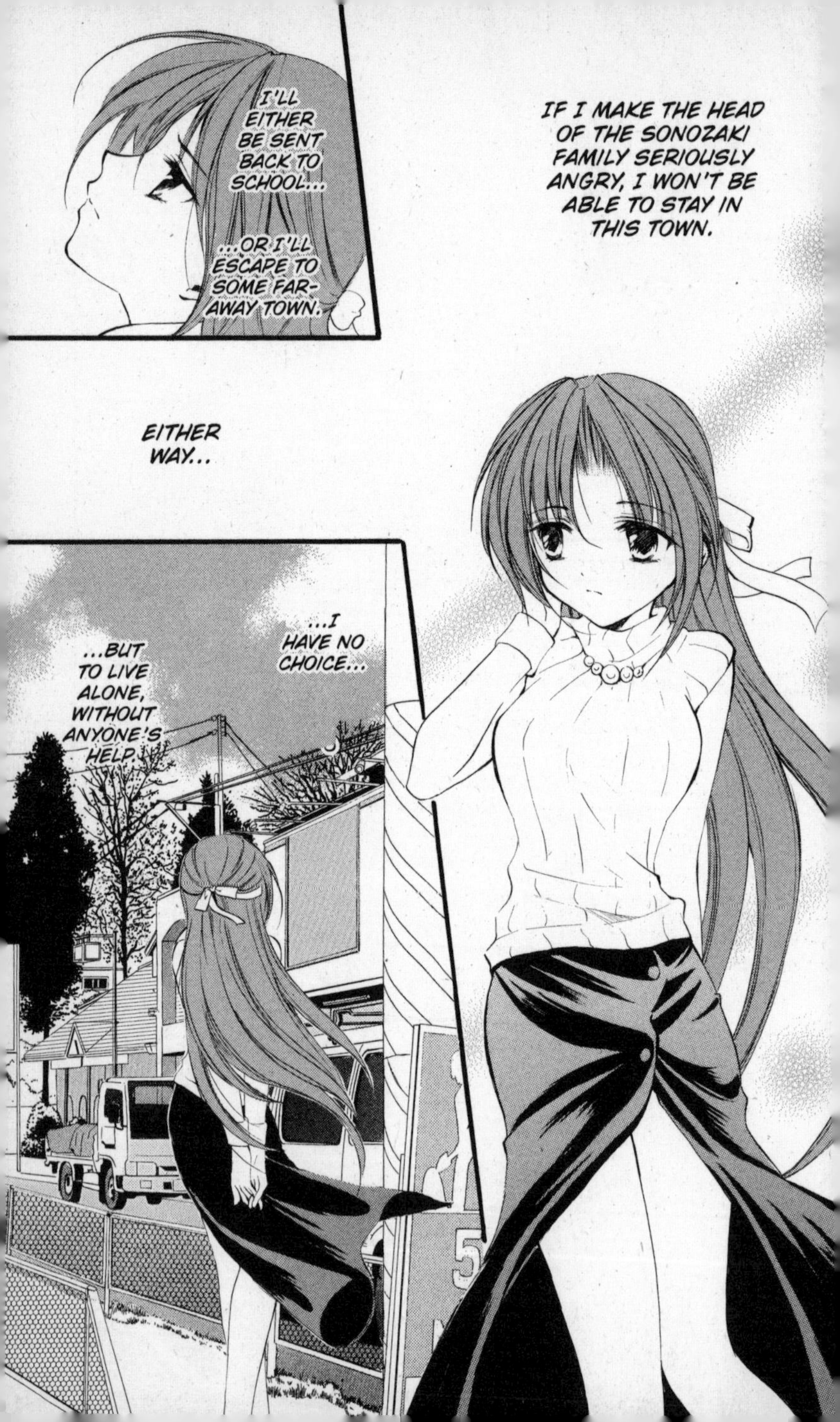
IF I MAKE THE HEAD OF THE SONOZAKI FAMILY SERIOUSLY ANGRY, I WON'T BE ABLE TO STAY IN THIS TOWN.
I'LL EITHER BE SENT BACK TO SCHOOL...
...OR I'LL ESCAPE TO SOME FAR-AWAY TOWN.
EITHER WAY...
...I HAVE NO CHOICE...
...BUT TO LIVE ALONE, WITHOUT ANYONE'S HELP.

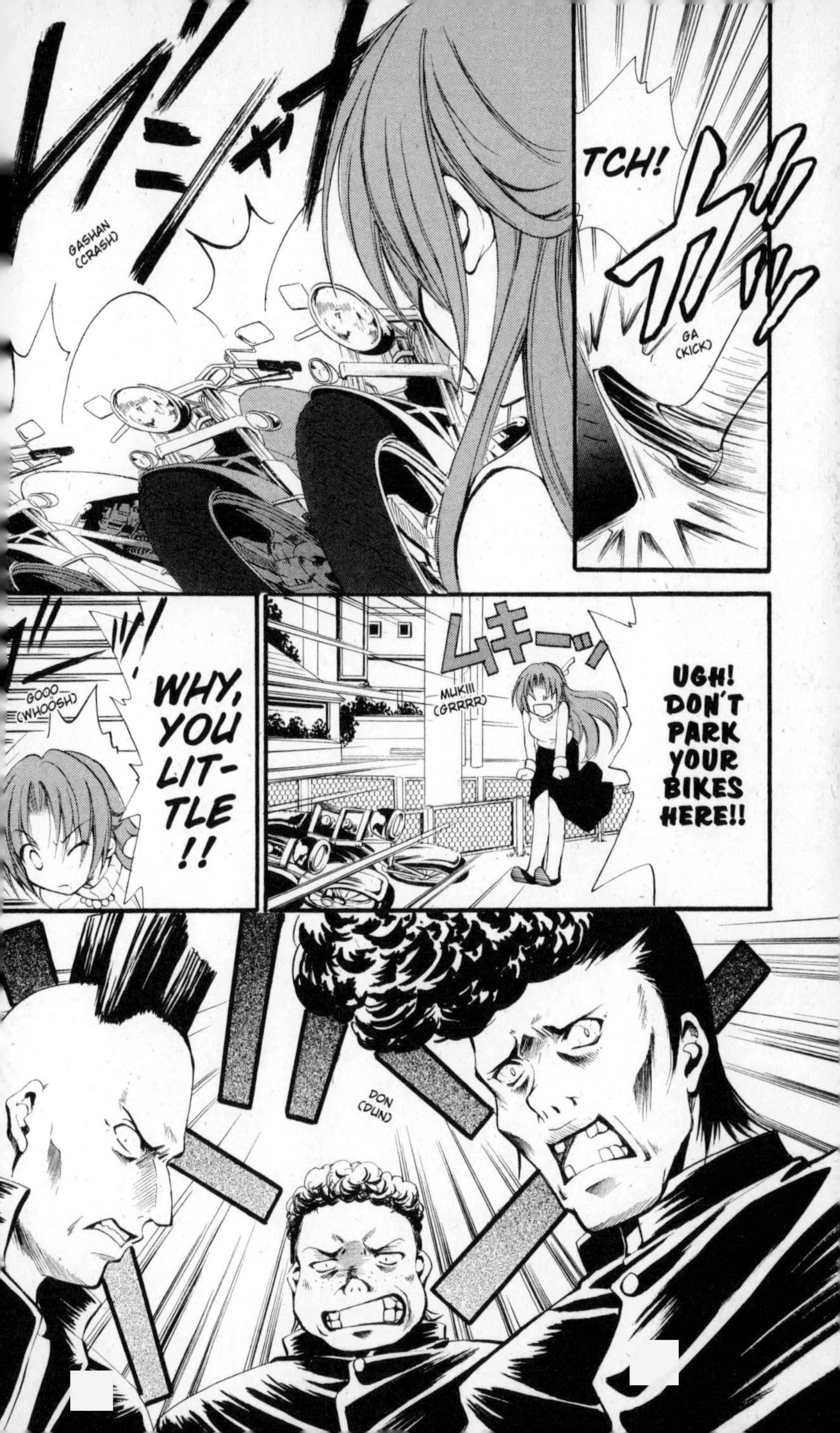
TCH!
GA (KICK)
GASHAN (CRASH)
UGH! DON'T PARK YOUR BIKES HERE!!
MUKIII (GRRRR)
WHY, YOU LIT-TLE!!
GOOO (WHOOSH)
DON (DUN)

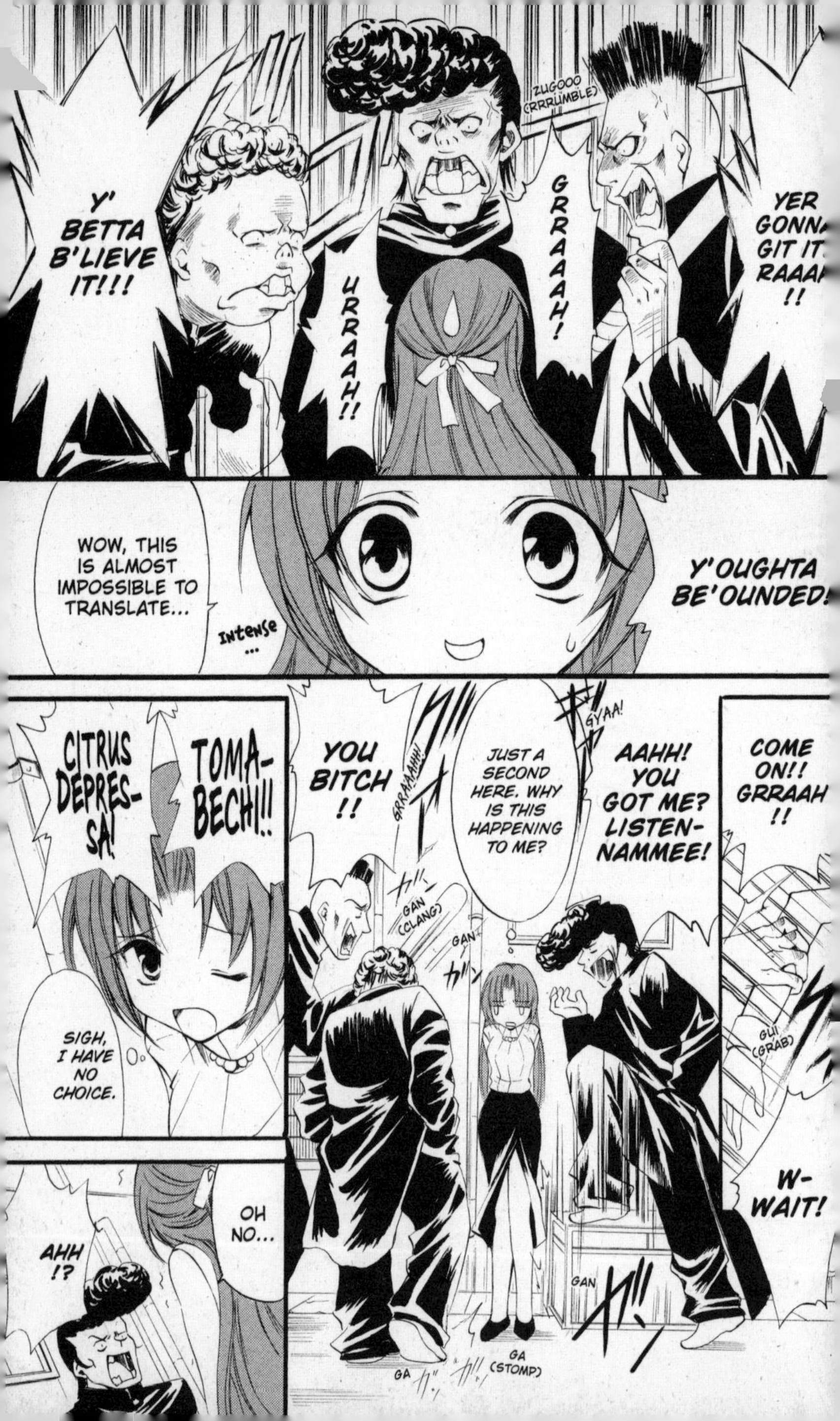

YER GONNA GIT IT RAAA
!!
ZUGOOO (RRRUMBLE)
GRRAAAH!
URRAAH!!
Y' BETTA B'LIEVE IT!!!
Y'OUGHTA BE'OUNDED!
Intense ...
WOW, THIS IS ALMOST IMPOSSIBLE TO TRANSLATE...
COME ON!! GRRAAH !!
GYAA!
AAHH! YOU GOT ME? LISTEN-NAMMEE!
JUST A SECOND HERE. WHY IS THIS HAPPENING TO ME?
GRRAAAHH!
YOU BITCH !!
GAN (CLANG)
GAN
GUI (GRAB)
W-WAIT!
GAN
GA (STOMP)
GA
TOMA-BECHI!!
CITRUS DEPRES-SA!
SIGH, I HAVE NO CHOICE.
OH NO...
AHH !?

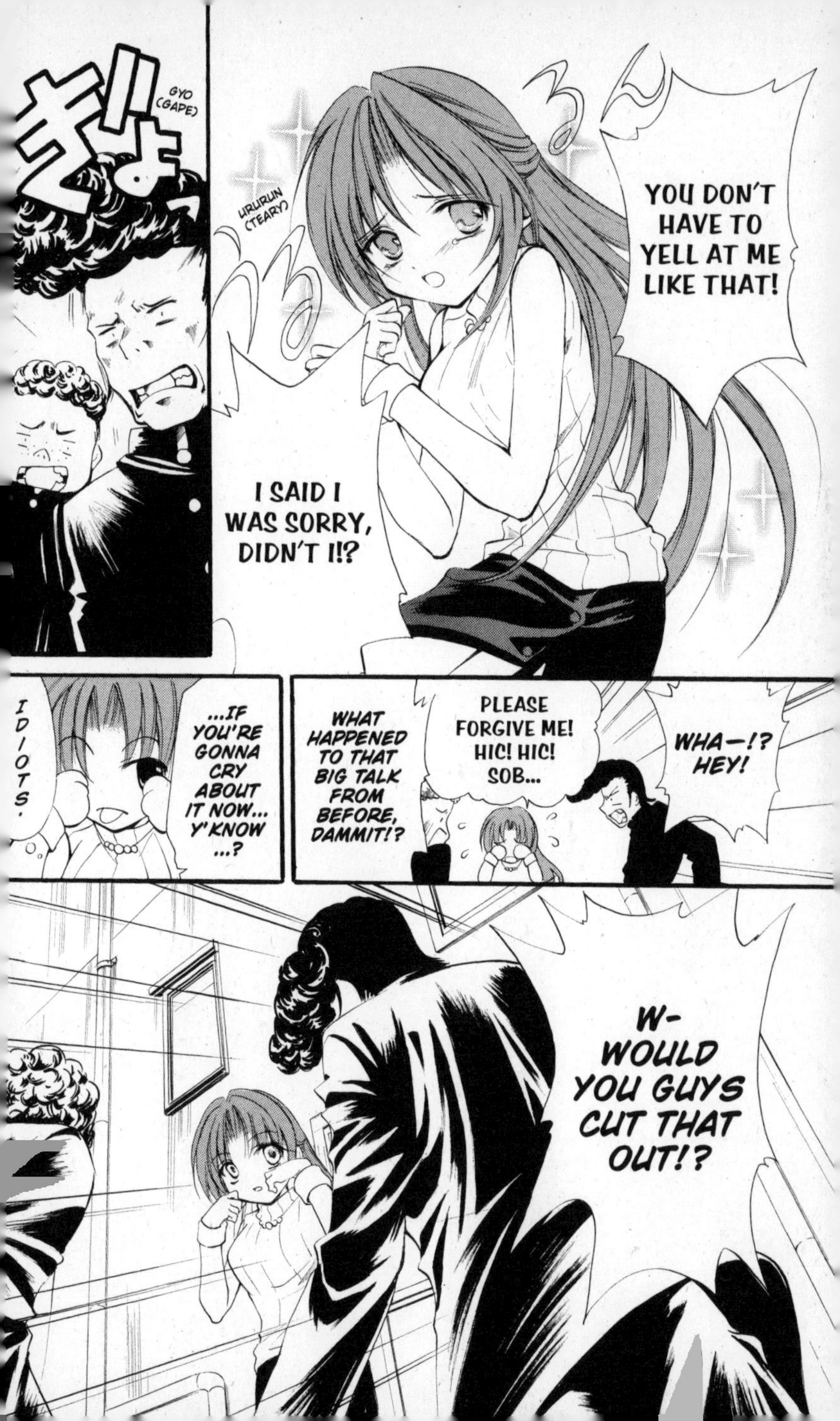
YOU DON'T HAVE TO YELL AT ME LIKE THAT!
URURUN (TEARY)
I SAID I WAS SORRY, DIDN'T I!?
GYO (GAPE)
WHA—!? HEY!
PLEASE FORGIVE ME! HIC! HIC! SOB...
WHAT HAPPENED TO THAT BIG TALK FROM BEFORE, DAMMIT!?
...IF YOU'RE GONNA CRY ABOUT IT NOW... Y'KNOW ...?
IDIOTS.
W-WOULD YOU GUYS CUT THAT OUT!?

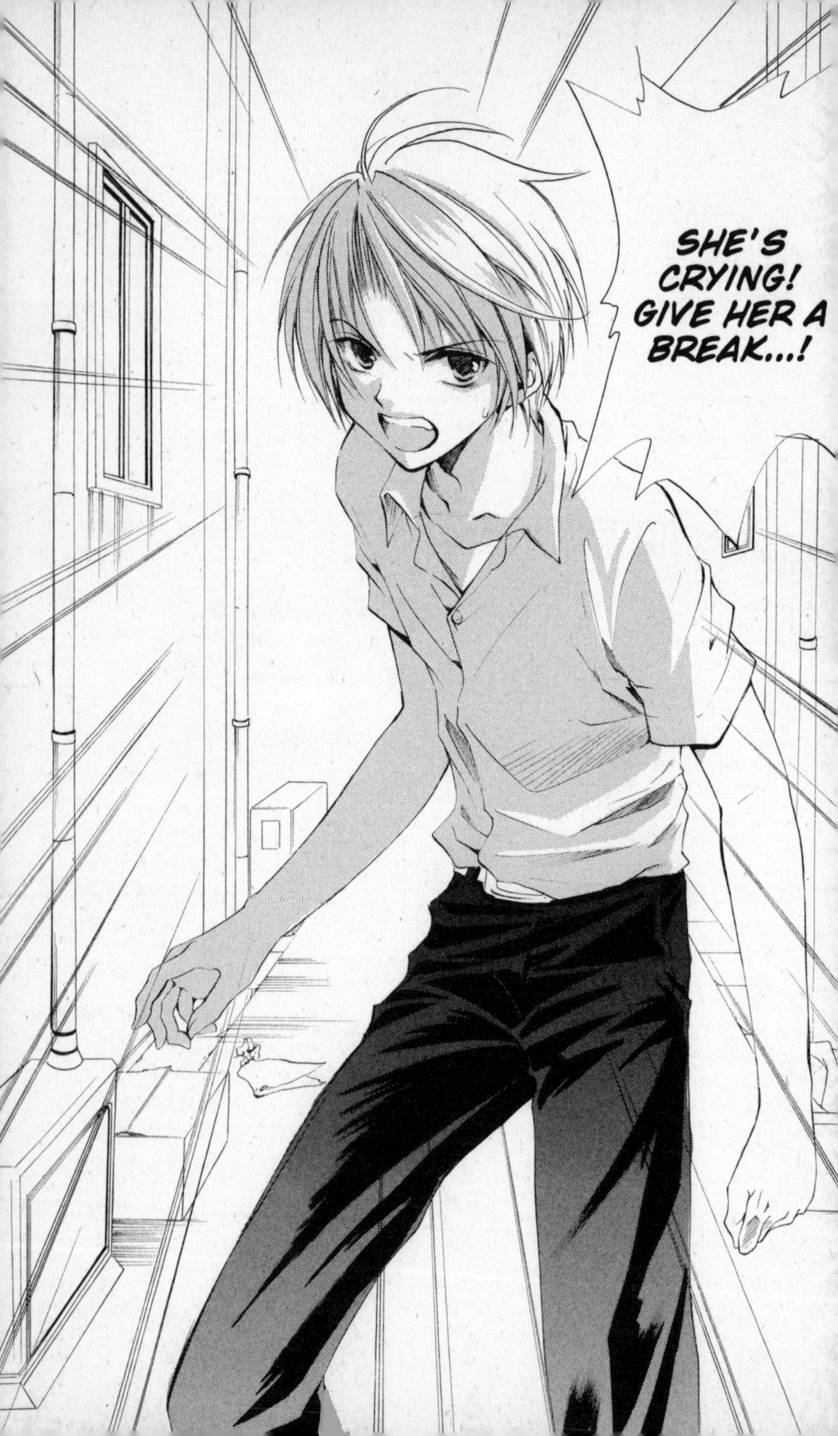
SHE'S CRYING! GIVE HER A BREAK...!

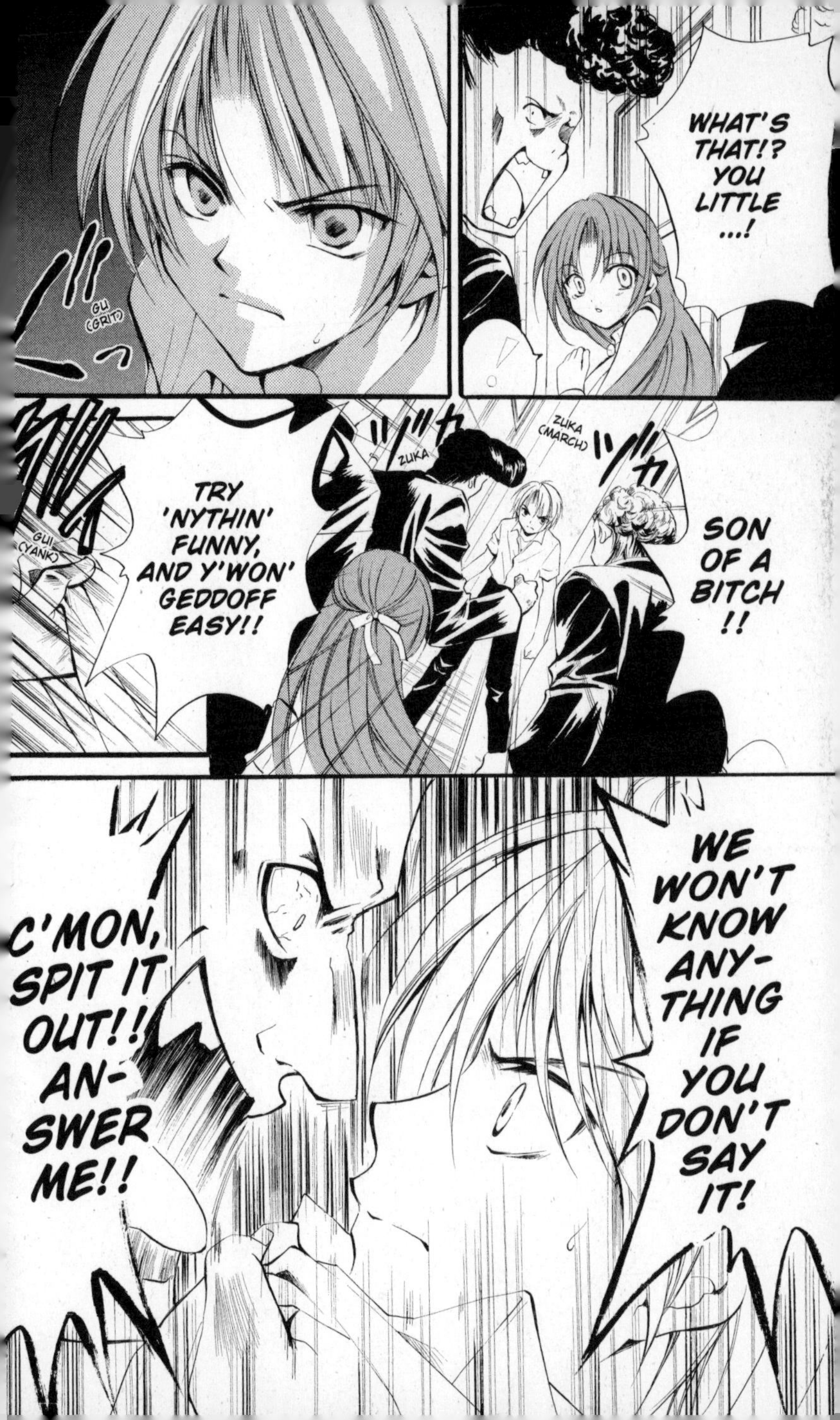
WHAT'S THAT!? YOU LITTLE ...!
GU (GRIT)
ZUKA (MARCH)
SON OF A BITCH!!
ZUKA
TRY 'NYTHIN' FUNNY, AND Y'WON' GEDDOFF EASY!!
GUI (YANK)
WE WON'T KNOW ANYTHING IF YOU DON'T SAY IT!
C'MON, SPIT IT OUT!! ANSWER ME!!

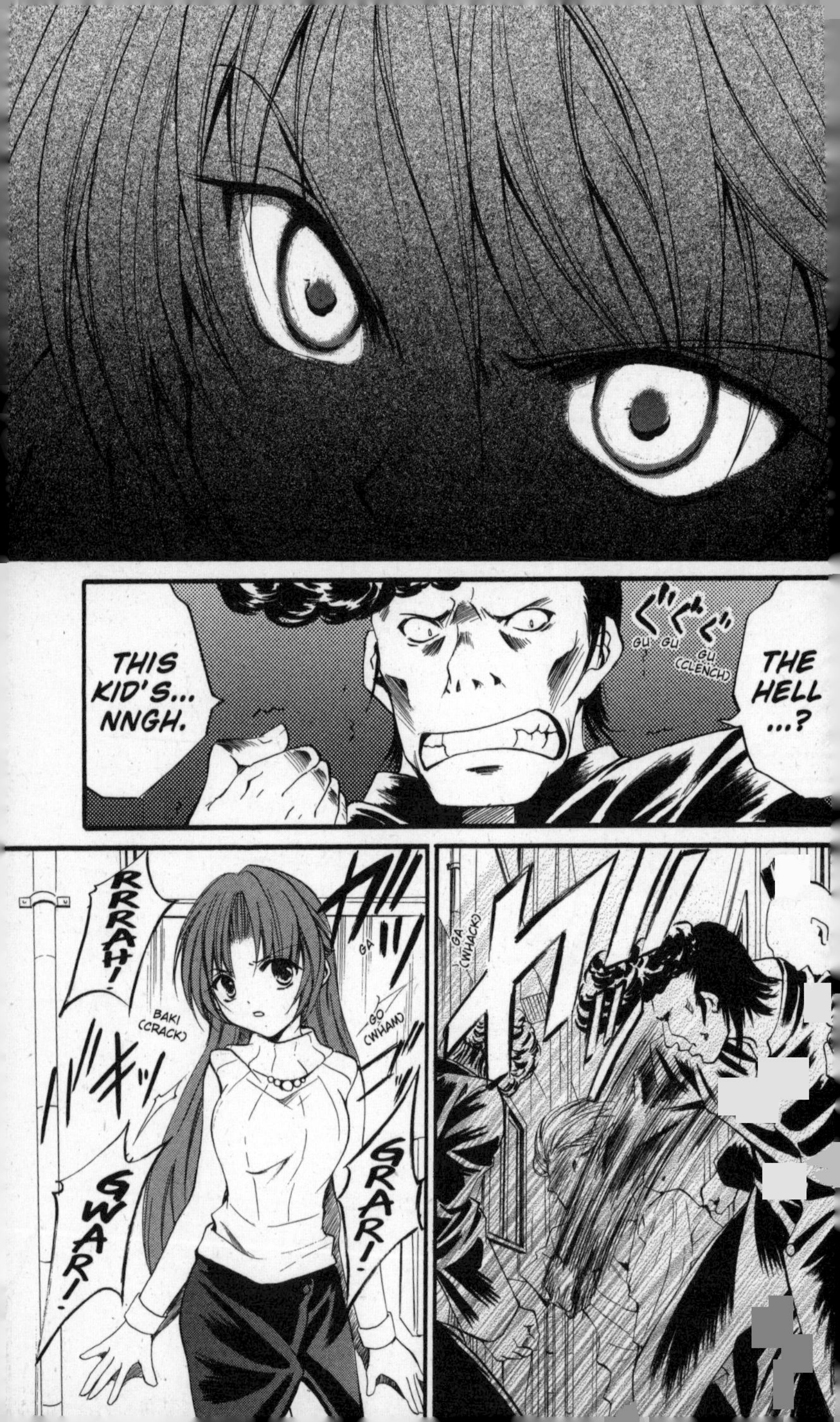
THE HELL ...?
ぐぐぐ
GU GU GU (CLENCH)
THIS KID'S... NNGH.
GA (WHACK)
GA
GO (WHAM)
RRRAH!
BAKI (CRACK)
GRAR!
GWAR!

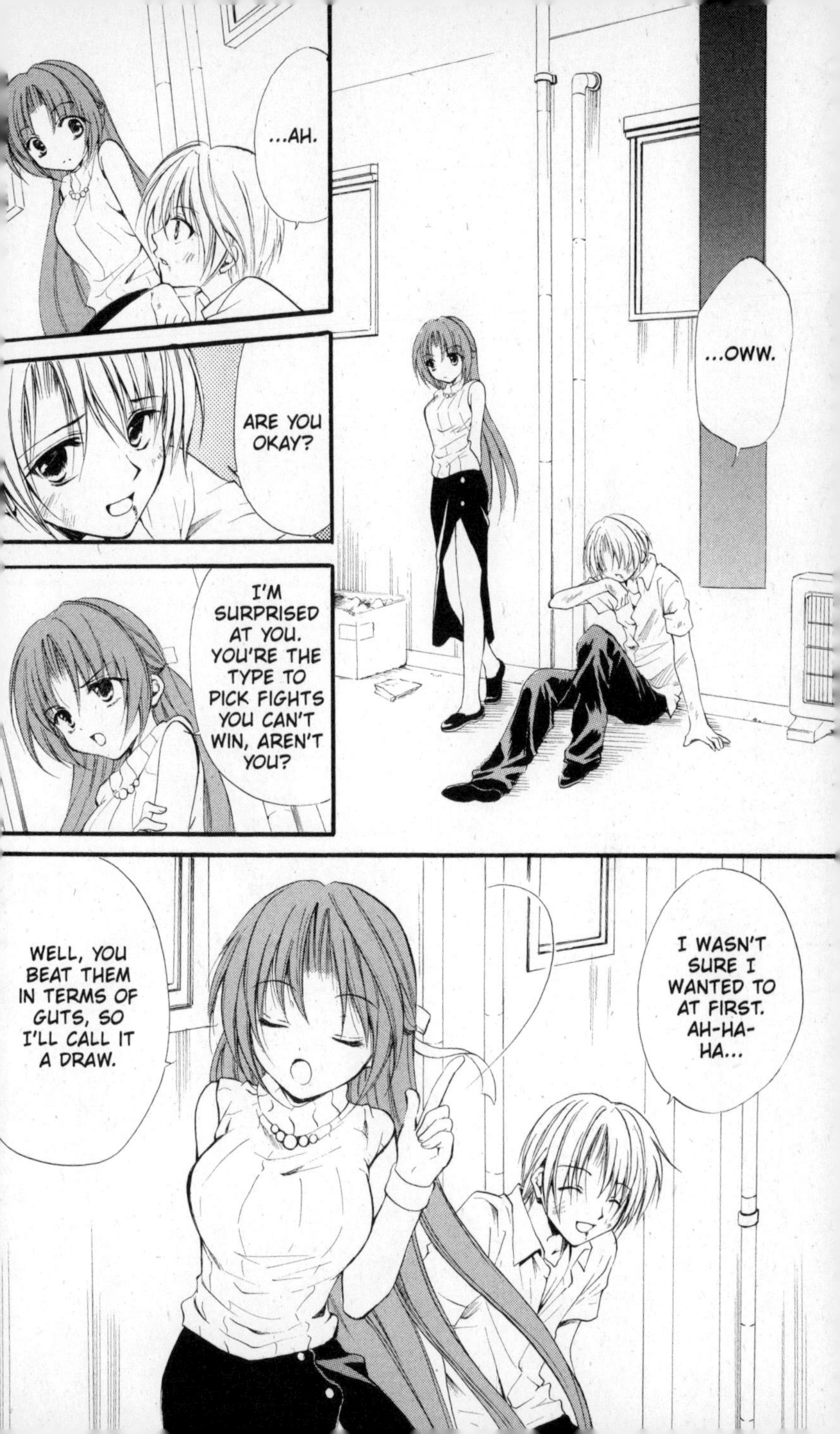
...OWW.
...AH.
ARE YOU OKAY?
I'M SURPRISED AT YOU. YOU'RE THE TYPE TO PICK FIGHTS YOU CAN'T WIN, AREN'T YOU?
I WASN'T SURE I WANTED TO AT FIRST. AH-HA-HA...
WELL, YOU BEAT THEM IN TERMS OF GUTS, SO I'LL CALL IT A DRAW.

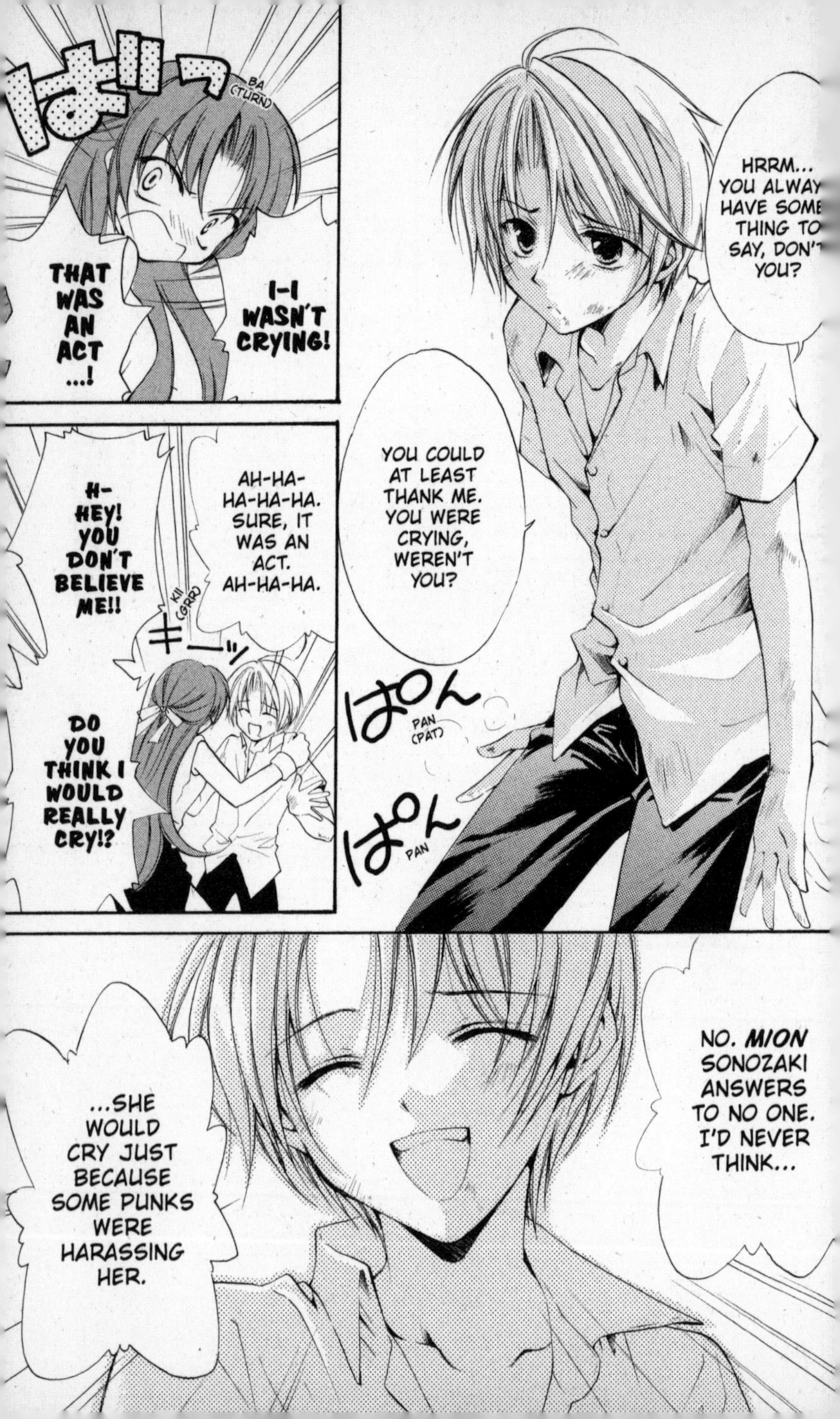
HRRM... YOU ALWAY HAVE SOME THING TO SAY, DON'T YOU?
YOU COULD AT LEAST THANK ME. YOU WERE CRYING, WEREN'T YOU?
ぱん
PAN (PAT)
ぱん
PAN
はっ
BA (TURN)
I-I WASN'T CRYING!
THAT WAS AN ACT ...!
AH-HA-HA-HA-HA. SURE, IT WAS AN ACT. AH-HA-HA.
H-HEY! YOU DON'T BELIEVE ME!!
キーッ
KII (GRR)
DO YOU THINK I WOULD REALLY CRY!?
NO. MION SONOZAKI ANSWERS TO NO ONE. I'D NEVER THINK...
...SHE WOULD CRY JUST BECAUSE SOME PUNKS WERE HARASSING HER.

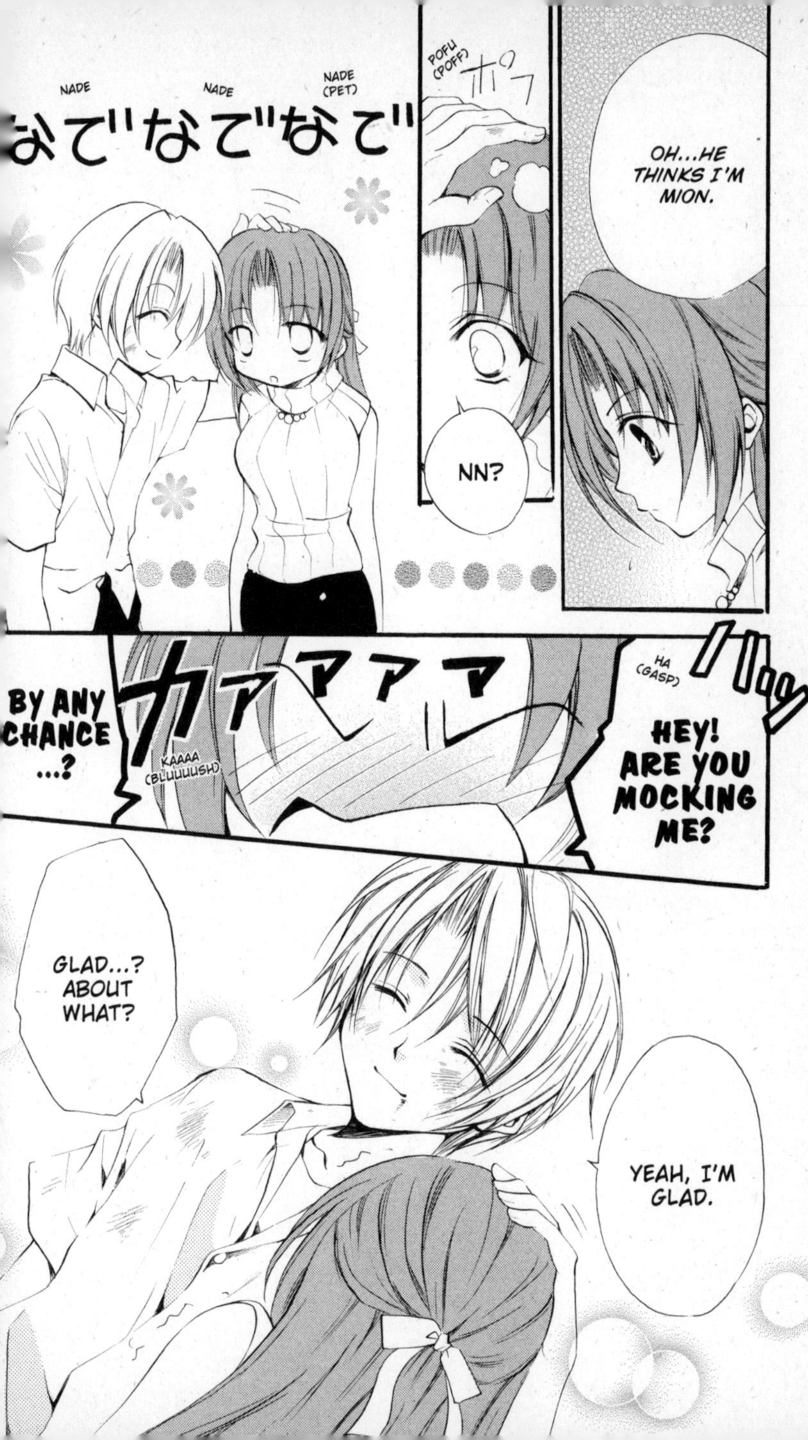
OH...HE THINKS I'M MION.
POFU (POFF)
ポフ
NN?
NADE (PET)
NADE
NADE
なでなでなで
HA (GASP)
HEY! ARE YOU MOCKING ME?
カァァァァ
KAAAA (BLUUUUSH)
BY ANY CHANCE ...?
YEAH, I'M GLAD.
GLAD...? ABOUT WHAT?

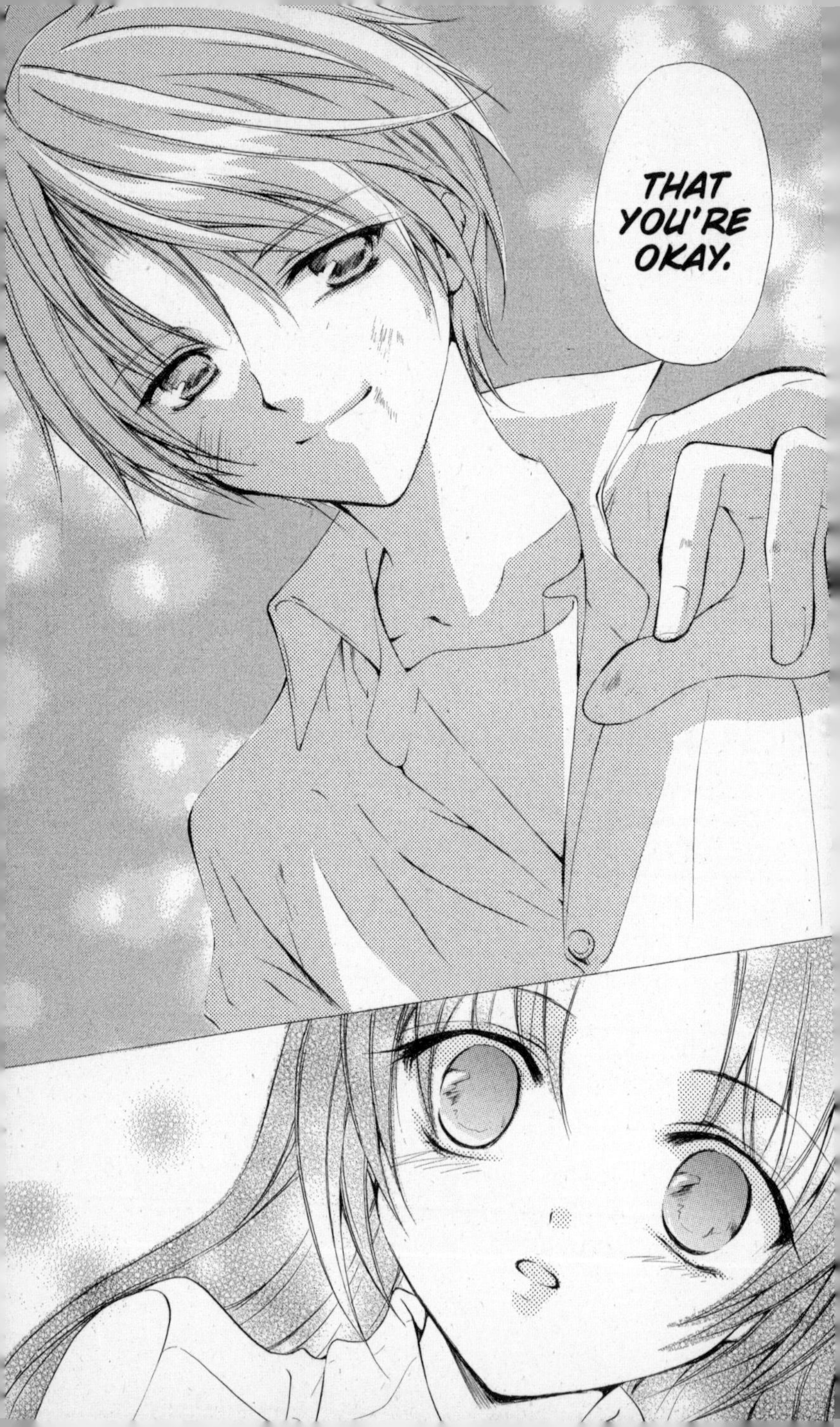
THAT YOU'RE OKAY.

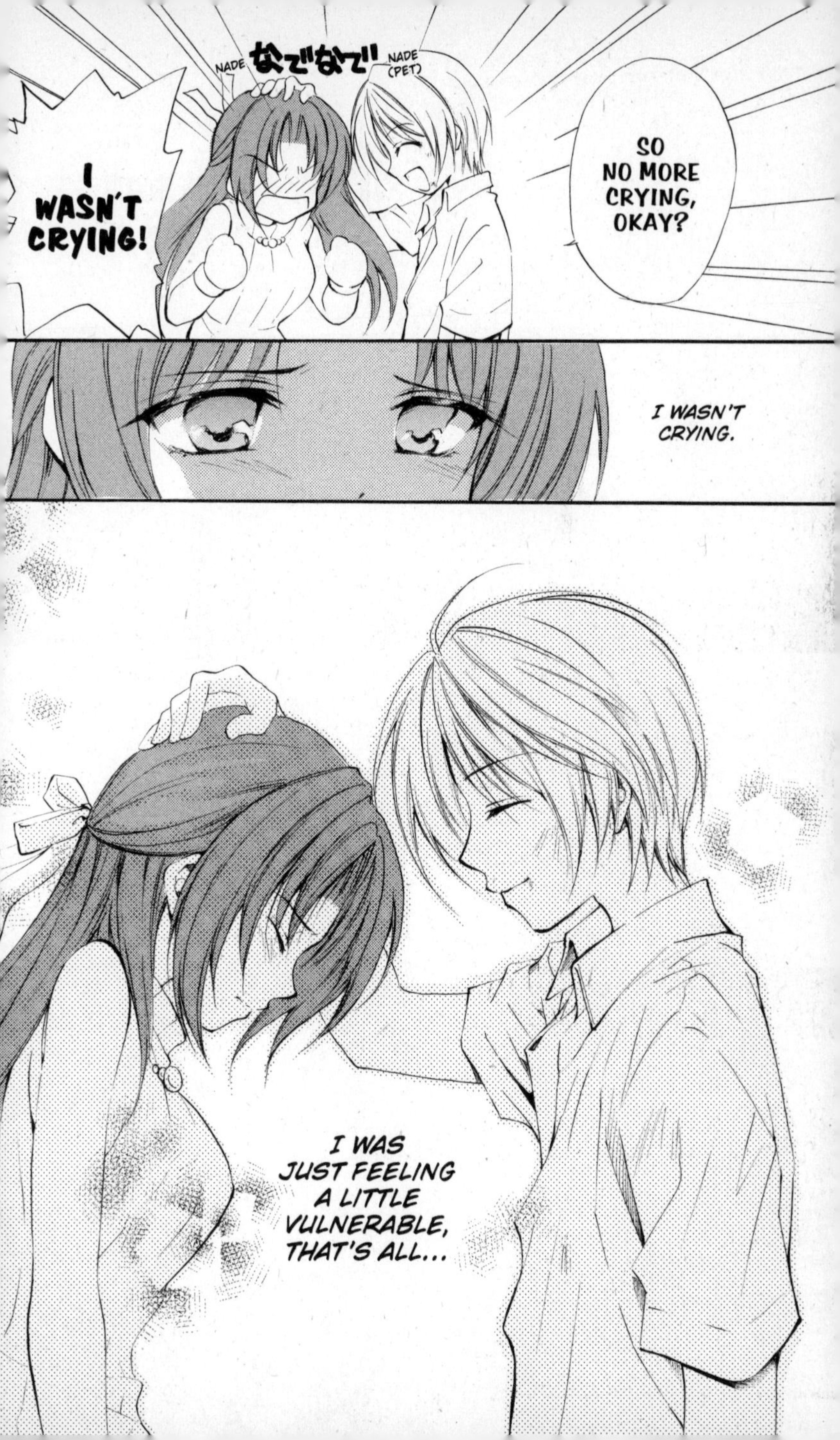
SO NO MORE CRYING, OKAY?
NADE なでなで NADE (PET)
I WASN'T CRYING!
I WASN'T CRYING.
I WAS JUST FEELING A LITTLE VULNERABLE, THAT'S ALL...

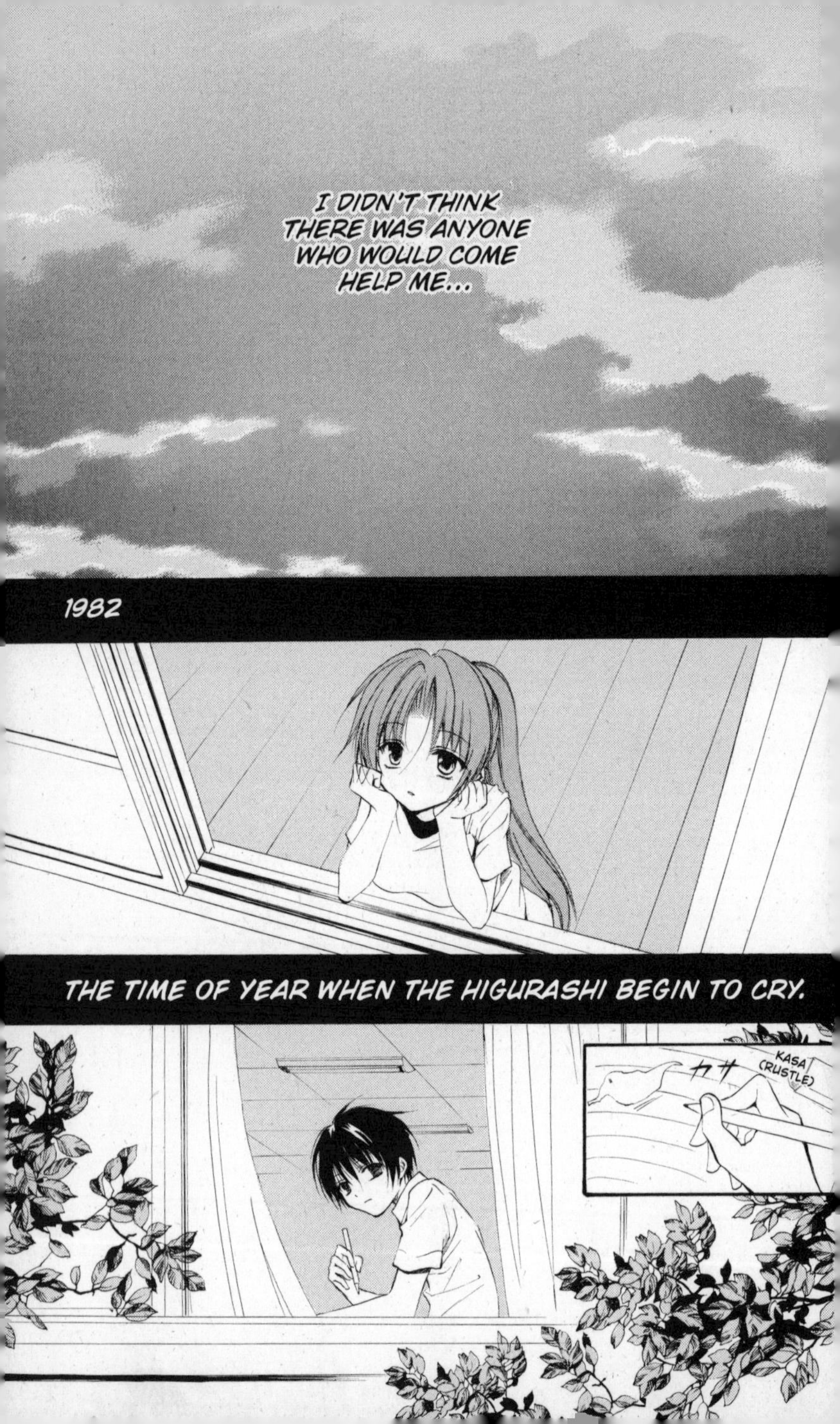
I DIDN'T THINK THERE WAS ANYONE WHO WOULD COME HELP ME...
1982
THE TIME OF YEAR WHEN THE HIGURASHI BEGIN TO CRY.
カサ
KASA (RUSTLE)

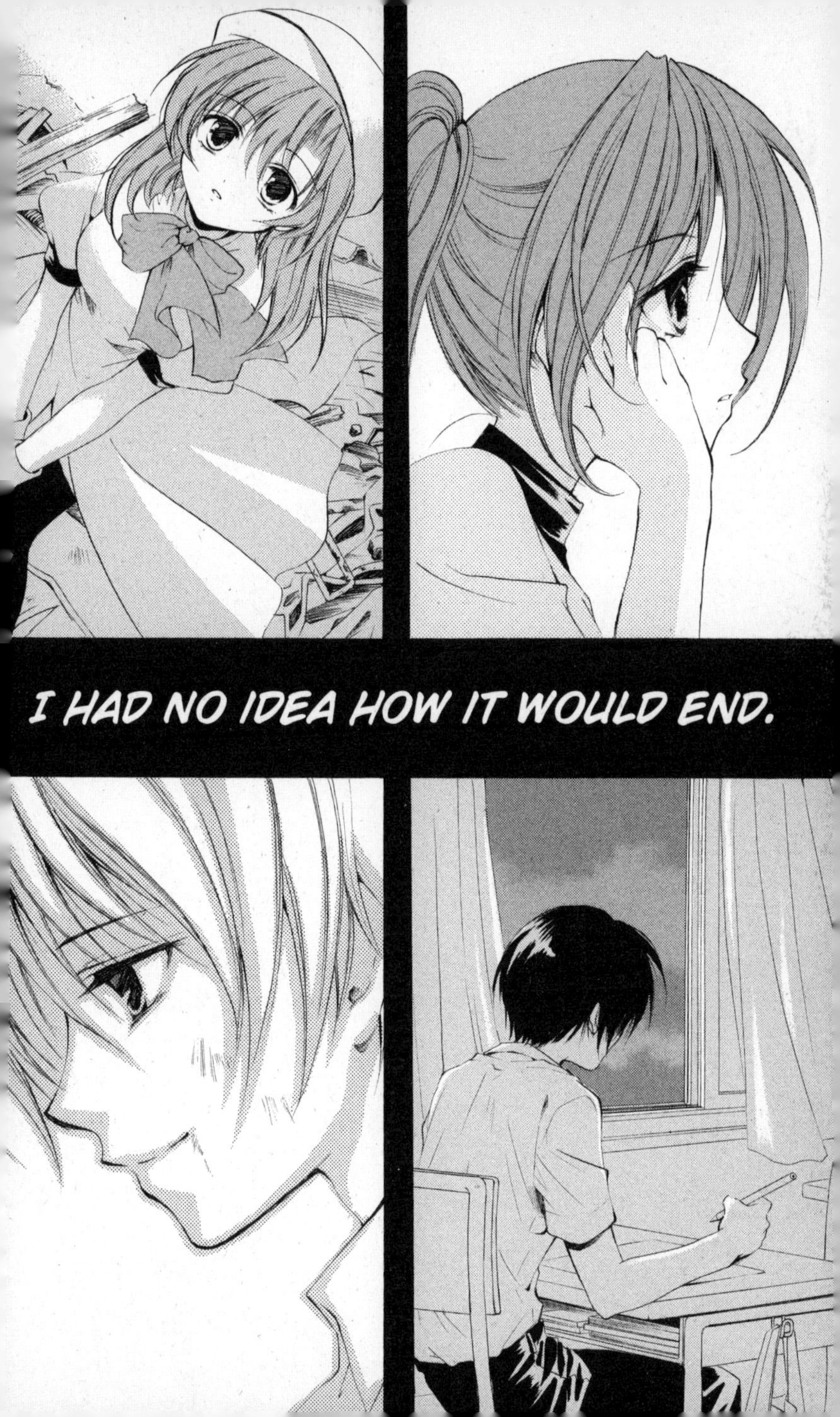
I HAD NO IDEA HOW IT WOULD END.

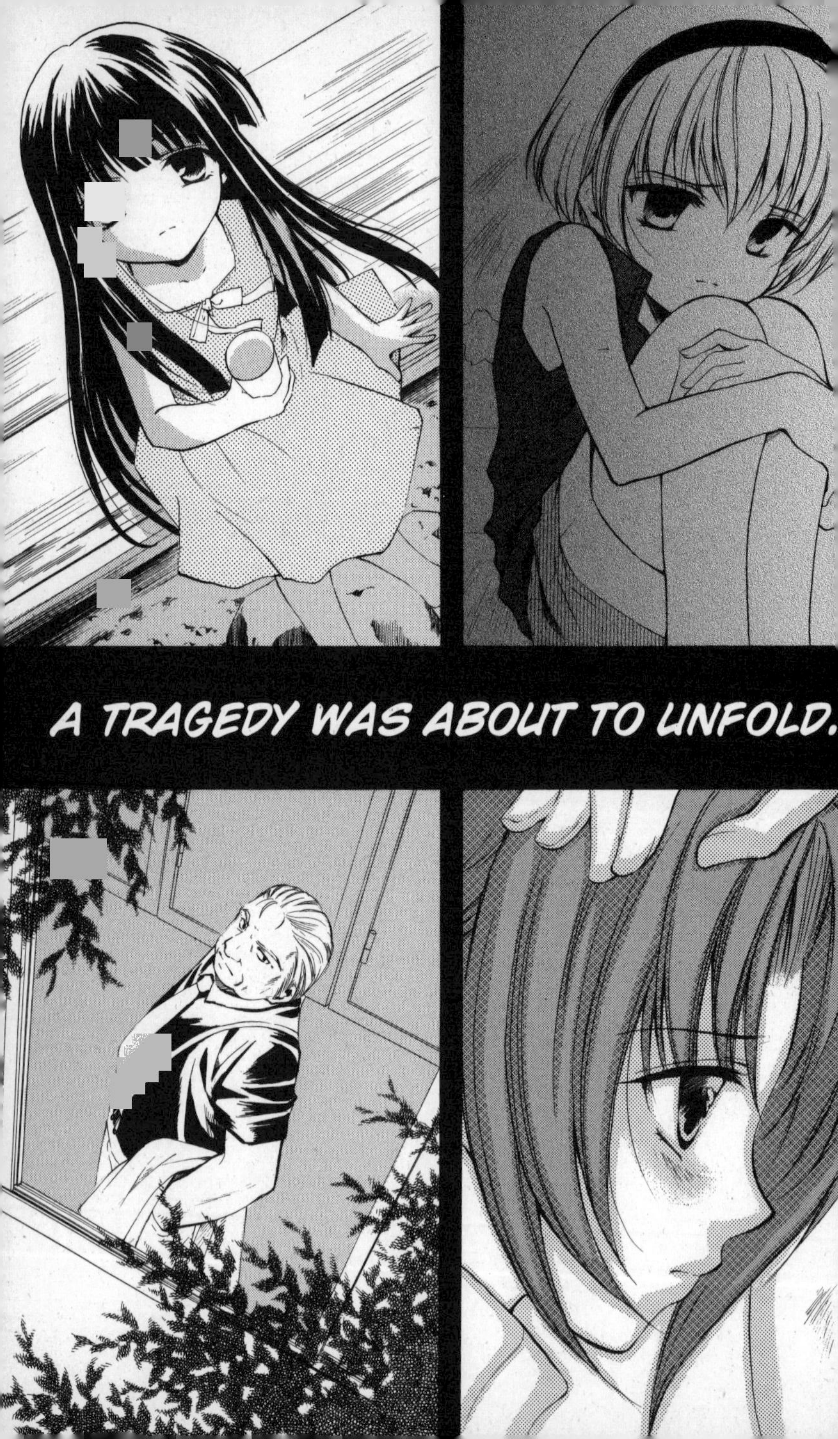
A TRAGEDY WAS ABOUT TO UNFOLD.

Higurashi
WHEN THEY CRY
EYE OPENING ARC

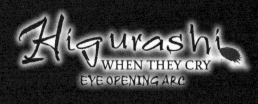

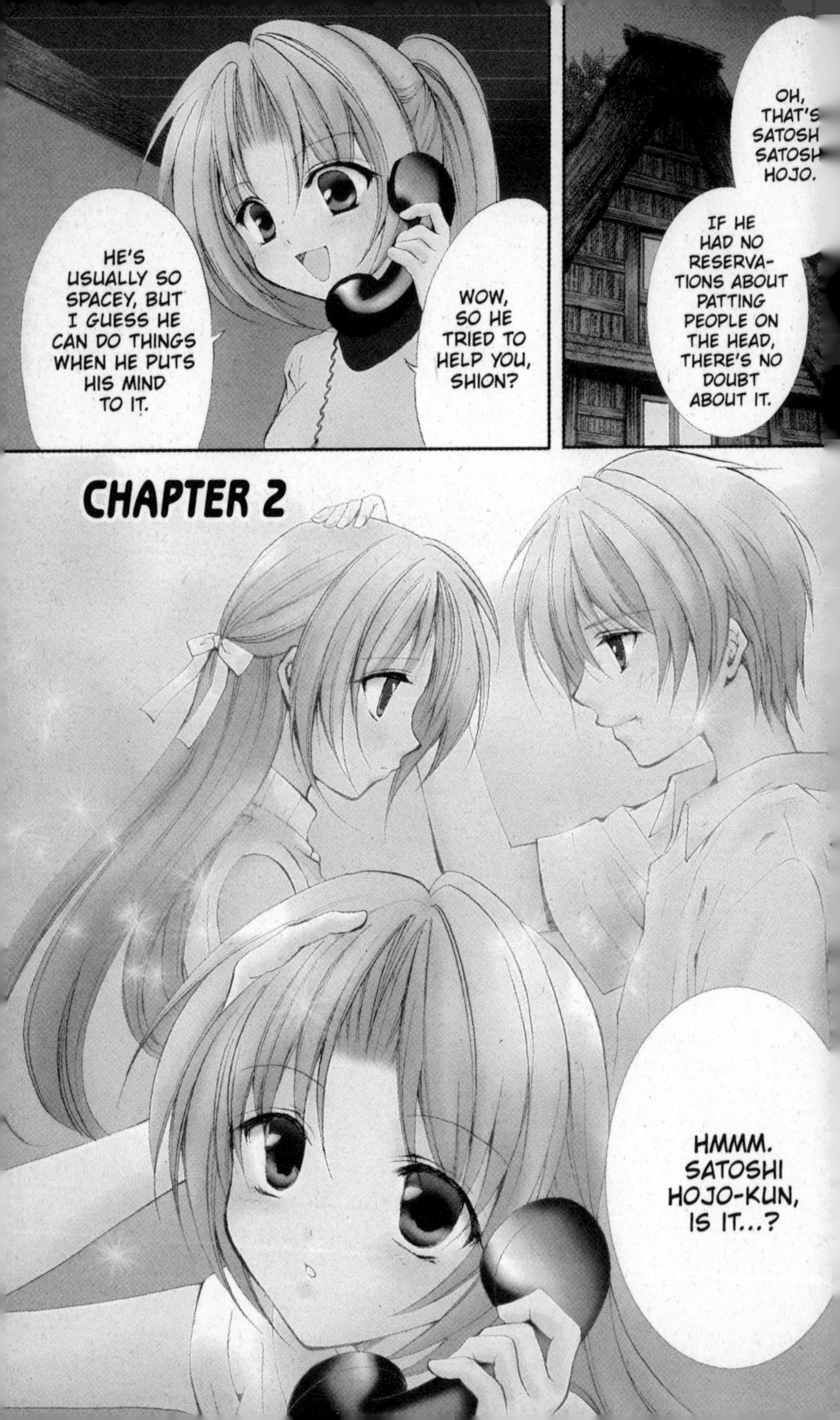
OH, THAT'S SATOSH SATOSH HOJO.
IF HE HAD NO RESERVATIONS ABOUT PATTING PEOPLE ON THE HEAD, THERE'S NO DOUBT ABOUT IT.
WOW, SO HE TRIED TO HELP YOU, SHION?
HE'S USUALLY SO SPACEY, BUT I GUESS HE CAN DO THINGS WHEN HE PUTS HIS MIND TO IT.
CHAPTER 2
HMMM. SATOSHI HOJO-KUN, IS IT...?

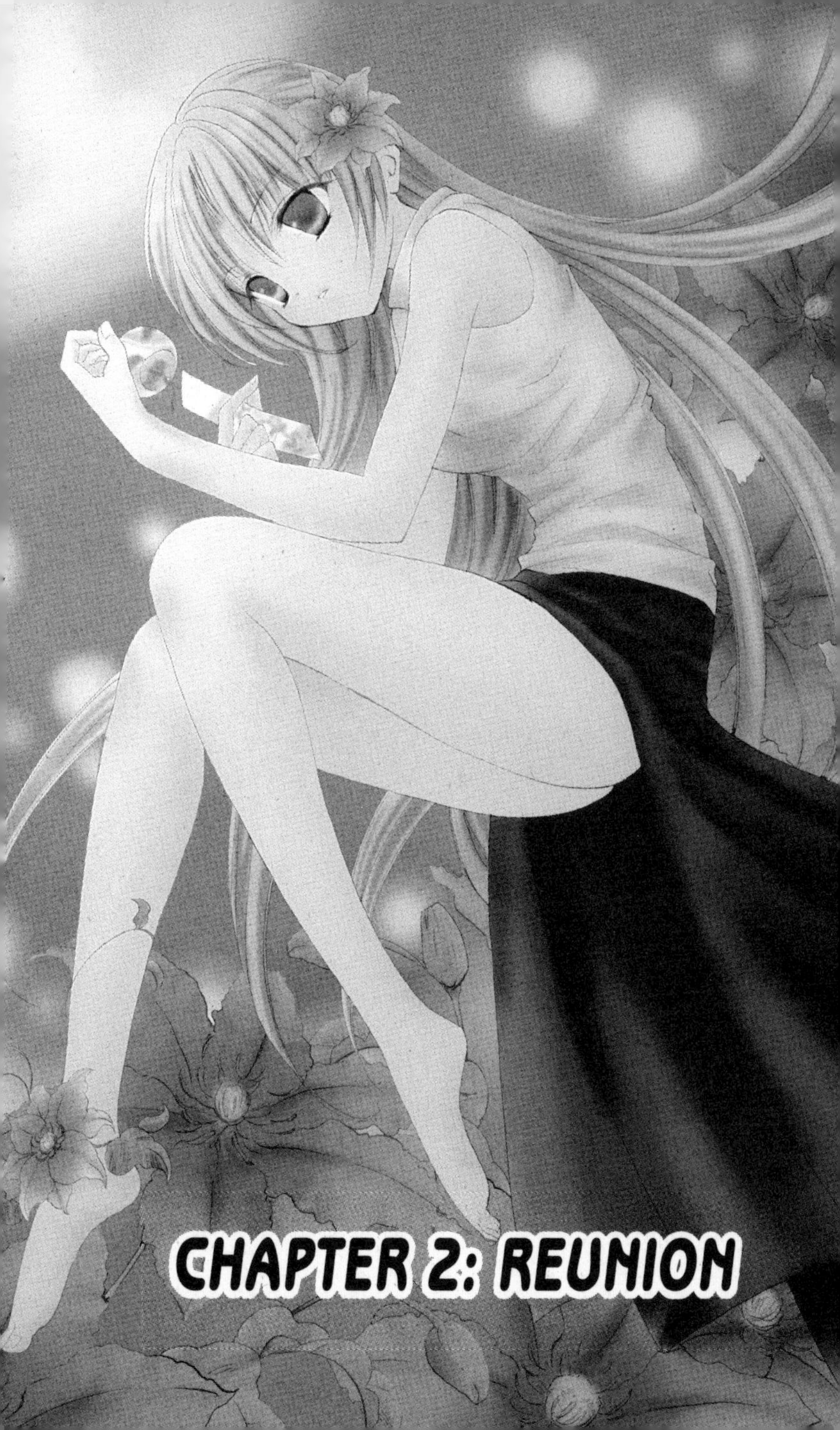
CHAPTER 2: REUNION

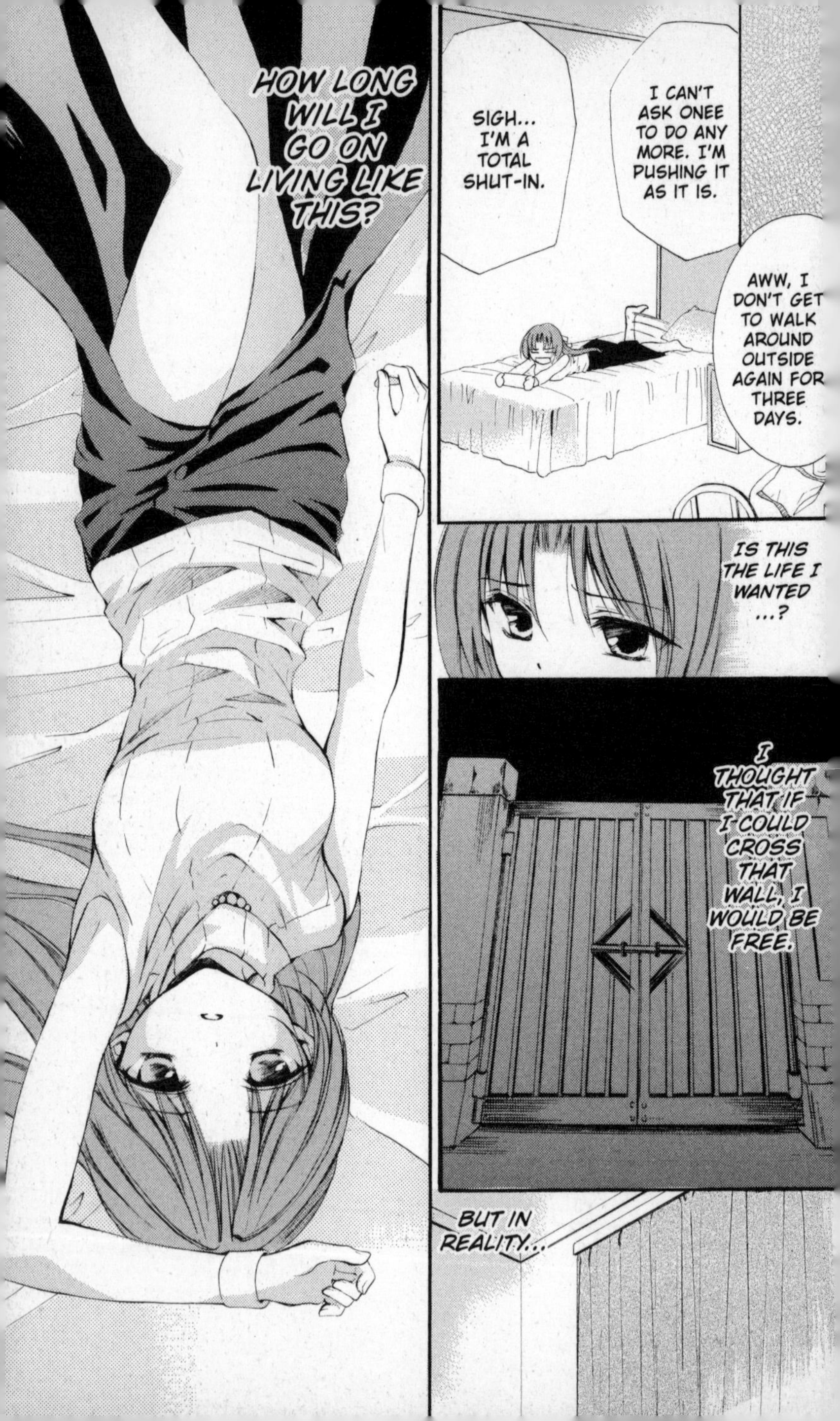
I CAN'T ASK ONEE TO DO ANY MORE. I'M PUSHING IT AS IT IS.
SIGH... I'M A TOTAL SHUT-IN.
AWW, I DON'T GET TO WALK AROUND OUTSIDE AGAIN FOR THREE DAYS.
IS THIS THE LIFE I WANTED ...?
I THOUGHT THAT IF I COULD CROSS THAT WALL, I WOULD BE FREE.
BUT IN REALITY...
HOW LONG WILL I GO ON LIVING LIKE THIS?

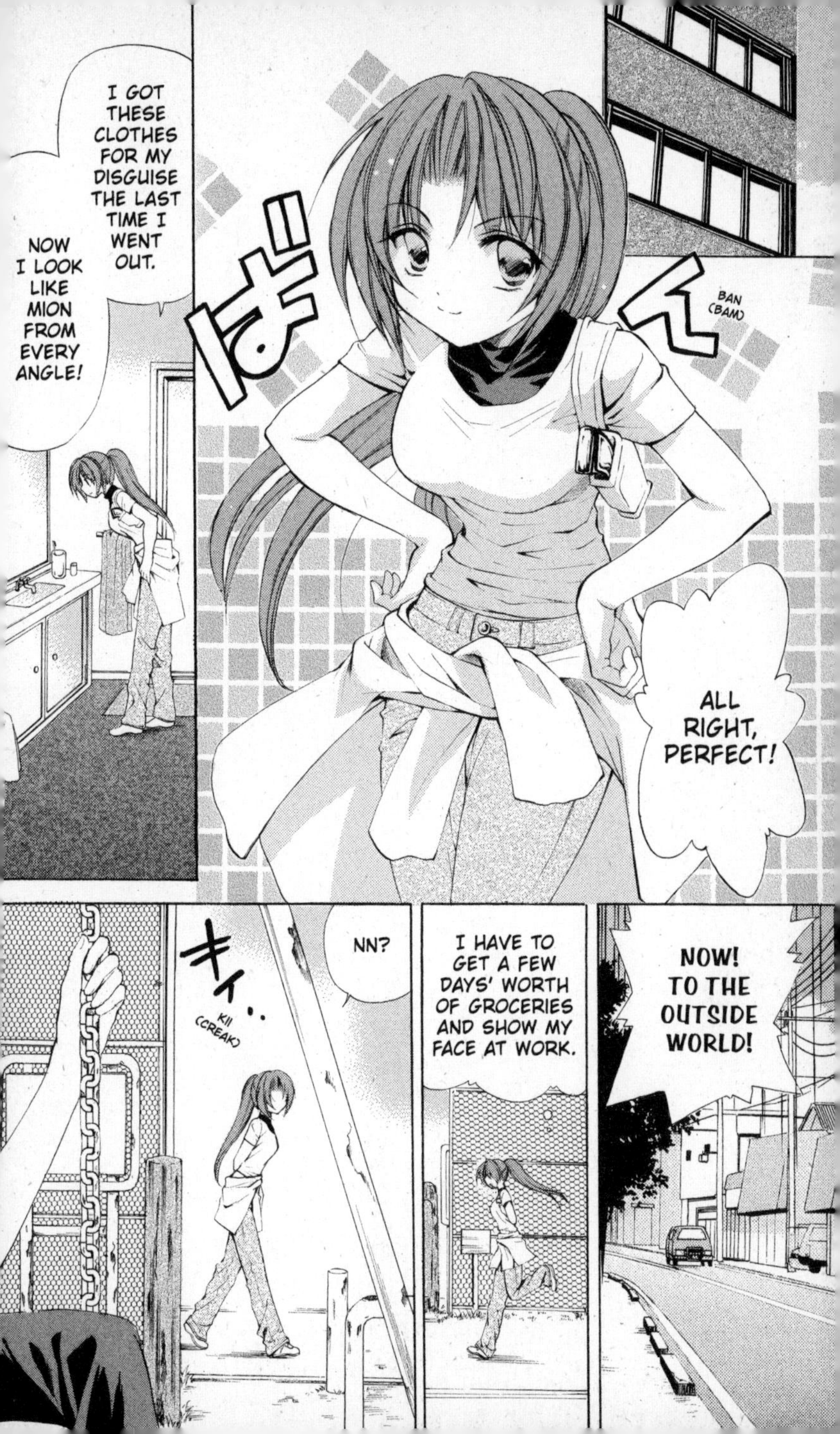
ぱん
BAN (BAM)
ALL RIGHT, PERFECT!
I GOT THESE CLOTHES FOR MY DISGUISE THE LAST TIME I WENT OUT.
NOW I LOOK LIKE MION FROM EVERY ANGLE!
NOW! TO THE OUTSIDE WORLD!
I HAVE TO GET A FEW DAYS' WORTH OF GROCERIES AND SHOW MY FACE AT WORK.
NN?
キィ..
KII (CREAK)

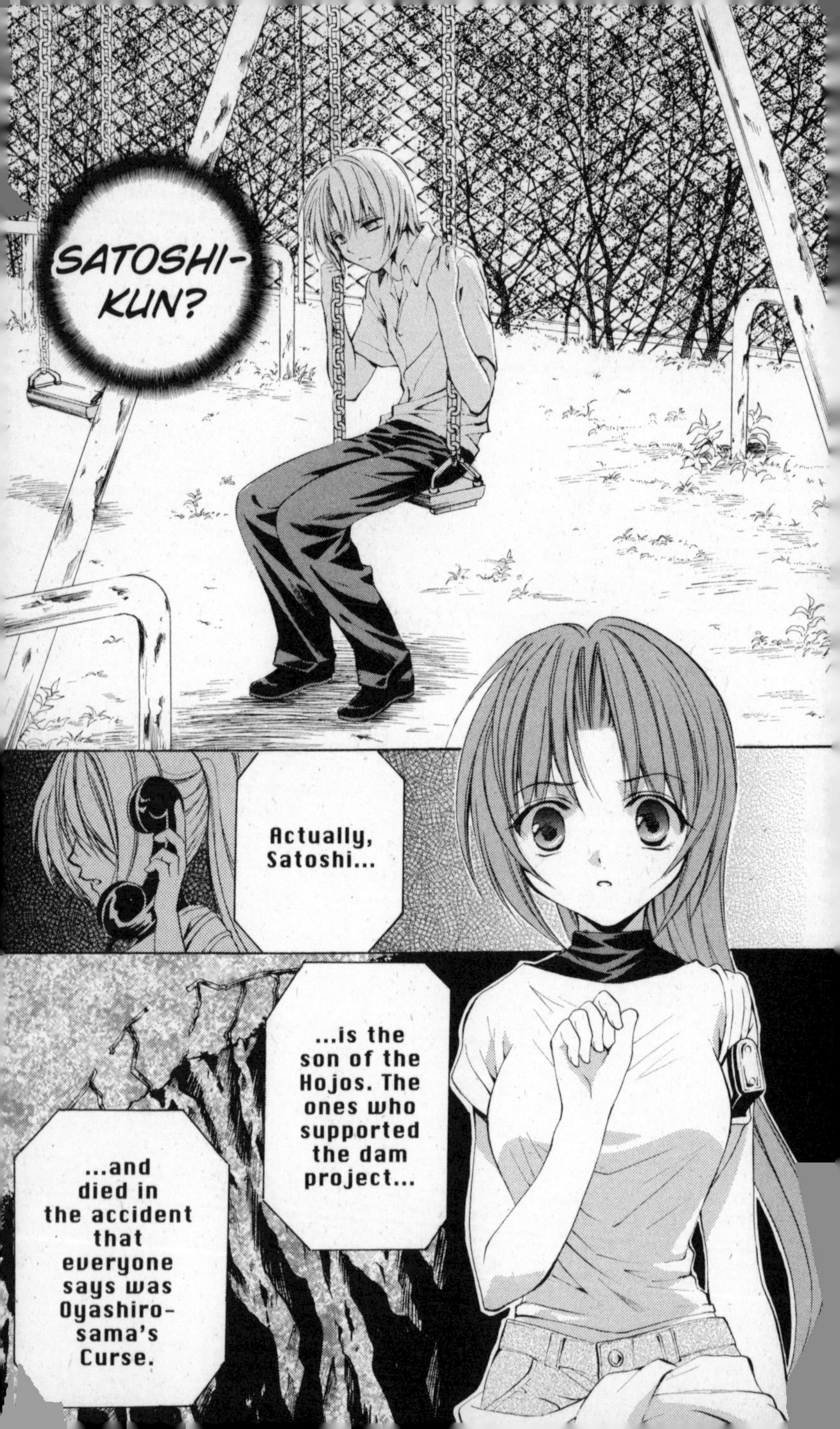
SATOSHI-KUN?
Actually, Satoshi...
...is the son of the Hojos. The ones who supported the dam project...
...and died in the accident that everyone says was Oyashiro-sama's Curse.

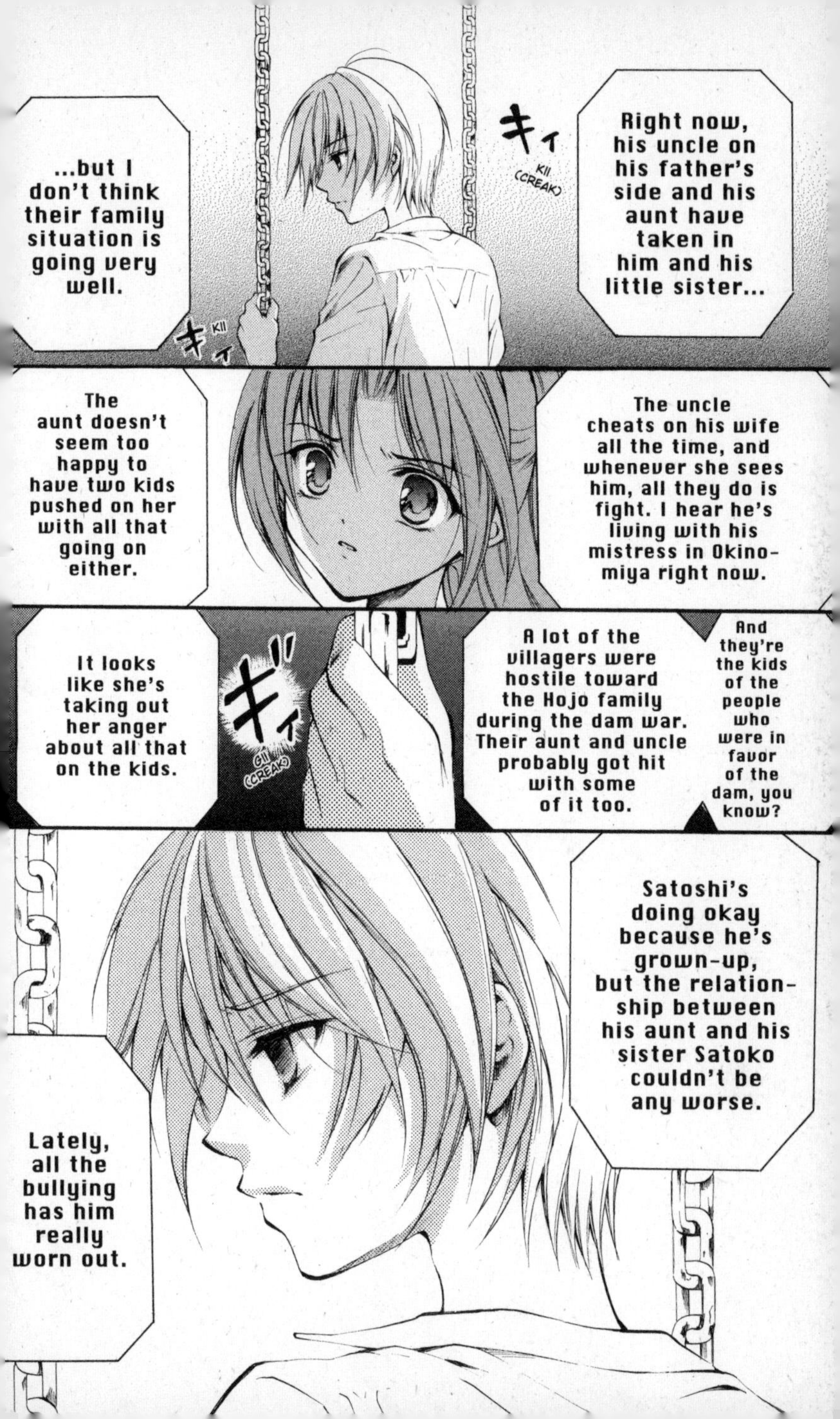

Right now, his uncle on his father's side and his aunt have taken in him and his little sister...
キィ
KII (CREAK)
...but I don't think their family situation is going very well.
キィ
KII
The uncle cheats on his wife all the time, and whenever she sees him, all they do is fight. I hear he's living with his mistress in Okino-miya right now.
The aunt doesn't seem too happy to have two kids pushed on her with all that going on either.
And they're the kids of the people who were in favor of the dam, you know?
A lot of the villagers were hostile toward the Hojo family during the dam war. Their aunt and uncle probably got hit with some of it too.
ギィ
GII (CREAK)
It looks like she's taking out her anger about all that on the kids.
Satoshi's doing okay because he's grown-up, but the relation-ship between his aunt and his sister Satoko couldn't be any worse.
Lately, all the bullying has him really worn out.

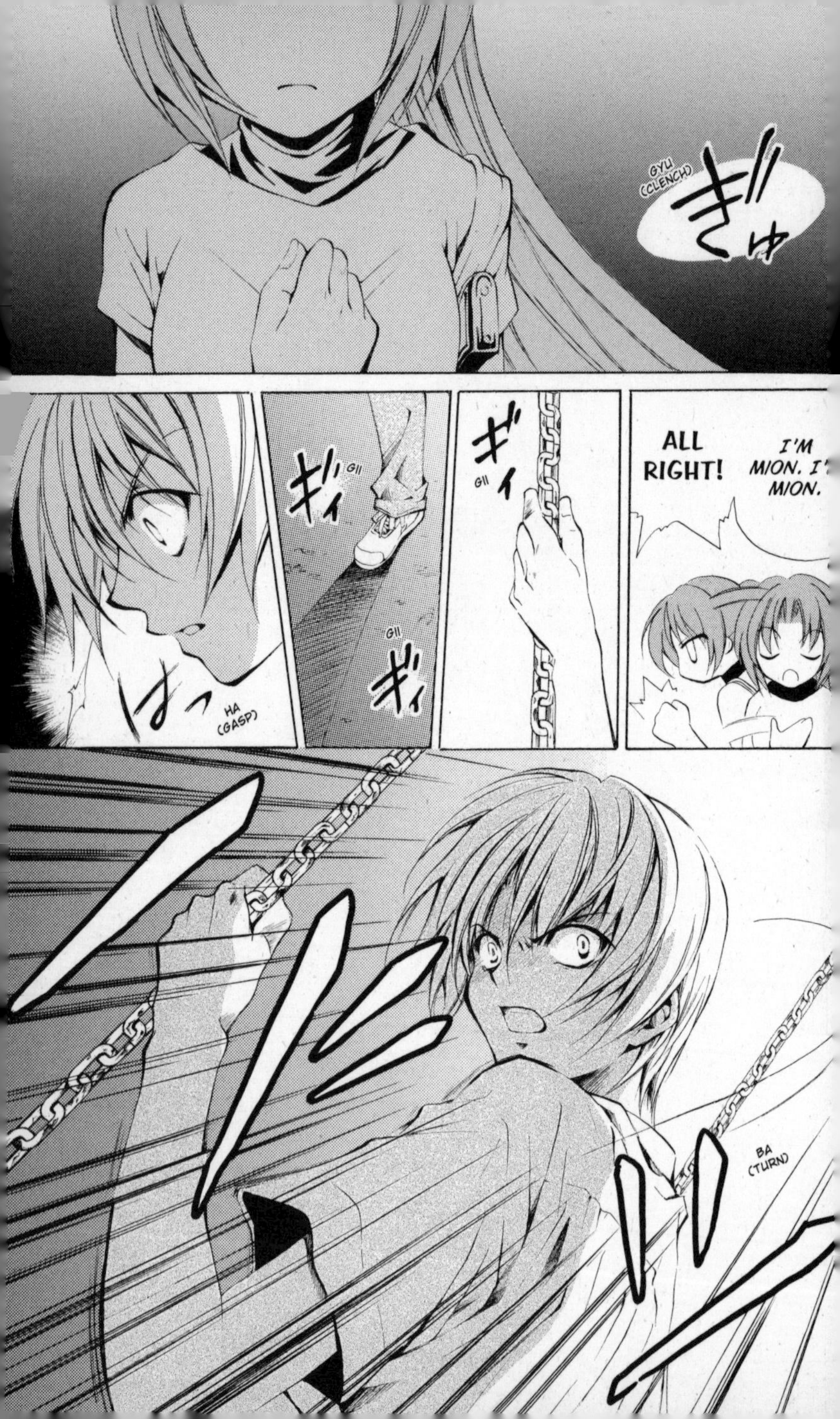

ぎゅ
GYU (CLENCH)
I'M MION. I'
MION.
ALL RIGHT!
ギィ
GII
ギィ
GII
ギィ
GII
はっ
HA (GASP)
BA (TURN)

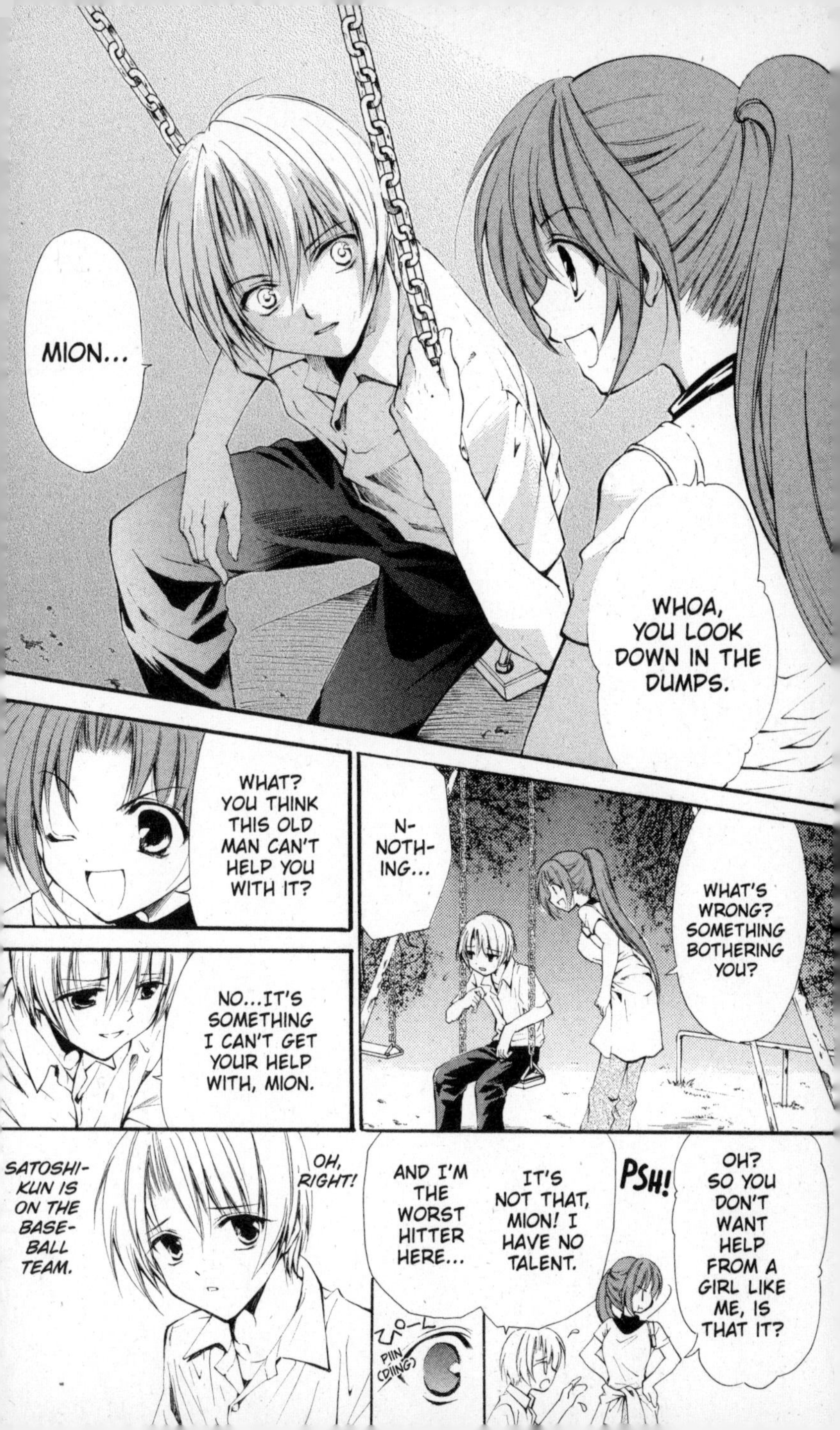
WHOA, YOU LOOK DOWN IN THE DUMPS.
MION...
WHAT'S WRONG? SOMETHING BOTHERING YOU?
N-NOTHING...
WHAT? YOU THINK THIS OLD MAN CAN'T HELP YOU WITH IT?
NO...IT'S SOMETHING I CAN'T GET YOUR HELP WITH, MION.
OH? SO YOU DON'T WANT HELP FROM A GIRL LIKE ME, IS THAT IT?
PSH!
IT'S NOT THAT, MION! I HAVE NO TALENT.
AND I'M THE WORST HITTER HERE...
PIIN (DIING)
OH, RIGHT!
SATOSHI-KUN IS ON THE BASEBALL TEAM.

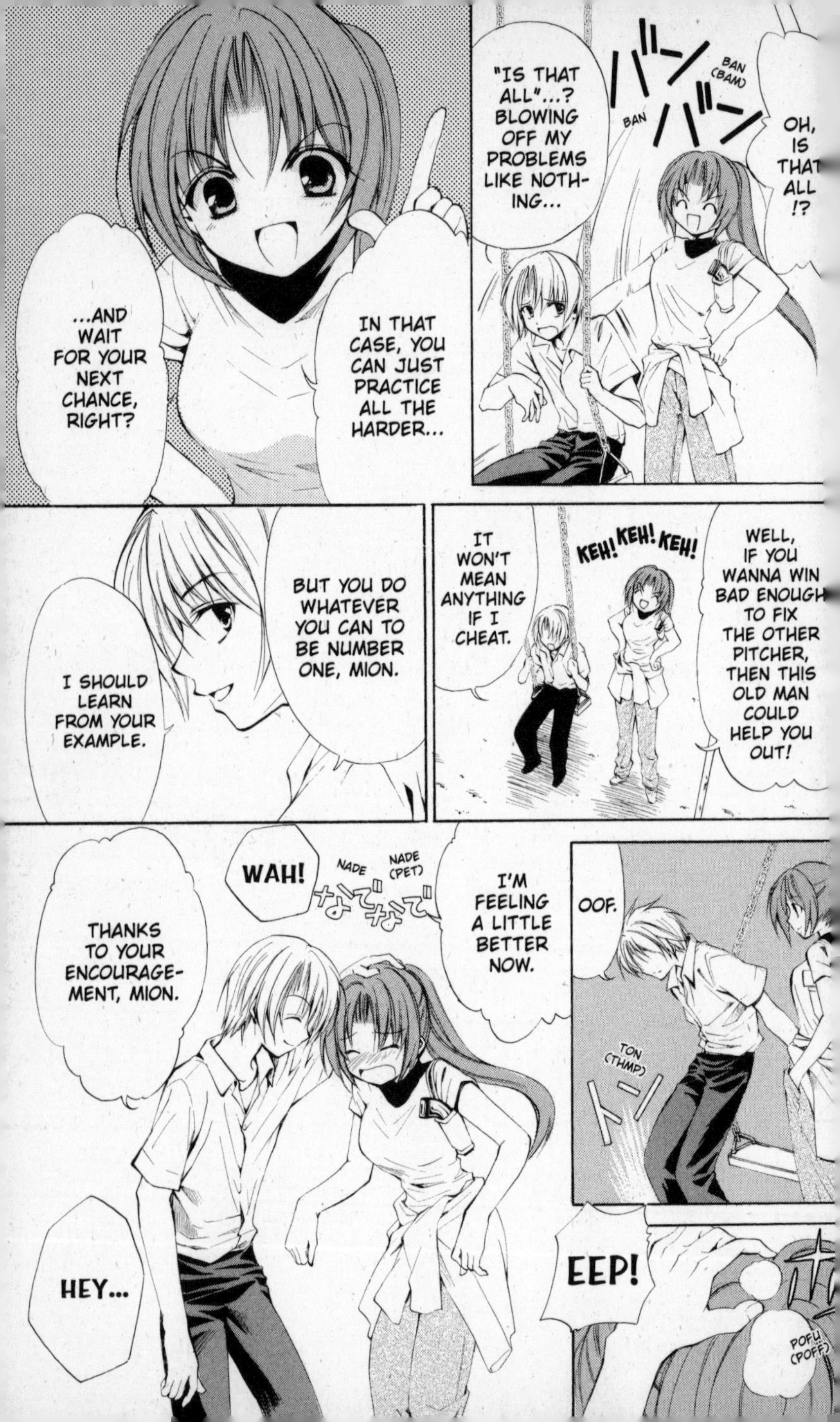
OH, IS THAT ALL!?
バン
BAN (BAM)
バン
BAN
"IS THAT ALL"...? BLOWING OFF MY PROBLEMS LIKE NOTHING...
IN THAT CASE, YOU CAN JUST PRACTICE ALL THE HARDER...
...AND WAIT FOR YOUR NEXT CHANCE, RIGHT?
WELL, IF YOU WANNA WIN BAD ENOUGH TO FIX THE OTHER PITCHER, THEN THIS OLD MAN COULD HELP YOU OUT!
KEH! KEH! KEH!
IT WON'T MEAN ANYTHING IF I CHEAT.
BUT YOU DO WHATEVER YOU CAN TO BE NUMBER ONE, MION.
I SHOULD LEARN FROM YOUR EXAMPLE.
OOF.
トン
TON (THMP)
EEP!
POFU (POFF)
I'M FEELING A LITTLE BETTER NOW.
なで
NADE (PET)
なで
NADE
WAH!
THANKS TO YOUR ENCOURAGEMENT, MION.
HEY...

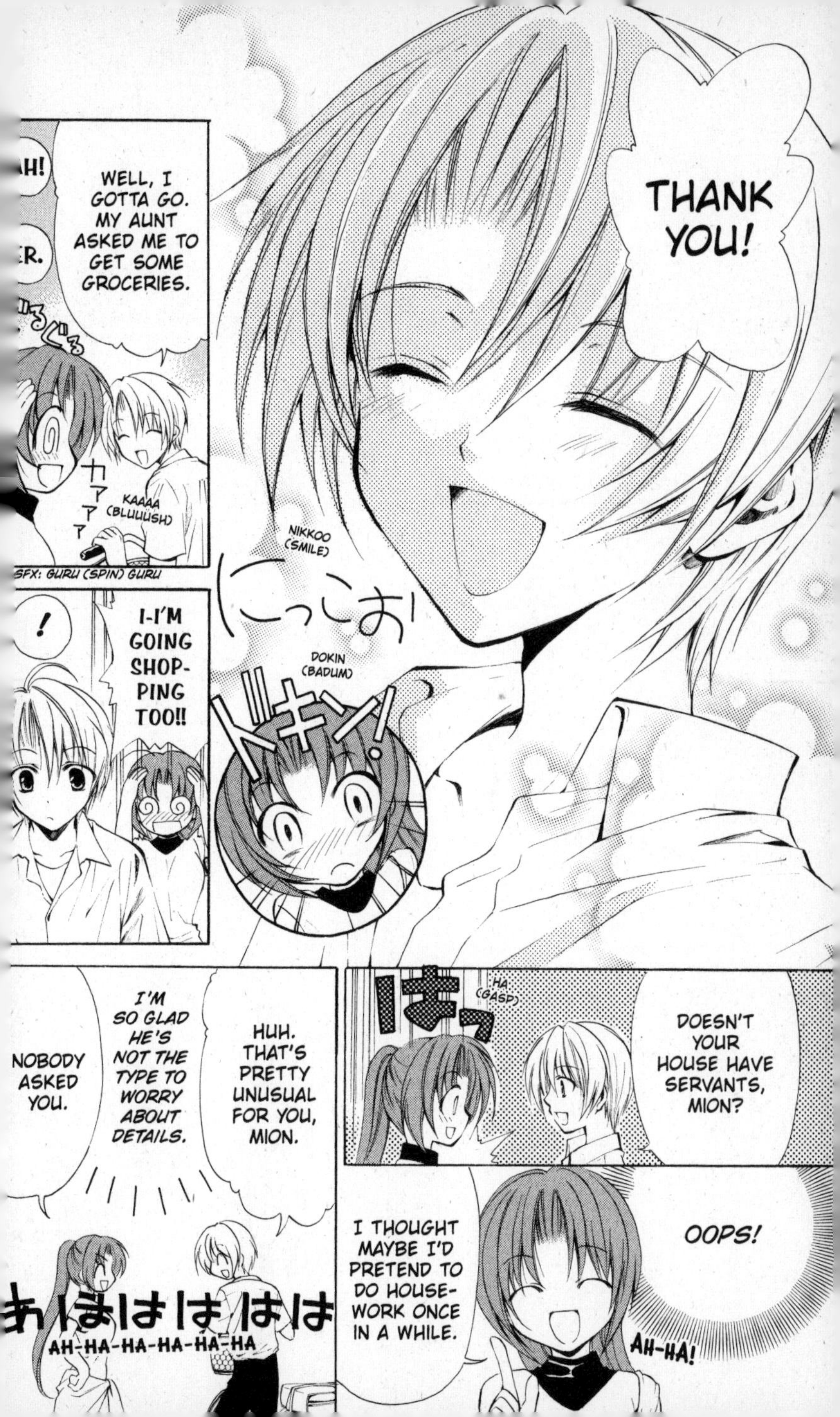

THANK YOU!
NIKKOO (SMILE)
DOKIN (BADUM)
WELL, I GOTTA GO. MY AUNT ASKED ME TO GET SOME GROCERIES.
KAAAA (BLUUUSH)
SFX: GURU (SPIN) GURU
!
I-I'M GOING SHOP-PING TOO!!
HA (GASP)
DOESN'T YOUR HOUSE HAVE SERVANTS, MION?
OOPS!
I THOUGHT MAYBE I'D PRETEND TO DO HOUSE-WORK ONCE IN A WHILE.
AH-HA!
HUH. THAT'S PRETTY UNUSUAL FOR YOU, MION.
I'M SO GLAD HE'S NOT THE TYPE TO WORRY ABOUT DETAILS.
NOBODY ASKED YOU.
AH-HA-HA-HA-HA-HA

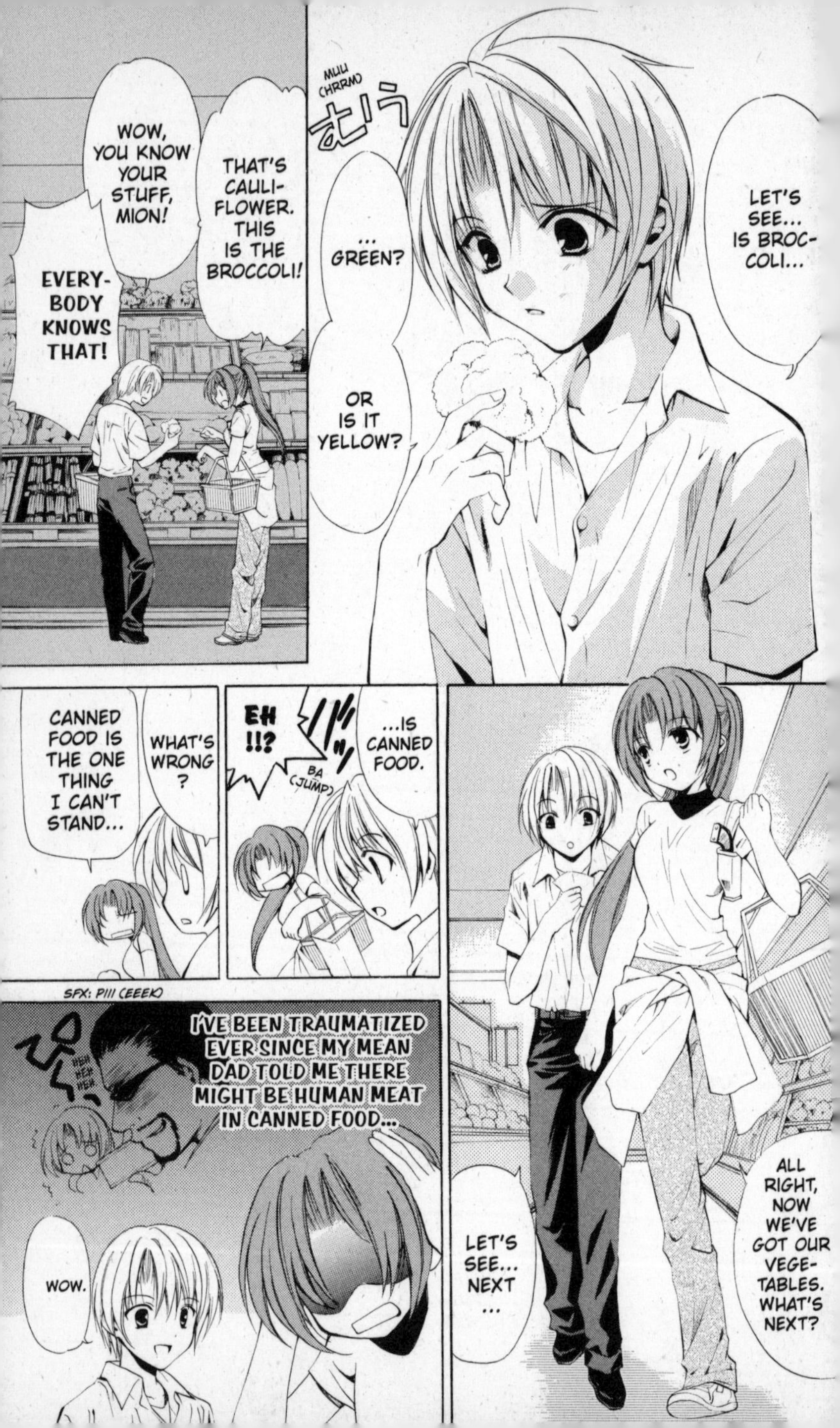
LET'S SEE... IS BROCCOLI...
MUU (HRRM)
...GREEN?
OR IS IT YELLOW?
THAT'S CAULIFLOWER. THIS IS THE BROCCOLI!
WOW, YOU KNOW YOUR STUFF, MION!
EVERYBODY KNOWS THAT!
ALL RIGHT, NOW WE'VE GOT OUR VEGETABLES. WHAT'S NEXT?
LET'S SEE... NEXT ...
...IS CANNED FOOD.
BA (JUMP)
EH !!?
WHAT'S WRONG?
CANNED FOOD IS THE ONE THING I CAN'T STAND...
SFX: PIII (EEEK)
I'VE BEEN TRAUMATIZED EVER SINCE MY MEAN DAD TOLD ME THERE MIGHT BE HUMAN MEAT IN CANNED FOOD...
HEH HEH HEH
WOW.

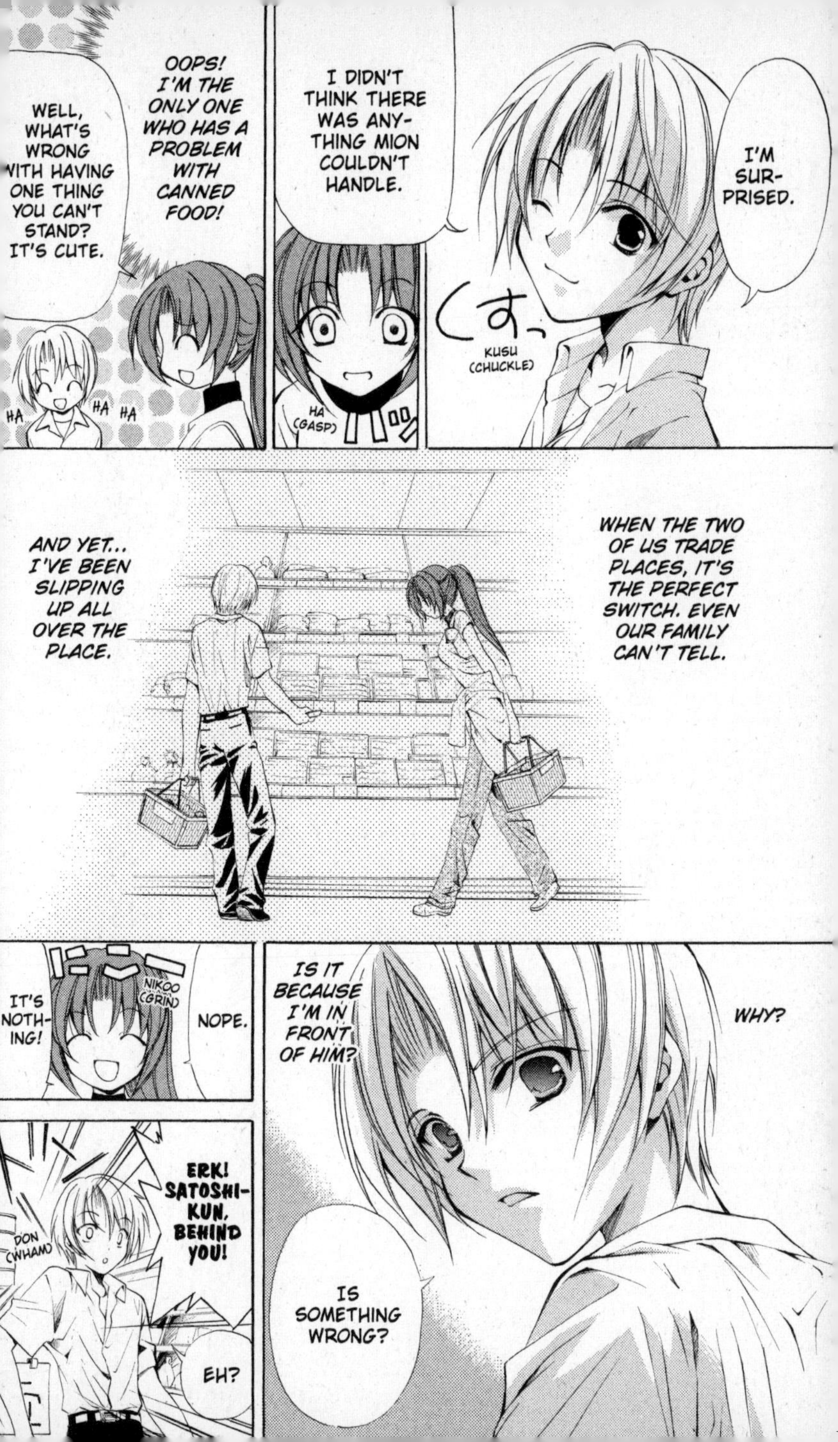

I'M SUR-PRISED.
くすっ
KUSU (CHUCKLE)
I DIDN'T THINK THERE WAS ANY-THING MION COULDN'T HANDLE.
HA (GASP)
OOPS! I'M THE ONLY ONE WHO HAS A PROBLEM WITH CANNED FOOD!
WELL, WHAT'S WRONG WITH HAVING ONE THING YOU CAN'T STAND? IT'S CUTE.
HA HA HA
WHEN THE TWO OF US TRADE PLACES, IT'S THE PERFECT SWITCH. EVEN OUR FAMILY CAN'T TELL.
AND YET... I'VE BEEN SLIPPING UP ALL OVER THE PLACE.
WHY?
IS IT BECAUSE I'M IN FRONT OF HIM?
IS SOMETHING WRONG?
NOPE.
NIKOO (GRIN)
IT'S NOTH-ING!
ERK! SATOSHI-KUN, BEHIND YOU!
DON (WHAM)
EH?

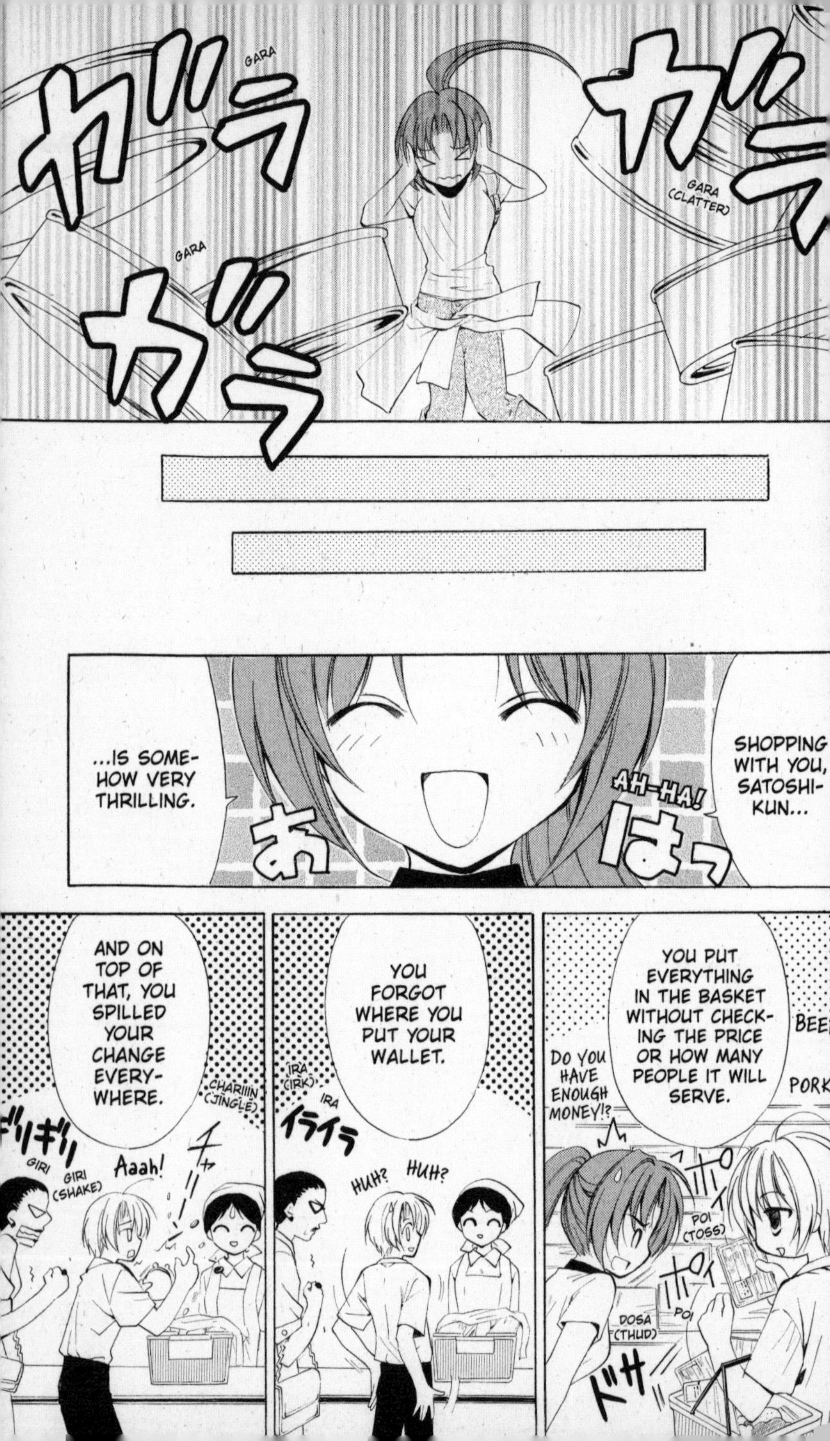
GARA (CLATTER)
GARA
GARA
SHOPPING WITH YOU, SATOSHI-KUN...
AH-HA!
...IS SOMEHOW VERY THRILLING.
BEEF
PORK.
YOU PUT EVERYTHING IN THE BASKET WITHOUT CHECKING THE PRICE OR HOW MANY PEOPLE IT WILL SERVE.
DO YOU HAVE ENOUGH MONEY!?
POI (TOSS)
POI
DOSA (THUD)
YOU FORGOT WHERE YOU PUT YOUR WALLET.
IRA (IRK)
IRA
HUH? HUH?
AND ON TOP OF THAT, YOU SPILLED YOUR CHANGE EVERYWHERE.
CHARIIIN (JINGLE)
Aaah!
GIRI
GIRI (SHAKE)

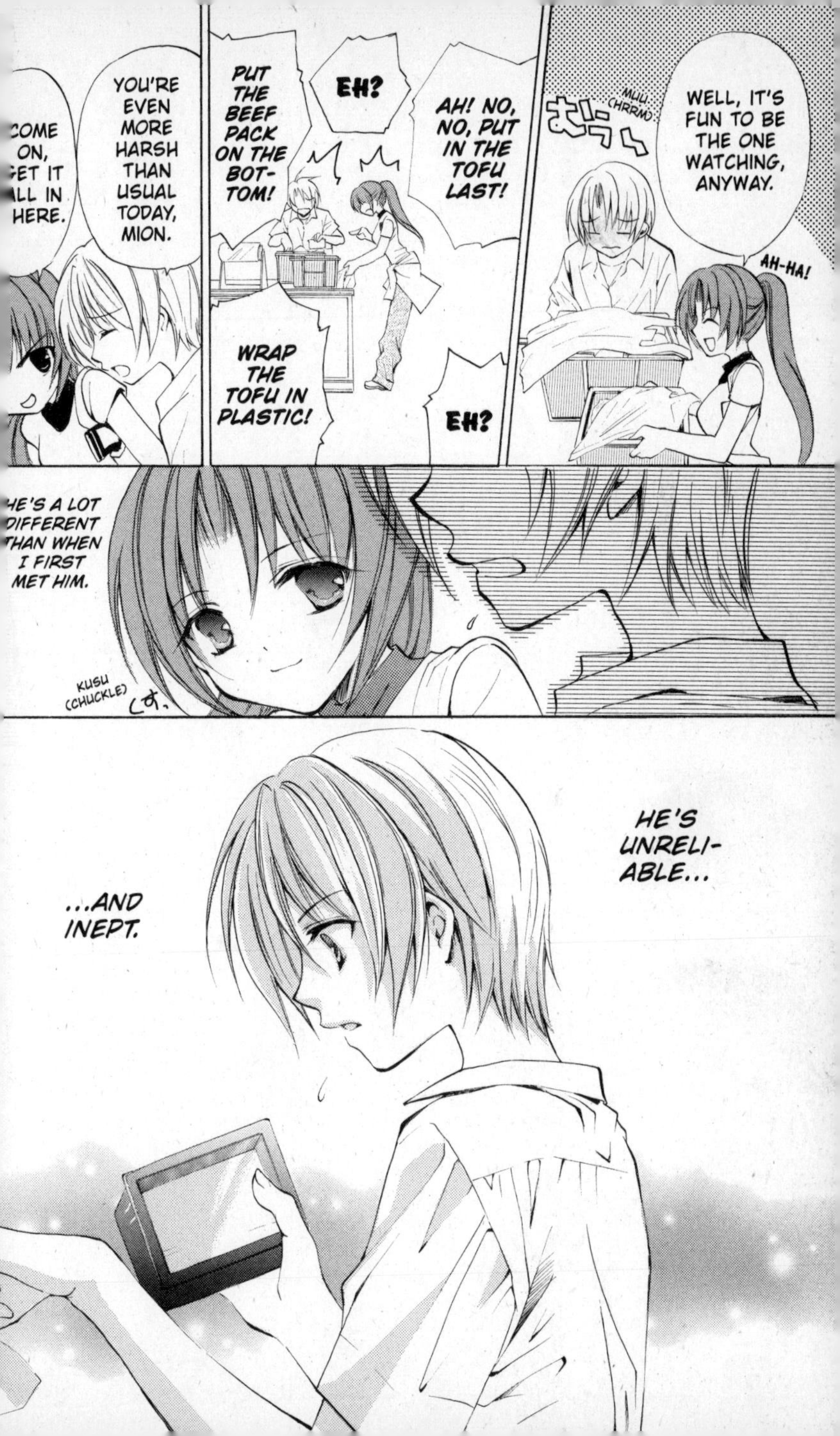
WELL, IT'S FUN TO BE THE ONE WATCHING, ANYWAY.
MUU (HRRM)
AH-HA!
AH! NO, NO, PUT IN THE TOFU LAST!
EH?
PUT THE BEEF PACK ON THE BOT-TOM!
EH?
WRAP THE TOFU IN PLASTIC!
YOU'RE EVEN MORE HARSH THAN USUAL TODAY, MION.
COME ON, GET IT ALL IN HERE.
HE'S A LOT DIFFERENT THAN WHEN I FIRST MET HIM.
KUSU (CHUCKLE)
くす.
HE'S UNRELI-ABLE...
...AND INEPT.

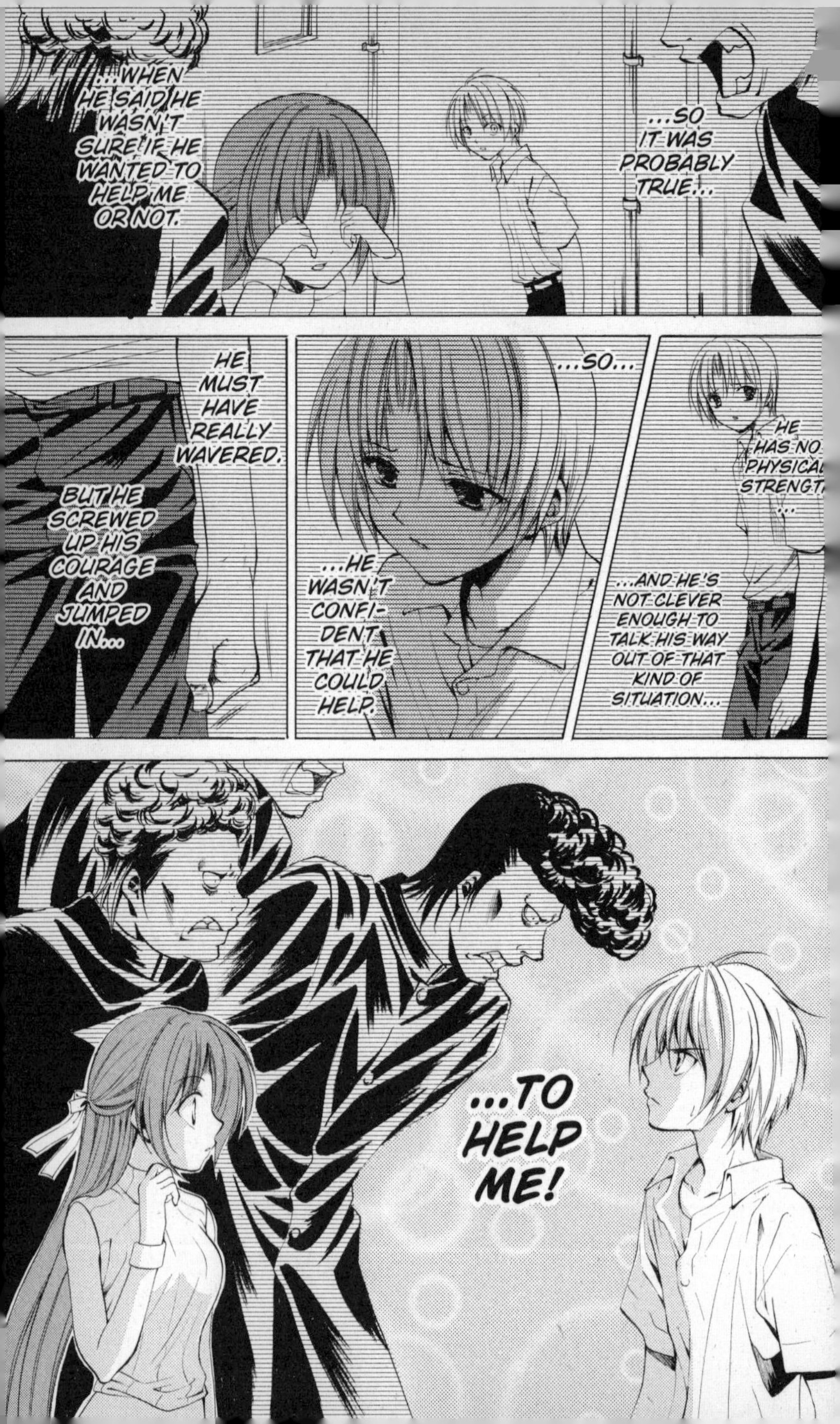
...SO IT WAS PROBABLY TRUE...
...WHEN HE SAID HE WASN'T SURE IF HE WANTED TO HELP ME OR NOT.
HE HAS NO PHYSICAL STRENGT...
...AND HE'S NOT CLEVER ENOUGH TO TALK HIS WAY OUT OF THAT KIND OF SITUATION...
...SO...
...HE WASN'T CONFI-DENT THAT HE COULD HELP.
HE MUST HAVE REALLY WAVERED.
BUT HE SCREWED UP HIS COURAGE AND JUMPED IN...
...TO HELP ME!

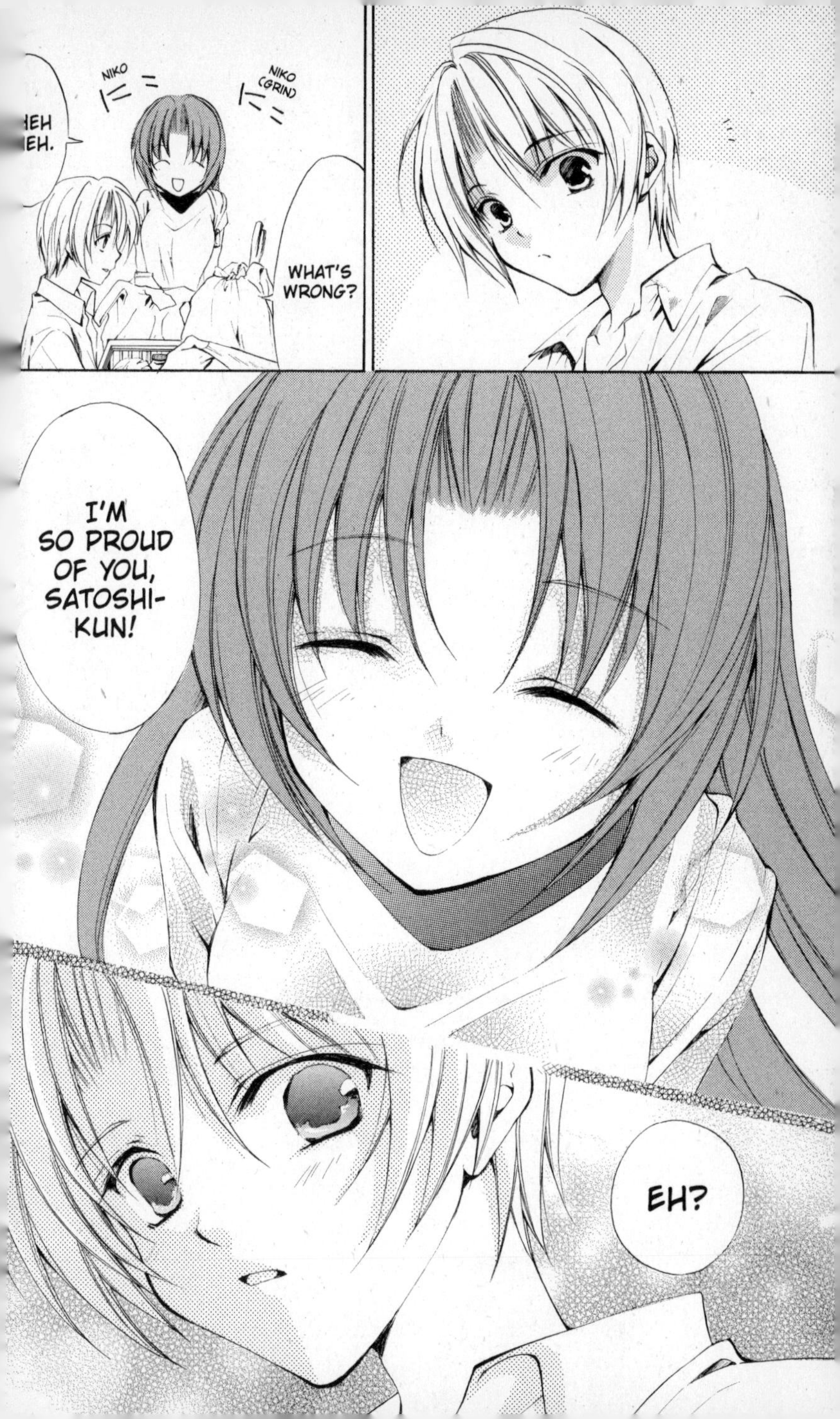
NIKO (GRIN)
NIKO
HEH HEH.
WHAT'S WRONG?
I'M SO PROUD OF YOU, SATOSHI-KUN!
EH?

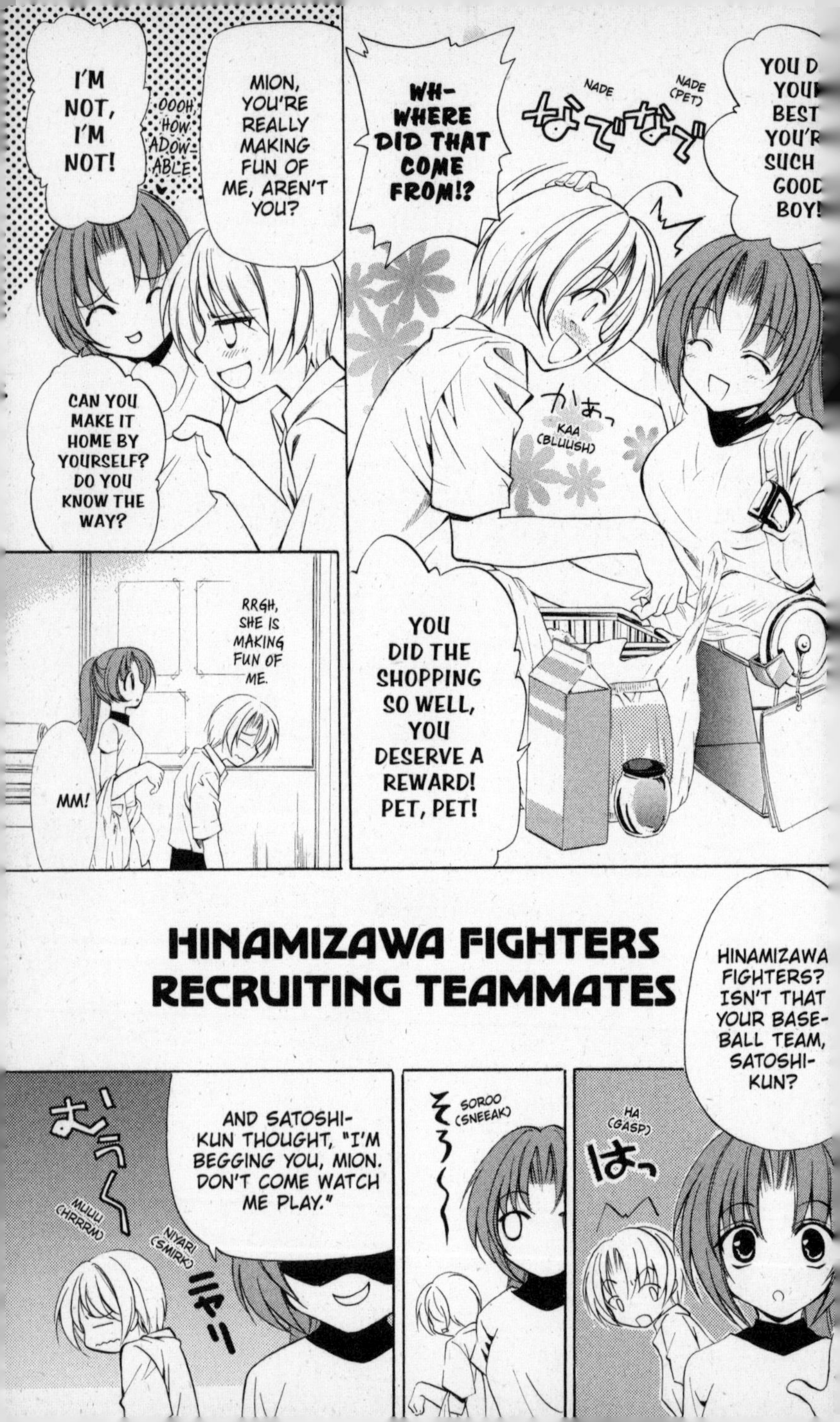
YOU D YOUR BEST YOU'R SUCH GOOD BOY!
NADE (PET)
NADE
WH-WHERE DID THAT COME FROM!?
KAA (BLUUSH)
YOU DID THE SHOPPING SO WELL, YOU DESERVE A REWARD! PET, PET!
MION, YOU'RE REALLY MAKING FUN OF ME, AREN'T YOU?
OOOH, HOW ADOWABLE
I'M NOT, I'M NOT!
CAN YOU MAKE IT HOME BY YOURSELF? DO YOU KNOW THE WAY?
RRGH, SHE IS MAKING FUN OF ME.
MM!
HINAMIZAWA FIGHTERS RECRUITING TEAMMATES
HINAMIZAWA FIGHTERS? ISN'T THAT YOUR BASE-BALL TEAM, SATOSHI-KUN?
HA (GASP)
SOROO (SNEEAK)
AND SATOSHI-KUN THOUGHT, "I'M BEGGING YOU, MION. DON'T COME WATCH ME PLAY."
MUUU (HRRRM)
NIYARI (SMIRK)

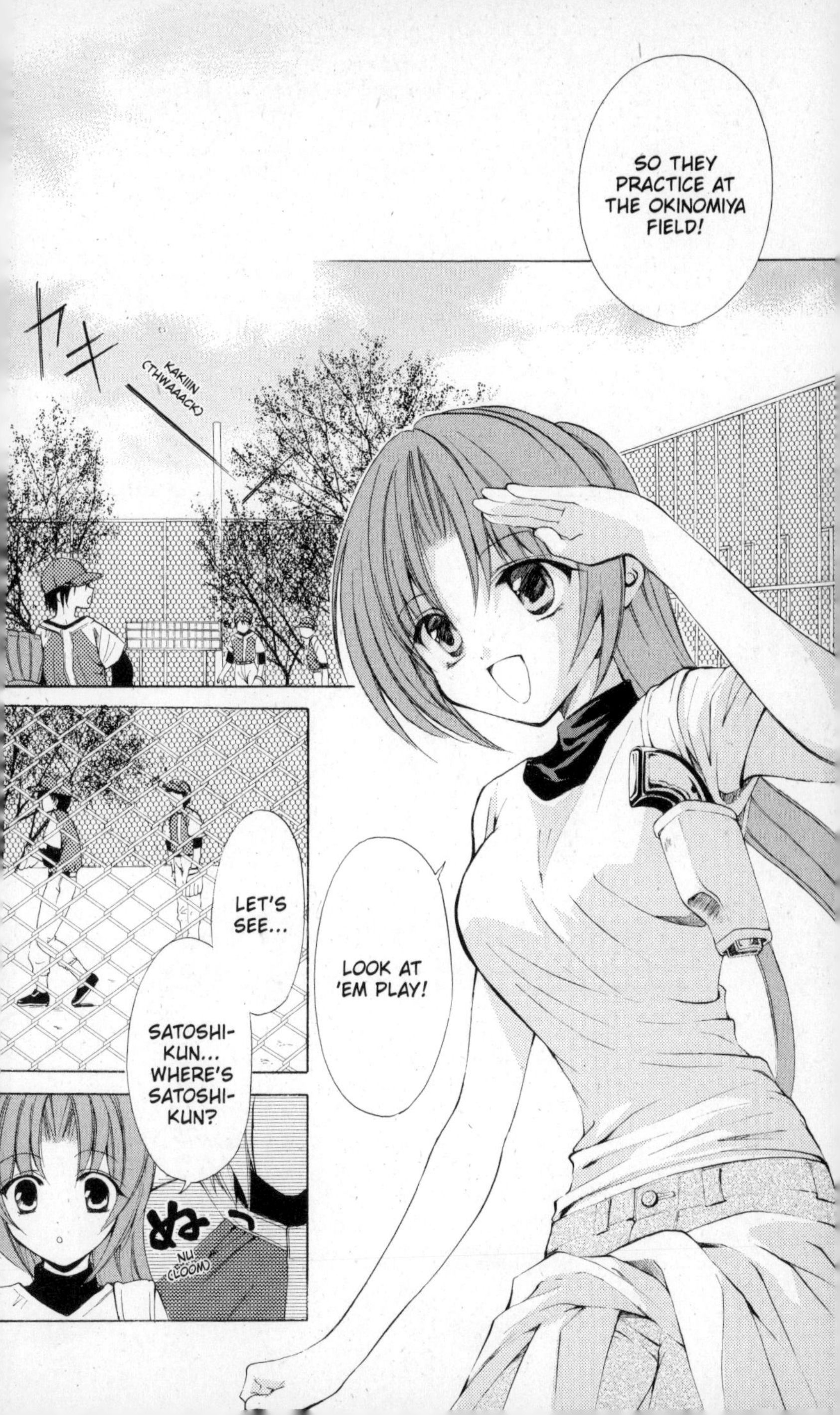
SO THEY PRACTICE AT THE OKINOMIYA FIELD!
KAKIIN (THWAAACK)
LOOK AT 'EM PLAY!
LET'S SEE...
SATOSHI-KUN... WHERE'S SATOSHI-KUN?
NU (LOOM)

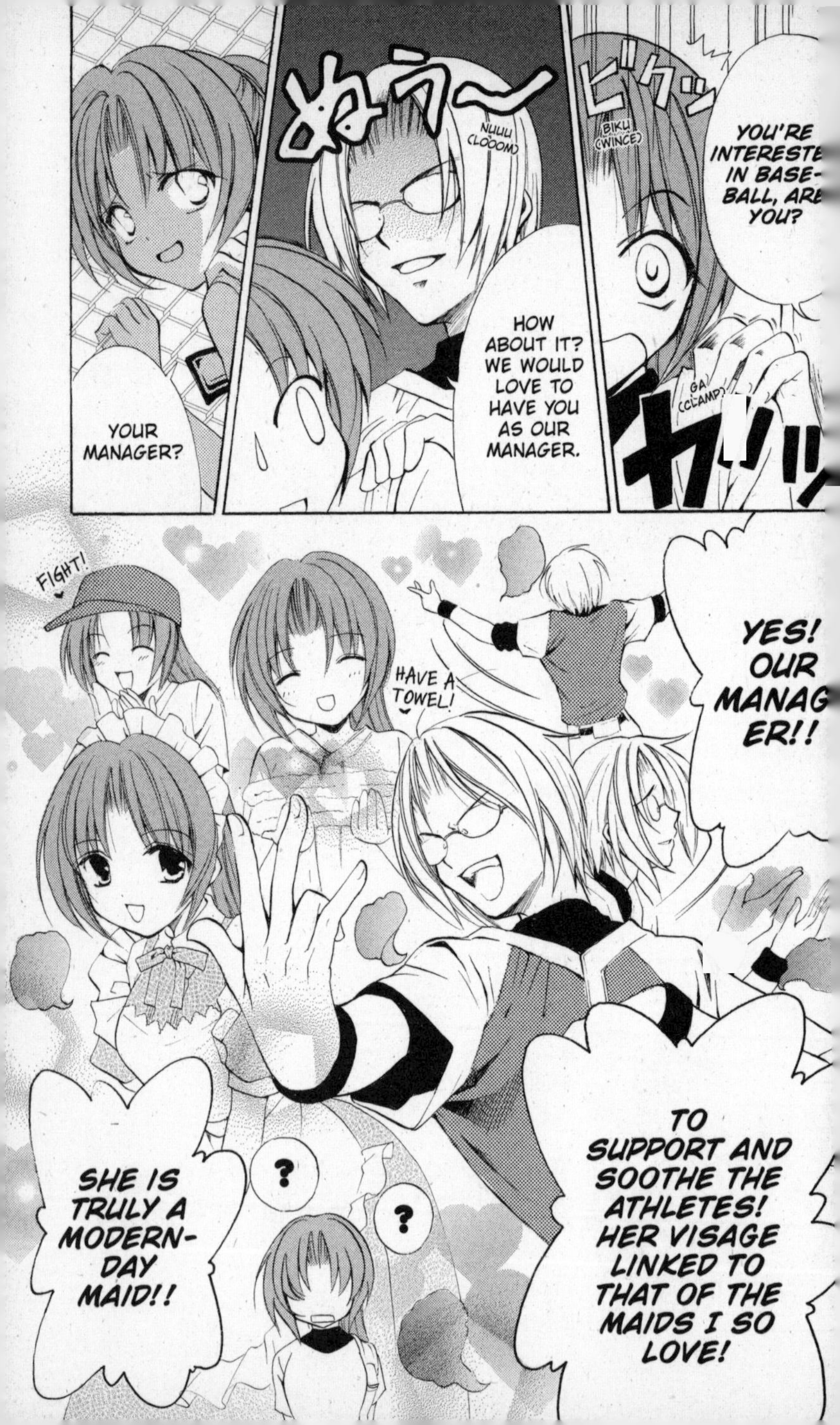

ビクッ
BIKU (WINCE)
YOU'RE INTERESTE IN BASE-BALL, ARE YOU?
ガッ
GA (CLAMP)
ぬう〜
NUUU (LOOOM)
HOW ABOUT IT? WE WOULD LOVE TO HAVE YOU AS OUR MANAGER.
YOUR MANAGER?
YES! OUR MANAGER!!
FIGHT!
HAVE A TOWEL!
TO SUPPORT AND SOOTHE THE ATHLETES! HER VISAGE LINKED TO THAT OF THE MAIDS I SO LOVE!
?
?
SHE IS TRULY A MODERN-DAY MAID!!

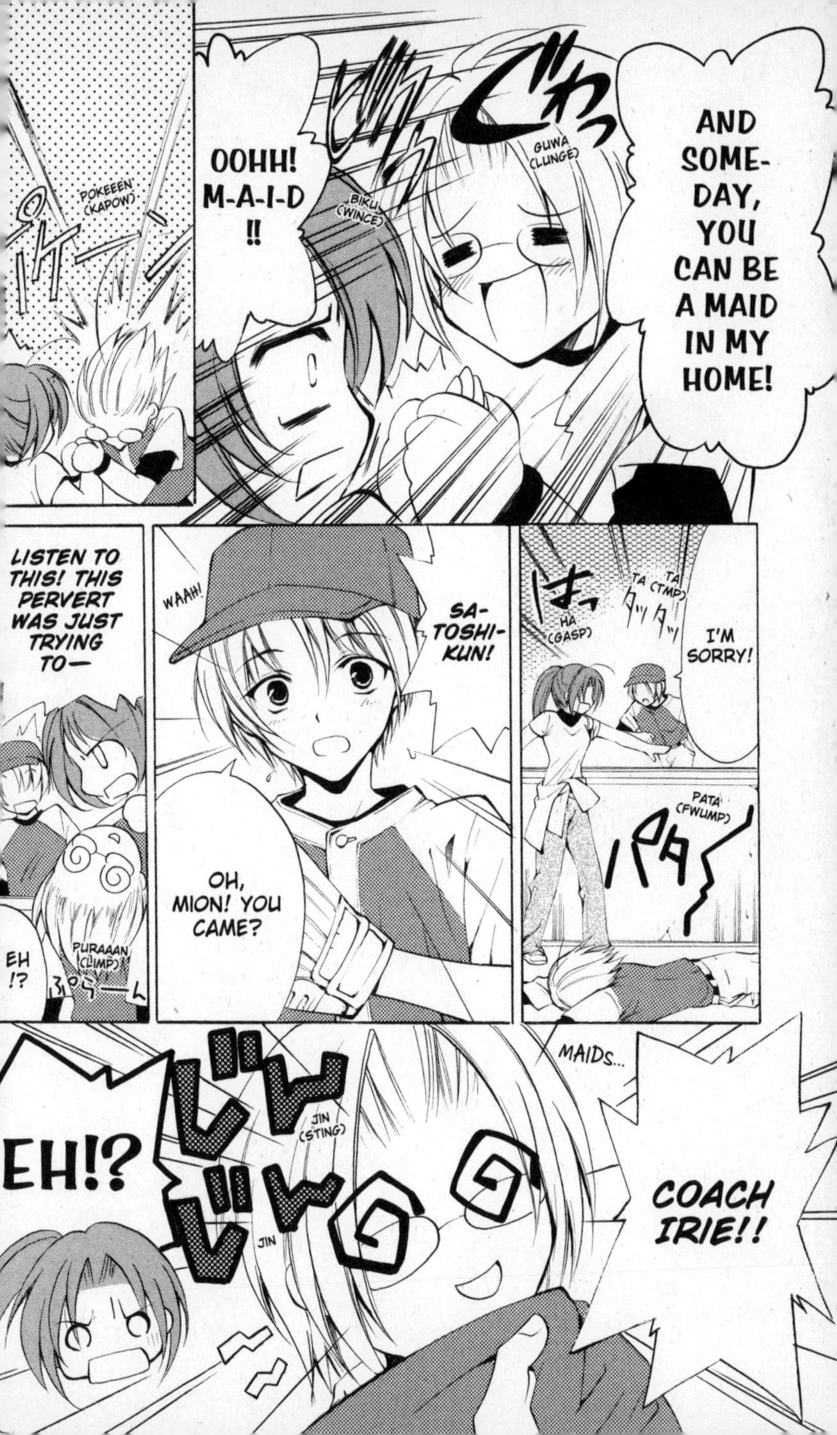
AND SOME-DAY, YOU CAN BE A MAID IN MY HOME!
GUWA (LUNGE)
BIKU (WINCE)
OOHH! M-A-I-D !!
POKEEEN (KAPOW)
I'M SORRY!
TA TA (TMP)
HA (GASP)
PATA (FWUMP)
SA-TOSHI-KUN!
WAAH!
OH, MION! YOU CAME?
LISTEN TO THIS! THIS PERVERT WAS JUST TRYING TO—
PURAAAN (LIMP)
EH !?
COACH IRIE!!
MAIDS...
JIN (STING)
JIN
EH!?

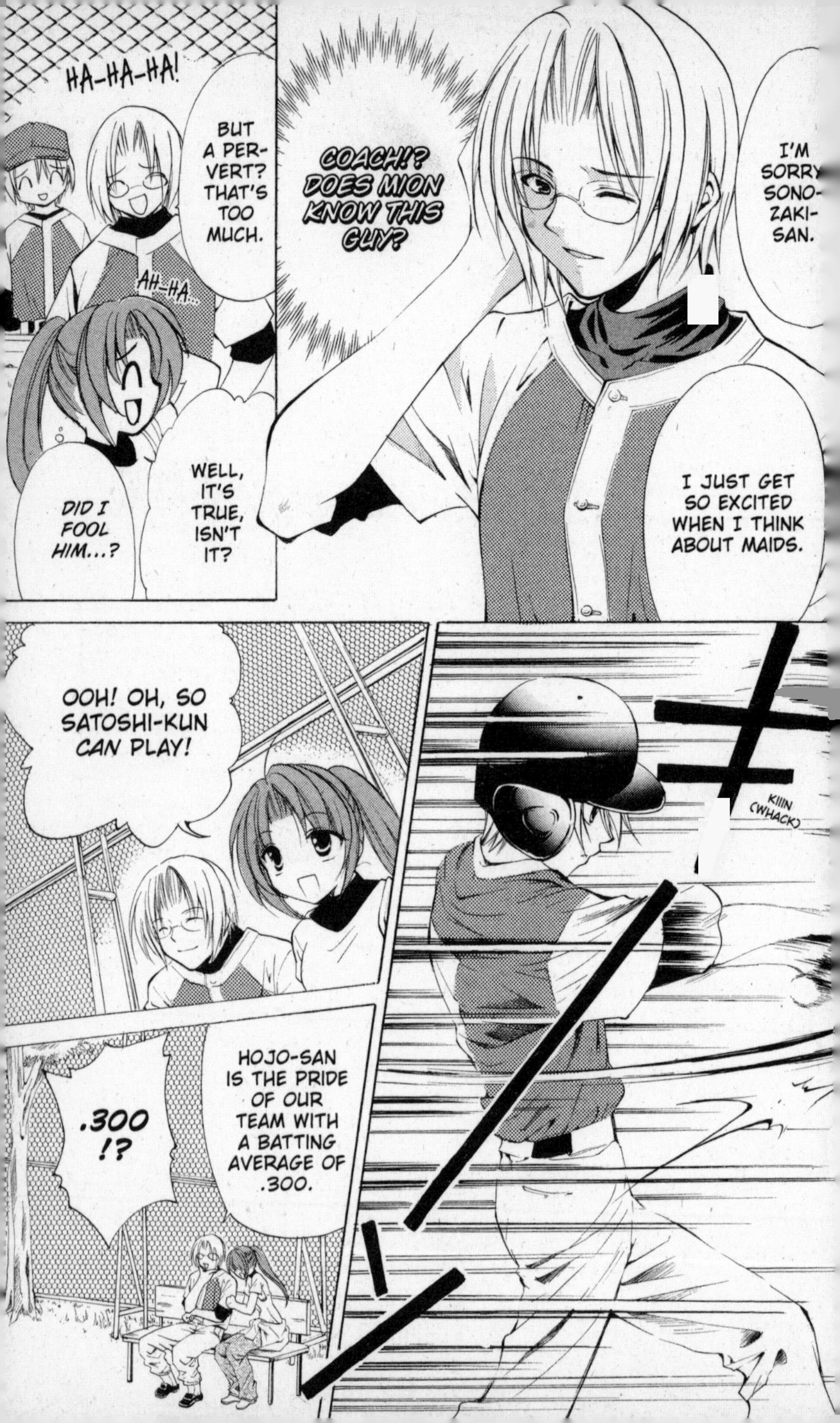
I'M SORRY SONO-ZAKI-SAN.
I JUST GET SO EXCITED WHEN I THINK ABOUT MAIDS.
COACH!? DOES MION KNOW THIS GUY?
HA-HA-HA!
BUT A PER-VERT? THAT'S TOO MUCH.
AH-HA...
WELL, IT'S TRUE, ISN'T IT?
DID I FOOL HIM...?
KIIIN (WHACK)
OOH! OH, SO SATOSHI-KUN CAN PLAY!
HOJO-SAN IS THE PRIDE OF OUR TEAM WITH A BATTING AVERAGE OF .300.
.300 !?

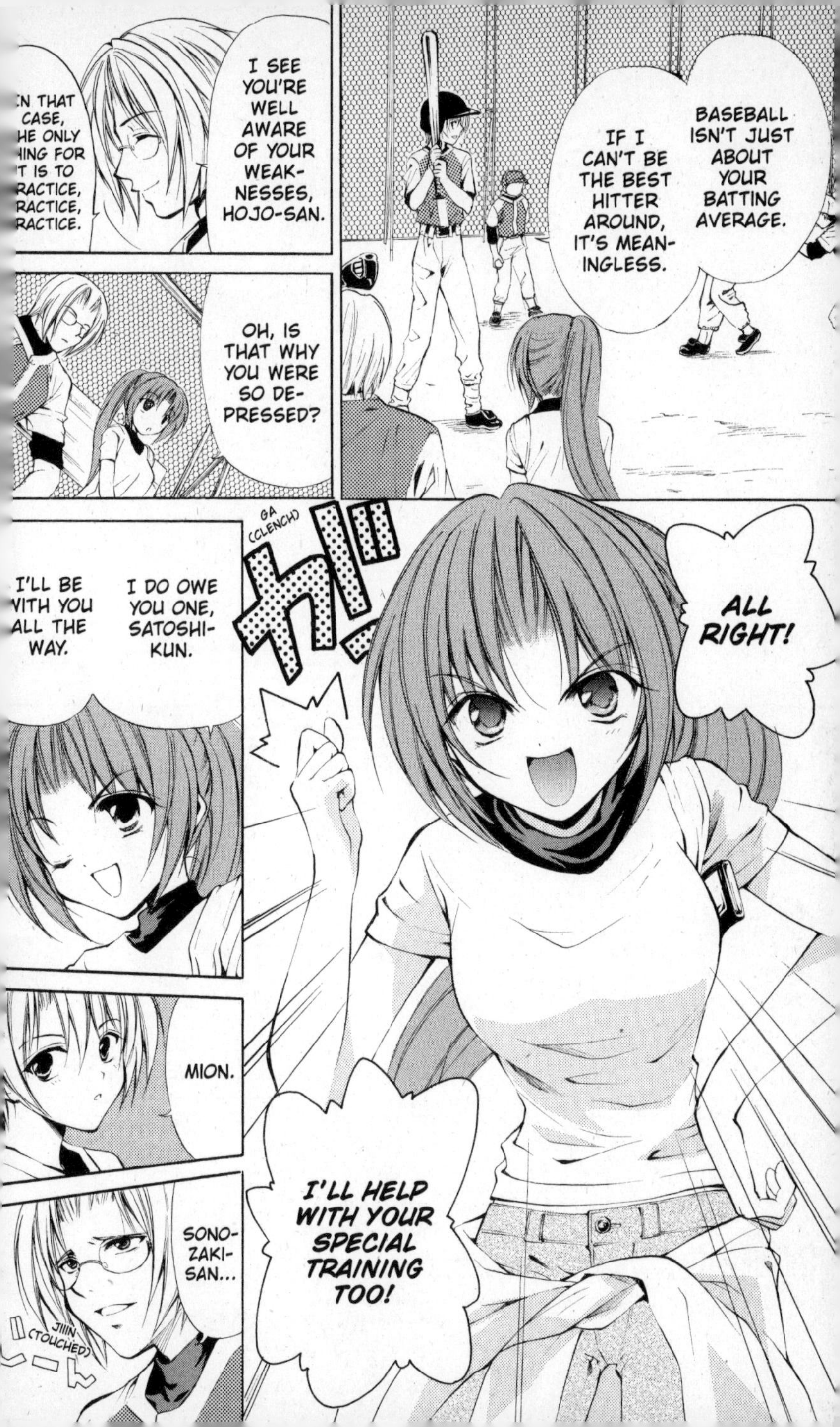

BASEBALL ISN'T JUST ABOUT YOUR BATTING AVERAGE.
IF I CAN'T BE THE BEST HITTER AROUND, IT'S MEANINGLESS.
I SEE YOU'RE WELL AWARE OF YOUR WEAK-NESSES, HOJO-SAN.
N THAT CASE, HE ONLY HING FOR T IS TO RACTICE, RACTICE, RACTICE.
OH, IS THAT WHY YOU WERE SO DE-PRESSED?
GA (CLENCH)
ALL RIGHT!
I'LL HELP WITH YOUR SPECIAL TRAINING TOO!
I DO OWE YOU ONE, SATOSHI-KUN.
I'LL BE ITH YOU ALL THE WAY.
MION.
SONO-ZAKI-SAN...
JIIIN (TOUCHED)

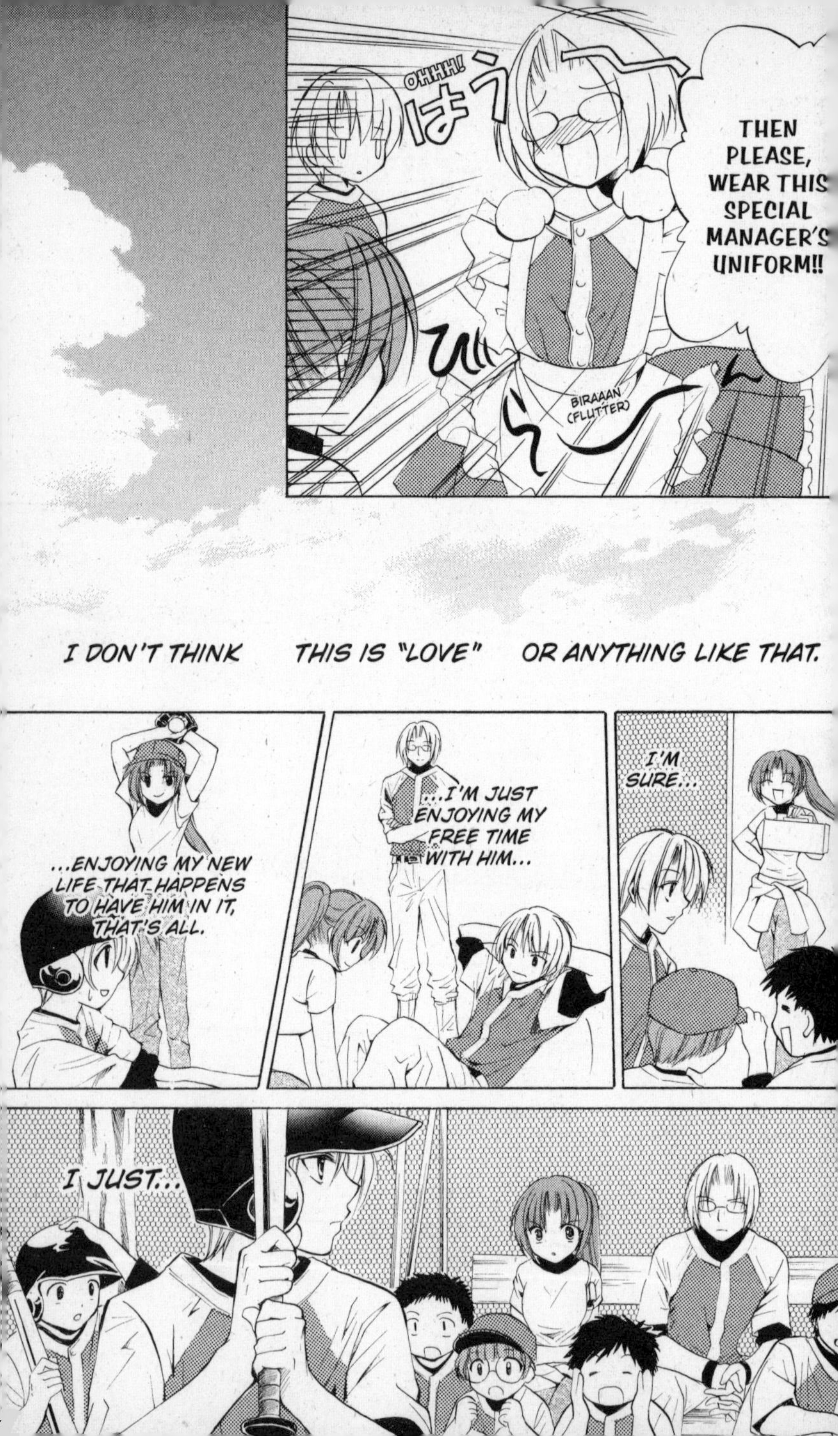
THEN PLEASE, WEAR THIS SPECIAL MANAGER'S UNIFORM!!
OHHH!
はう
BIRAAAN (FLUTTER)
I DON'T THINK THIS IS "LOVE" OR ANYTHING LIKE THAT.
I'M SURE...
...I'M JUST ENJOYING MY FREE TIME WITH HIM...
...ENJOYING MY NEW LIFE THAT HAPPENS TO HAVE HIM IN IT, THAT'S ALL.
I JUST...

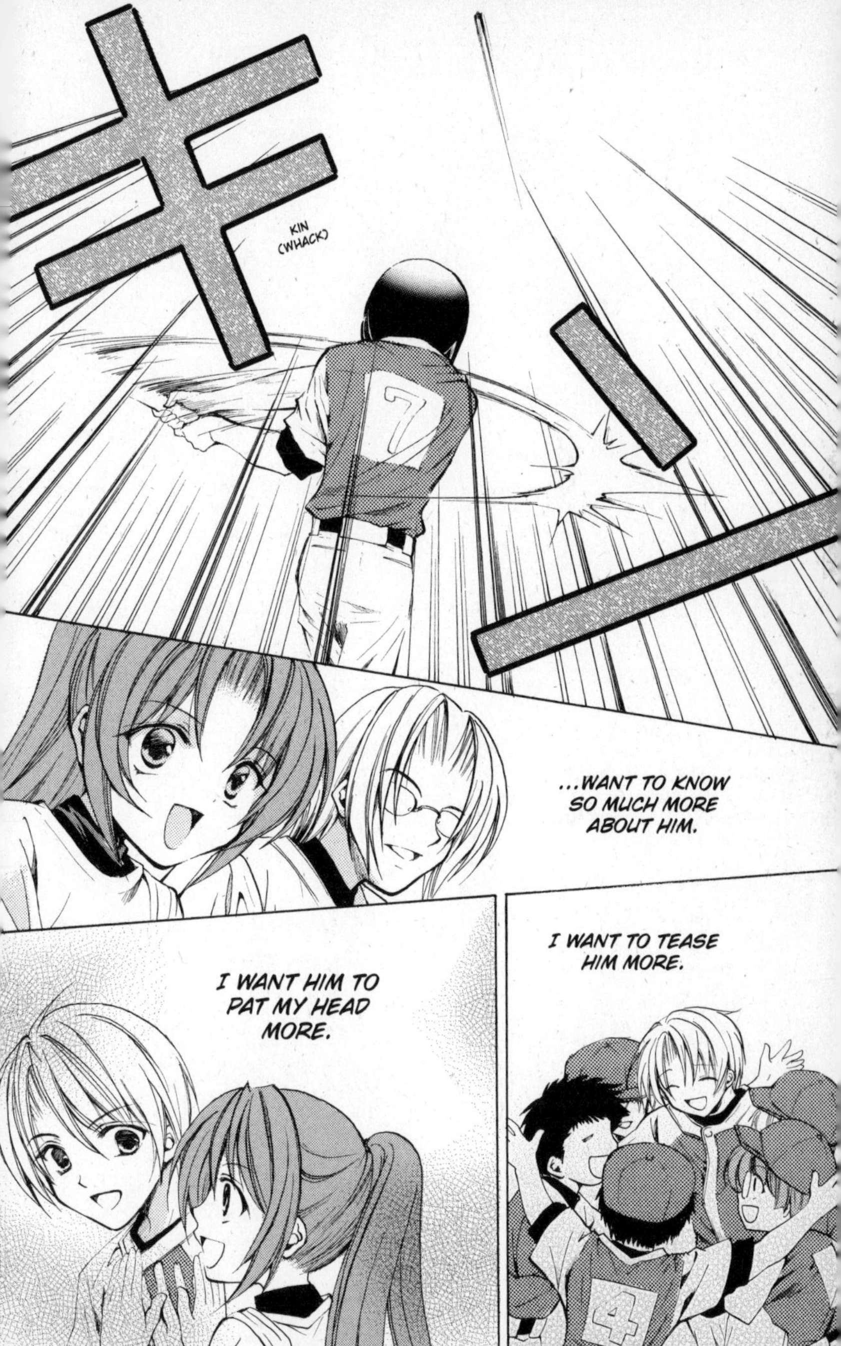
KIN
(WHACK)
...WANT TO KNOW SO MUCH MORE ABOUT HIM.
I WANT TO TEASE HIM MORE.
I WANT HIM TO PAT MY HEAD MORE.

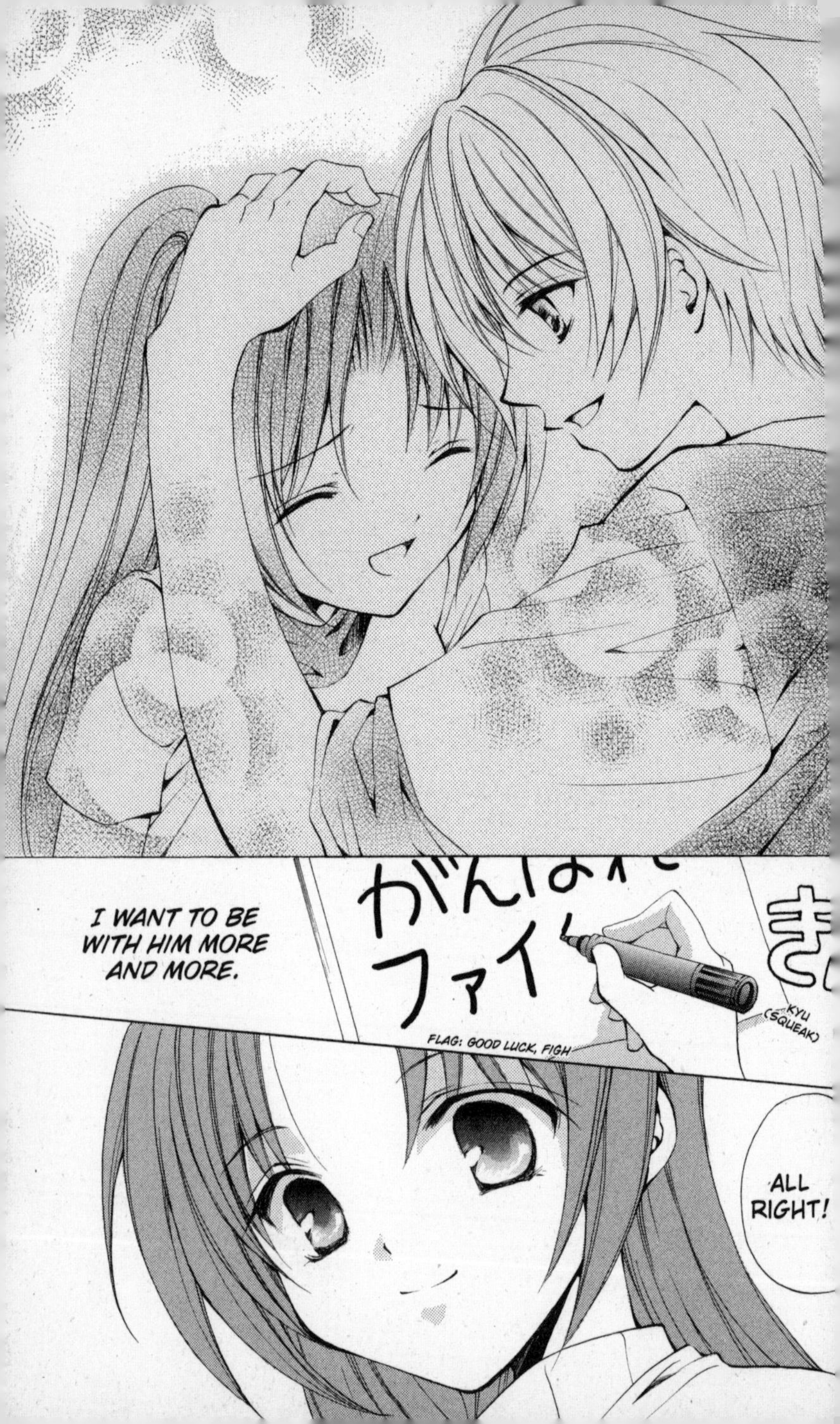

KYU (SQUEAK)
ファイ
FLAG: GOOD LUCK, FIGH
I WANT TO BE WITH HIM MORE AND MORE.
ALL RIGHT!

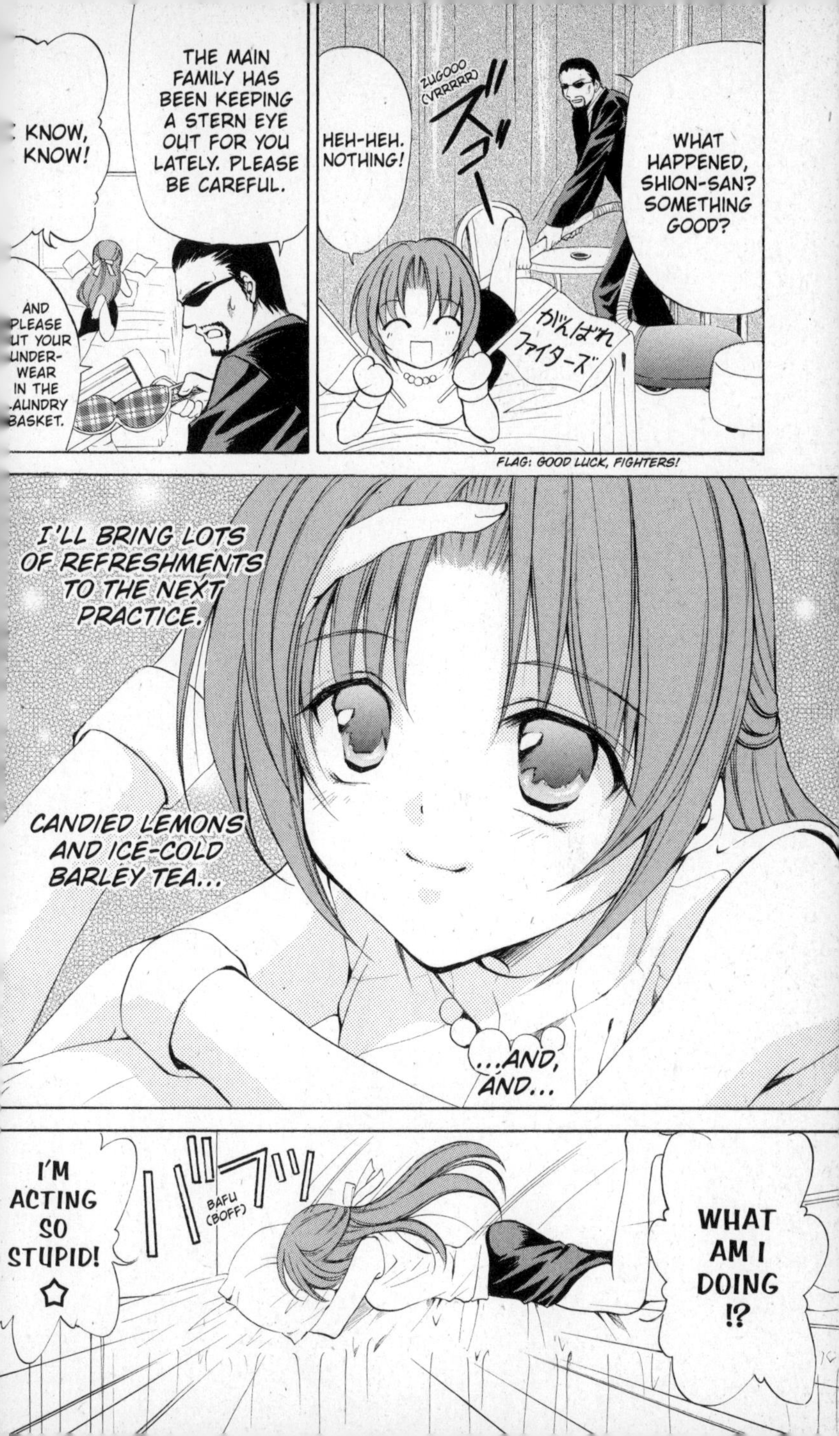
WHAT HAPPENED, SHION-SAN? SOMETHING GOOD?
ZUGOOO (VRRRRR)
HEH-HEH. NOTHING!
がんばれ ファイターズ
FLAG: GOOD LUCK, FIGHTERS!
THE MAIN FAMILY HAS BEEN KEEPING A STERN EYE OUT FOR YOU LATELY. PLEASE BE CAREFUL.
KNOW, KNOW!
AND PLEASE UT YOUR UNDER-WEAR IN THE AUNDRY BASKET.
I'LL BRING LOTS OF REFRESHMENTS TO THE NEXT PRACTICE.
CANDIED LEMONS AND ICE-COLD BARLEY TEA...
...AND, AND...
WHAT AM I DOING !?
BAFU (BOFF)
I'M ACTING SO STUPID! ☆

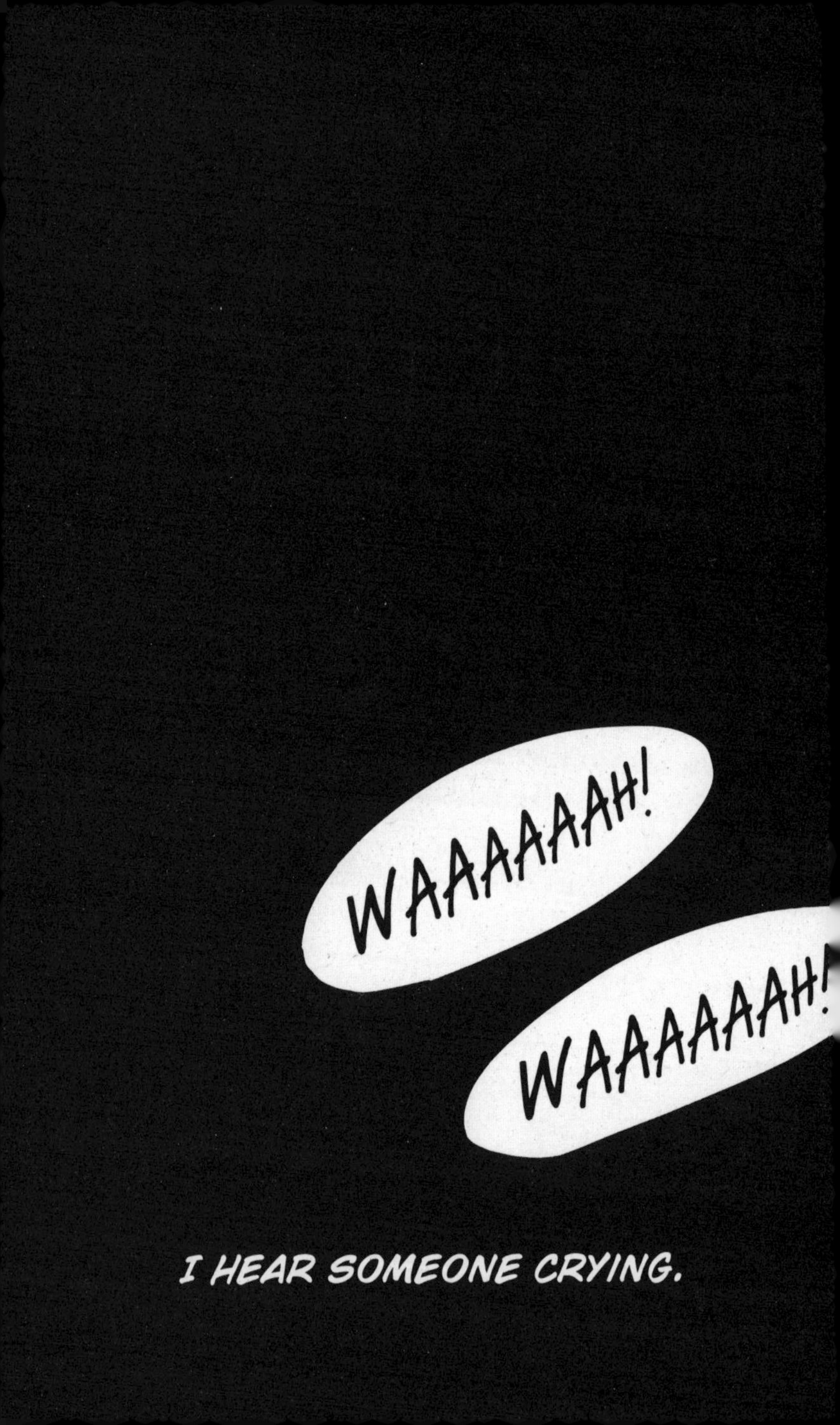
WAAAAAAH!
WAAAAAAH!
I HEAR SOMEONE CRYING.

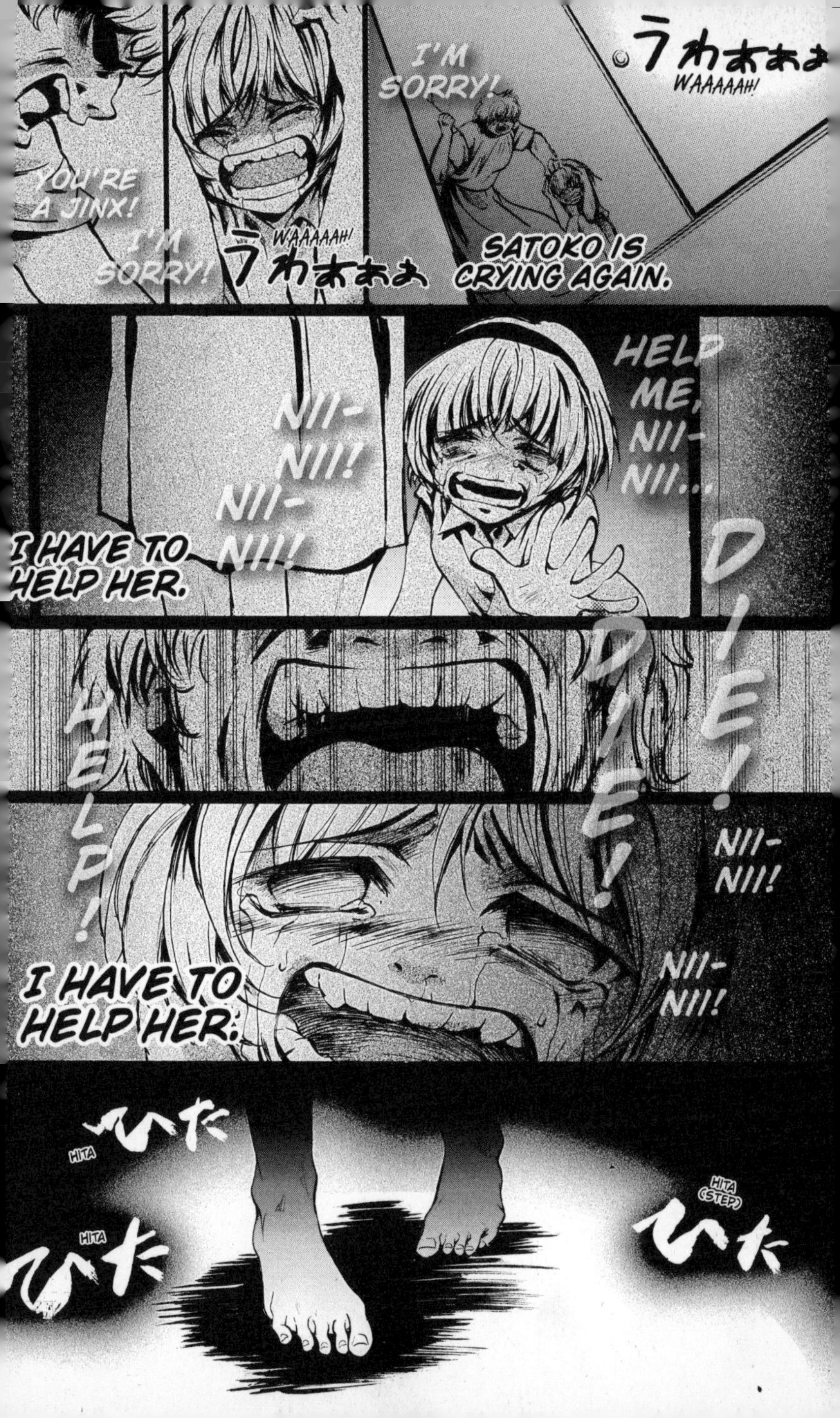
うわあああ
WAAAAAH!
I'M SORRY!
SATOKO IS CRYING AGAIN.
WAAAAAH!
うわあああ
I'M SORRY!
YOU'RE A JINX!
HELP ME, NII-NII...
NII-NII!
NII-NII!
I HAVE TO HELP HER.
DIE!
DIE!
HELP!
NII-NII!
NII-NII!
I HAVE TO HELP HER.
HITA (STEP)
ひた
HITA
ひた
HITA
ひた

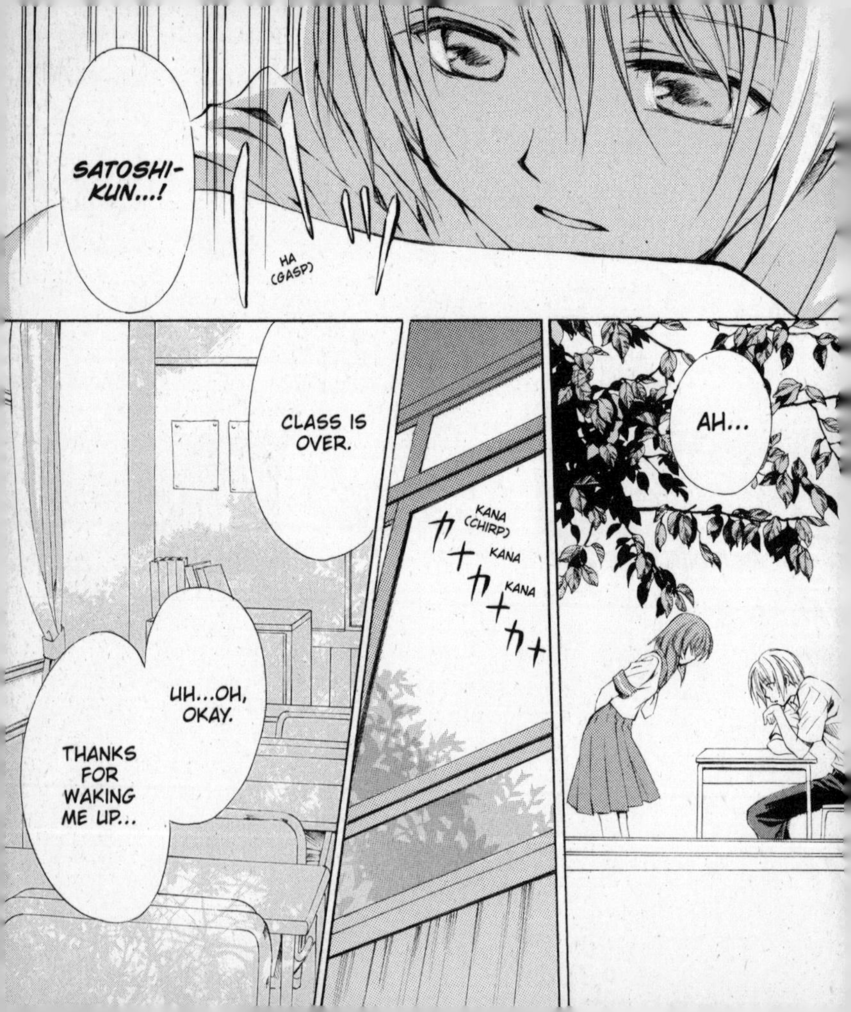
SATOSHI-KUN...!
HA (GASP)
AH...
カナカナカナ
KANA (CHIRP)
KANA
KANA
CLASS IS OVER.
UH...OH, OKAY.
THANKS FOR WAKING ME UP...

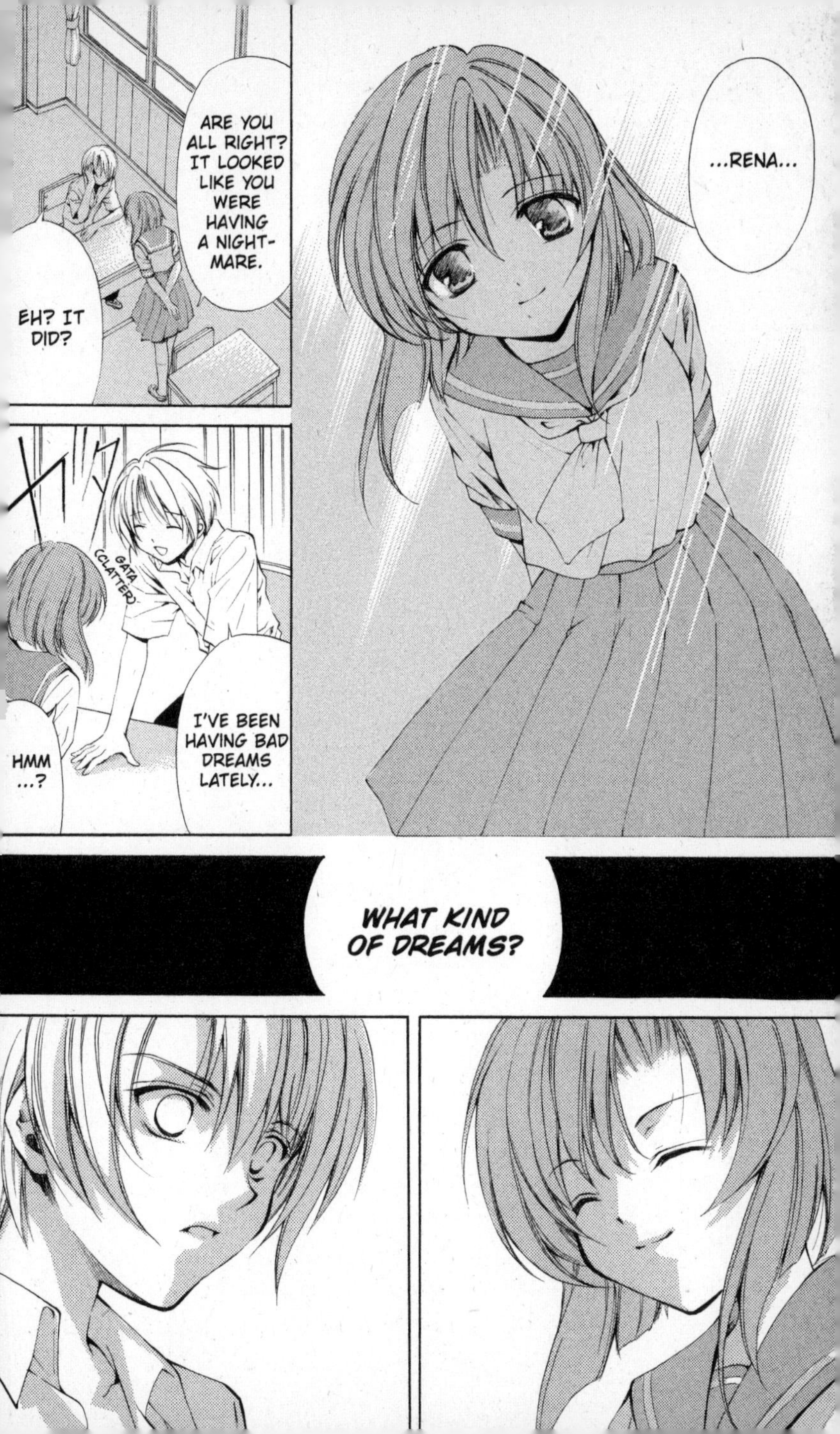
...RENA...
ARE YOU ALL RIGHT? IT LOOKED LIKE YOU WERE HAVING A NIGHT-MARE.
EH? IT DID?
GATA (CLATTER)
I'VE BEEN HAVING BAD DREAMS LATELY...
HMM ...?
WHAT KIND OF DREAMS?

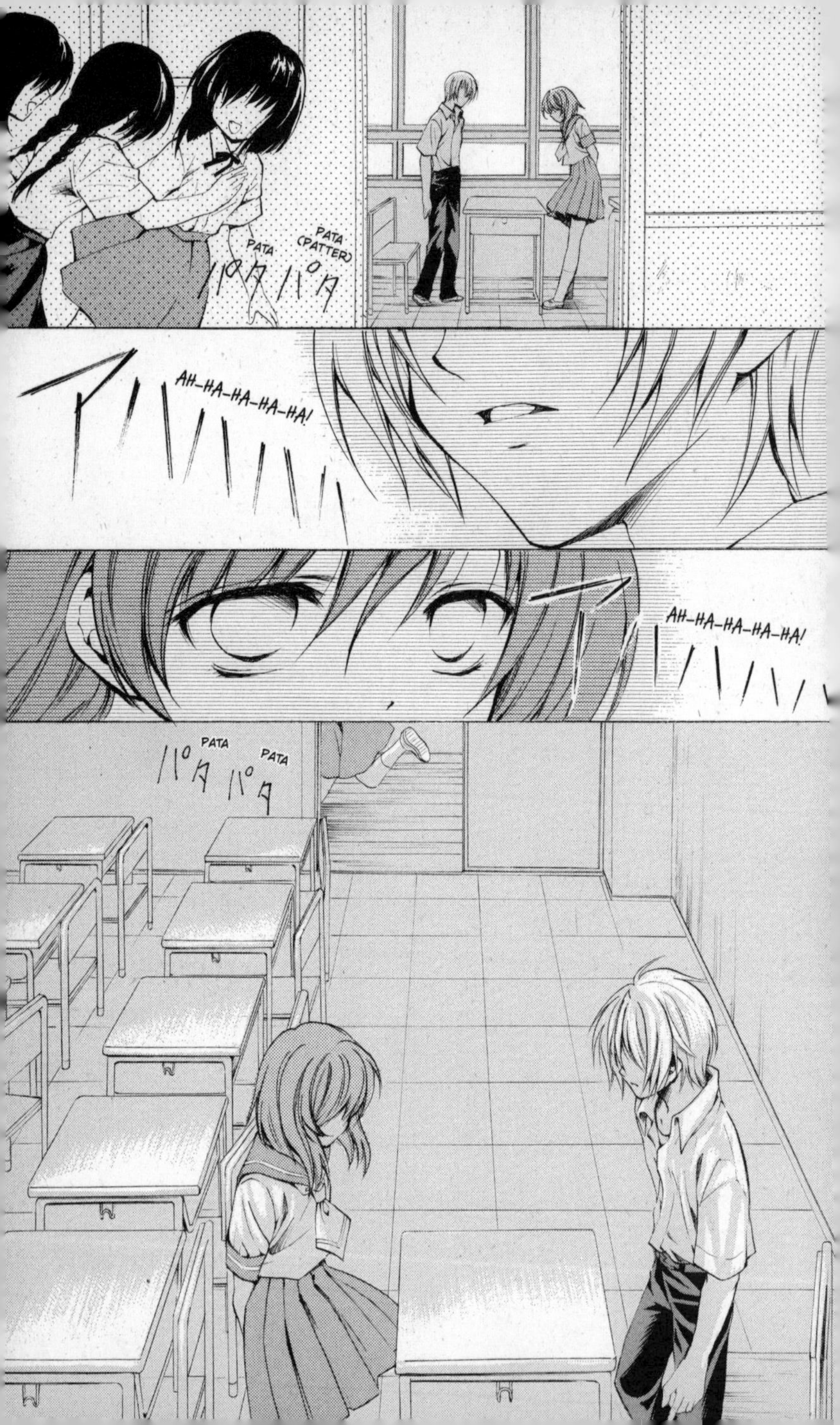

PATA (PATTER)
PATA
AH-HA-HA-HA-HA!
AH-HA-HA-HA-HA!
PATA
PATA

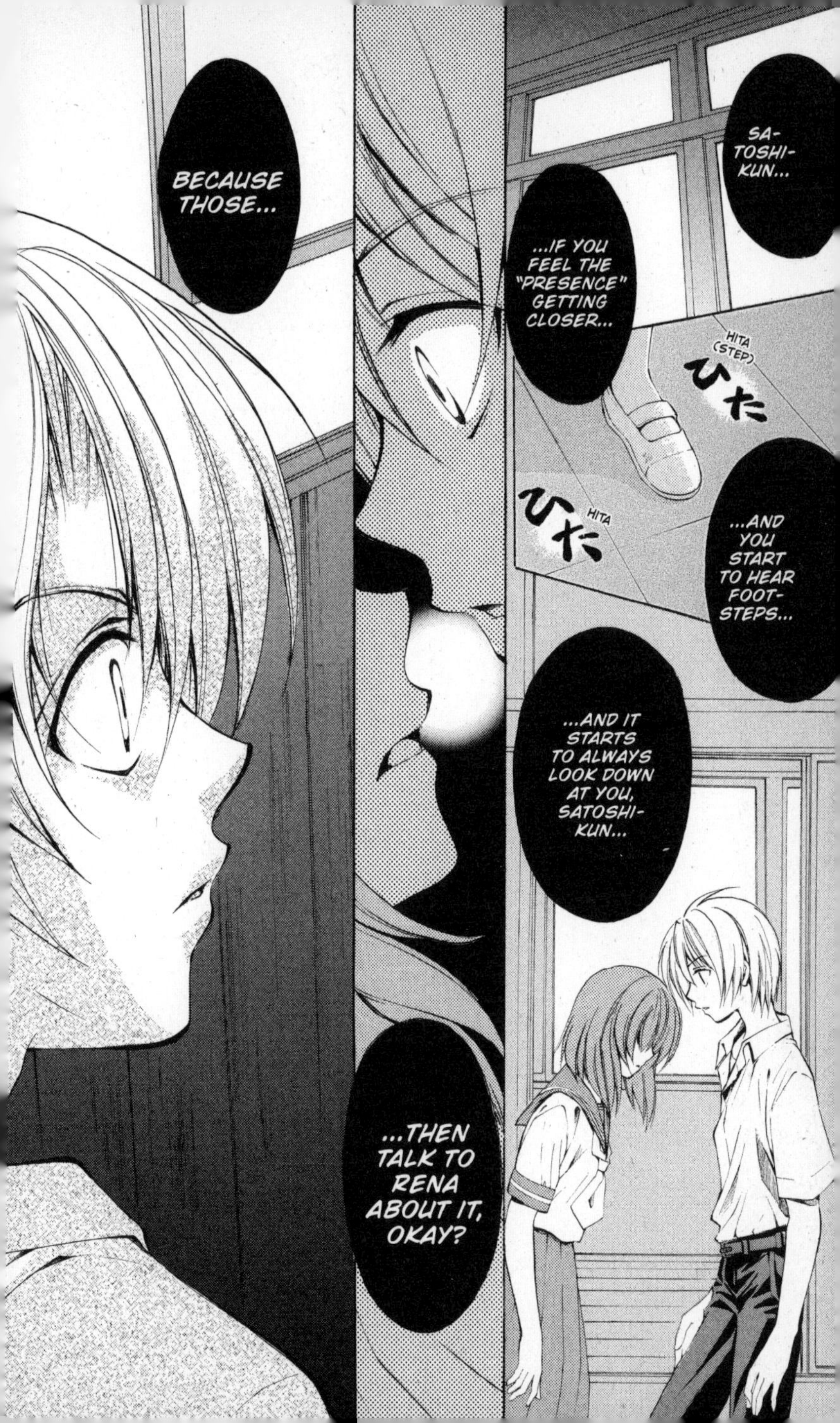
SA-TOSHI-KUN...
...IF YOU FEEL THE "PRESENCE" GETTING CLOSER...
HITA (STEP)
ひた
ひた
HITA
...AND YOU START TO HEAR FOOT-STEPS...
...AND IT STARTS TO ALWAYS LOOK DOWN AT YOU, SATOSHI-KUN...
...THEN TALK TO RENA ABOUT IT, OKAY?
BECAUSE THOSE...

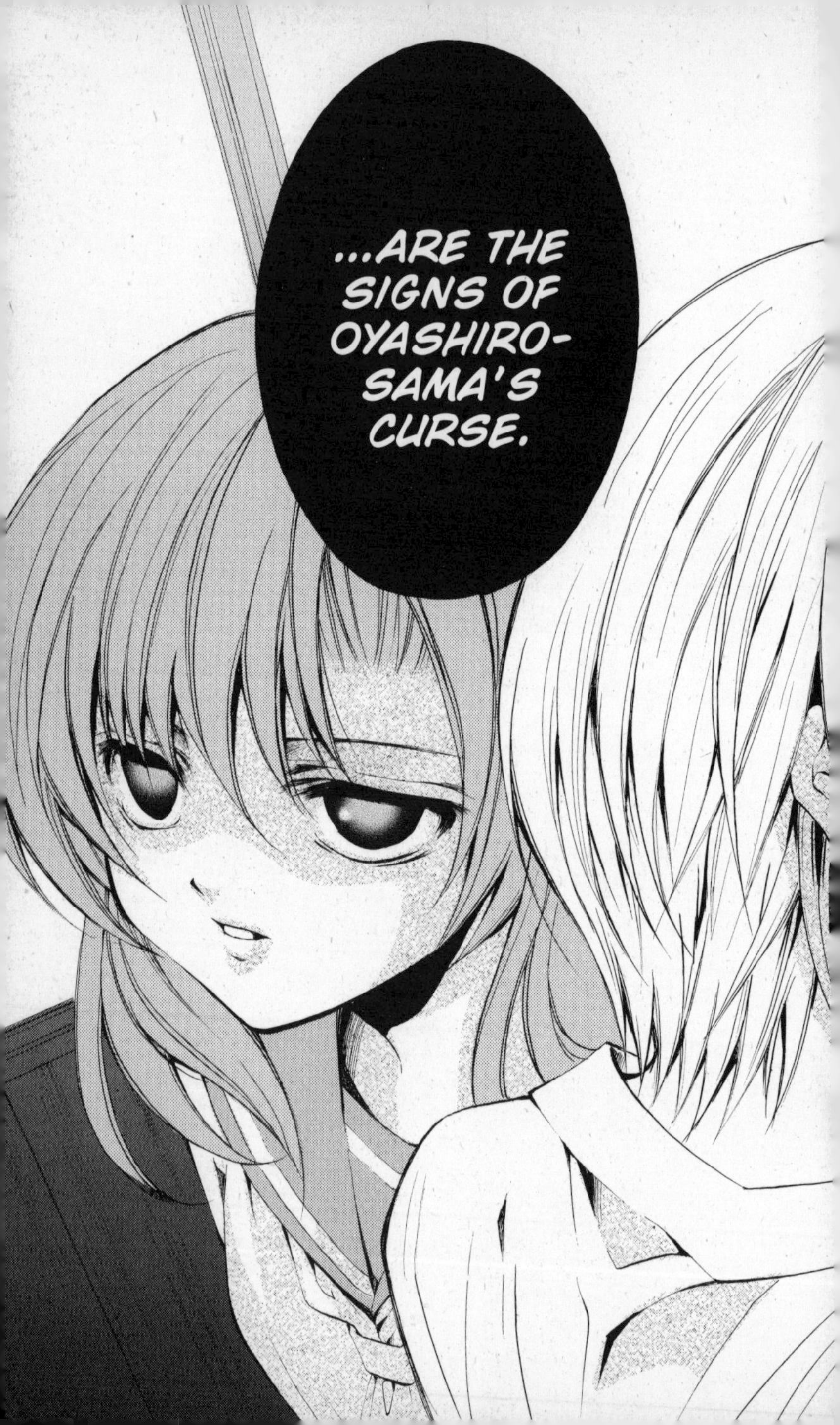
...ARE THE SIGNS OF OYASHIRO-SAMA'S CURSE.

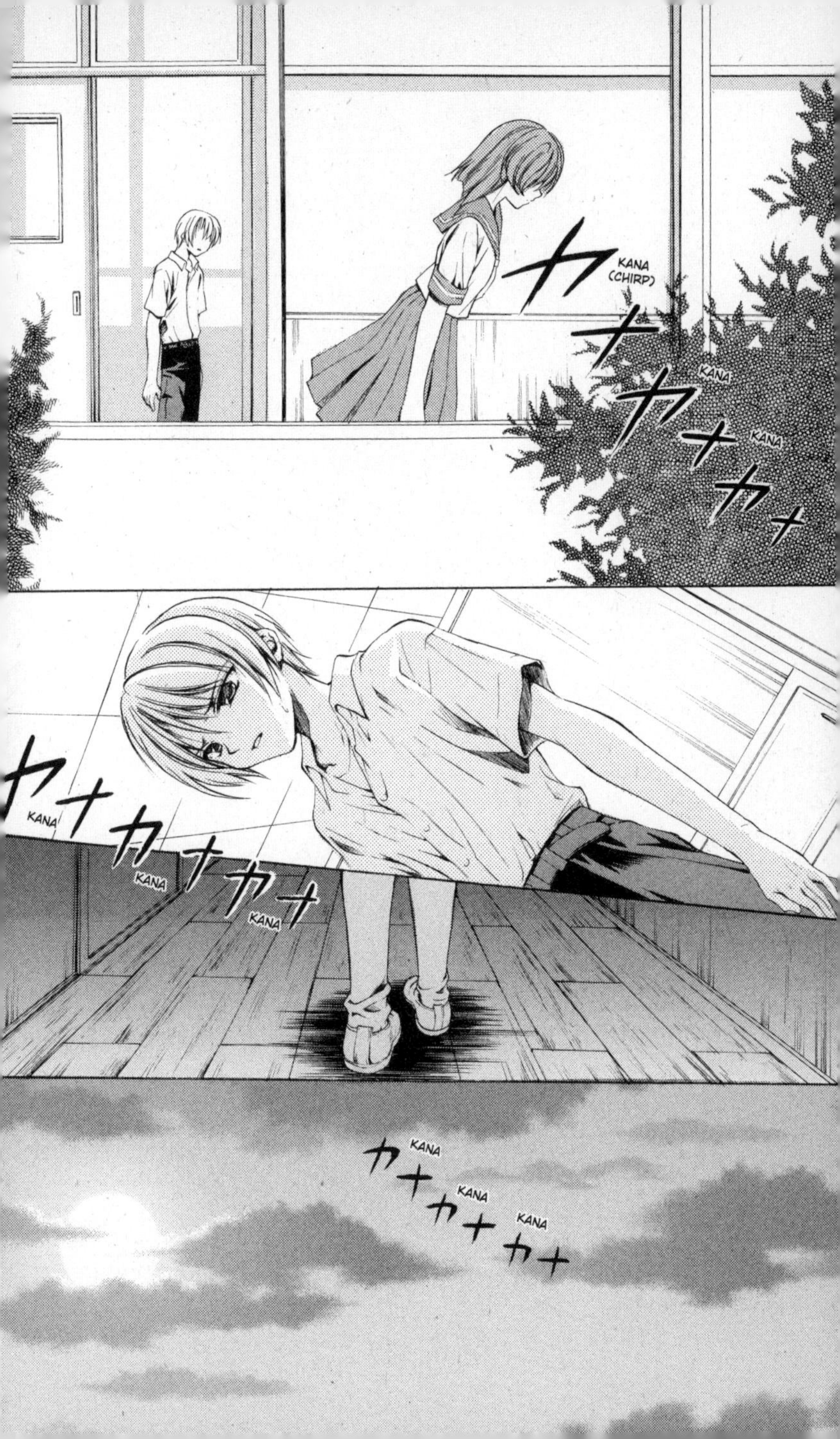
KANA (CHIRP)
KANA
KANA
KANA
KANA
KANA
KANA
KANA
KANA

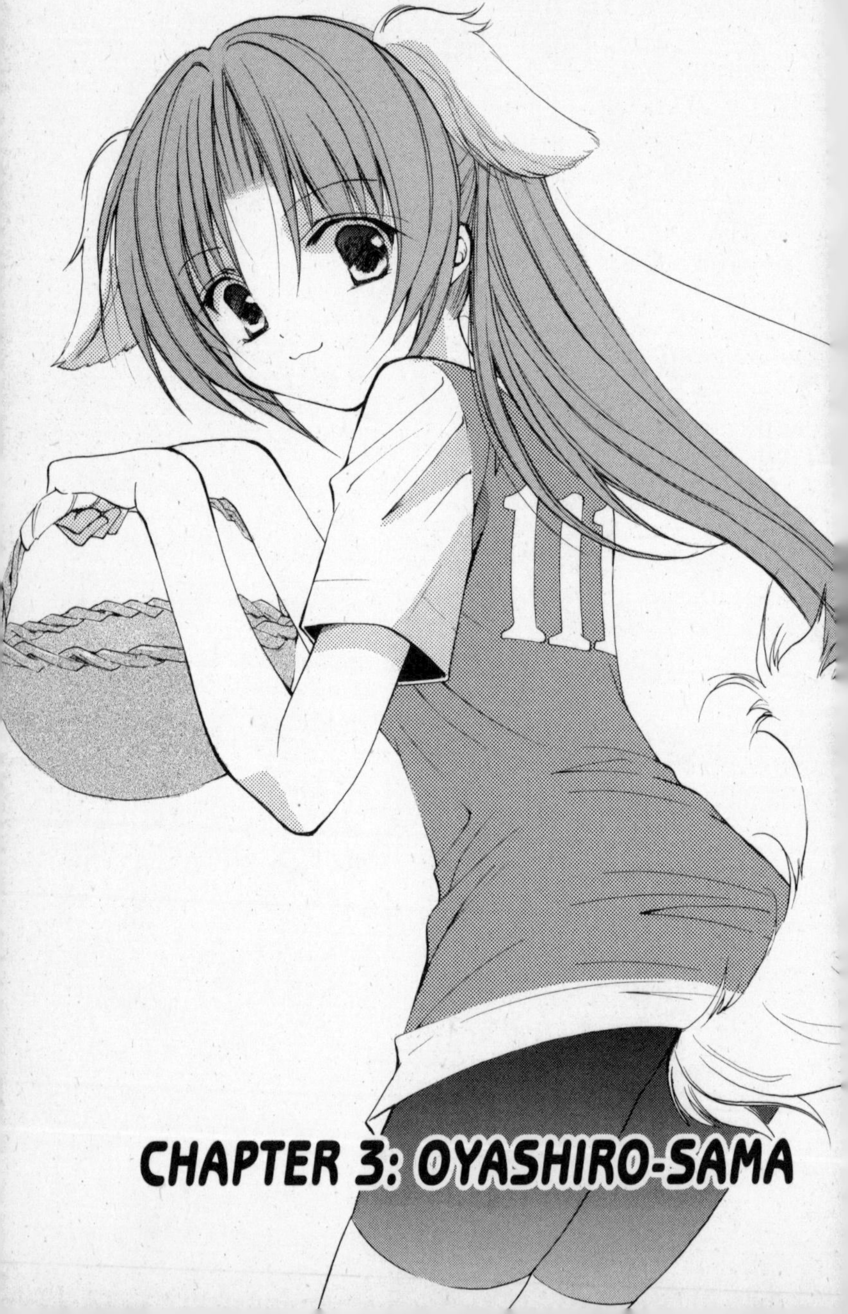

CHAPTER 3: OYASHIRO-SAMA

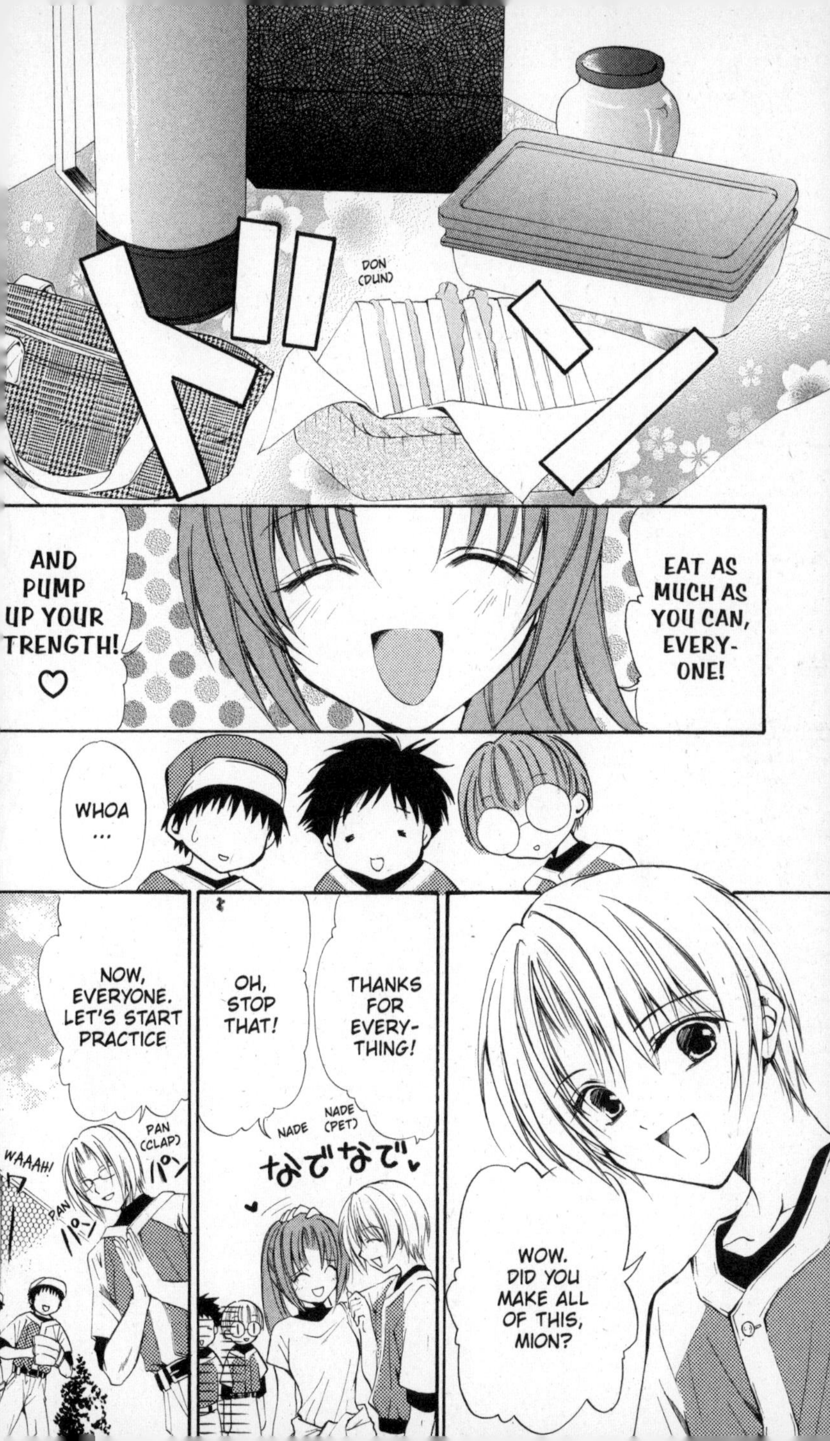
DON (DUN)
EAT AS MUCH AS YOU CAN, EVERYONE!
AND PUMP UP YOUR TRENGTH! ♡
WHOA ...
WOW. DID YOU MAKE ALL OF THIS, MION?
THANKS FOR EVERYTHING!
OH, STOP THAT!
NADE NADE (PET)
なでなで
NOW, EVERYONE. LET'S START PRACTICE
PAN (CLAP)
パン
PAN
パン
WAAAH!

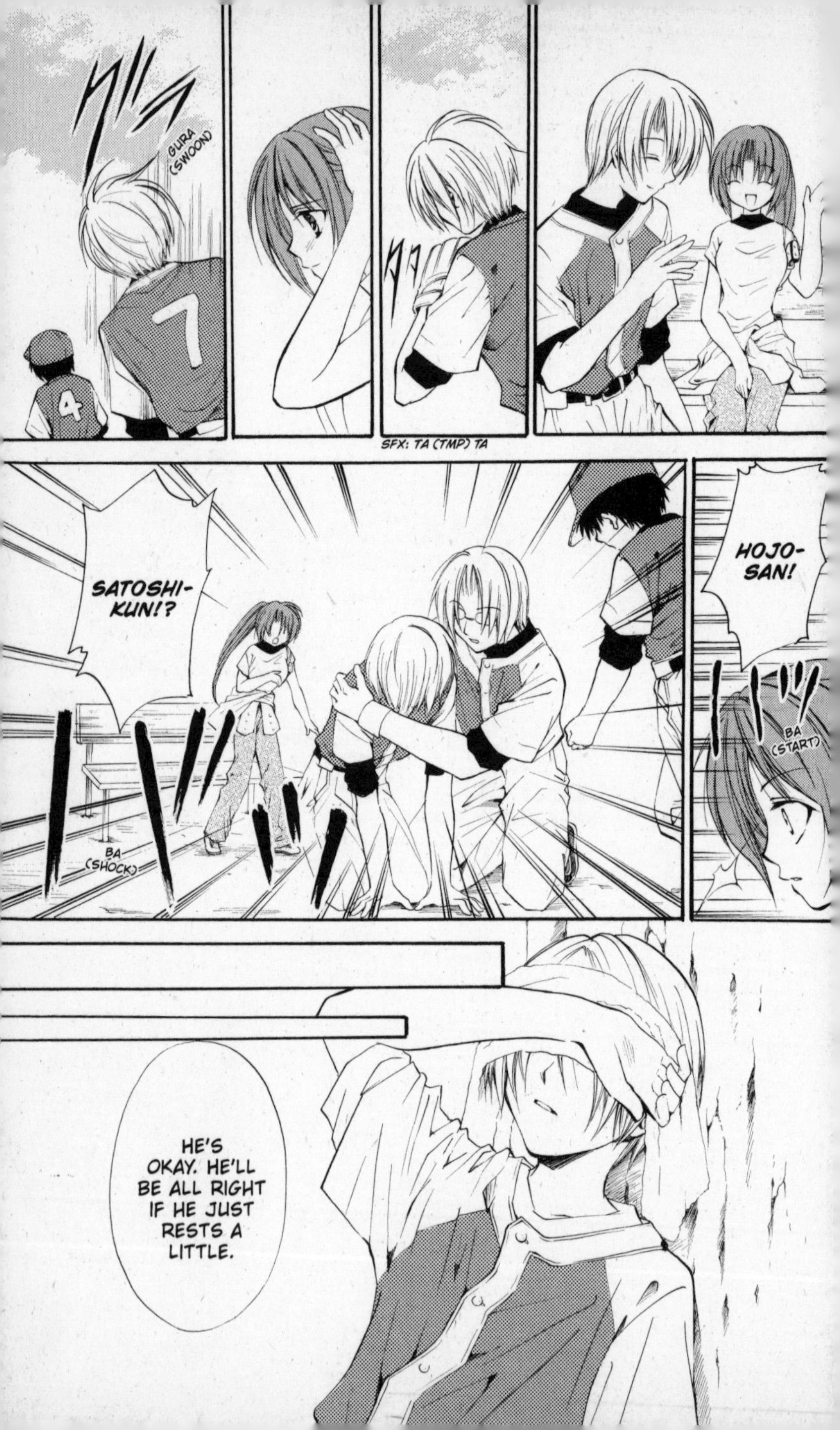
SFX: TA (TMP) TA
GURA (SWOON)
HOJO-SAN!
BA (START)
SATOSHI-KUN!?
BA (SHOCK)
HE'S OKAY. HE'LL BE ALL RIGHT IF HE JUST RESTS A LITTLE.

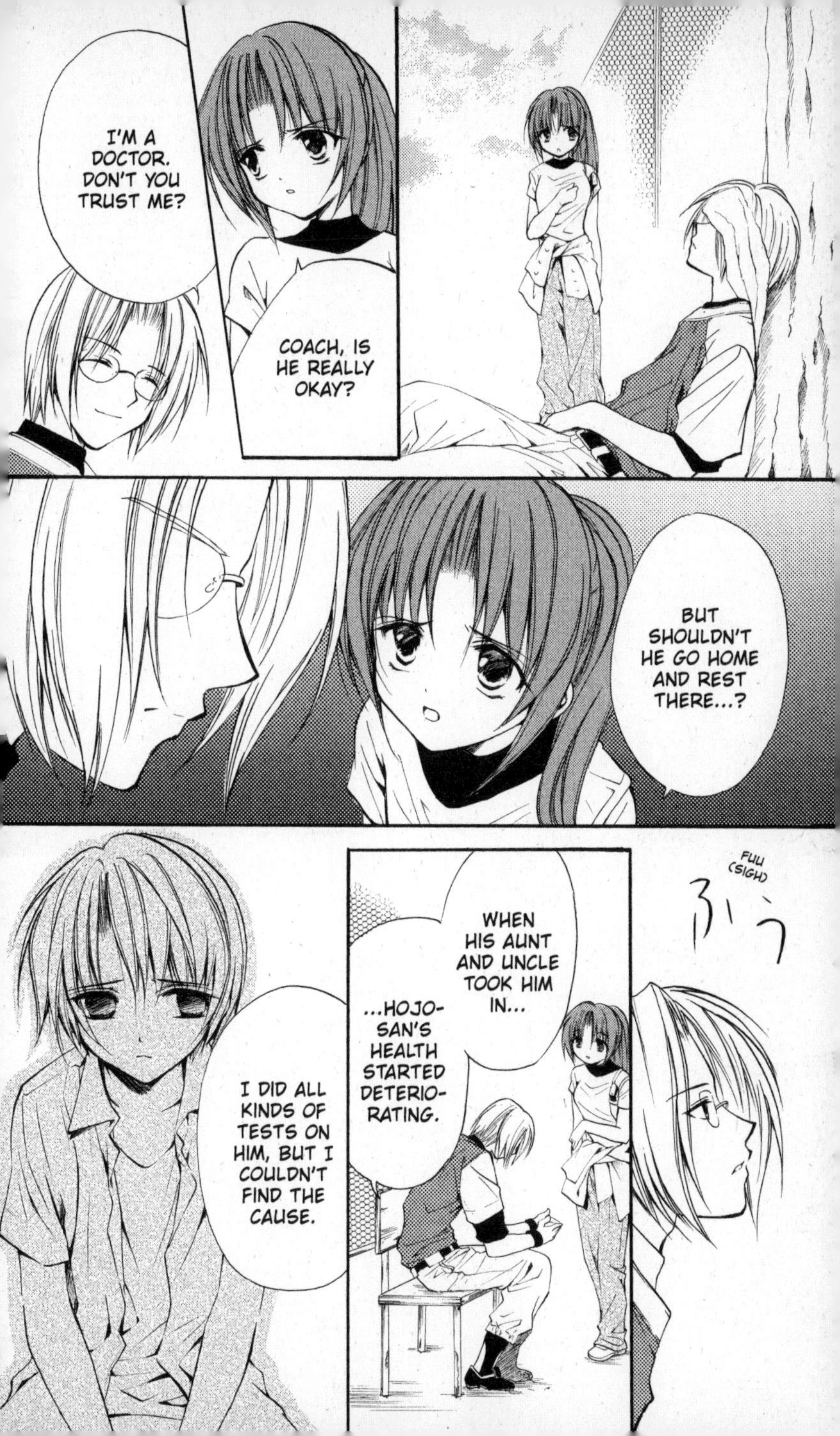
COACH, IS HE REALLY OKAY?
I'M A DOCTOR. DON'T YOU TRUST ME?
BUT SHOULDN'T HE GO HOME AND REST THERE...?
ふぅ
FUU (SIGH)
WHEN HIS AUNT AND UNCLE TOOK HIM IN...
...HOJO-SAN'S HEALTH STARTED DETERIO-RATING.
I DID ALL KINDS OF TESTS ON HIM, BUT I COULDN'T FIND THE CAUSE.

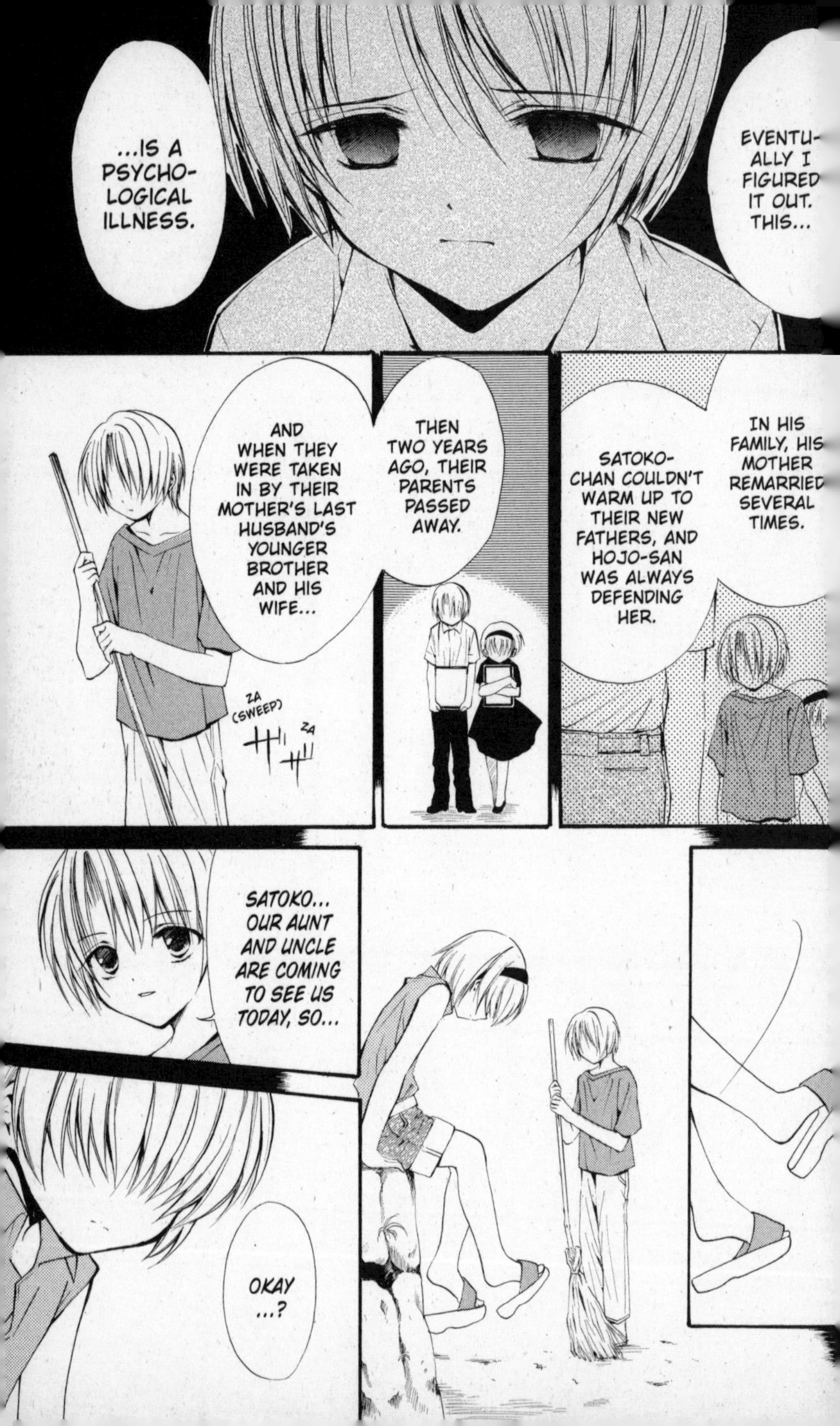
EVENTUALLY I FIGURED IT OUT. THIS...
...IS A PSYCHOLOGICAL ILLNESS.
IN HIS FAMILY, HIS MOTHER REMARRIED SEVERAL TIMES.
SATOKO-CHAN COULDN'T WARM UP TO THEIR NEW FATHERS, AND HOJO-SAN WAS ALWAYS DEFENDING HER.
THEN TWO YEARS AGO, THEIR PARENTS PASSED AWAY.
AND WHEN THEY WERE TAKEN IN BY THEIR MOTHER'S LAST HUSBAND'S YOUNGER BROTHER AND HIS WIFE...
ZA (SWEEP)
ZA
SATOKO... OUR AUNT AND UNCLE ARE COMING TO SEE US TODAY, SO...
OKAY ...?

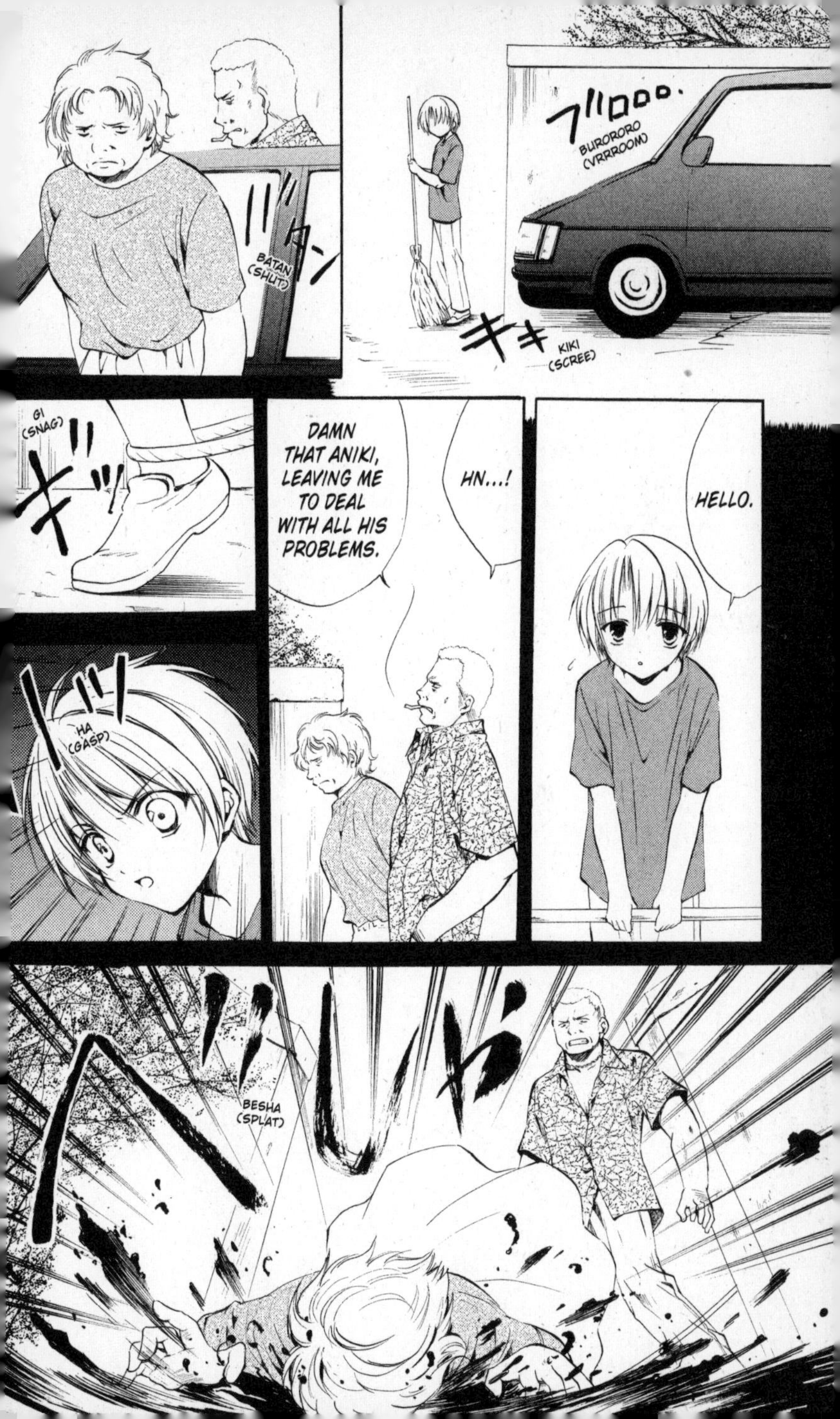
BURORORO (VRRROOM)
KIKI (SCREE)
BATAN (SHUT)
HELLO.
HN...!
DAMN THAT ANIKI, LEAVING ME TO DEAL WITH ALL HIS PROBLEMS.
GI (SNAG)
HA (GASP)
BESHA (SPLAT)

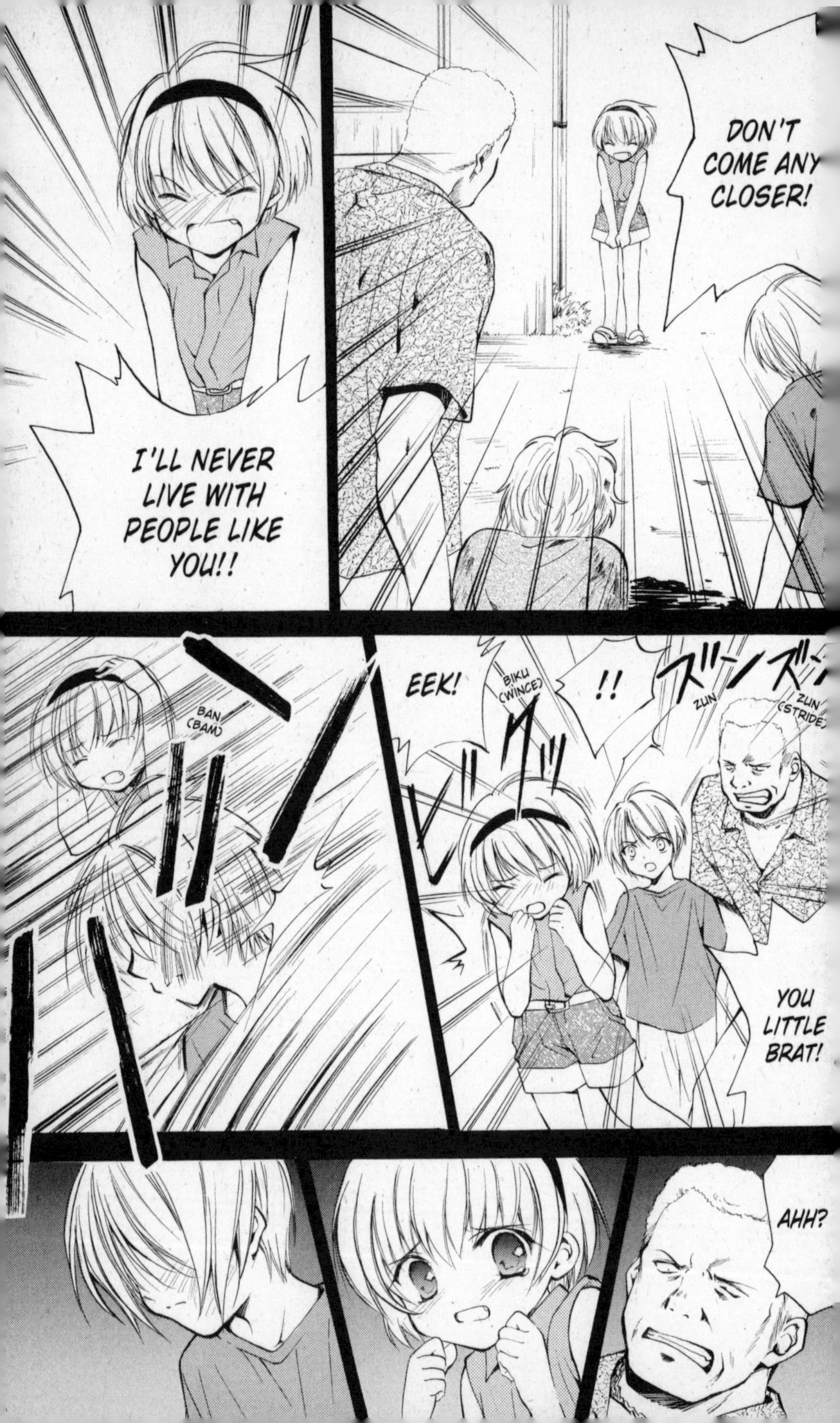
DON'T COME ANY CLOSER!
I'LL NEVER LIVE WITH PEOPLE LIKE YOU!!
ZUN
ZUN (STRIDE)
!!
BIKU (WINCE)
EEK!
YOU LITTLE BRAT!
BAN (BAM)
AHH?

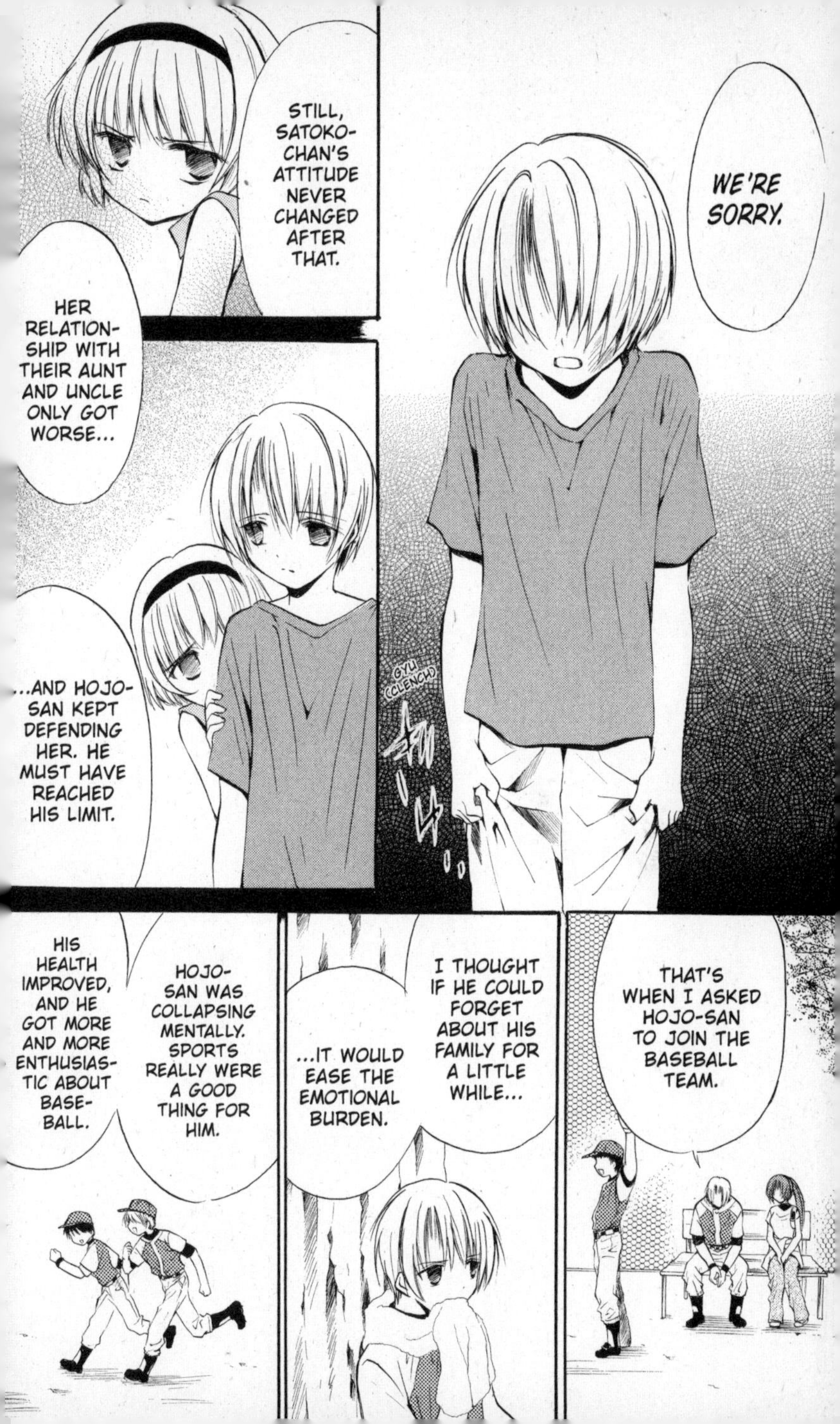
WE'RE SORRY.
GYU (CLENCH)
STILL, SATOKO-CHAN'S ATTITUDE NEVER CHANGED AFTER THAT.
HER RELATIONSHIP WITH THEIR AUNT AND UNCLE ONLY GOT WORSE...
...AND HOJO-SAN KEPT DEFENDING HER. HE MUST HAVE REACHED HIS LIMIT.
THAT'S WHEN I ASKED HOJO-SAN TO JOIN THE BASEBALL TEAM.
I THOUGHT IF HE COULD FORGET ABOUT HIS FAMILY FOR A LITTLE WHILE...
...IT WOULD EASE THE EMOTIONAL BURDEN.
HOJO-SAN WAS COLLAPSING MENTALLY. SPORTS REALLY WERE A GOOD THING FOR HIM.
HIS HEALTH IMPROVED, AND HE GOT MORE AND MORE ENTHUSIASTIC ABOUT BASEBALL.

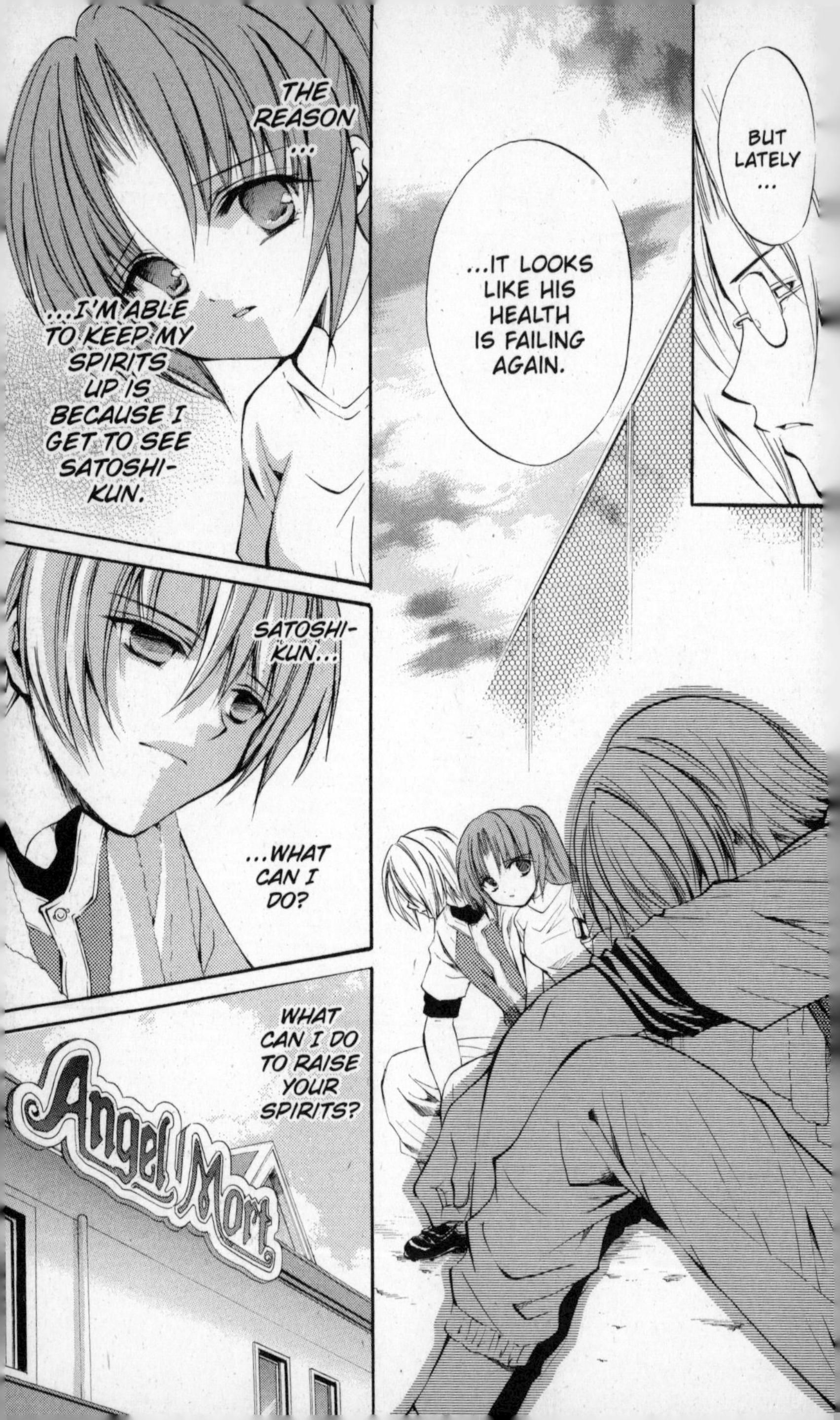
BUT LATELY ...
...IT LOOKS LIKE HIS HEALTH IS FAILING AGAIN.
THE REASON ...
...I'M ABLE TO KEEP MY SPIRITS UP IS BECAUSE I GET TO SEE SATOSHI-KUN.
SATOSHI-KUN...
...WHAT CAN I DO?
WHAT CAN I DO TO RAISE YOUR SPIRITS?
Angel Mort

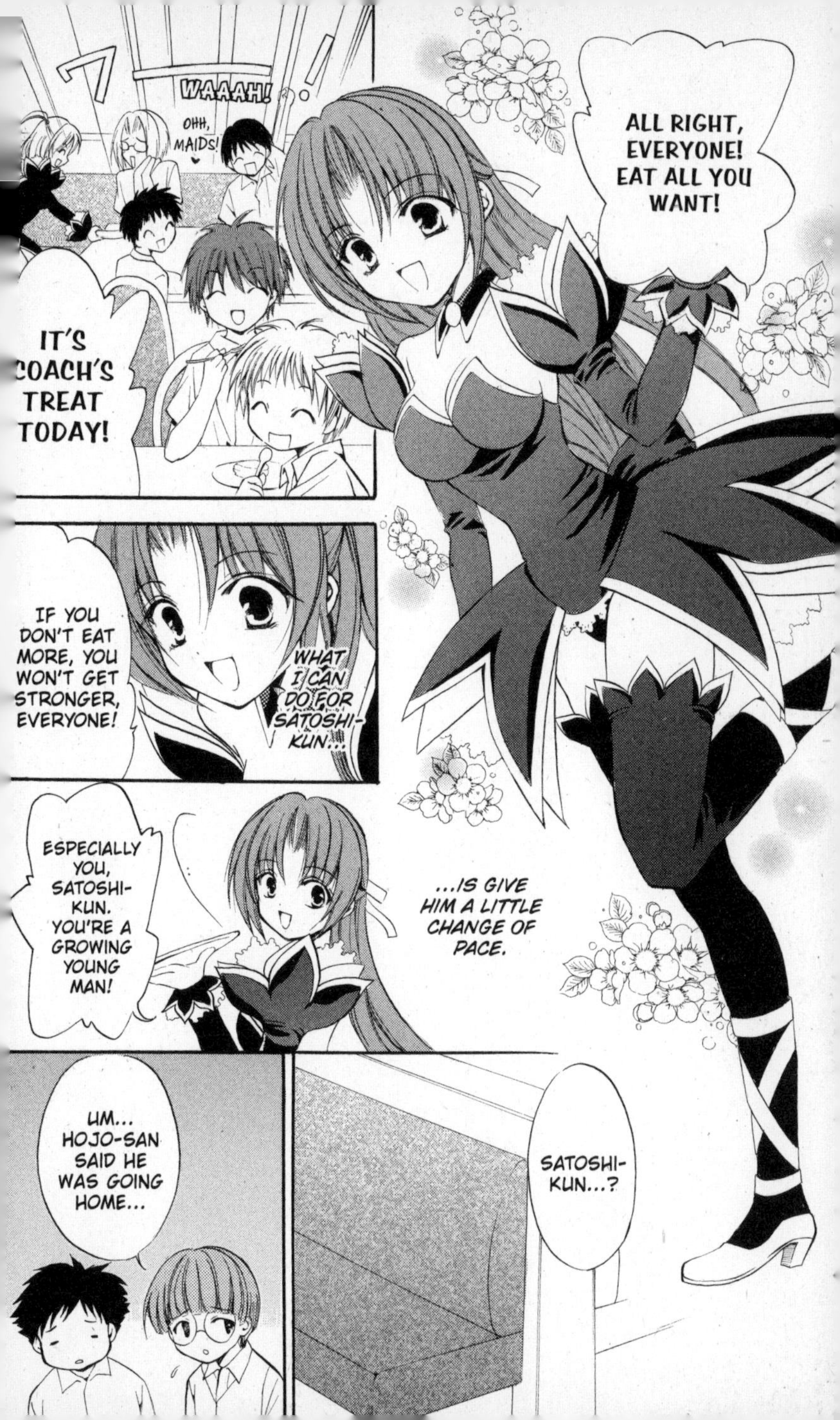
ALL RIGHT, EVERYONE! EAT ALL YOU WANT!
WAAAH!
OHH, MAIDS!
IT'S COACH'S TREAT TODAY!
WHAT I CAN DO FOR SATOSHI-KUN...
IF YOU DON'T EAT MORE, YOU WON'T GET STRONGER, EVERYONE!
...IS GIVE HIM A LITTLE CHANGE OF PACE.
ESPECIALLY YOU, SATOSHI-KUN. YOU'RE A GROWING YOUNG MAN!
SATOSHI-KUN...?
UM... HOJO-SAN SAID HE WAS GOING HOME...

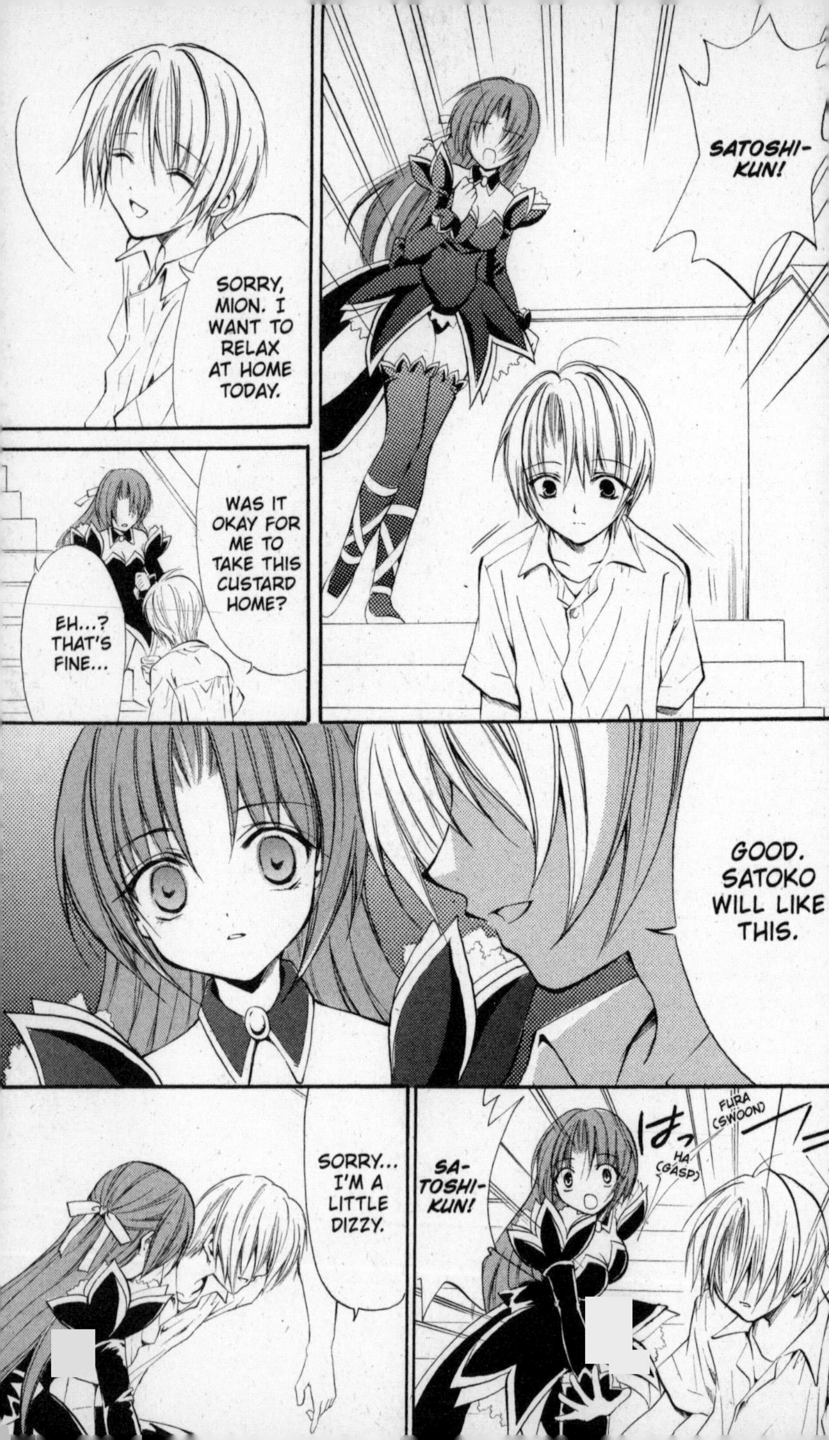
SATOSHI-KUN!
SORRY, MION. I WANT TO RELAX AT HOME TODAY.
WAS IT OKAY FOR ME TO TAKE THIS CUSTARD HOME?
EH...? THAT'S FINE...
GOOD. SATOKO WILL LIKE THIS.
FURA (SWOON)
はっ
HA (GASP)
SA-TOSHI-KUN!
SORRY... I'M A LITTLE DIZZY.

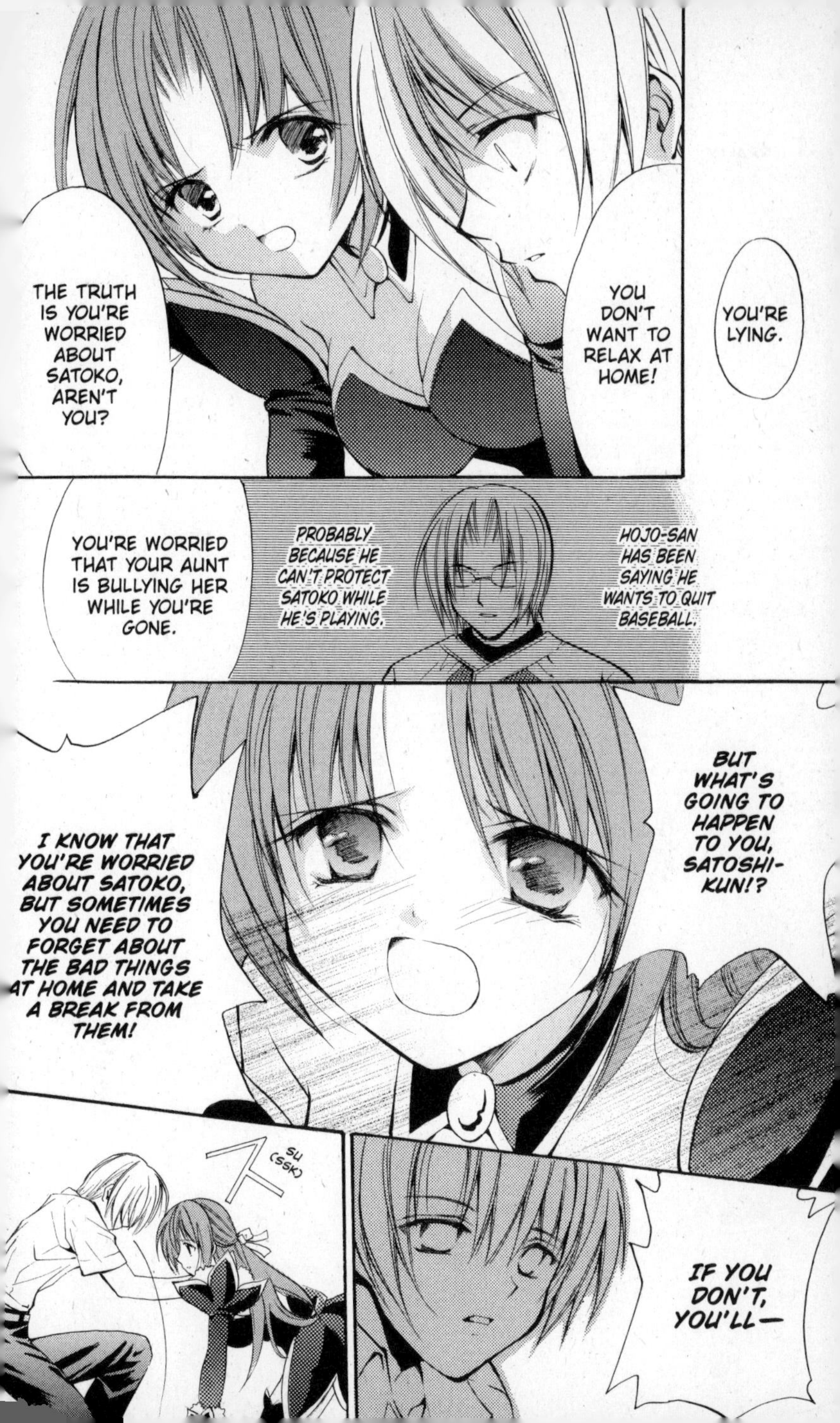
YOU'RE LYING.
YOU DON'T WANT TO RELAX AT HOME!
THE TRUTH IS YOU'RE WORRIED ABOUT SATOKO, AREN'T YOU?
HOJO-SAN HAS BEEN SAYING HE WANTS TO QUIT BASEBALL.
PROBABLY BECAUSE HE CAN'T PROTECT SATOKO WHILE HE'S PLAYING.
YOU'RE WORRIED THAT YOUR AUNT IS BULLYING HER WHILE YOU'RE GONE.
BUT WHAT'S GOING TO HAPPEN TO YOU, SATOSHI-KUN!?
I KNOW THAT YOU'RE WORRIED ABOUT SATOKO, BUT SOMETIMES YOU NEED TO FORGET ABOUT THE BAD THINGS AT HOME AND TAKE A BREAK FROM THEM!
IF YOU DON'T, YOU'LL—
SU (SSK)

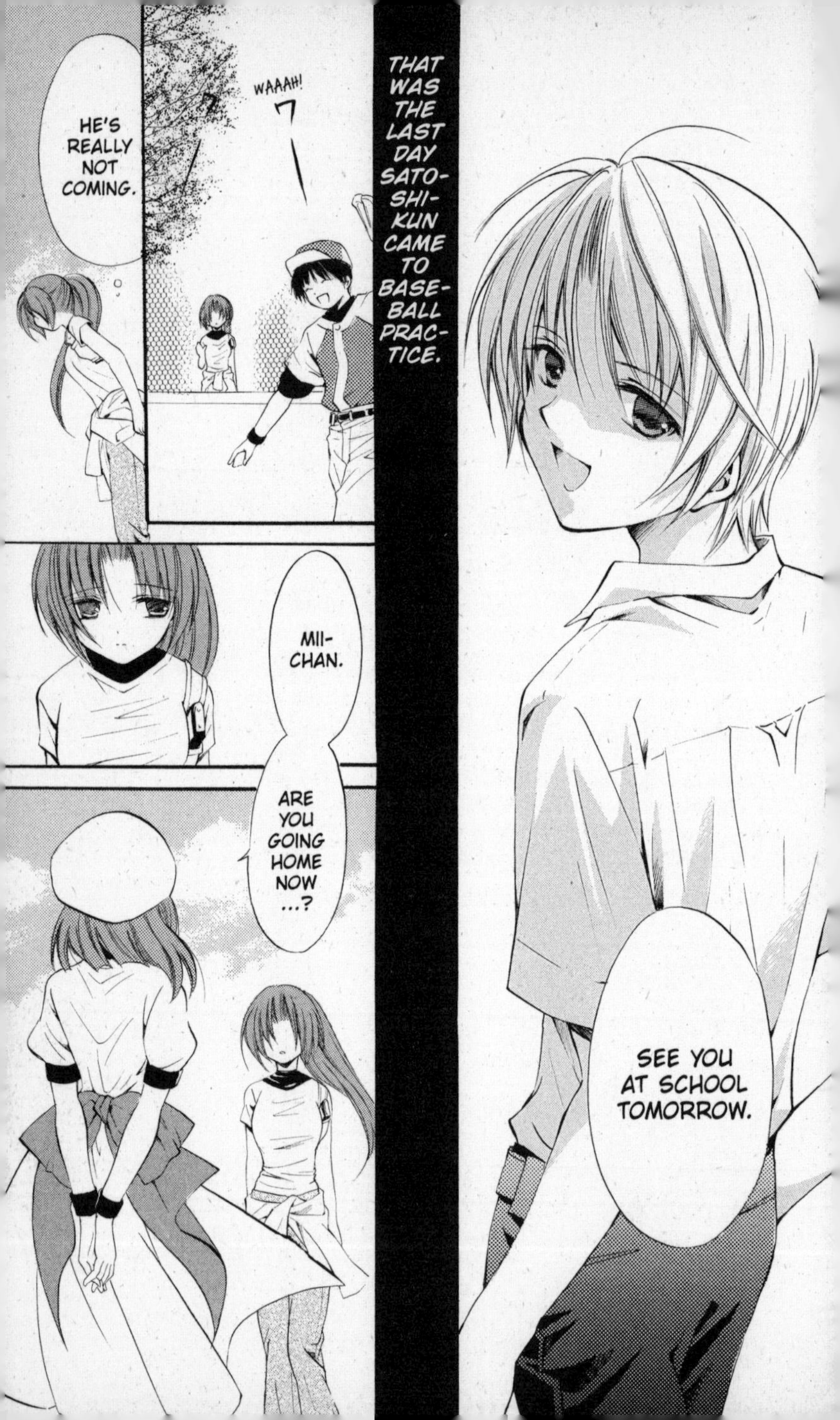
SEE YOU AT SCHOOL TOMORROW.
THAT WAS THE LAST DAY SATOSHI-KUN CAME TO BASEBALL PRACTICE.
WAAAH!
HE'S REALLY NOT COMING.
MII-CHAN.
ARE YOU GOING HOME NOW ...?

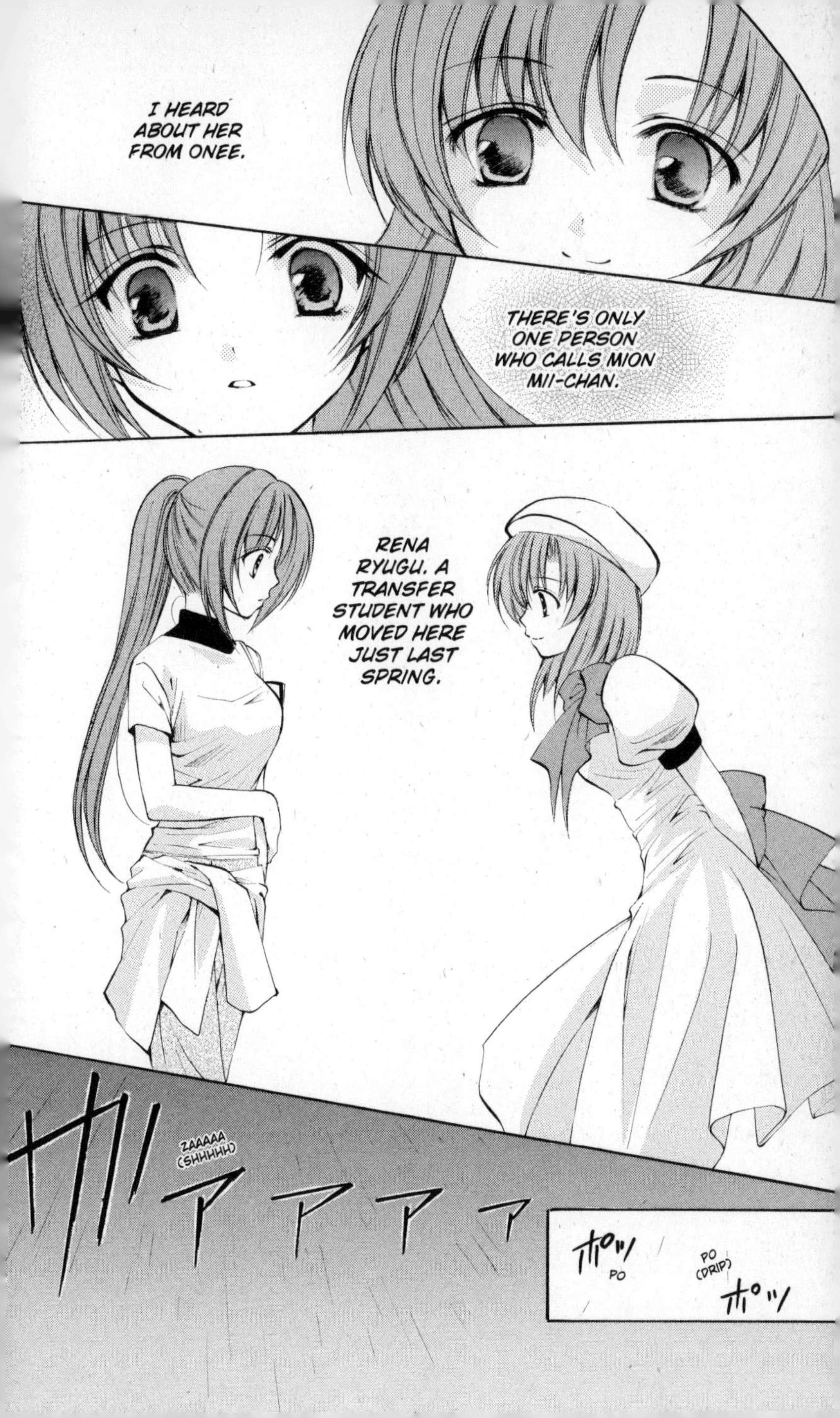
I HEARD ABOUT HER FROM ONEE.
THERE'S ONLY ONE PERSON WHO CALLS MION MII-CHAN.
RENA RYUGU. A TRANSFER STUDENT WHO MOVED HERE JUST LAST SPRING.
ZAAAAA (SHHHHH)
PO PO (DRIP)

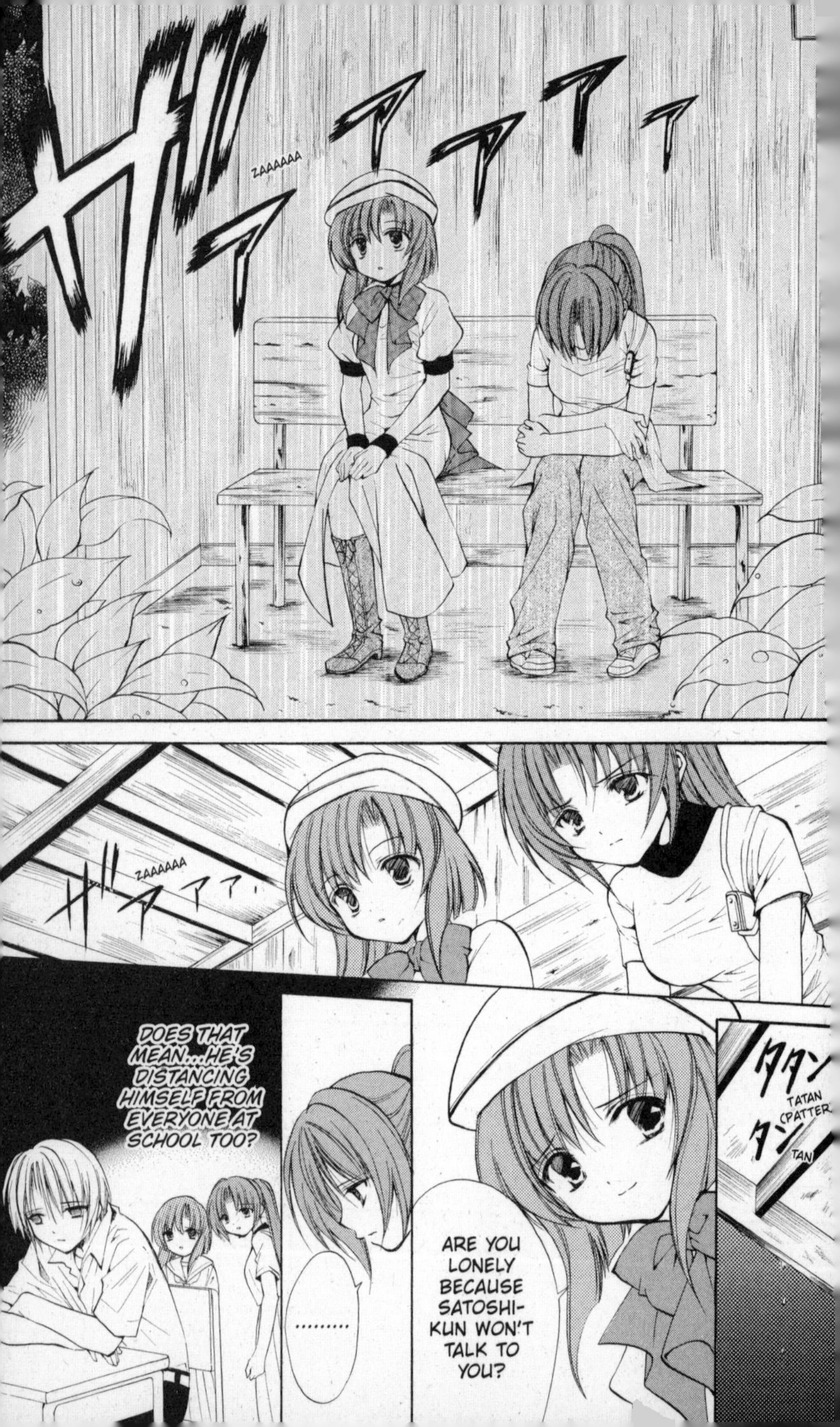
ZAAAAAA
ZAAAAAA
TATAN (PATTER)
TAN
ARE YOU LONELY BECAUSE SATOSHI-KUN WON'T TALK TO YOU?
....
DOES THAT MEAN...HE'S DISTANCING HIMSELF FROM EVERYONE AT SCHOOL TOO?

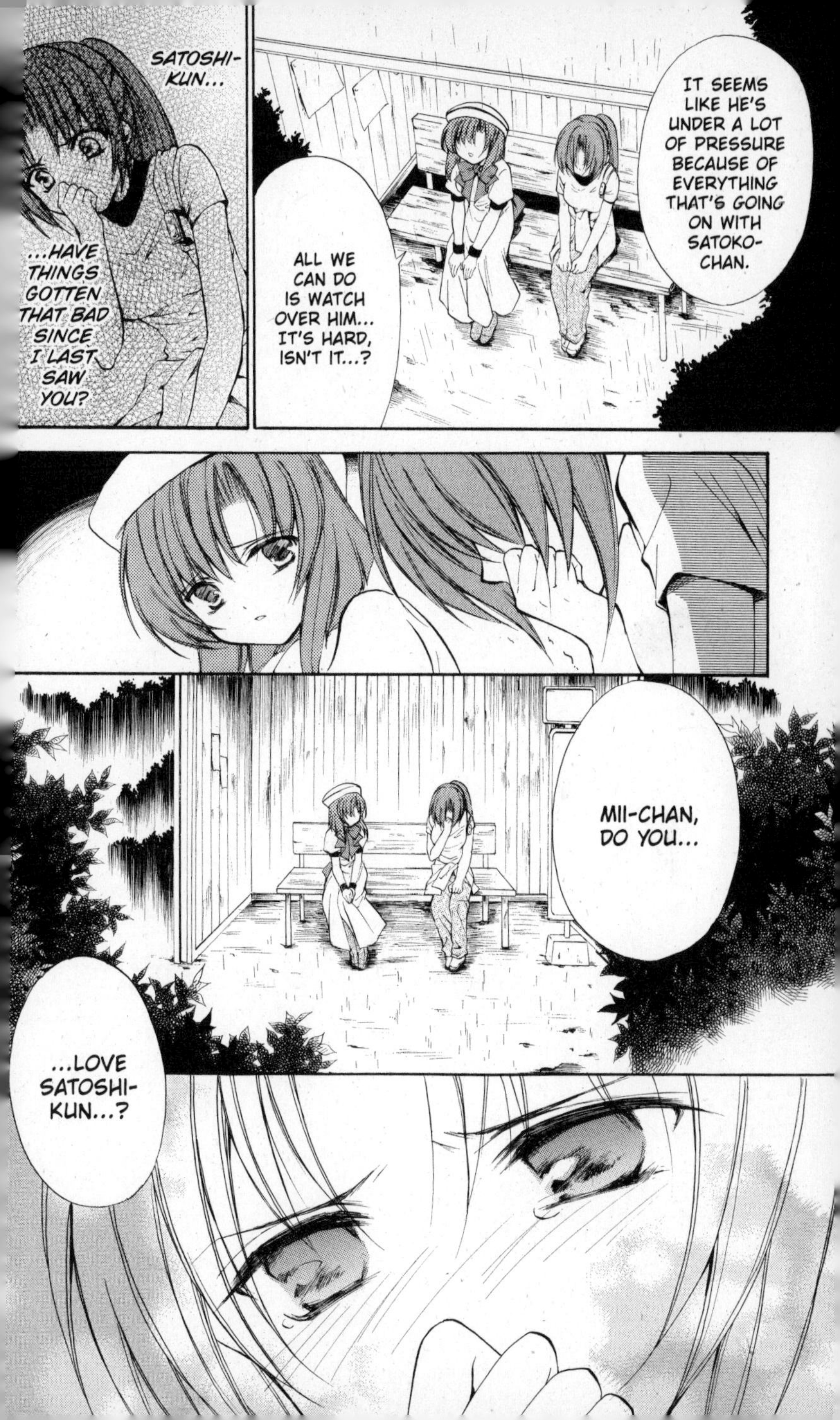
IT SEEMS LIKE HE'S UNDER A LOT OF PRESSURE BECAUSE OF EVERYTHING THAT'S GOING ON WITH SATOKO-CHAN.
ALL WE CAN DO IS WATCH OVER HIM... IT'S HARD, ISN'T IT...?
SATOSHI-KUN...
...HAVE THINGS GOTTEN THAT BAD SINCE I LAST SAW YOU?
MII-CHAN, DO YOU...
...LOVE SATOSHI-KUN...?

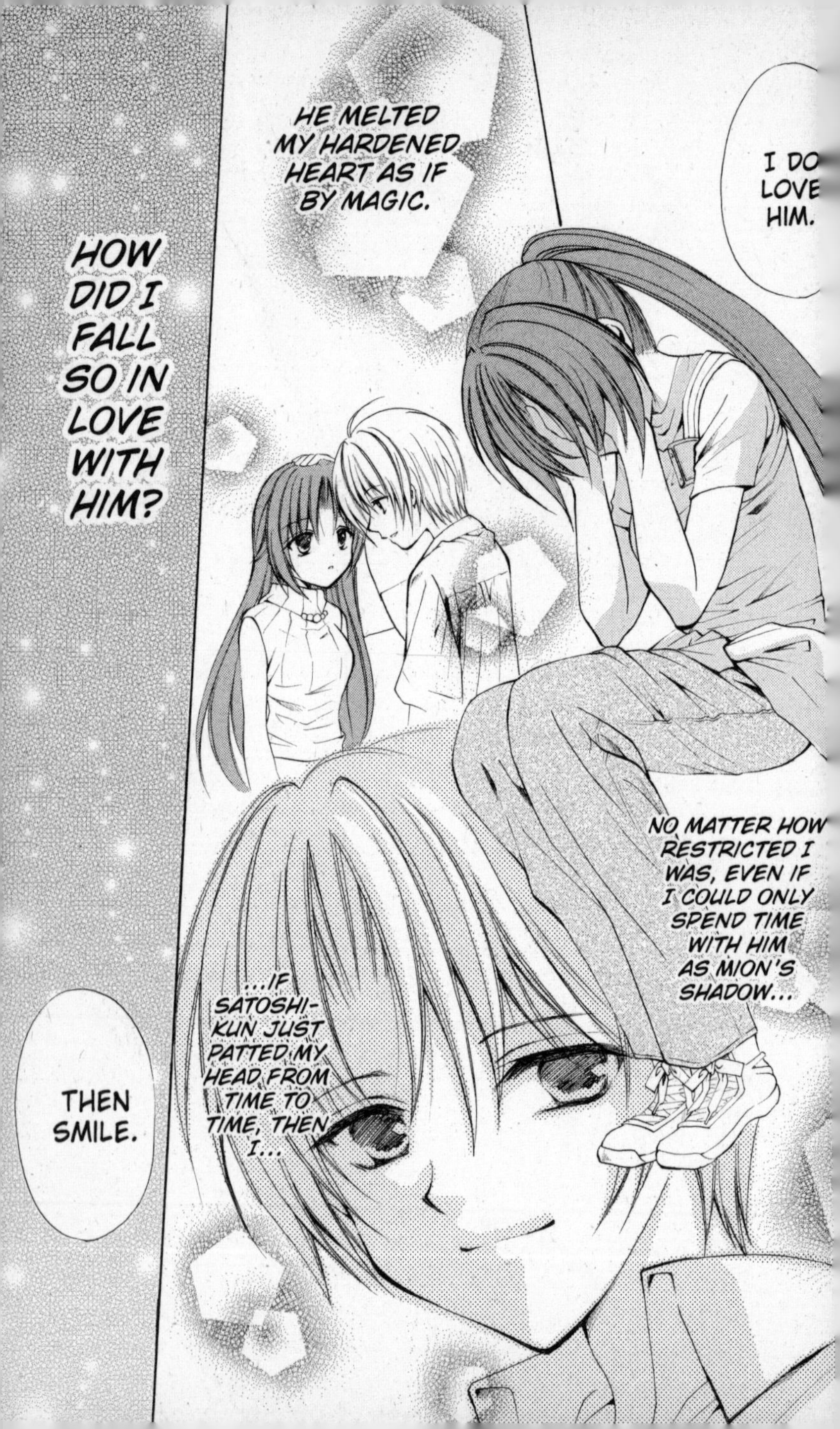
I DO LOVE HIM.
HE MELTED MY HARDENED HEART AS IF BY MAGIC.
NO MATTER HOW RESTRICTED I WAS, EVEN IF I COULD ONLY SPEND TIME WITH HIM AS MION'S SHADOW...
...IF SATOSHI-KUN JUST PATTED MY HEAD FROM TIME TO TIME, THEN I...
HOW DID I FALL SO IN LOVE WITH HIM?
THEN SMILE.

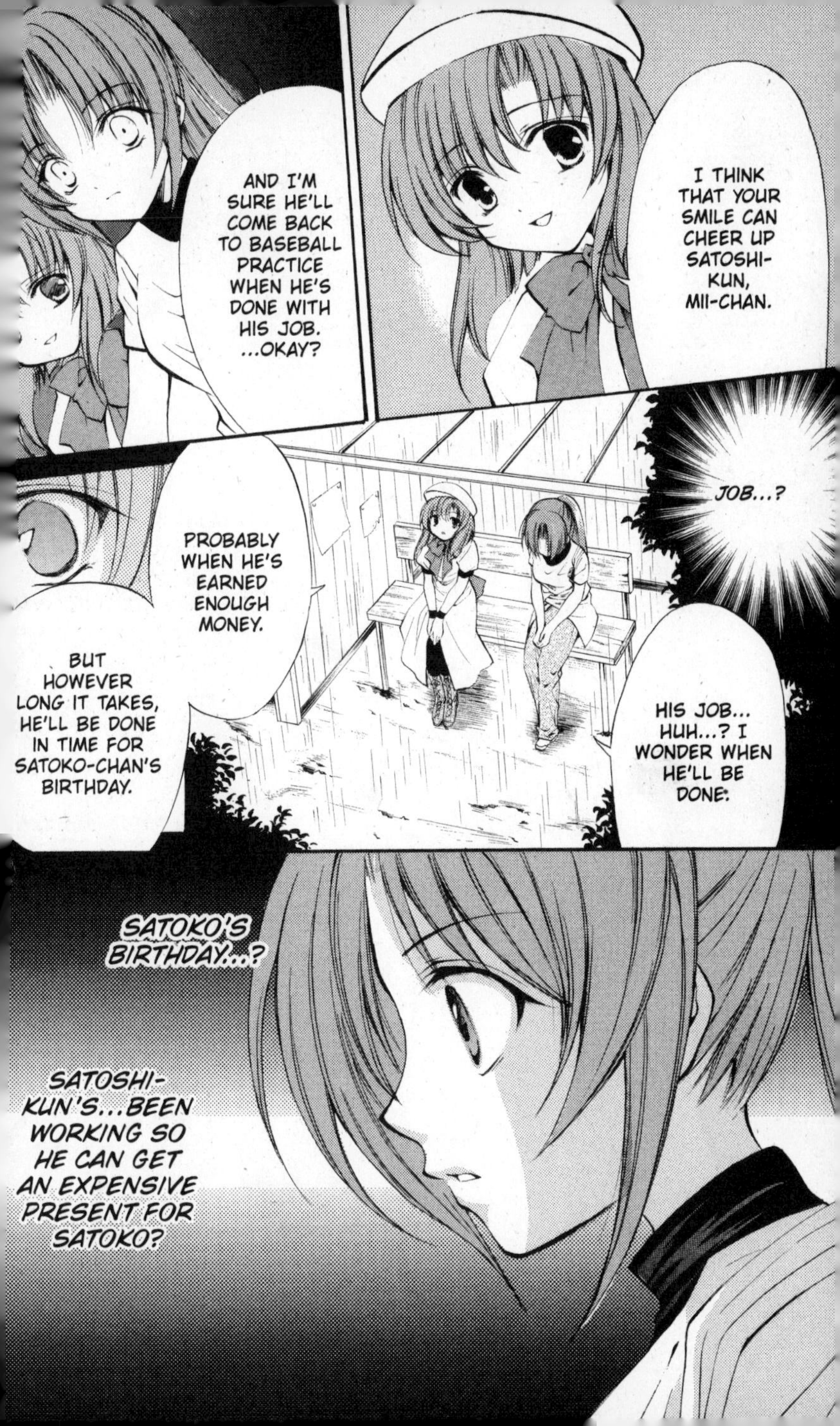
I THINK THAT YOUR SMILE CAN CHEER UP SATOSHI-KUN, MII-CHAN.
AND I'M SURE HE'LL COME BACK TO BASEBALL PRACTICE WHEN HE'S DONE WITH HIS JOB. ...OKAY?
JOB...?
HIS JOB... HUH...? I WONDER WHEN HE'LL BE DONE.
PROBABLY WHEN HE'S EARNED ENOUGH MONEY.
BUT HOWEVER LONG IT TAKES, HE'LL BE DONE IN TIME FOR SATOKO-CHAN'S BIRTHDAY.
SATOKO'S BIRTHDAY...?
SATOSHI-KUN'S...BEEN WORKING SO HE CAN GET AN EXPENSIVE PRESENT FOR SATOKO?

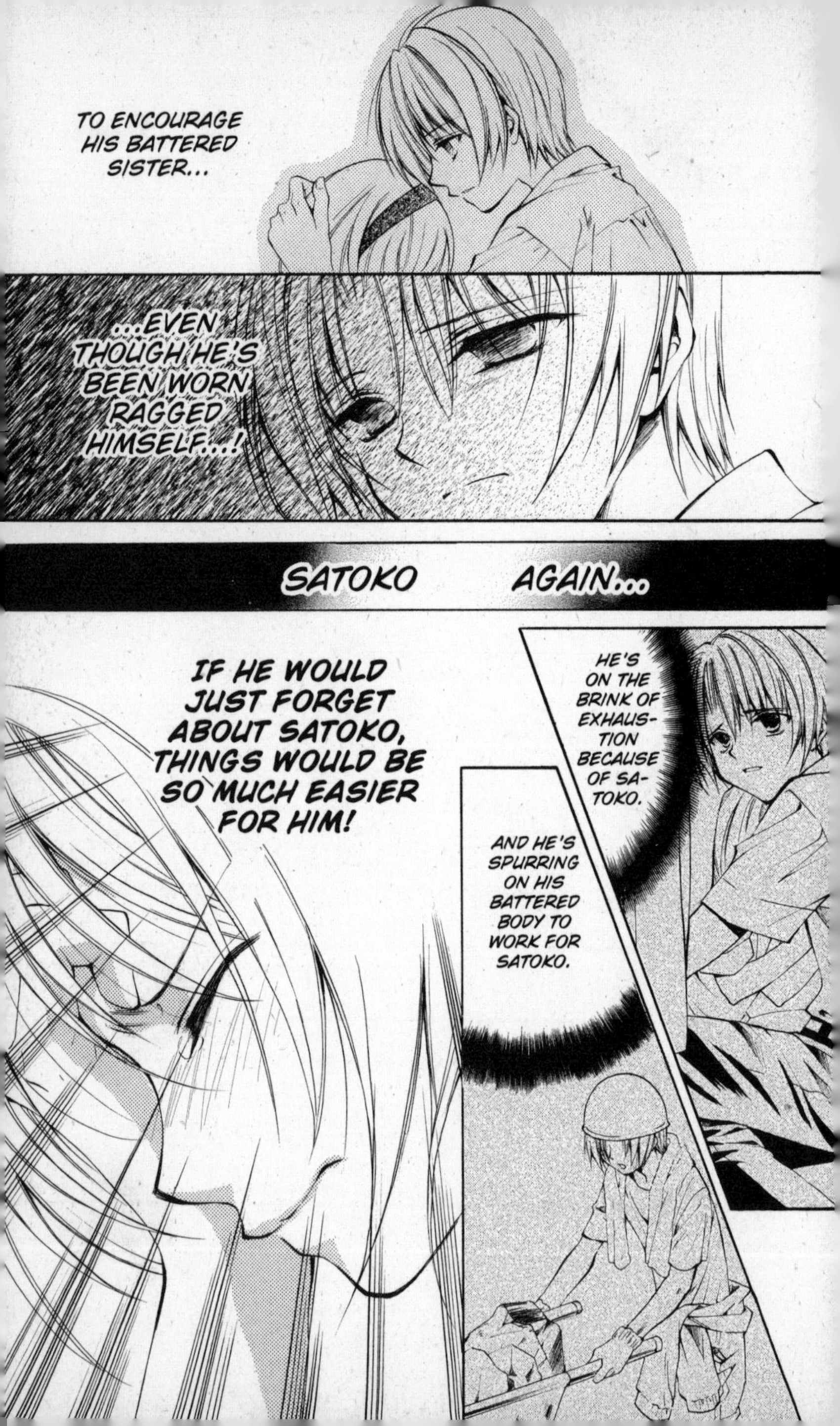
TO ENCOURAGE HIS BATTERED SISTER...
...EVEN THOUGH HE'S BEEN WORN RAGGED HIMSELF...!
SATOKO AGAIN...
HE'S ON THE BRINK OF EXHAUS-TION BECAUSE OF SA-TOKO.
AND HE'S SPURRING ON HIS BATTERED BODY TO WORK FOR SATOKO.
IF HE WOULD JUST FORGET ABOUT SATOKO, THINGS WOULD BE SO MUCH EASIER FOR HIM!

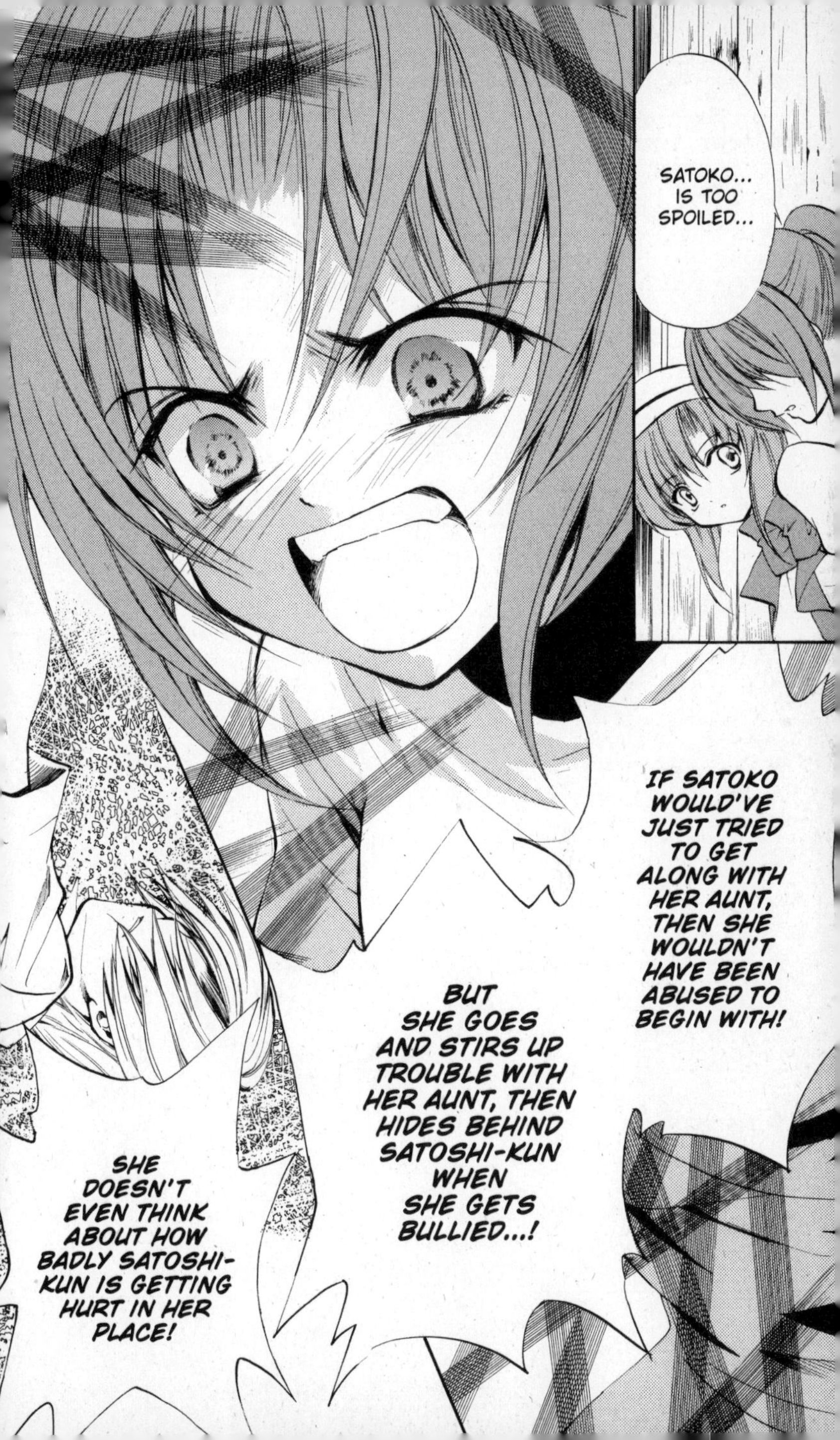
SATOKO... IS TOO SPOILED...
IF SATOKO WOULD'VE JUST TRIED TO GET ALONG WITH HER AUNT, THEN SHE WOULDN'T HAVE BEEN ABUSED TO BEGIN WITH!
BUT SHE GOES AND STIRS UP TROUBLE WITH HER AUNT, THEN HIDES BEHIND SATOSHI-KUN WHEN SHE GETS BULLIED...!
SHE DOESN'T EVEN THINK ABOUT HOW BADLY SATOSHI-KUN IS GETTING HURT IN HER PLACE!

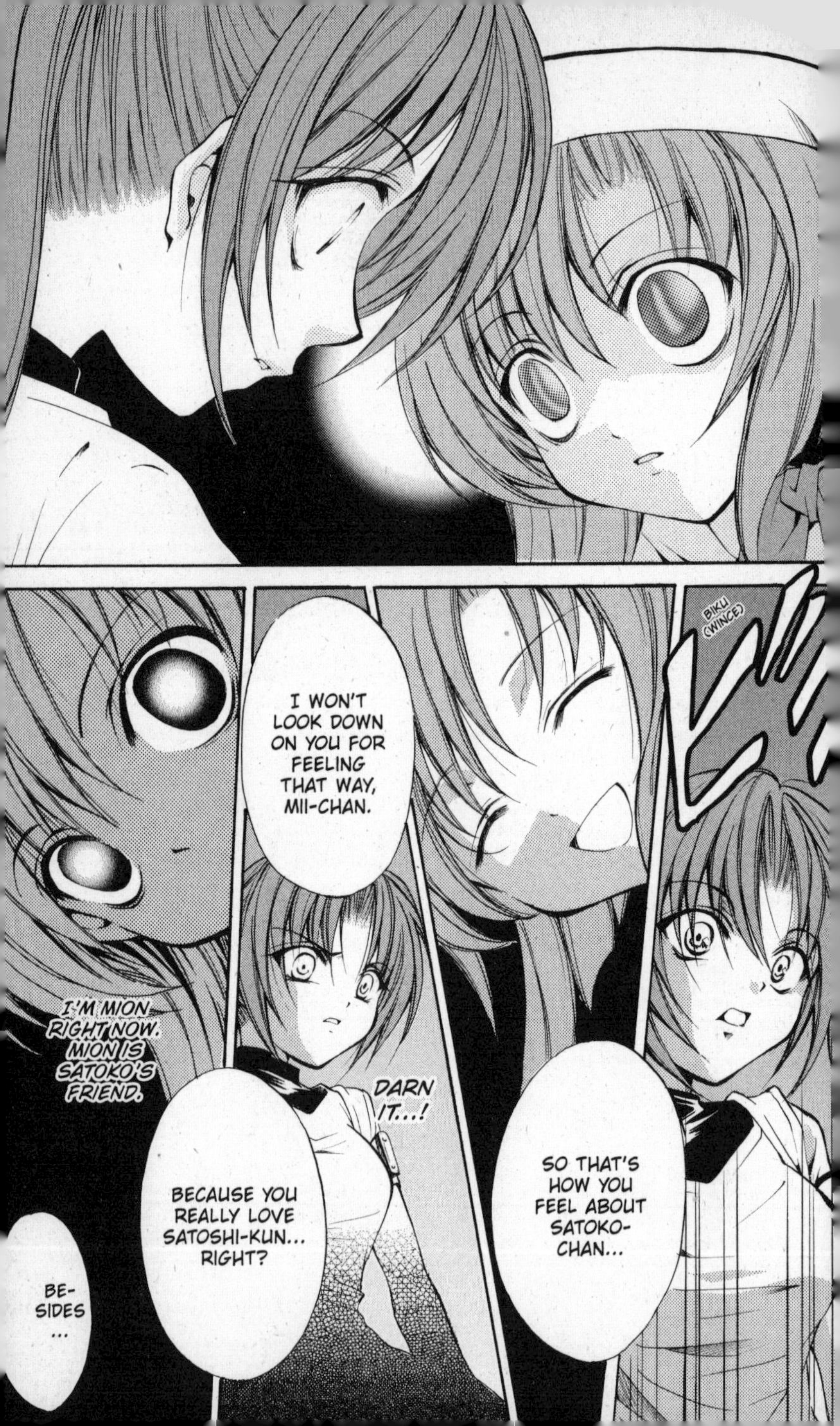
BIKU (WINCE)
I WON'T LOOK DOWN ON YOU FOR FEELING THAT WAY, MII-CHAN.
SO THAT'S HOW YOU FEEL ABOUT SATOKO-CHAN...
DARN IT...!
BECAUSE YOU REALLY LOVE SATOSHI-KUN... RIGHT?
I'M MION RIGHT NOW. MION IS SATOKO'S FRIEND.
BE-SIDES ...

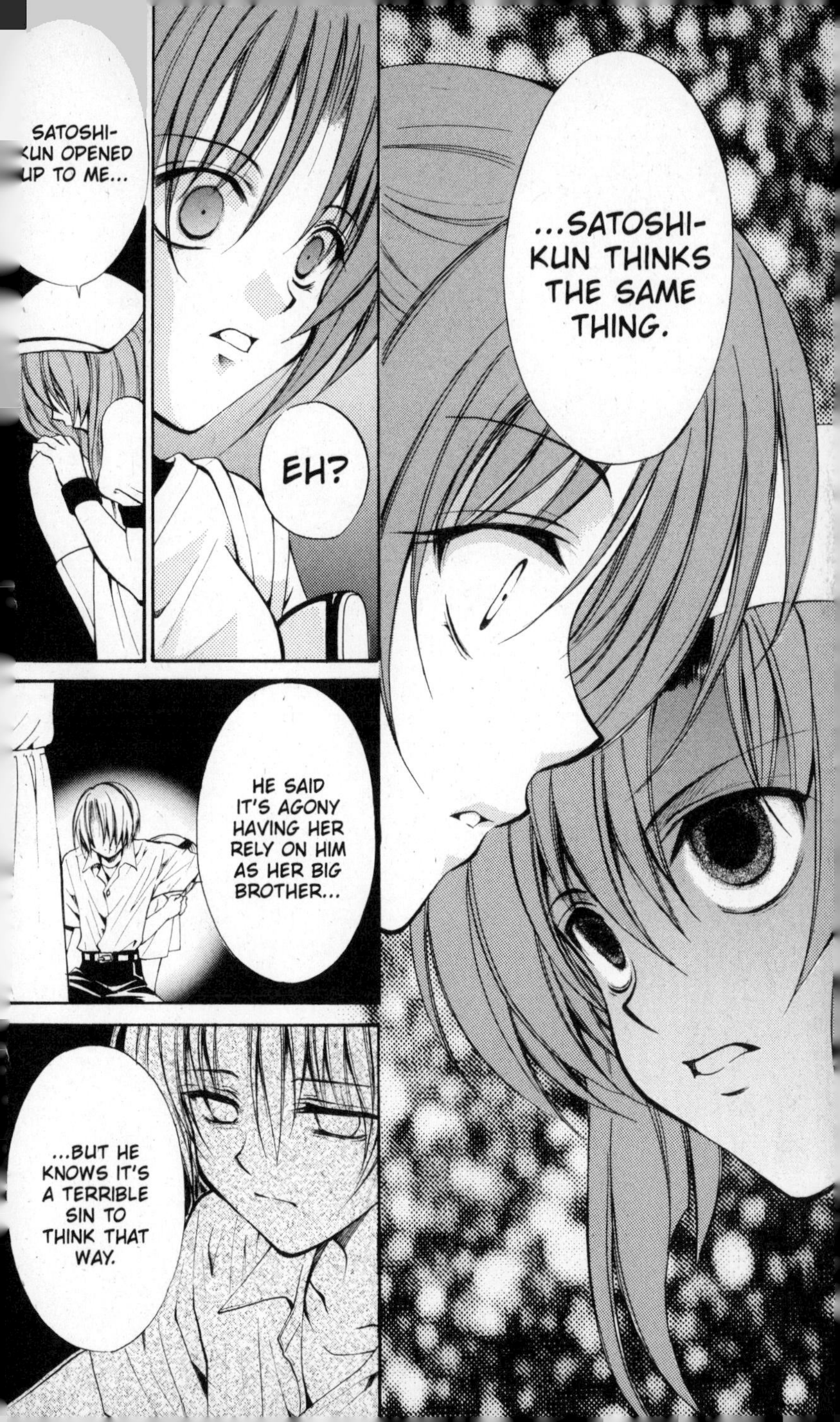
...SATOSHI-KUN THINKS THE SAME THING.
EH?
SATOSHI-KUN OPENED UP TO ME...
HE SAID IT'S AGONY HAVING HER RELY ON HIM AS HER BIG BROTHER...
...BUT HE KNOWS IT'S A TERRIBLE SIN TO THINK THAT WAY.

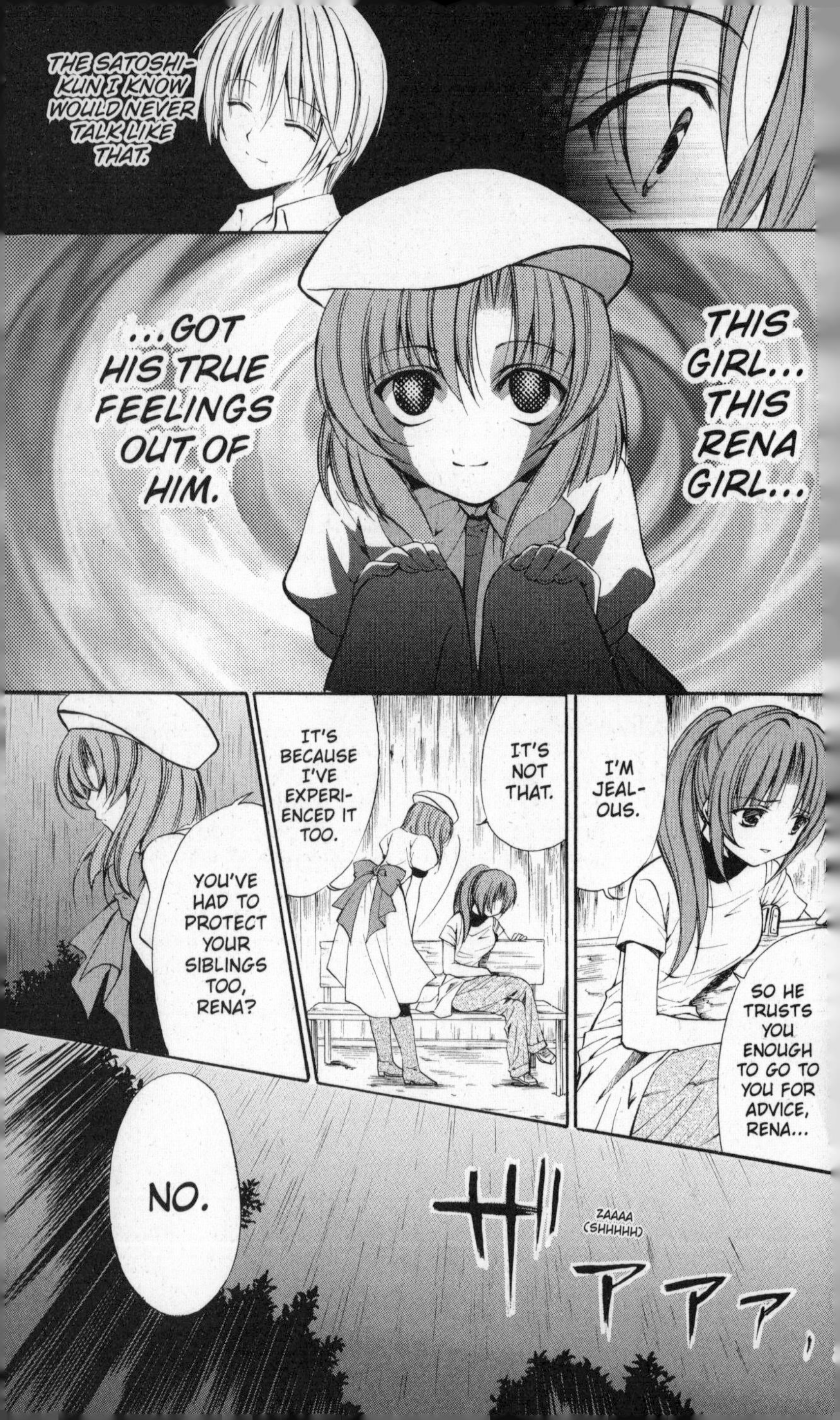
THE SATOSHI-KUN I KNOW WOULD NEVER TALK LIKE THAT.
THIS GIRL... THIS RENA GIRL...
...GOT HIS TRUE FEELINGS OUT OF HIM.
SO HE TRUSTS YOU ENOUGH TO GO TO YOU FOR ADVICE, RENA...
I'M JEAL-OUS.
IT'S NOT THAT.
IT'S BECAUSE I'VE EXPERI-ENCED IT TOO.
YOU'VE HAD TO PROTECT YOUR SIBLINGS TOO, RENA?
NO.
ZAAAA (SHHHHH)

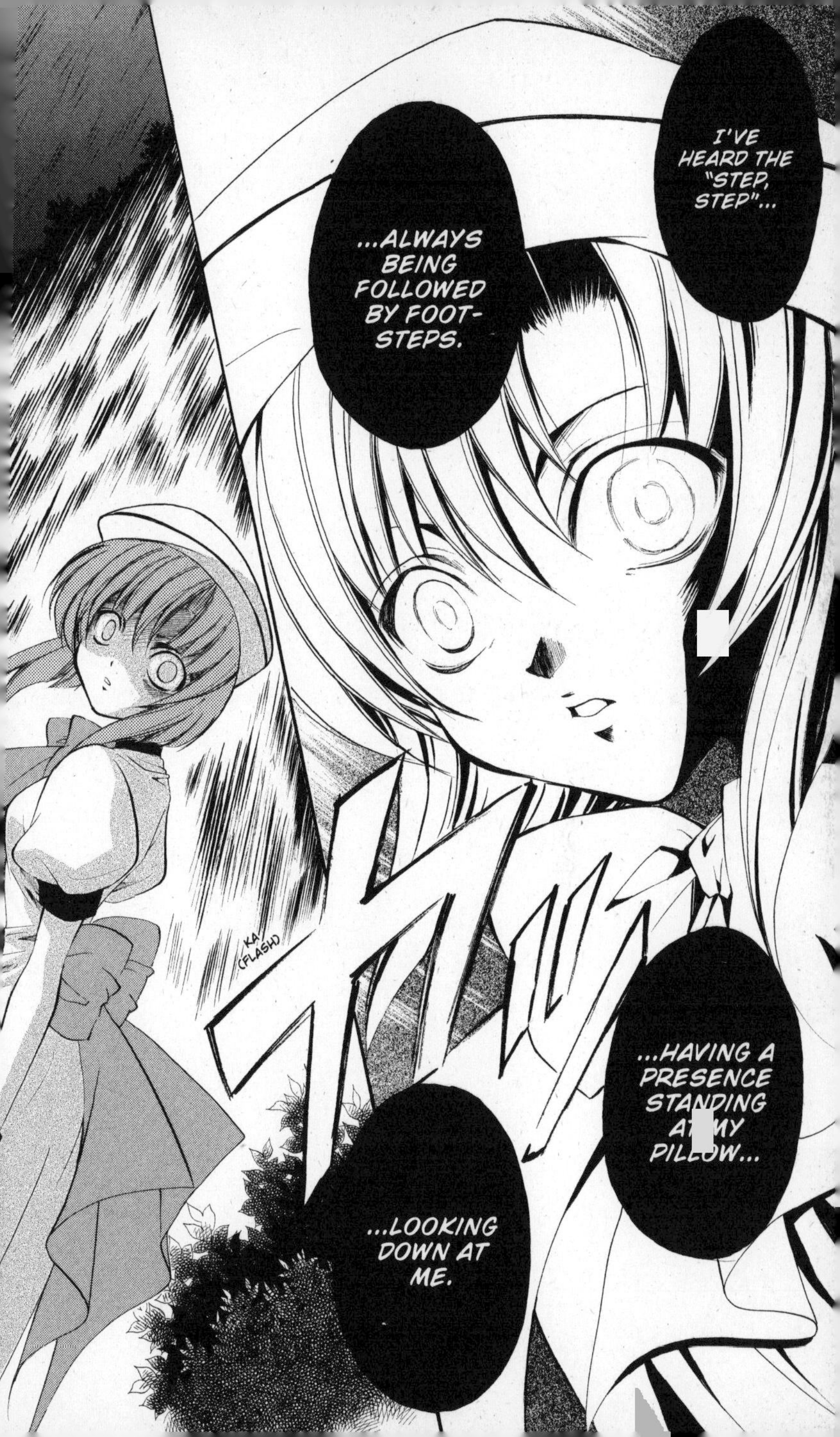
I'VE HEARD THE "STEP, STEP"...
...ALWAYS BEING FOLLOWED BY FOOT-STEPS.
KA (FLASH)
...HAVING A PRESENCE STANDING AT MY PILLOW...
...LOOKING DOWN AT ME.

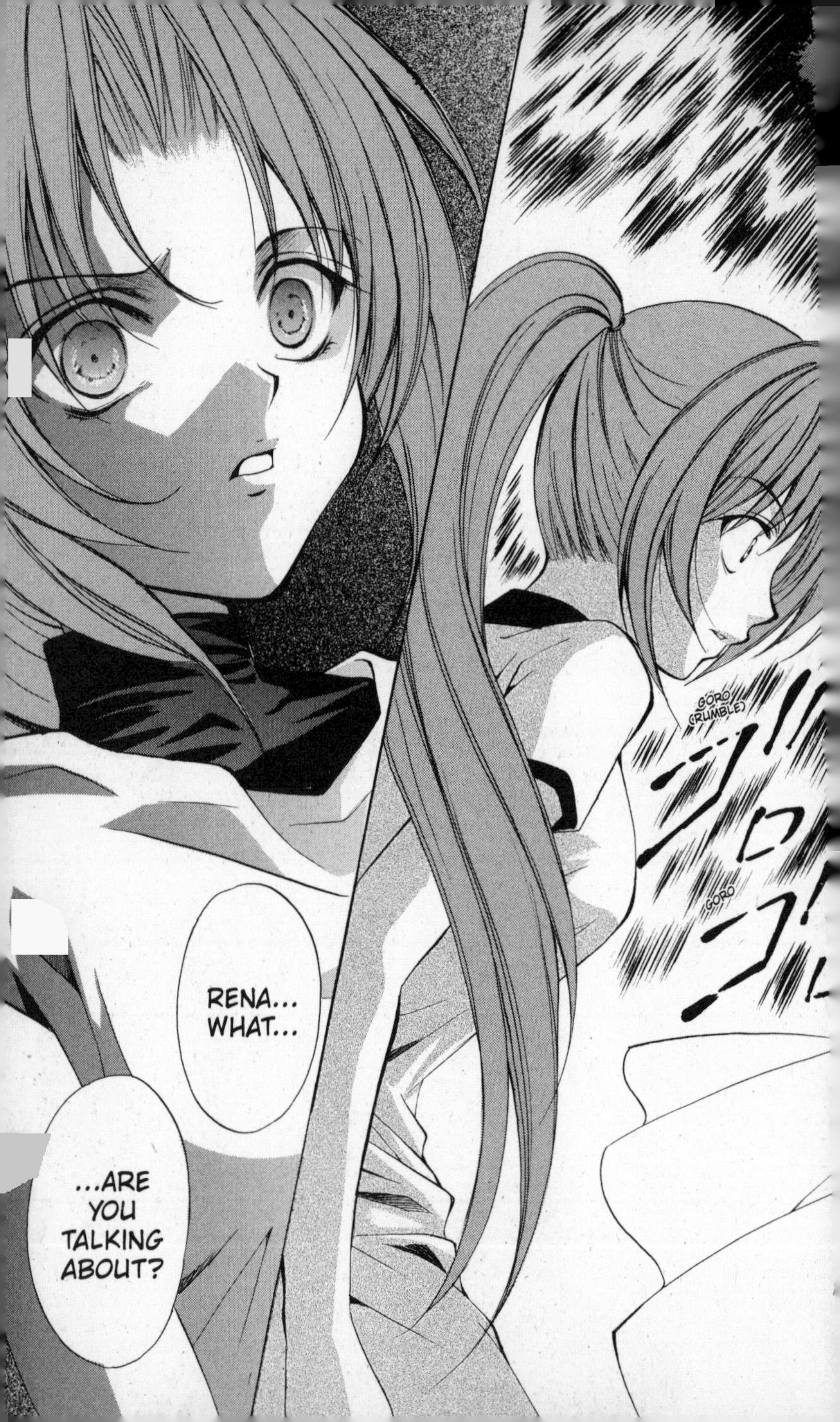
GORO (RUMBLE)
GORO
RENA... WHAT...
...ARE YOU TALKING ABOUT?

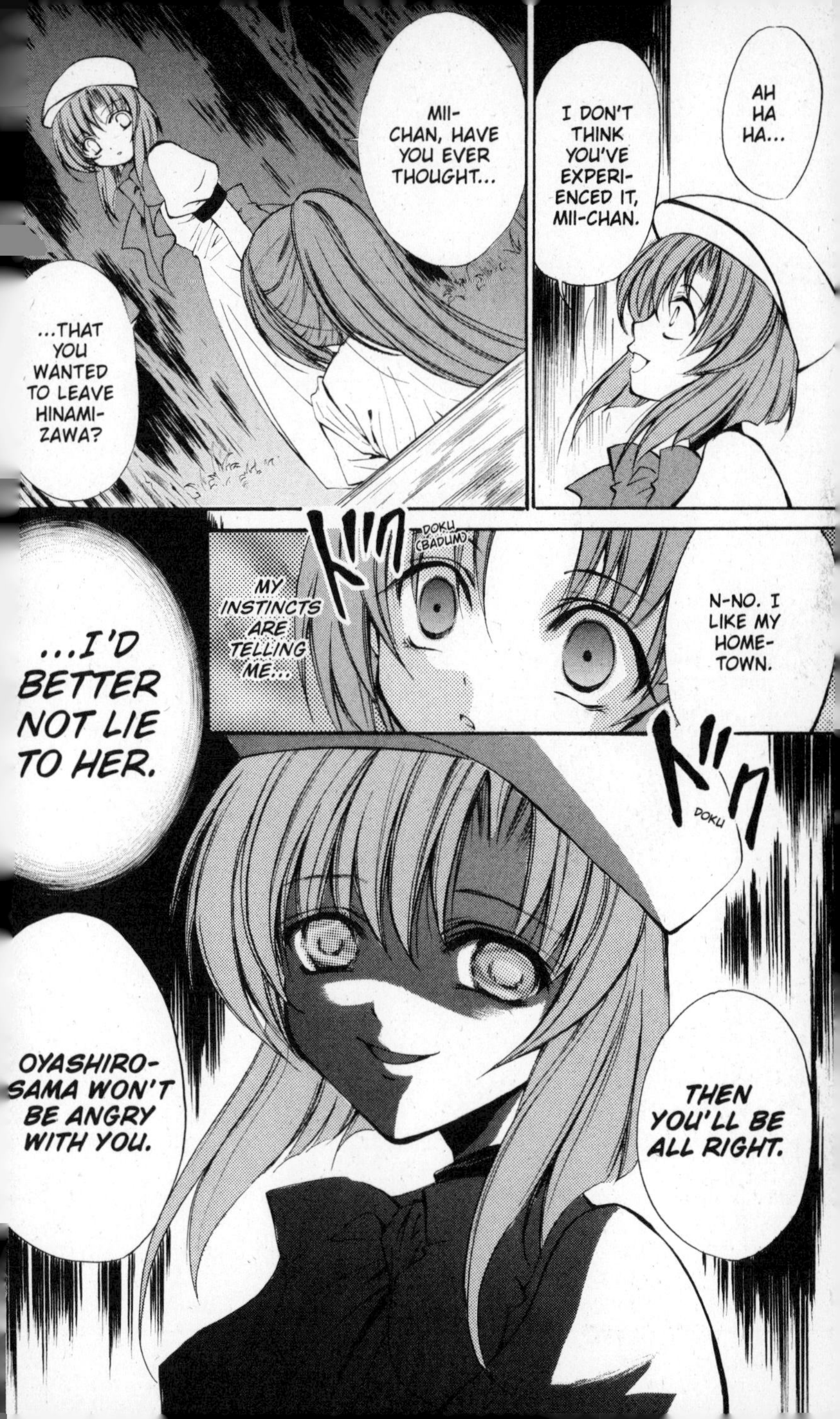
AH HA HA...
I DON'T THINK YOU'VE EXPERIENCED IT, MII-CHAN.
MII-CHAN, HAVE YOU EVER THOUGHT...
...THAT YOU WANTED TO LEAVE HINAMIZAWA?
N-NO. I LIKE MY HOMETOWN.
DOKU (BADUM)
MY INSTINCTS ARE TELLING ME...
...I'D BETTER NOT LIE TO HER.
DOKU
THEN YOU'LL BE ALL RIGHT.
OYASHIRO-SAMA WON'T BE ANGRY WITH YOU.

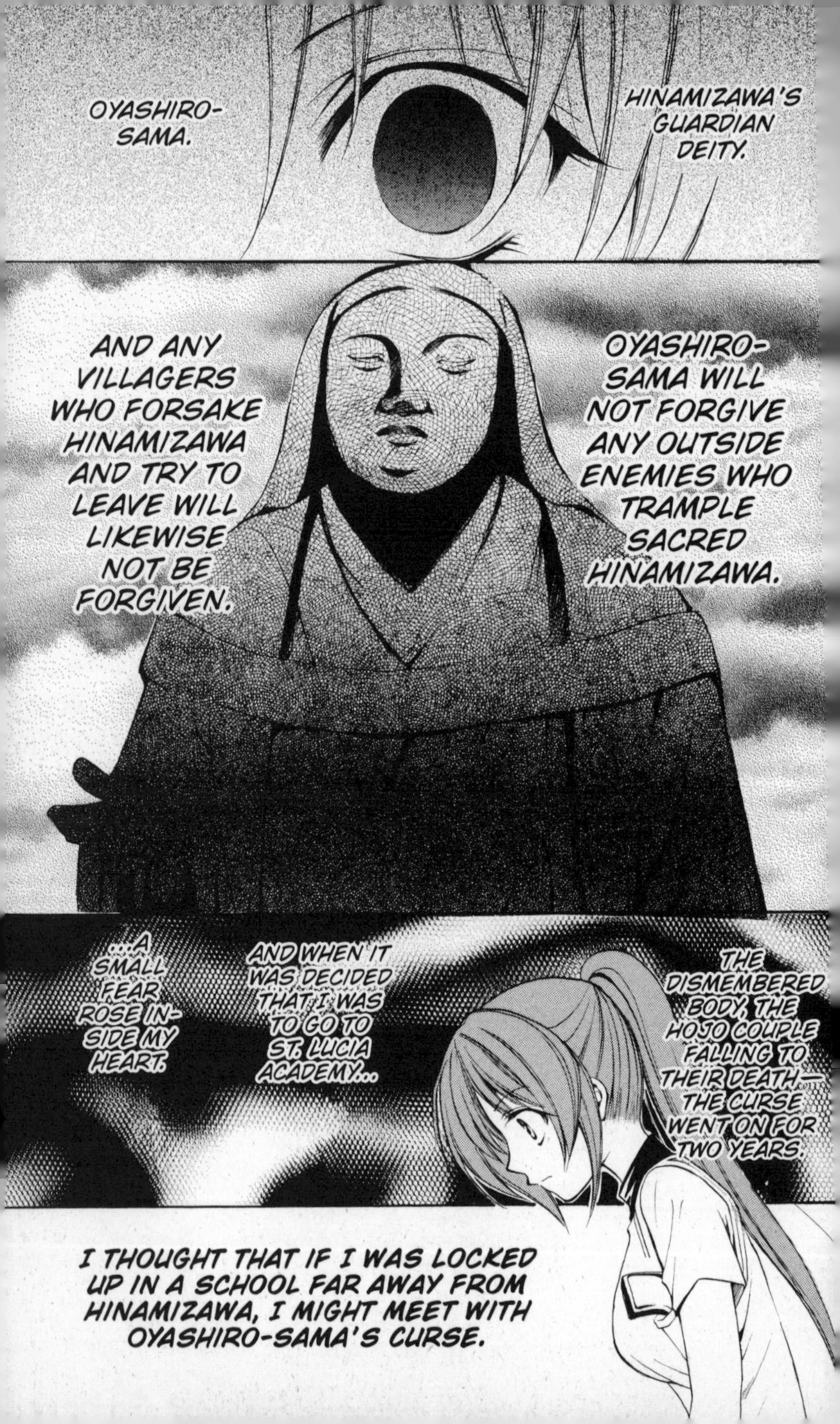
HINAMIZAWA'S GUARDIAN DEITY.
OYASHIRO-SAMA.
OYASHIRO-SAMA WILL NOT FORGIVE ANY OUTSIDE ENEMIES WHO TRAMPLE SACRED HINAMIZAWA.
AND ANY VILLAGERS WHO FORSAKE HINAMIZAWA AND TRY TO LEAVE WILL LIKEWISE NOT BE FORGIVEN.
THE DISMEMBERED BODY, THE HOJO COUPLE FALLING TO THEIR DEATH—THE CURSE WENT ON FOR TWO YEARS.
AND WHEN IT WAS DECIDED THAT I WAS TO GO TO ST. LUCIA ACADEMY...
...A SMALL FEAR ROSE INSIDE MY HEART.
I THOUGHT THAT IF I WAS LOCKED UP IN A SCHOOL FAR AWAY FROM HINAMIZAWA, I MIGHT MEET WITH OYASHIRO-SAMA'S CURSE.

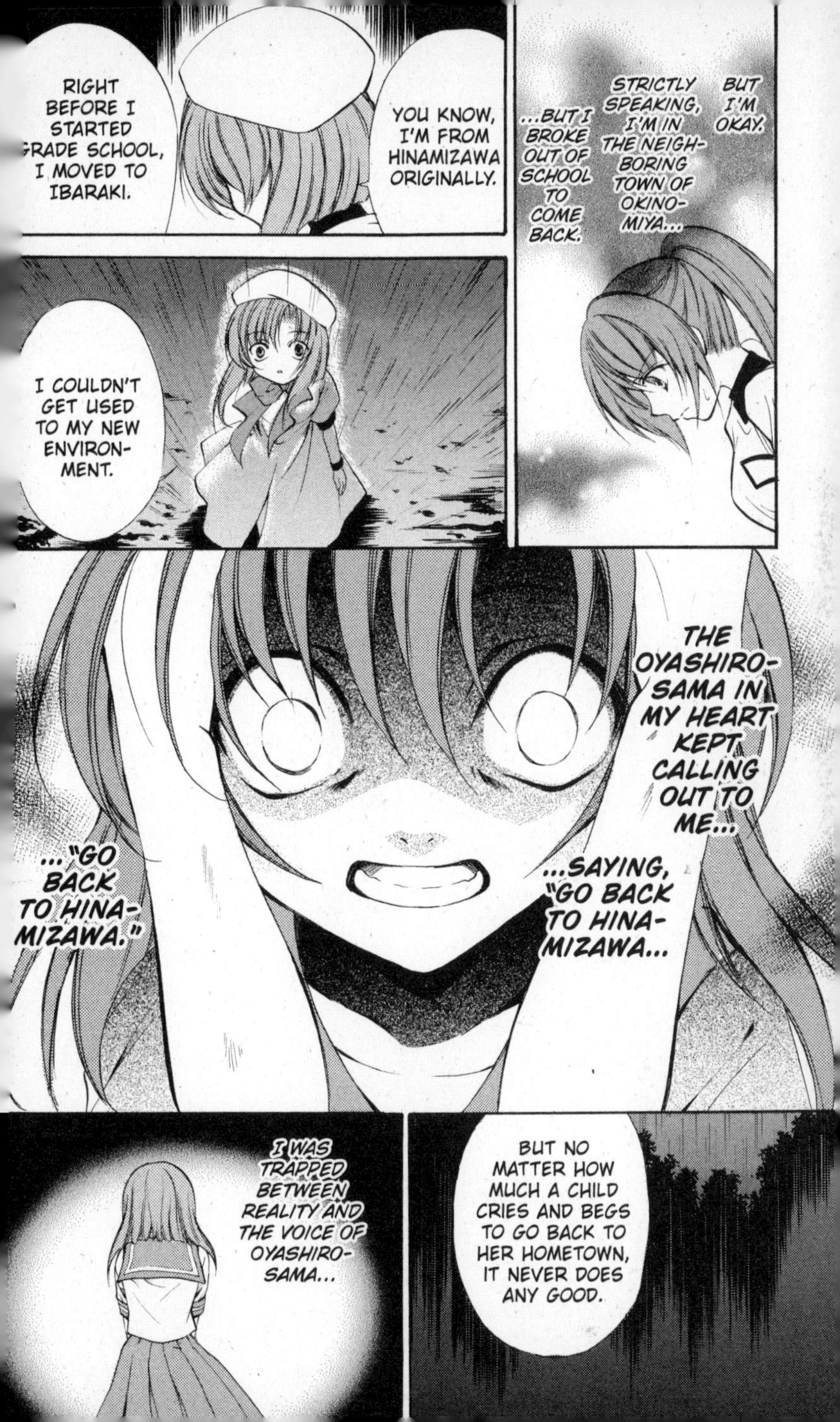
BUT I'M OKAY.
STRICTLY SPEAKING, I'M IN THE NEIGHBORING TOWN OF OKINOMIYA...
...BUT I BROKE OUT OF SCHOOL TO COME BACK.
YOU KNOW, I'M FROM HINAMIZAWA ORIGINALLY.
RIGHT BEFORE I STARTED GRADE SCHOOL, I MOVED TO IBARAKI.
I COULDN'T GET USED TO MY NEW ENVIRONMENT.
THE OYASHIRO-SAMA IN MY HEART KEPT CALLING OUT TO ME...
...SAYING, "GO BACK TO HINAMIZAWA...
..."GO BACK TO HINAMIZAWA."
BUT NO MATTER HOW MUCH A CHILD CRIES AND BEGS TO GO BACK TO HER HOMETOWN, IT NEVER DOES ANY GOOD.
I WAS TRAPPED BETWEEN REALITY AND THE VOICE OF OYASHIRO-SAMA...

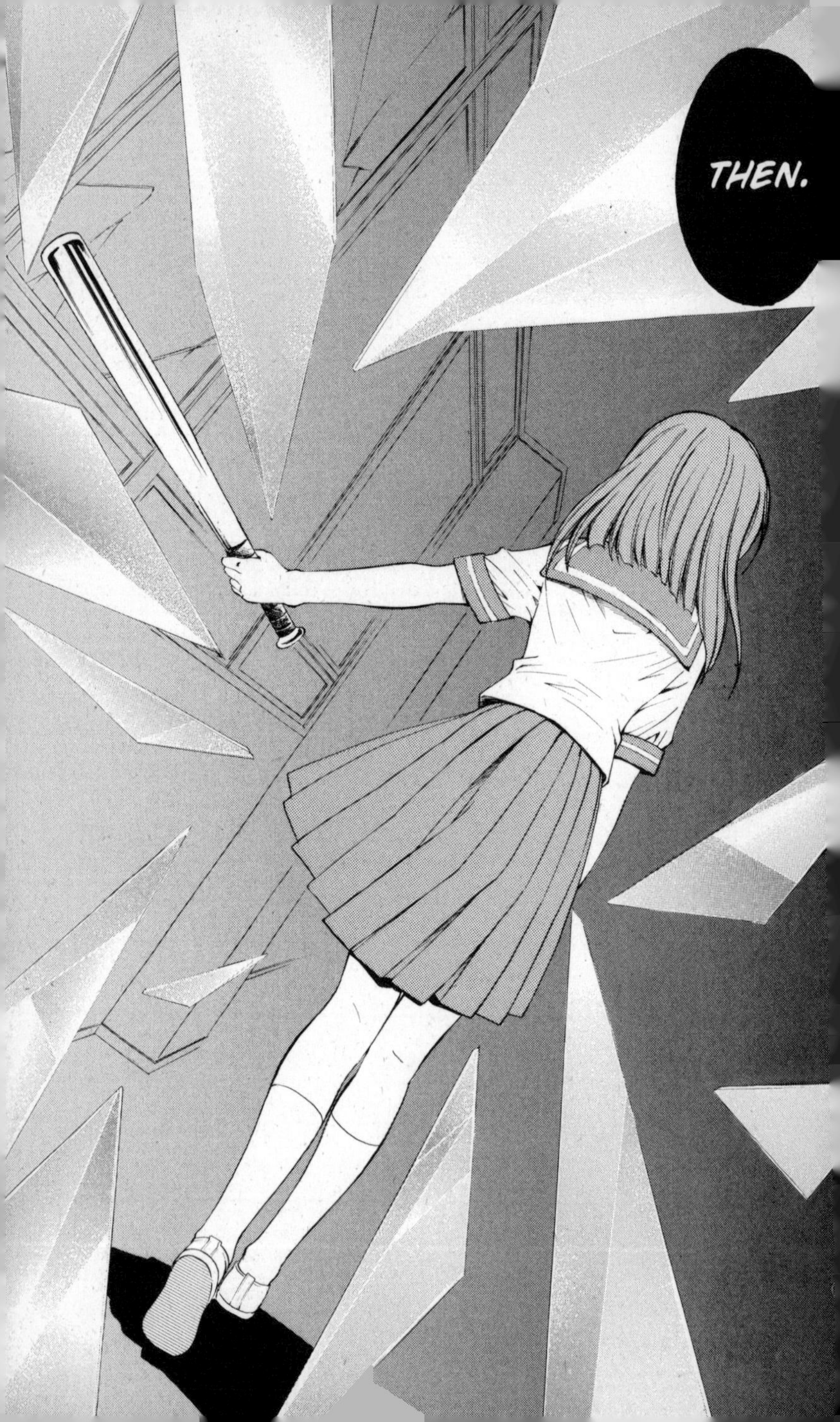
THEN.

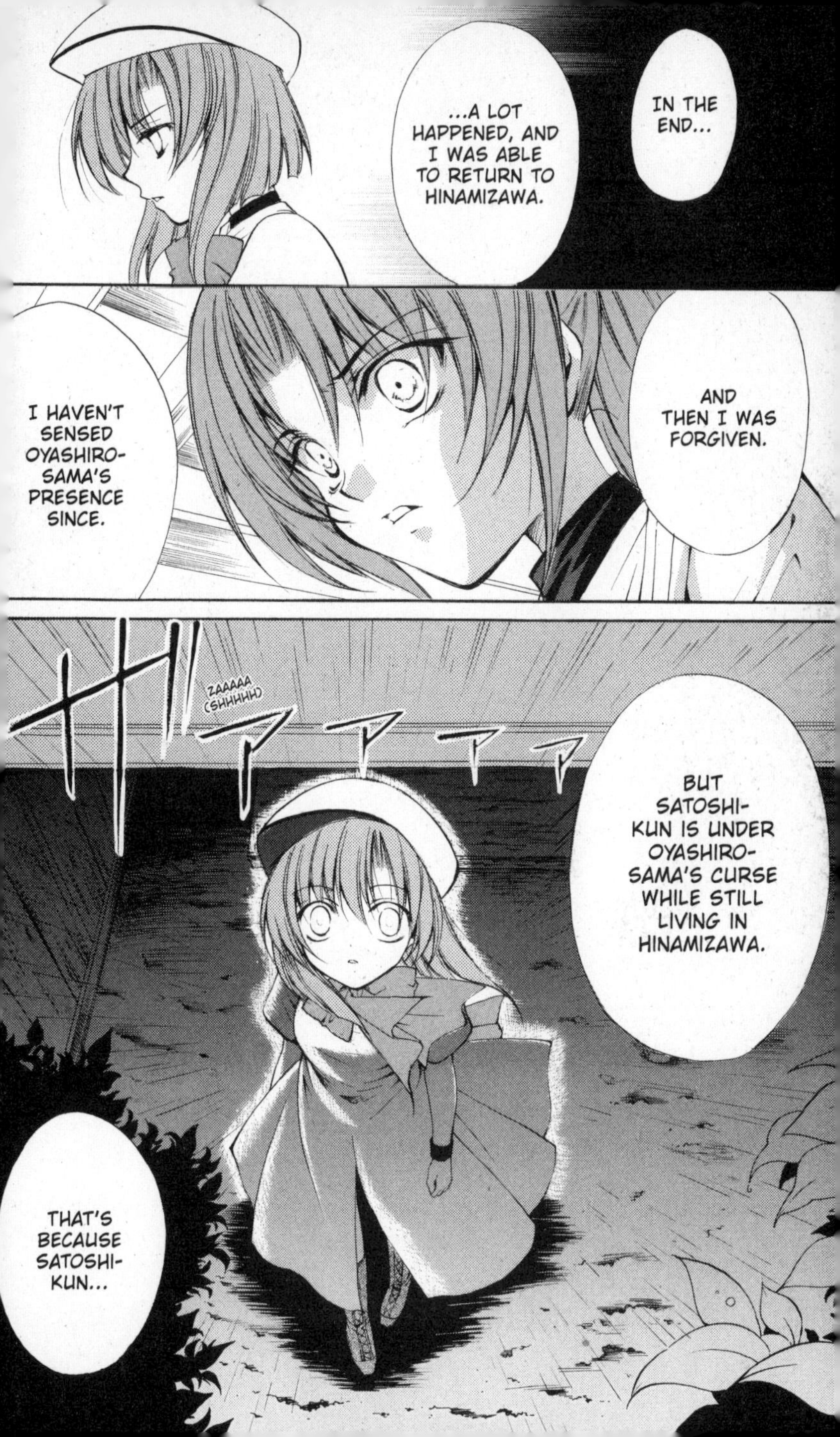
IN THE END...
...A LOT HAPPENED, AND I WAS ABLE TO RETURN TO HINAMIZAWA.
AND THEN I WAS FORGIVEN.
I HAVEN'T SENSED OYASHIRO-SAMA'S PRESENCE SINCE.
ZAAAAA (SHHHHH)
BUT SATOSHI-KUN IS UNDER OYASHIRO-SAMA'S CURSE WHILE STILL LIVING IN HINAMIZAWA.
THAT'S BECAUSE SATOSHI-KUN...

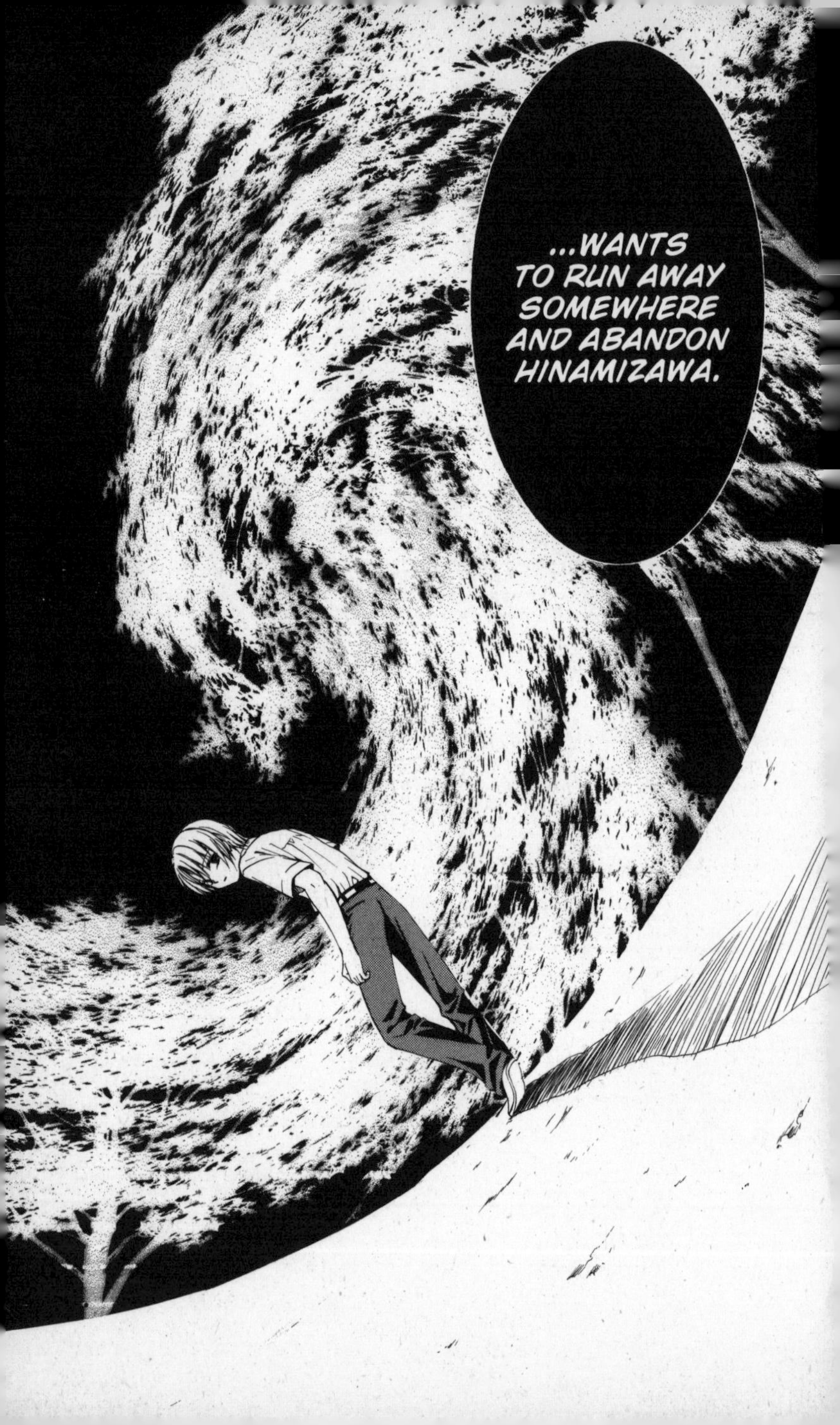
...WANTS TO RUN AWAY SOMEWHERE AND ABANDON HINAMIZAWA.

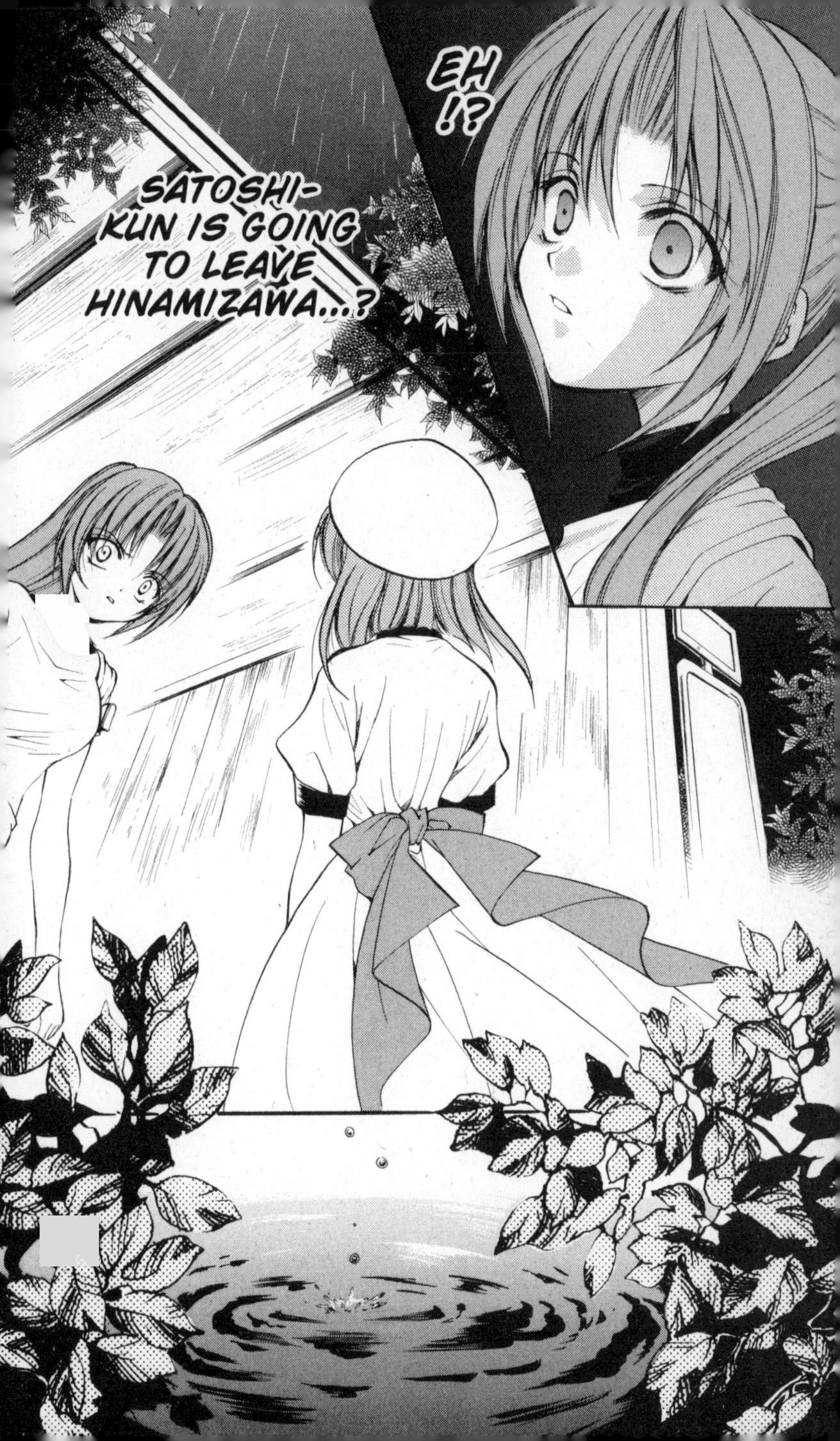
EH !?
SATOSHI-KUN IS GOING TO LEAVE HINAMIZAWA...?

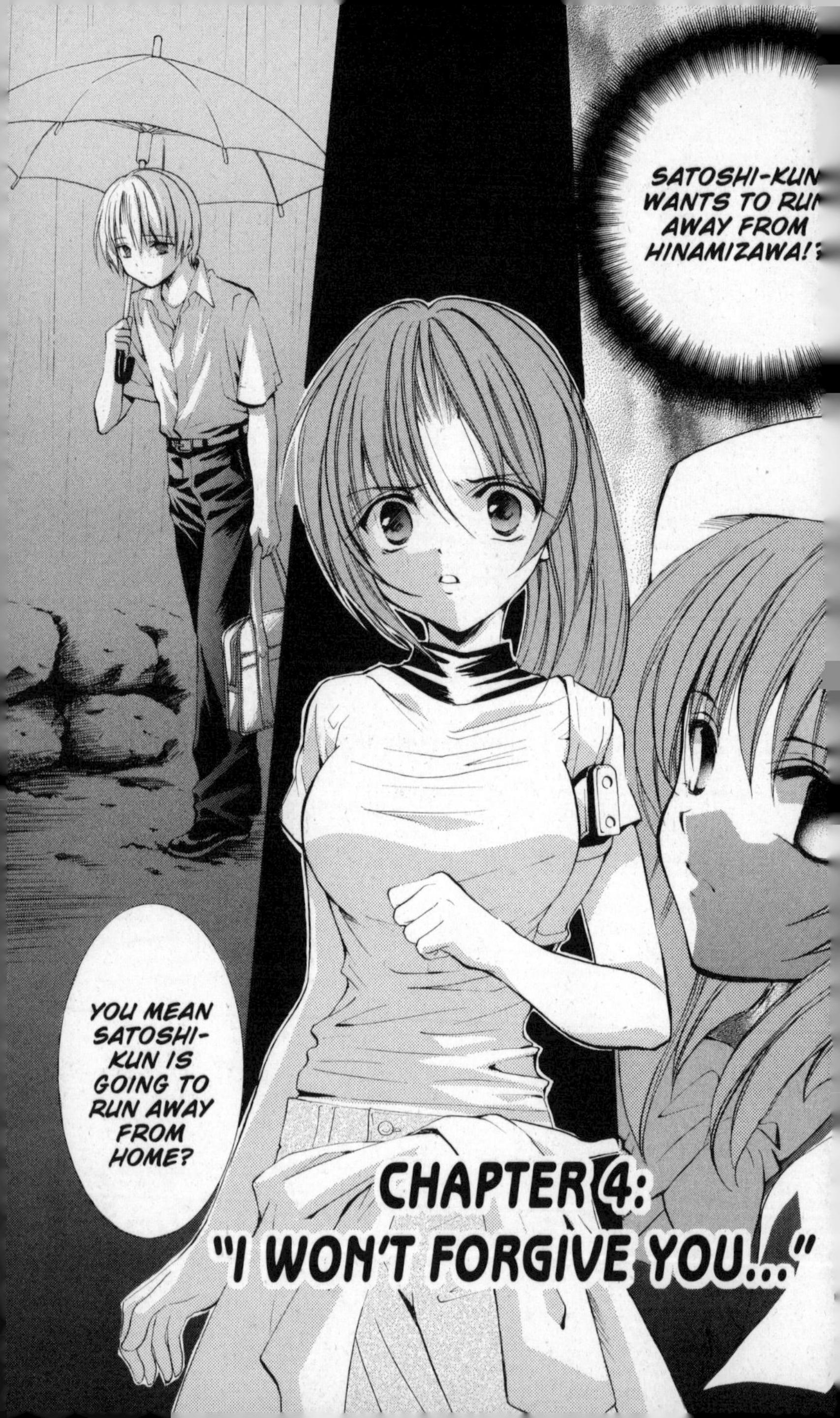
SATOSHI-KUN WANTS TO RUN AWAY FROM HINAMIZAWA!?
YOU MEAN SATOSHI-KUN IS GOING TO RUN AWAY FROM HOME?
CHAPTER 4: "I WON'T FORGIVE YOU..."

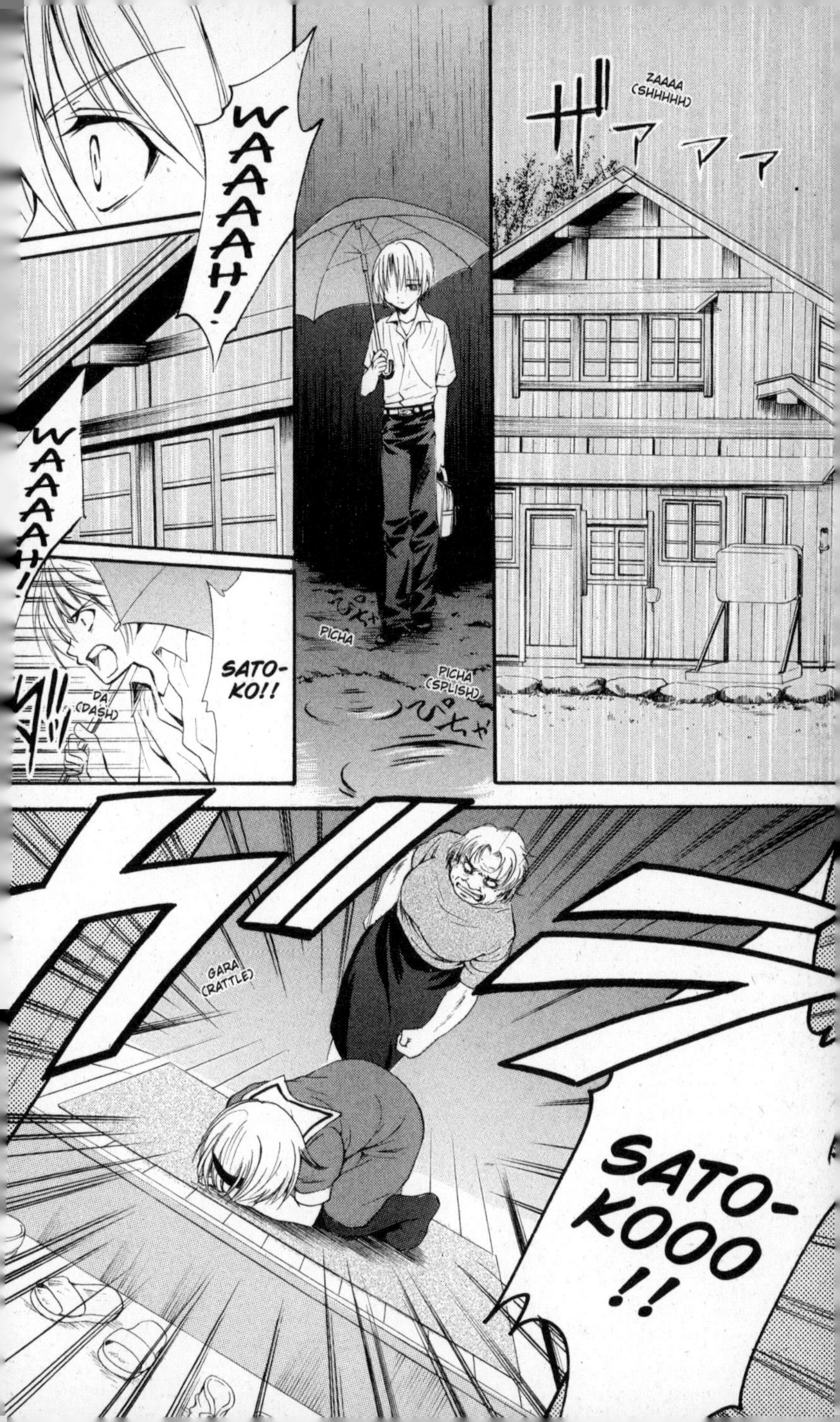

ザァァァ
ZAAAA (SHHHHH)
PICHA
PICHA (SPLISH)
WAAAAAH!
WAAAAAH!
SATO-KO!!
DA (DASH)
GARA (RATTLE)
SATO-KOOO!!

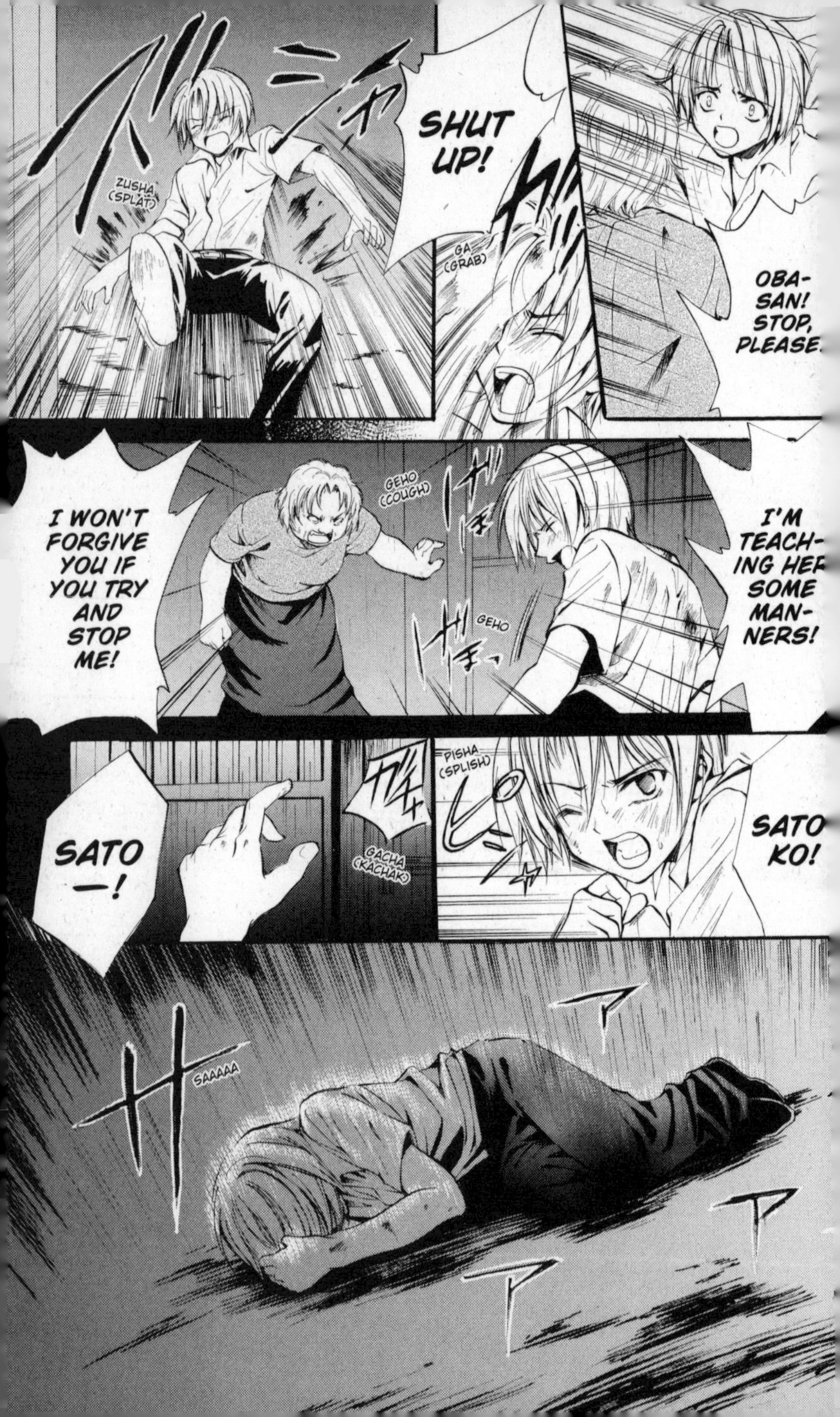
OBA-SAN! STOP, PLEASE.
SHUT UP!
GA (GRAB)
ZUSHA (SPLAT)
I'M TEACHING HER SOME MANNERS!
GEHO (COUGH)
GEHO
I WON'T FORGIVE YOU IF YOU TRY AND STOP ME!
SATOKO!
PISHA (SPLISH)
GACHA (KACHAK)
SATO—!
SAAAAA

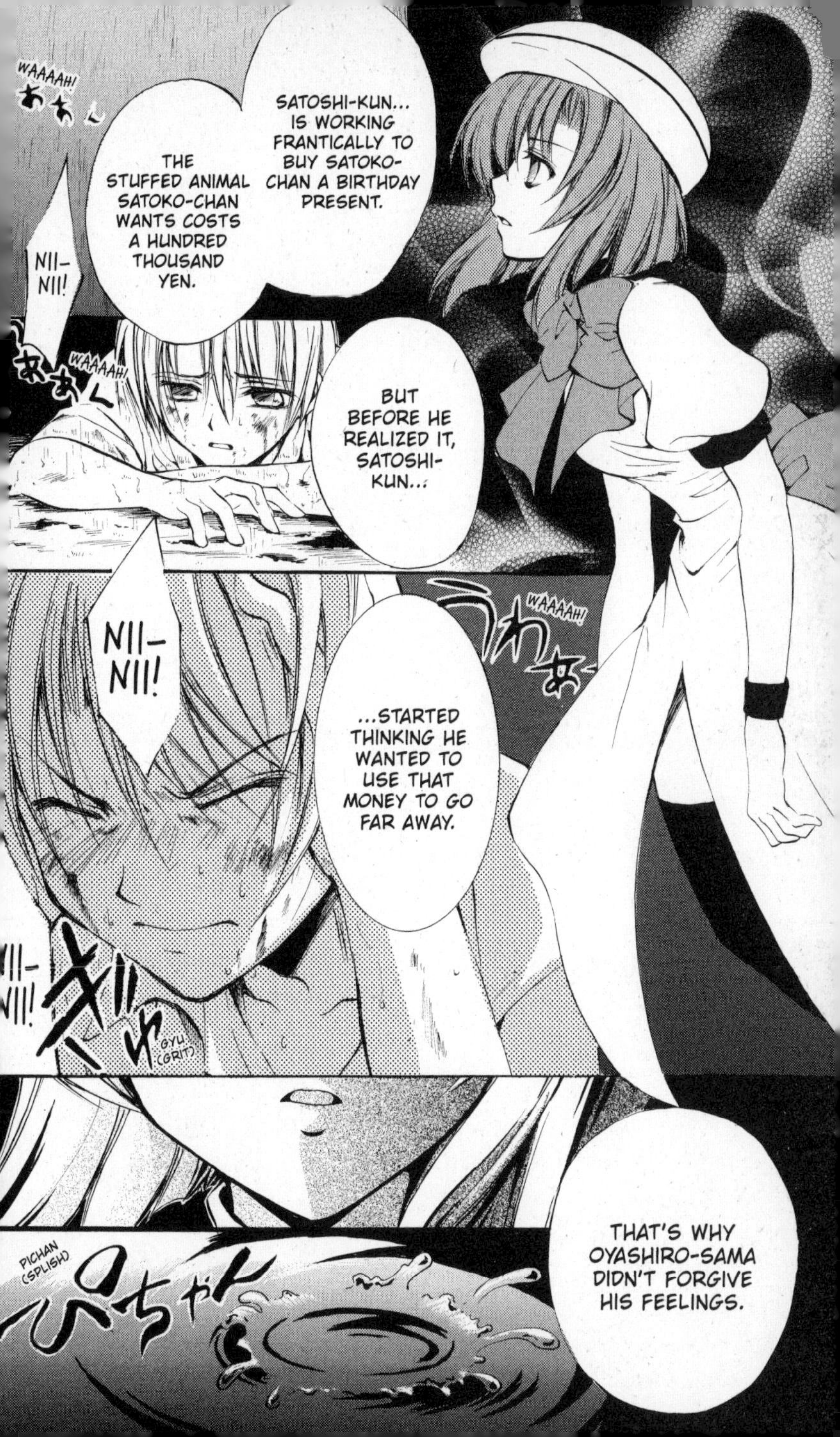
SATOSHI-KUN... IS WORKING FRANTICALLY TO BUY SATOKO-CHAN A BIRTHDAY PRESENT.
THE STUFFED ANIMAL SATOKO-CHAN WANTS COSTS A HUNDRED THOUSAND YEN.
WAAAAH!
NII-NII!
BUT BEFORE HE REALIZED IT, SATOSHI-KUN...
WAAAAH!
WAAAAH!
...STARTED THINKING HE WANTED TO USE THAT MONEY TO GO FAR AWAY.
NII-NII!
GYU (GRIT)
THAT'S WHY OYASHIRO-SAMA DIDN'T FORGIVE HIS FEELINGS.
PICHAN (SPLISH)

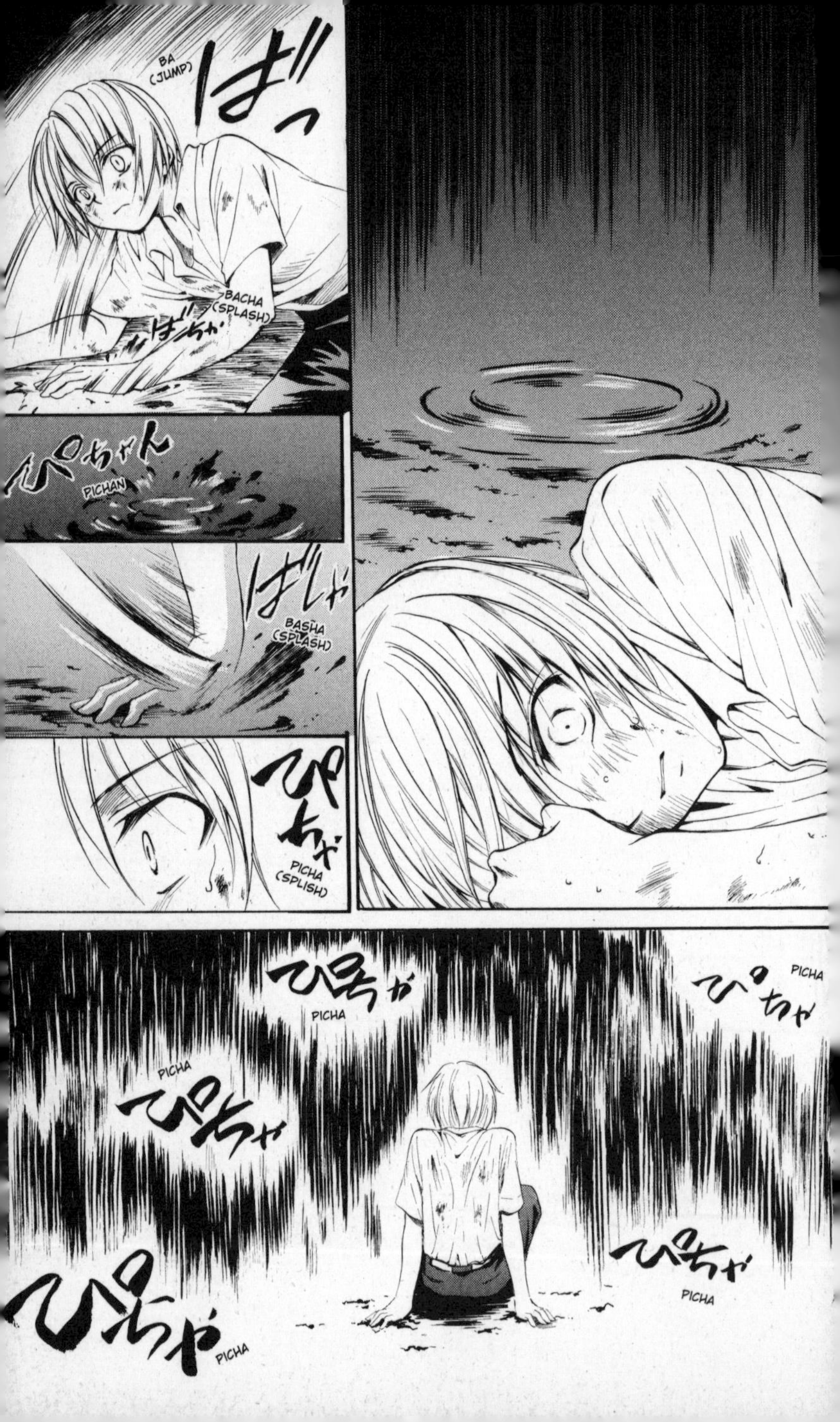
ばっ
BA (JUMP)
ばちゃ
BACHA (SPLASH)
ぴちゃん
PICHAN
ばしゃ
BASHA (SPLASH)
ぴちゃ
PICHA (SPLASH)
ぴちゃ
PICHA
ぴちゃ
PICHA
ぴちゃ
PICHA
ぴちゃ
PICHA
ぴちゃ
PICHA

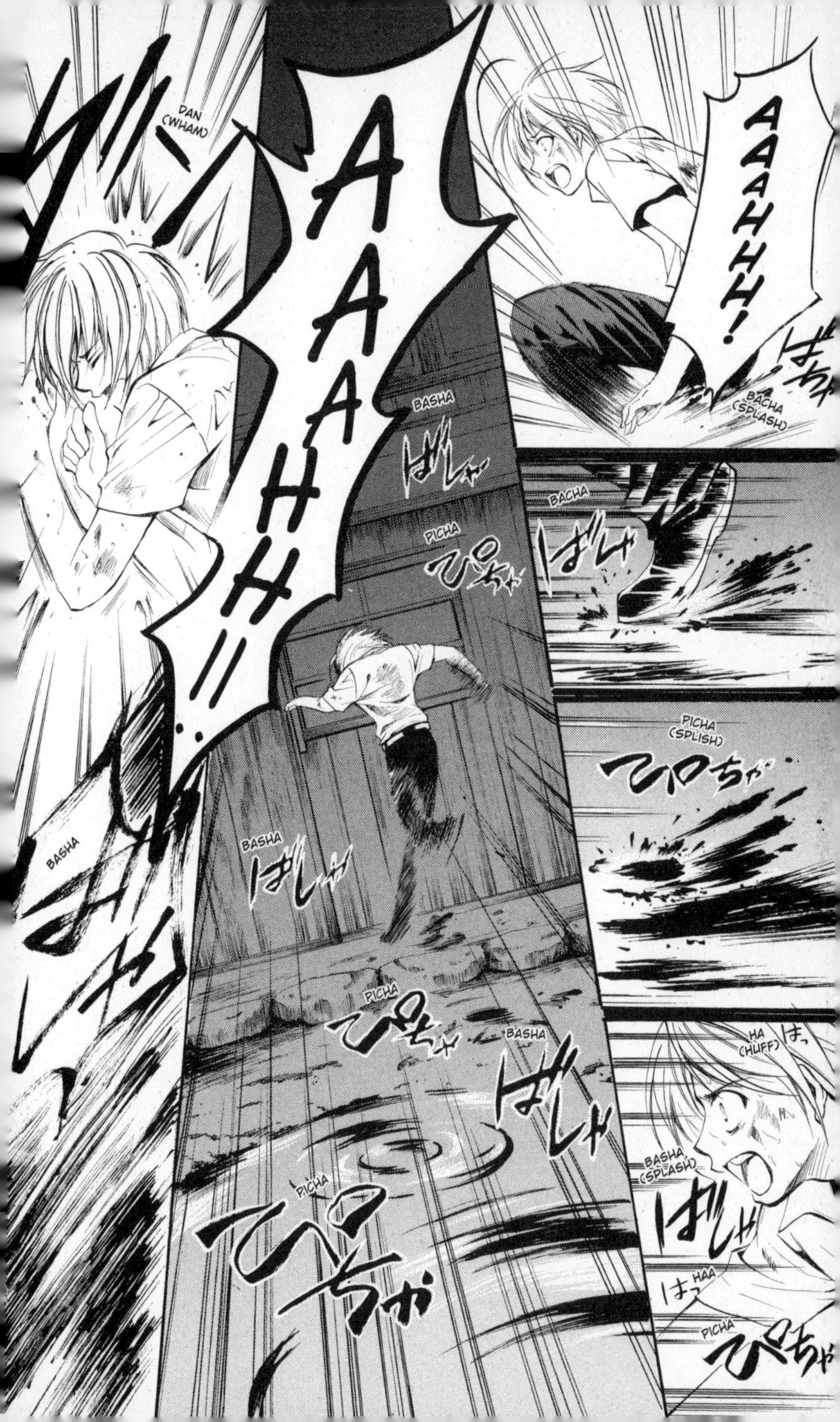

AAAAHHHH!
BACHA (SPLASH)
BACHA
PICHA (SPLISH)
HA (HUFF)
BASHA (SPLASH)
HAA
PICHA
AAAHHH!!
BASHA
PICHA
BASHA
PICHA
BASHA
PICHA
DAN (WHAM)
BASHA

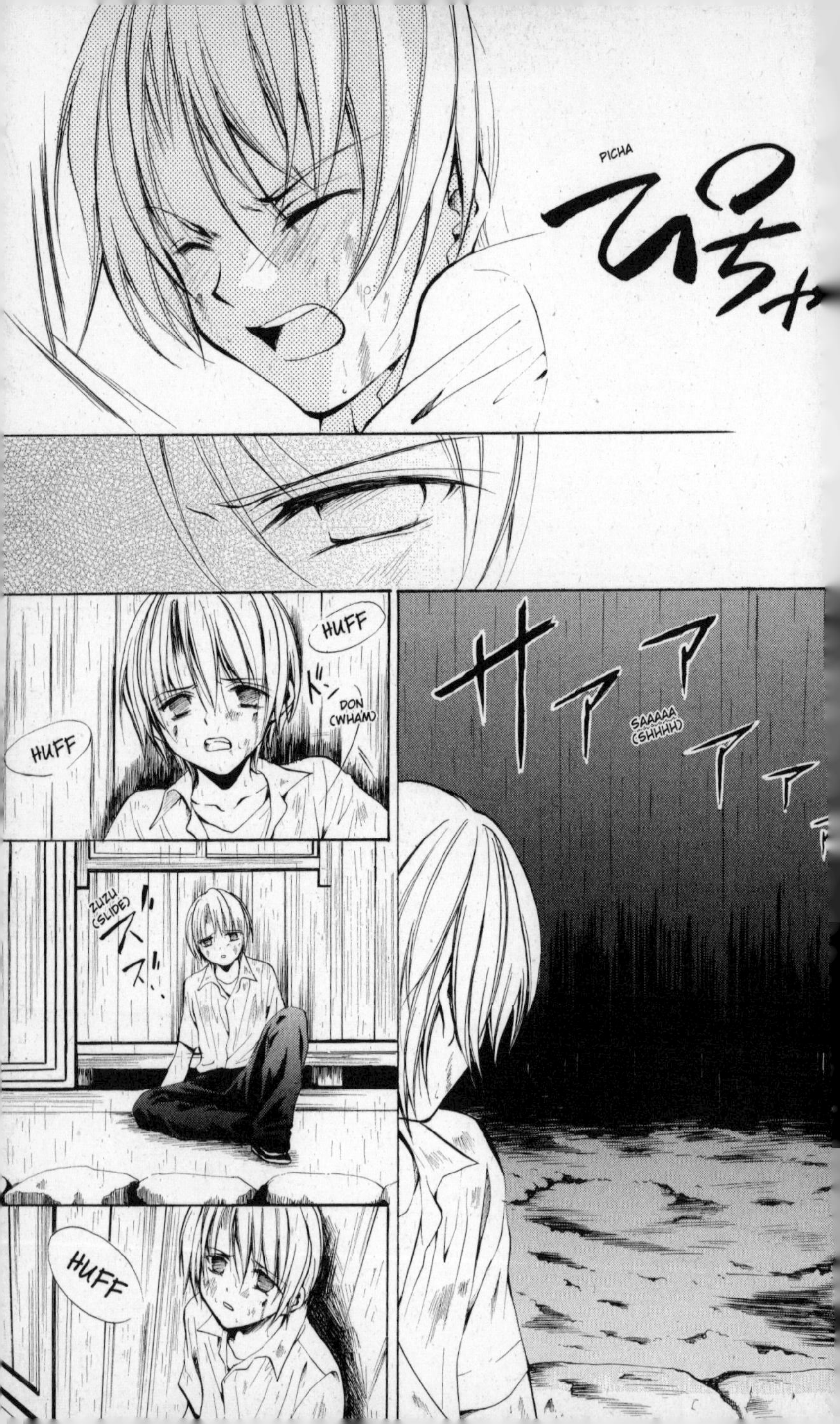
ぴちゃ
PICHA
サァァァァ
SAAAAA (SHHHH)
HUFF
ドン
DON (WHAM)
HUFF
ズズ
ZUZU (SLIDE)
HUFF

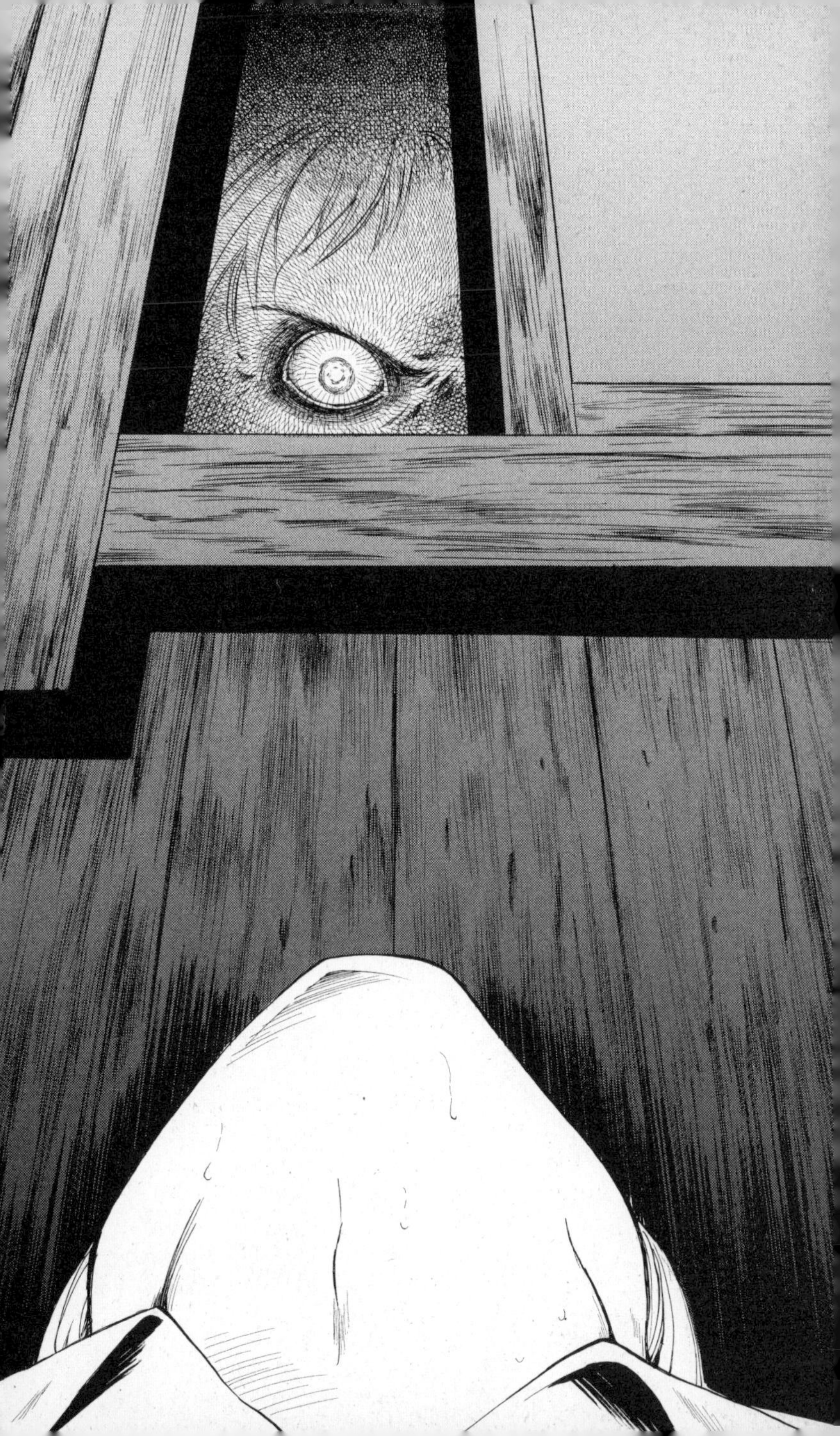

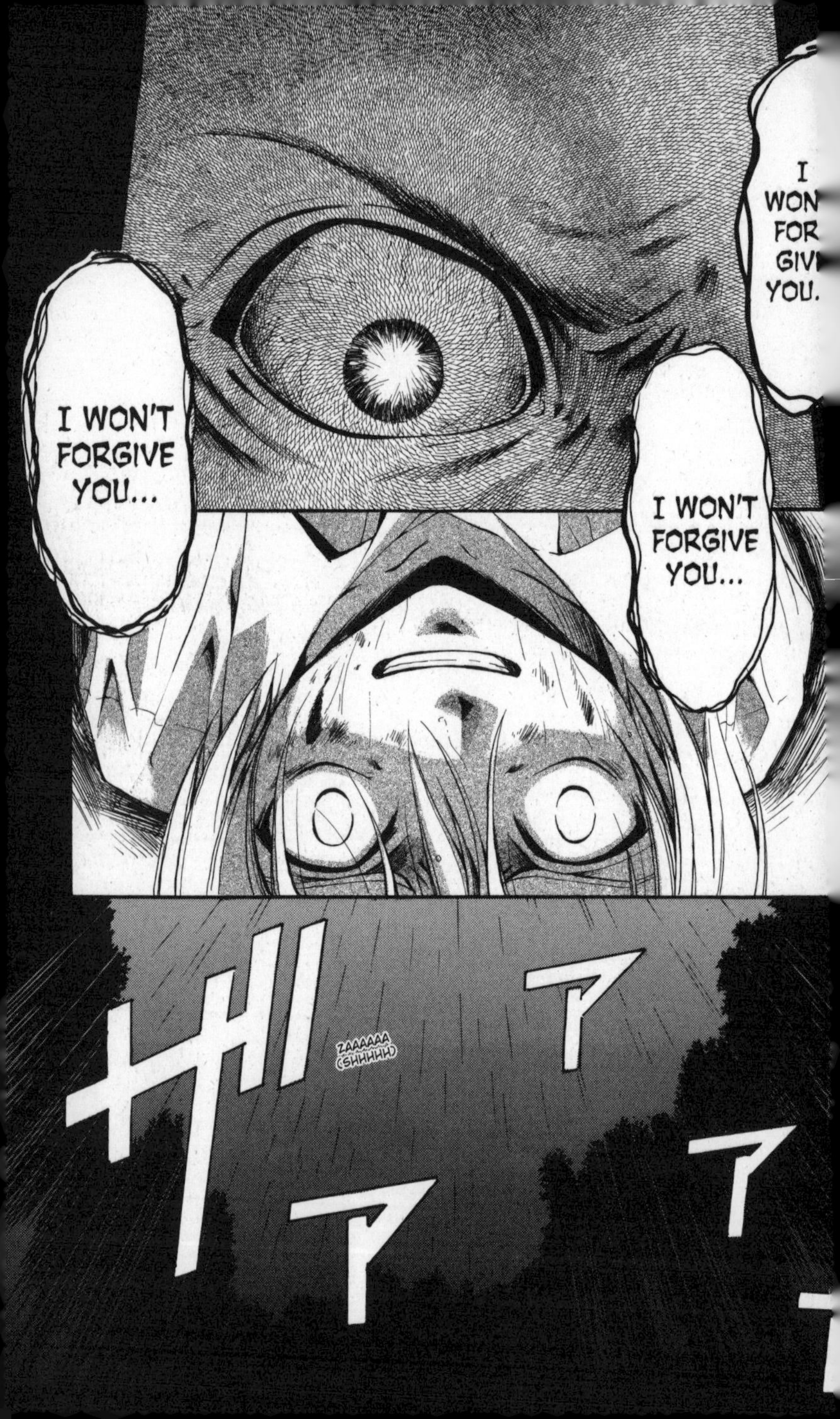
I WON FOR GIV YOU.
I WON'T FORGIVE YOU...
I WON'T FORGIVE YOU...
ZAAAAAA (SHHHHH)

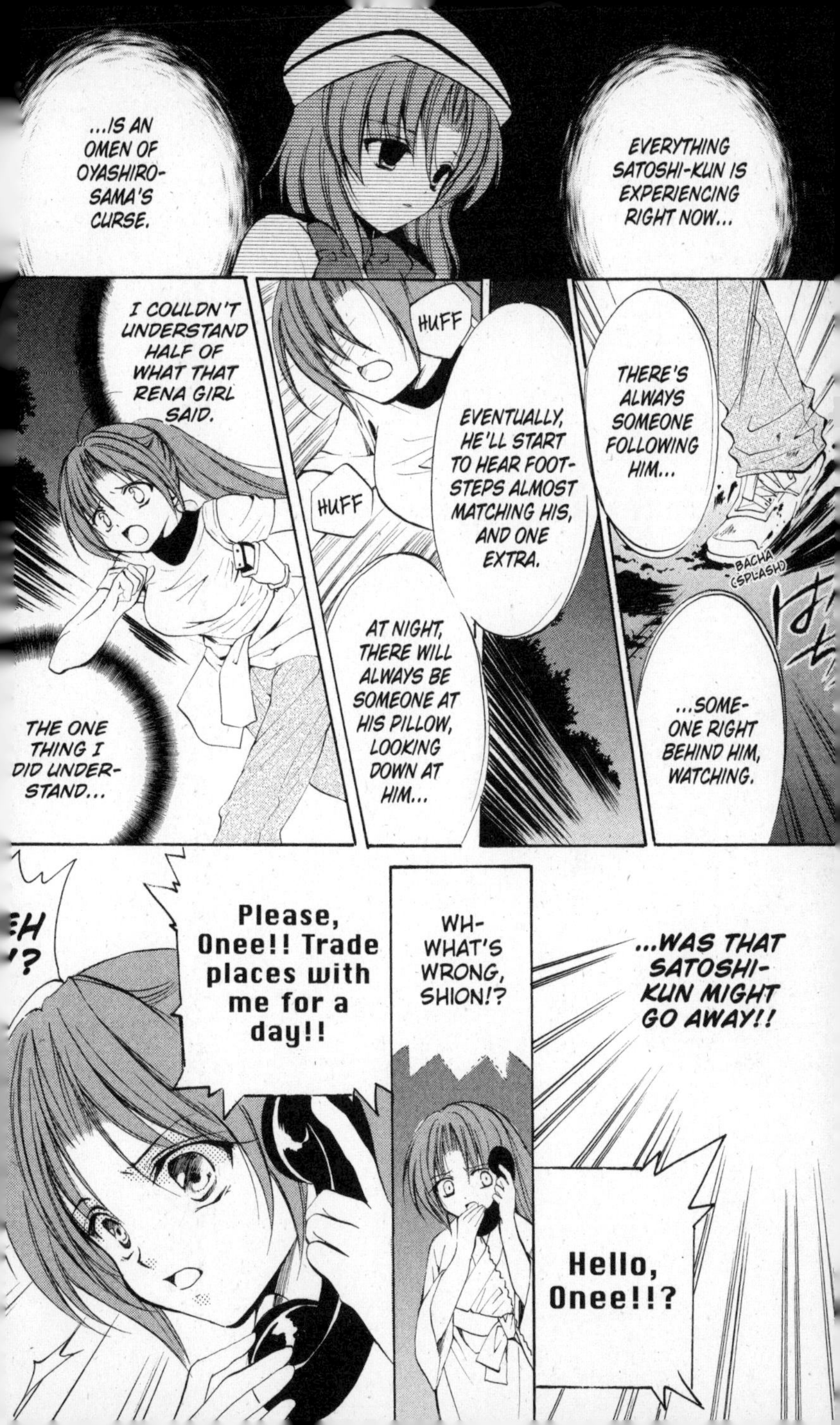
EVERYTHING SATOSHI-KUN IS EXPERIENCING RIGHT NOW...
...IS AN OMEN OF OYASHIRO-SAMA'S CURSE.
THERE'S ALWAYS SOMEONE FOLLOWING HIM...
BACHA (SPLASH)
...SOME-ONE RIGHT BEHIND HIM, WATCHING.
HUFF
EVENTUALLY, HE'LL START TO HEAR FOOT-STEPS ALMOST MATCHING HIS, AND ONE EXTRA.
HUFF
AT NIGHT, THERE WILL ALWAYS BE SOMEONE AT HIS PILLOW, LOOKING DOWN AT HIM...
I COULDN'T UNDERSTAND HALF OF WHAT THAT RENA GIRL SAID.
THE ONE THING I DID UNDER-STAND...
...WAS THAT SATOSHI-KUN MIGHT GO AWAY!!
Hello, Onee!!?
WH-WHAT'S WRONG, SHION!?
Please, Onee!! Trade places with me for a day!!

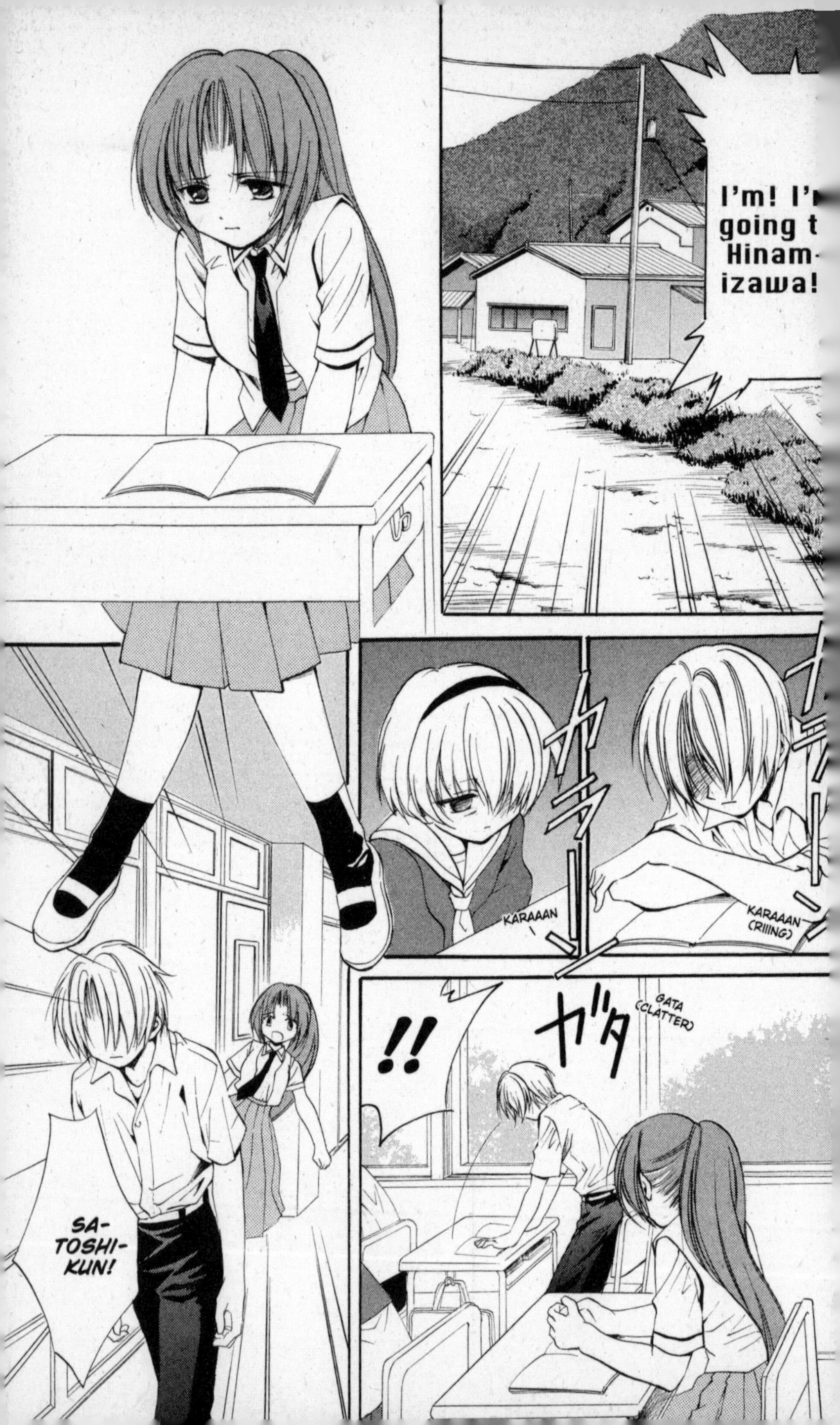

I'm! I' going t Hinam-izawa!
KARAAAN (RIIING)
KARAAAN
!!
GATA (CLATTER)
SA-TOSHI-KUN!

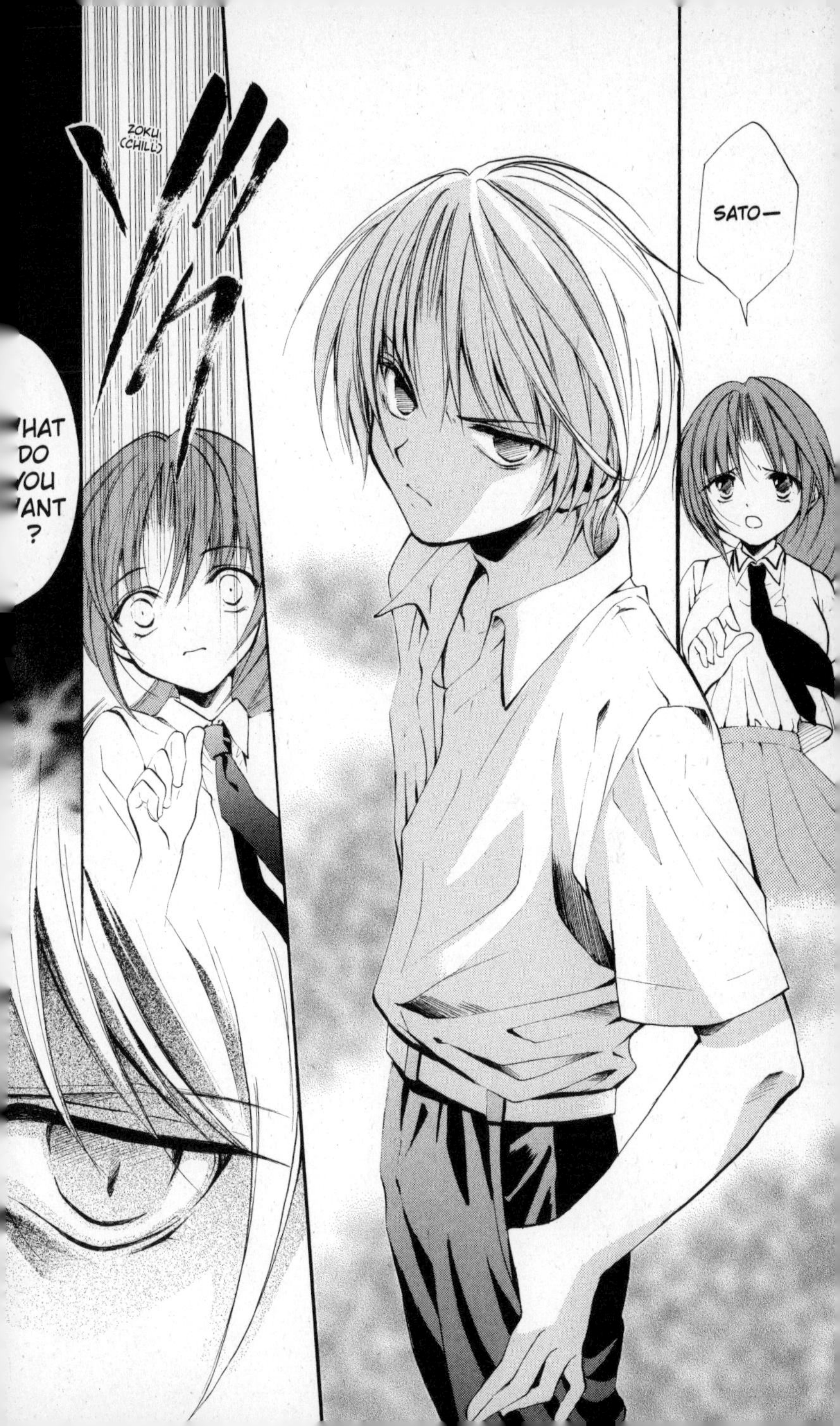
SATO—
ZOKU (CHILL)
WHAT DO YOU WANT?

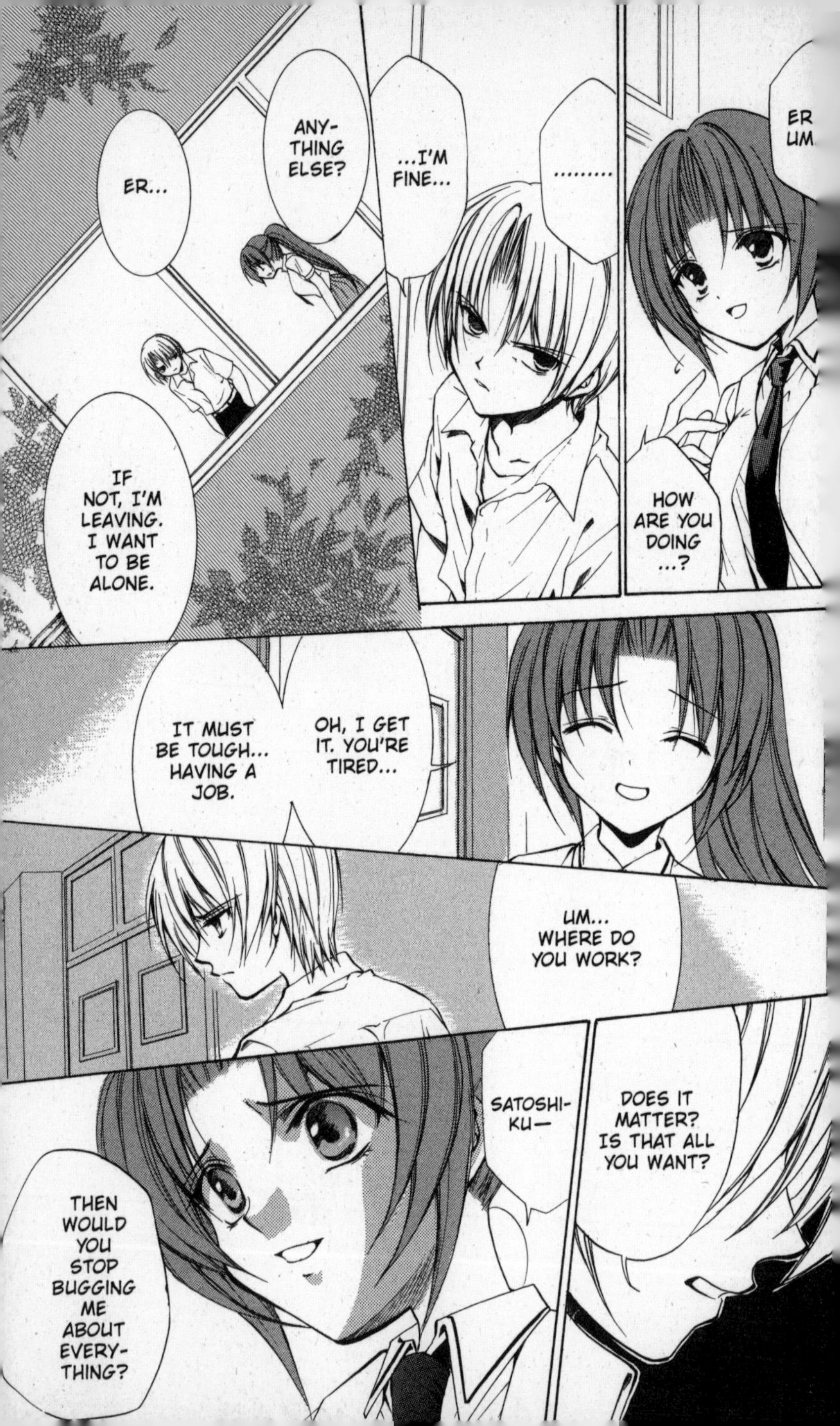
ER UM
HOW ARE YOU DOING ...?
....
...I'M FINE...
ANY-THING ELSE?
ER...
IF NOT, I'M LEAVING. I WANT TO BE ALONE.
OH, I GET IT. YOU'RE TIRED...
IT MUST BE TOUGH... HAVING A JOB.
UM... WHERE DO YOU WORK?
DOES IT MATTER? IS THAT ALL YOU WANT?
SATOSHI-KU—
THEN WOULD YOU STOP BUGGING ME ABOUT EVERY-THING?

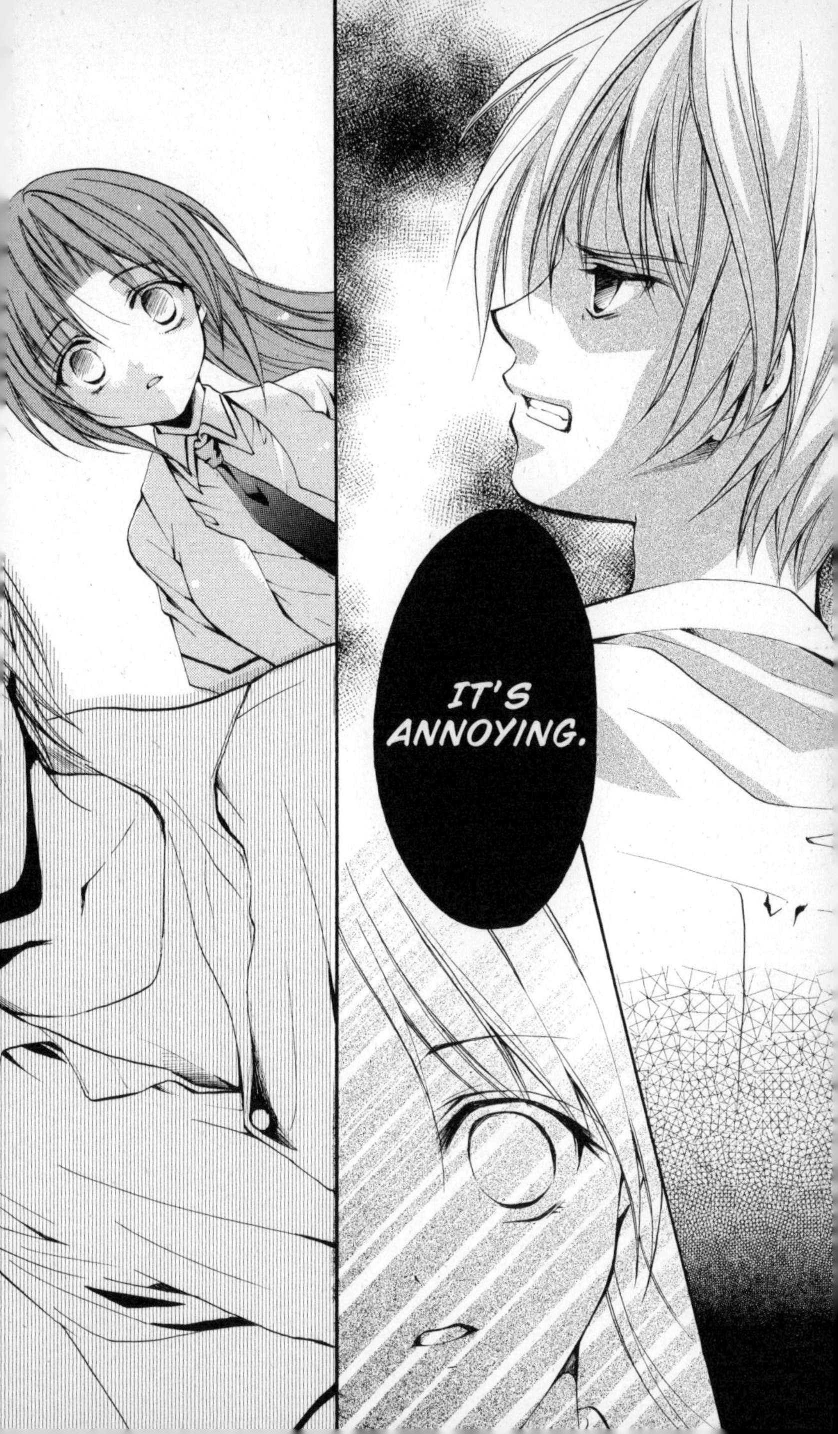
IT'S ANNOYING.

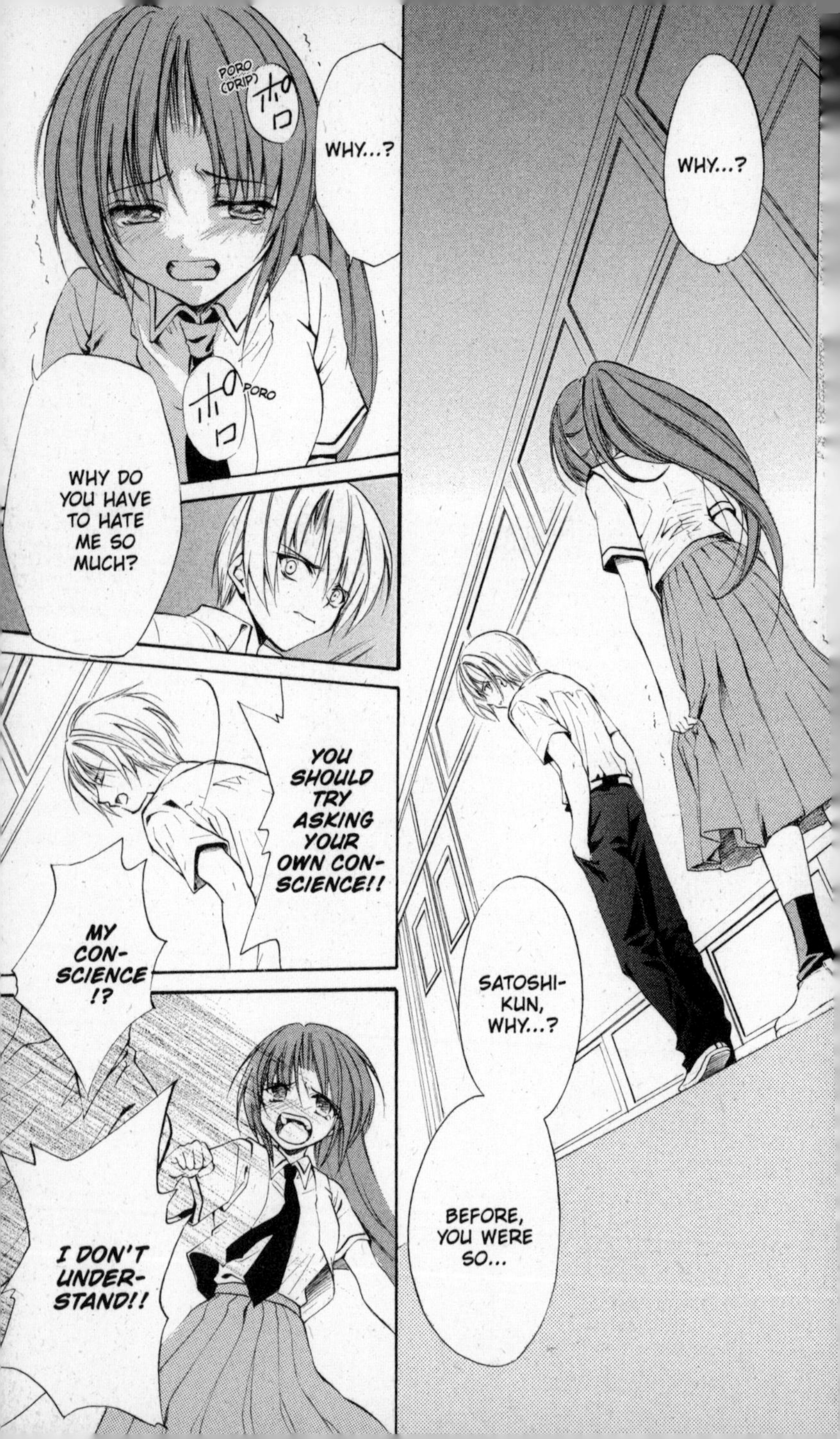
WHY...?
SATOSHI-KUN, WHY...?
BEFORE, YOU WERE SO...
ホロ
PORO (DRIP)
WHY...?
ホロ
PORO
WHY DO YOU HAVE TO HATE ME SO MUCH?
YOU SHOULD TRY ASKING YOUR OWN CON-SCIENCE!!
MY CON-SCIENCE!?
I DON'T UNDER-STAND!!

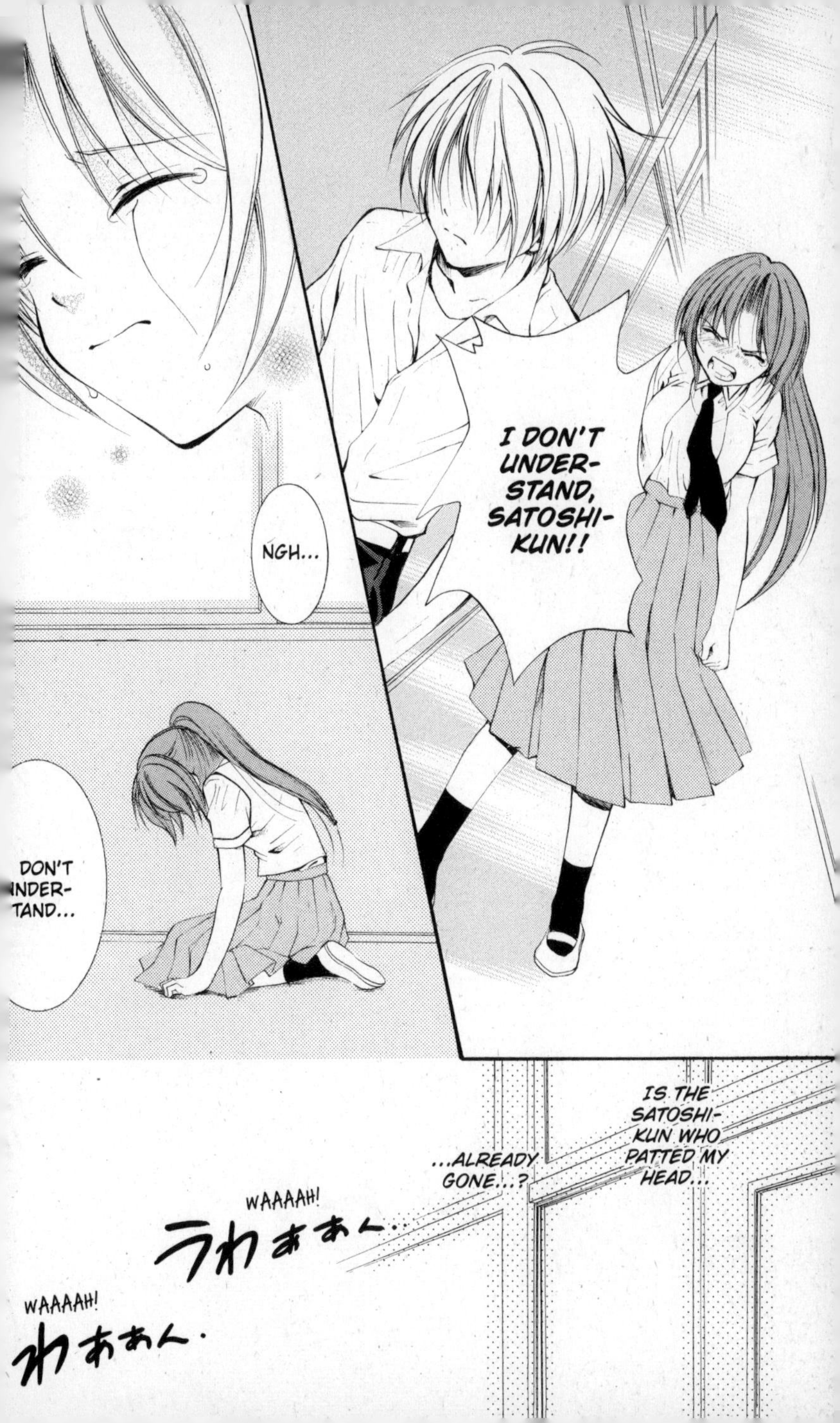
I DON'T UNDER-STAND, SATOSHI-KUN!!
NGH...
DON'T NDER-TAND...
IS THE SATOSHI-KUN WHO PATTED MY HEAD...
...ALREADY GONE...?
WAAAAH!
うわぁあん..
WAAAAH!
わぁあん.

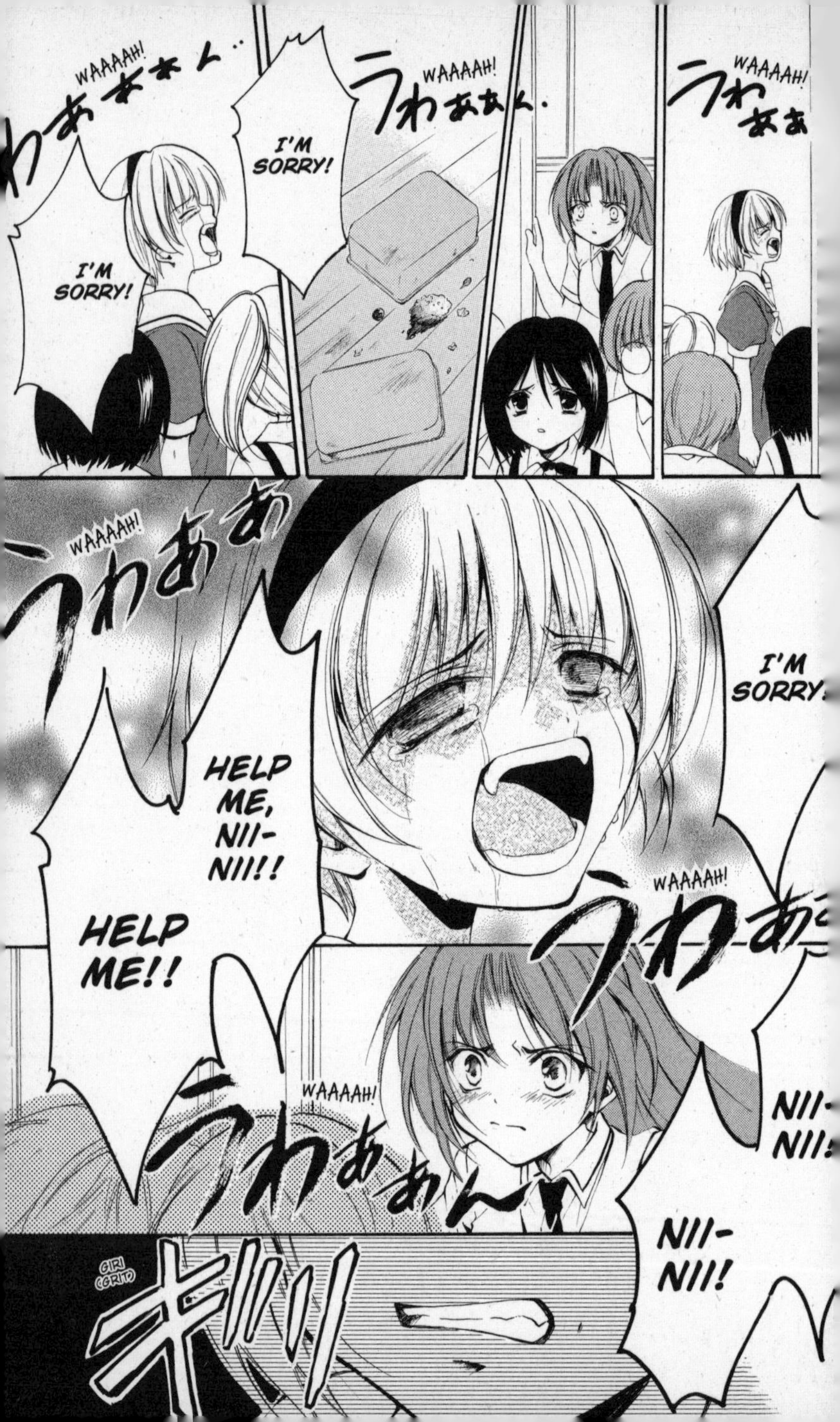

WAAAAH!
うわあぁ
WAAAAH!
うわあぁん.
I'M SORRY!
WAAAAH!
わあぁぁん…
I'M SORRY!
I'M SORRY!
WAAAAH!
うわあぁ
WAAAAH!
うわあぁあ
HELP ME, NII-NII!!
HELP ME!!
NII-NII!
NII-NII!
WAAAAH!
うわあぁん
GIRI (GRIT)
ギリッ

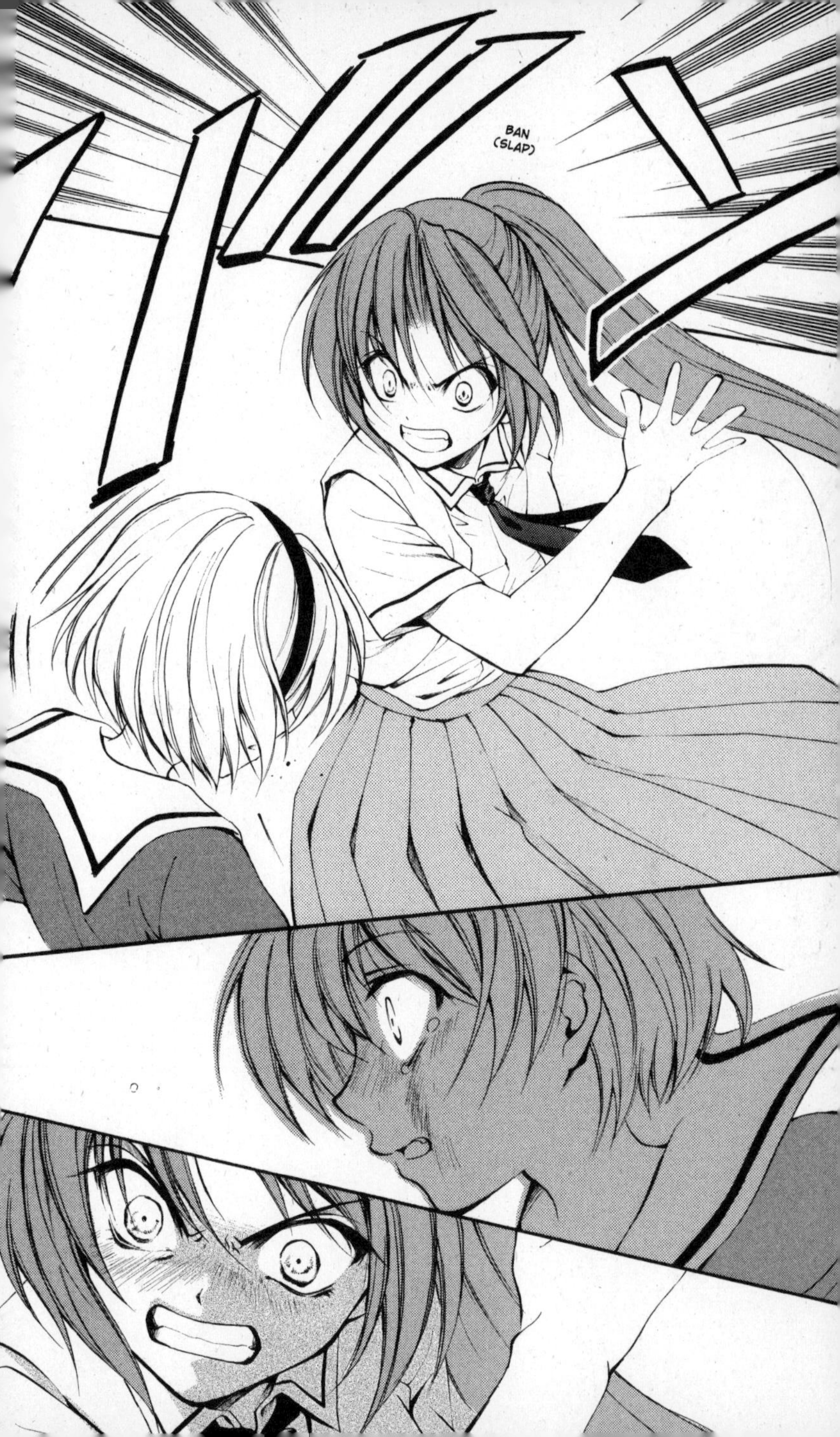
BAN
(SLAP)

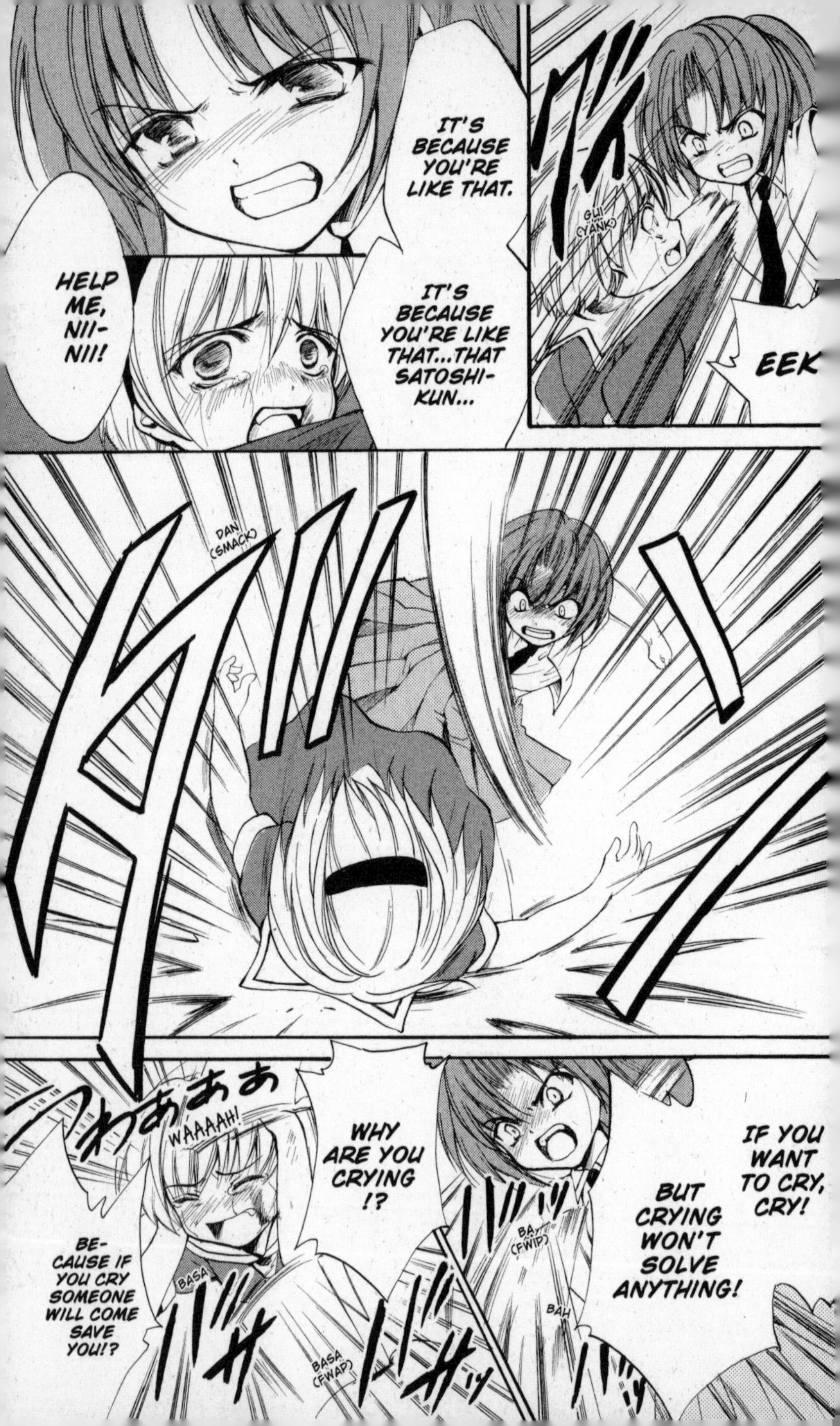

GUI (YANK)
EEK
IT'S BECAUSE YOU'RE LIKE THAT.
IT'S BECAUSE YOU'RE LIKE THAT...THAT SATOSHI-KUN...
HELP ME, NII-NII!
DAN (SMACK)
IF YOU WANT TO CRY, CRY!
BUT CRYING WON'T SOLVE ANYTHING!
BA (FWIP)
BAH
WHY ARE YOU CRYING!?
BE-CAUSE IF YOU CRY SOMEONE WILL COME SAVE YOU!?
うわあああ
WAAAAH!
BASA
BASA (FWAP)

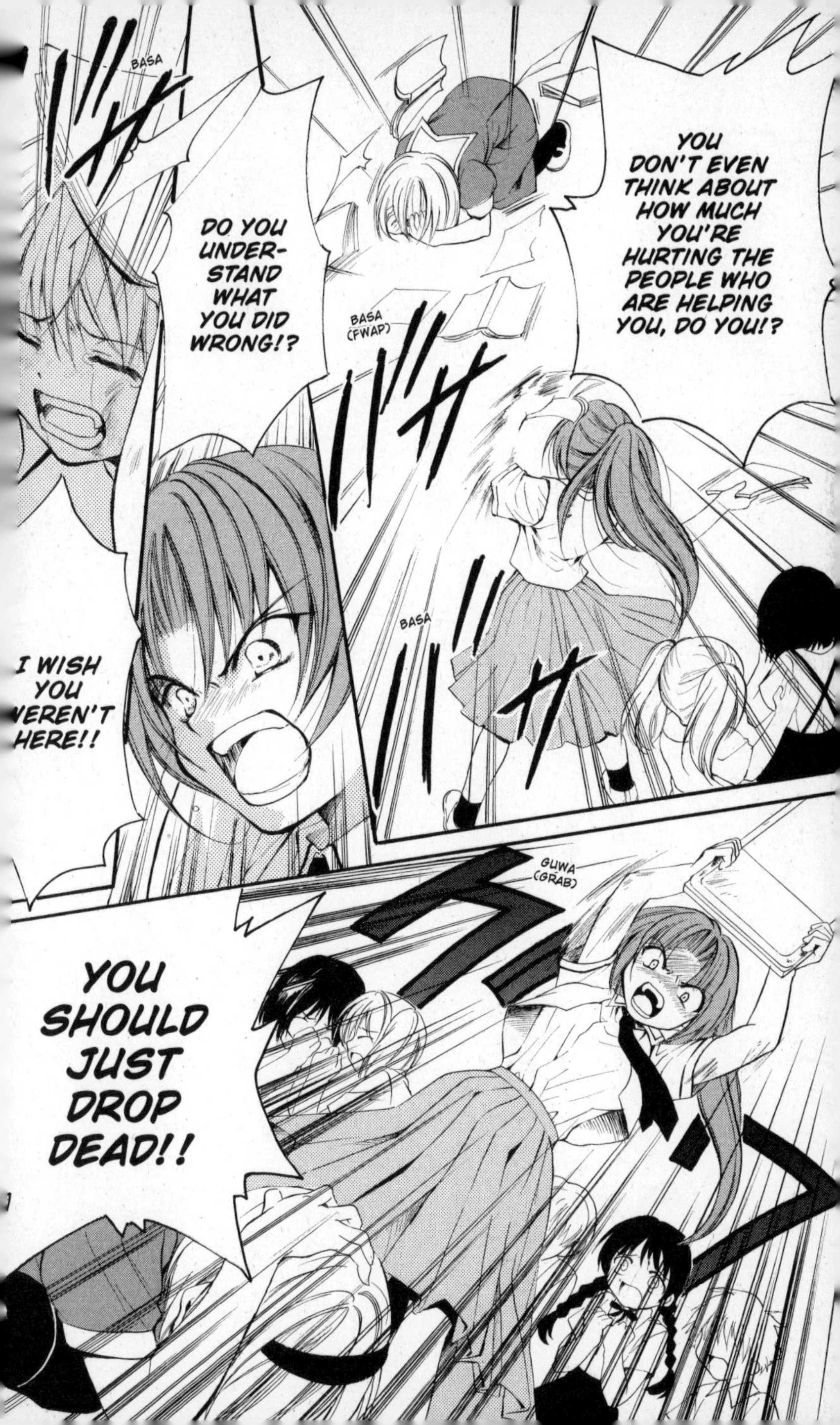
YOU DON'T EVEN THINK ABOUT HOW MUCH YOU'RE HURTING THE PEOPLE WHO ARE HELPING YOU, DO YOU!?
BASA (FWAP)
BASA
BASA
DO YOU UNDER-STAND WHAT YOU DID WRONG!?
I WISH YOU WEREN'T HERE!!
GUWA (GRAB)
YOU SHOULD JUST DROP DEAD!!

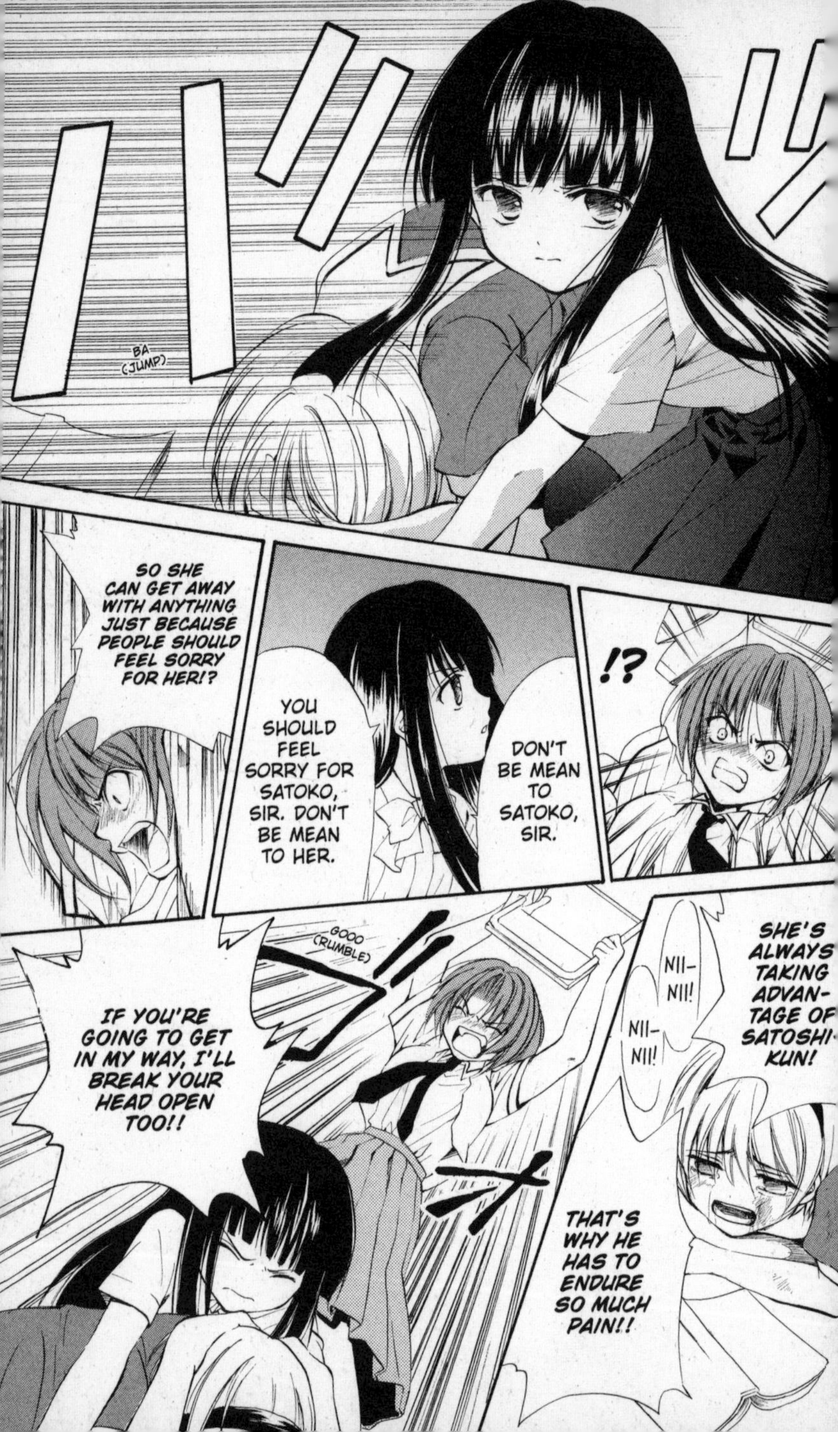

BA (JUMP)
!?
DON'T BE MEAN TO SATOKO, SIR.
YOU SHOULD FEEL SORRY FOR SATOKO, SIR. DON'T BE MEAN TO HER.
SO SHE CAN GET AWAY WITH ANYTHING JUST BECAUSE PEOPLE SHOULD FEEL SORRY FOR HER!?
SHE'S ALWAYS TAKING ADVANTAGE OF SATOSHI-KUN!
NII-NII!
NII-NII!
GOOO (RUMBLE)
IF YOU'RE GOING TO GET IN MY WAY, I'LL BREAK YOUR HEAD OPEN TOO!!
THAT'S WHY HE HAS TO ENDURE SO MUCH PAIN!!

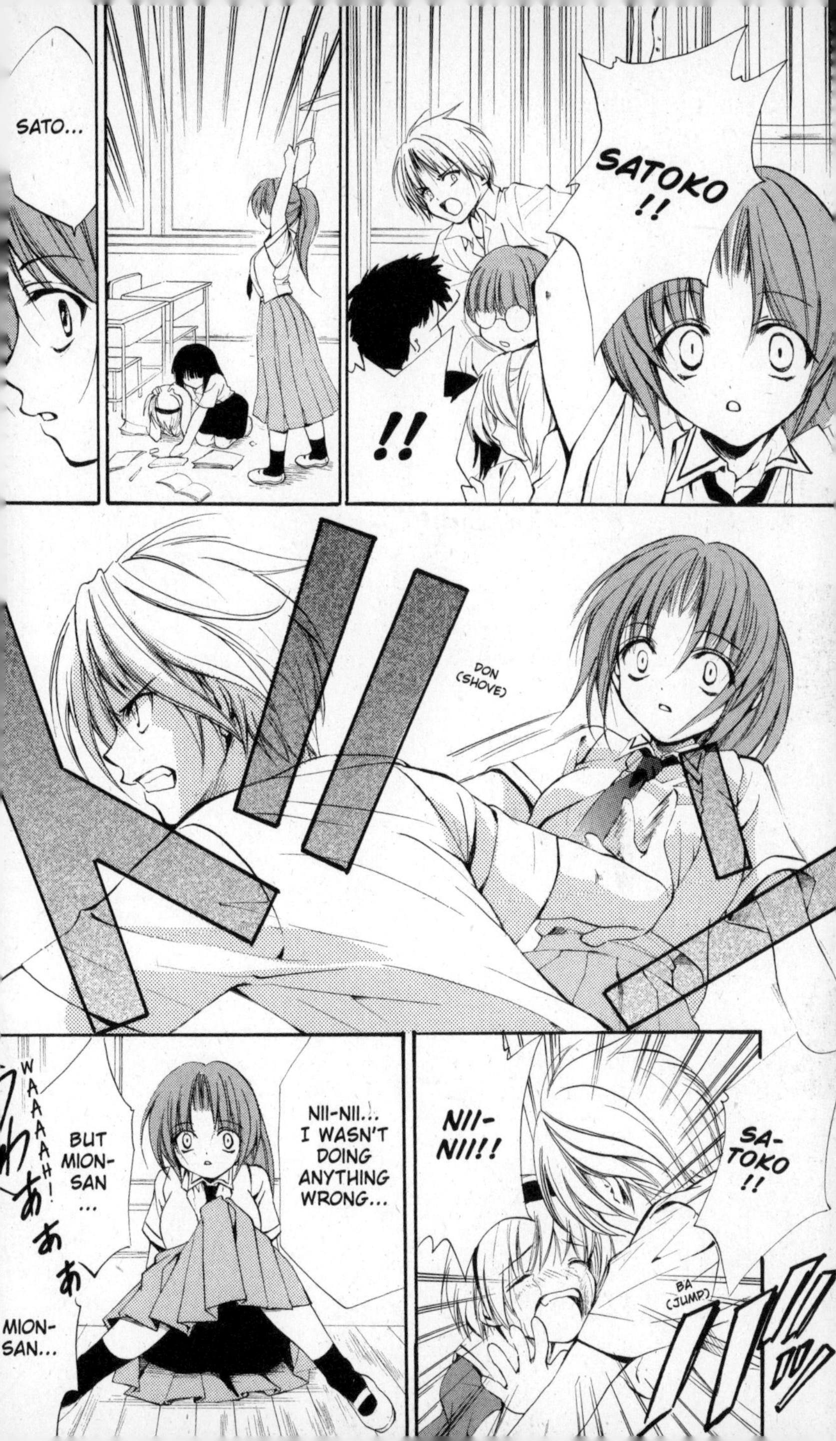
SATOKO!!
!!
SATO...
DON (SHOVE)
SA-TOKO!!
NII-NII!!
BA (JUMP)
NII-NII... I WASN'T DOING ANYTHING WRONG...
BUT MION-SAN...
WAAAAAH!
うわあああ
MION-SAN...

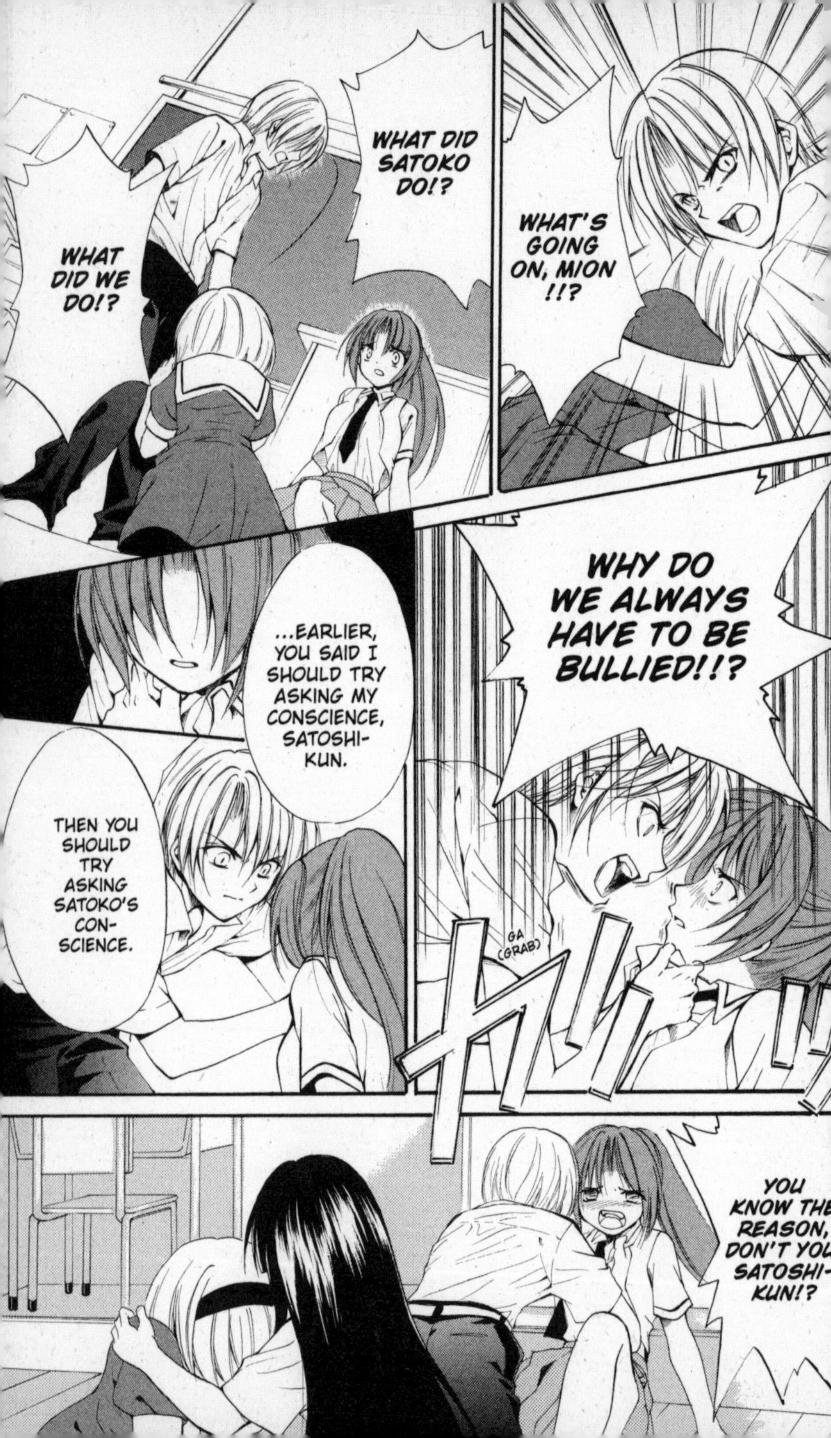
WHAT'S GOING ON, MION !!?
WHAT DID SATOKO DO!?
WHAT DID WE DO!?
WHY DO WE ALWAYS HAVE TO BE BULLIED!!?
GA (GRAB)
...EARLIER, YOU SAID I SHOULD TRY ASKING MY CONSCIENCE, SATOSHI-KUN.
THEN YOU SHOULD TRY ASKING SATOKO'S CON-SCIENCE.
YOU KNOW THE REASON, DON'T YOU, SATOSHI-KUN!?

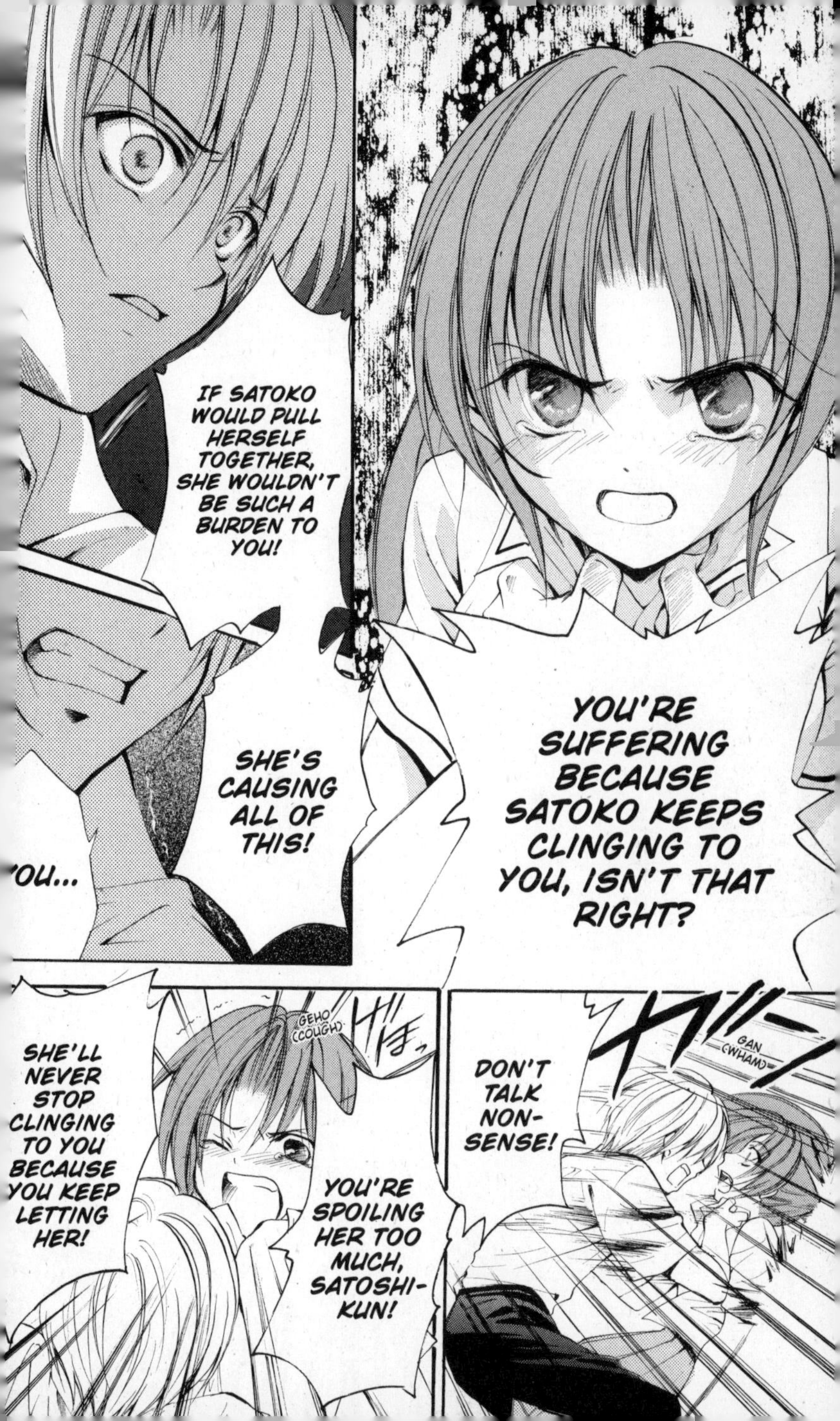
YOU'RE SUFFERING BECAUSE SATOKO KEEPS CLINGING TO YOU, ISN'T THAT RIGHT?
IF SATOKO WOULD PULL HERSELF TOGETHER, SHE WOULDN'T BE SUCH A BURDEN TO YOU!
SHE'S CAUSING ALL OF THIS!
OU...
GAN (WHAM)
DON'T TALK NON-SENSE!
GEHO (COUGH)
YOU'RE SPOILING HER TOO MUCH, SATOSHI-KUN!
SHE'LL NEVER STOP CLINGING TO YOU BECAUSE YOU KEEP LETTING HER!

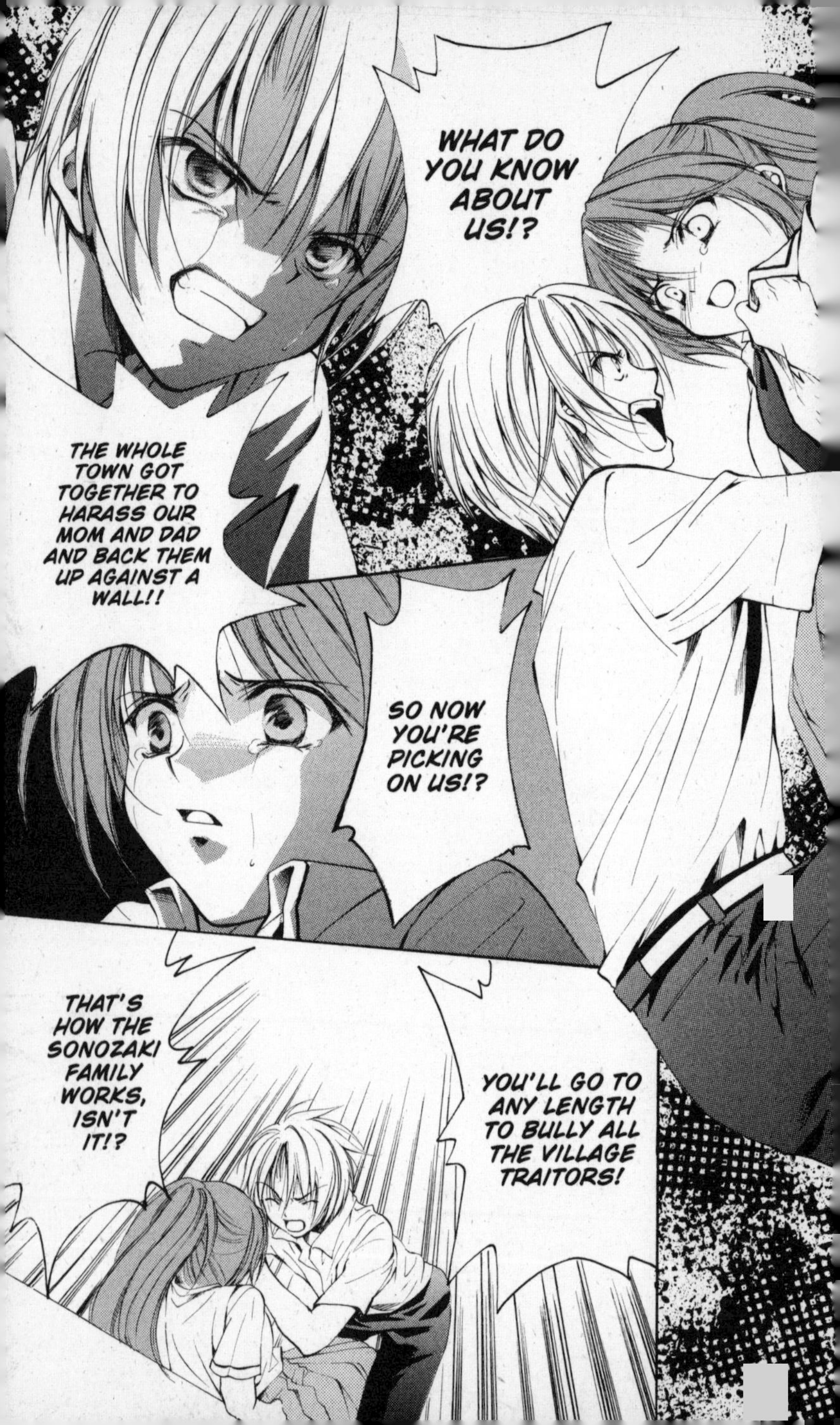
WHAT DO YOU KNOW ABOUT US!?
THE WHOLE TOWN GOT TOGETHER TO HARASS OUR MOM AND DAD AND BACK THEM UP AGAINST A WALL!!
SO NOW YOU'RE PICKING ON US!?
YOU'LL GO TO ANY LENGTH TO BULLY ALL THE VILLAGE TRAITORS!
THAT'S HOW THE SONOZAKI FAMILY WORKS, ISN'T IT!?

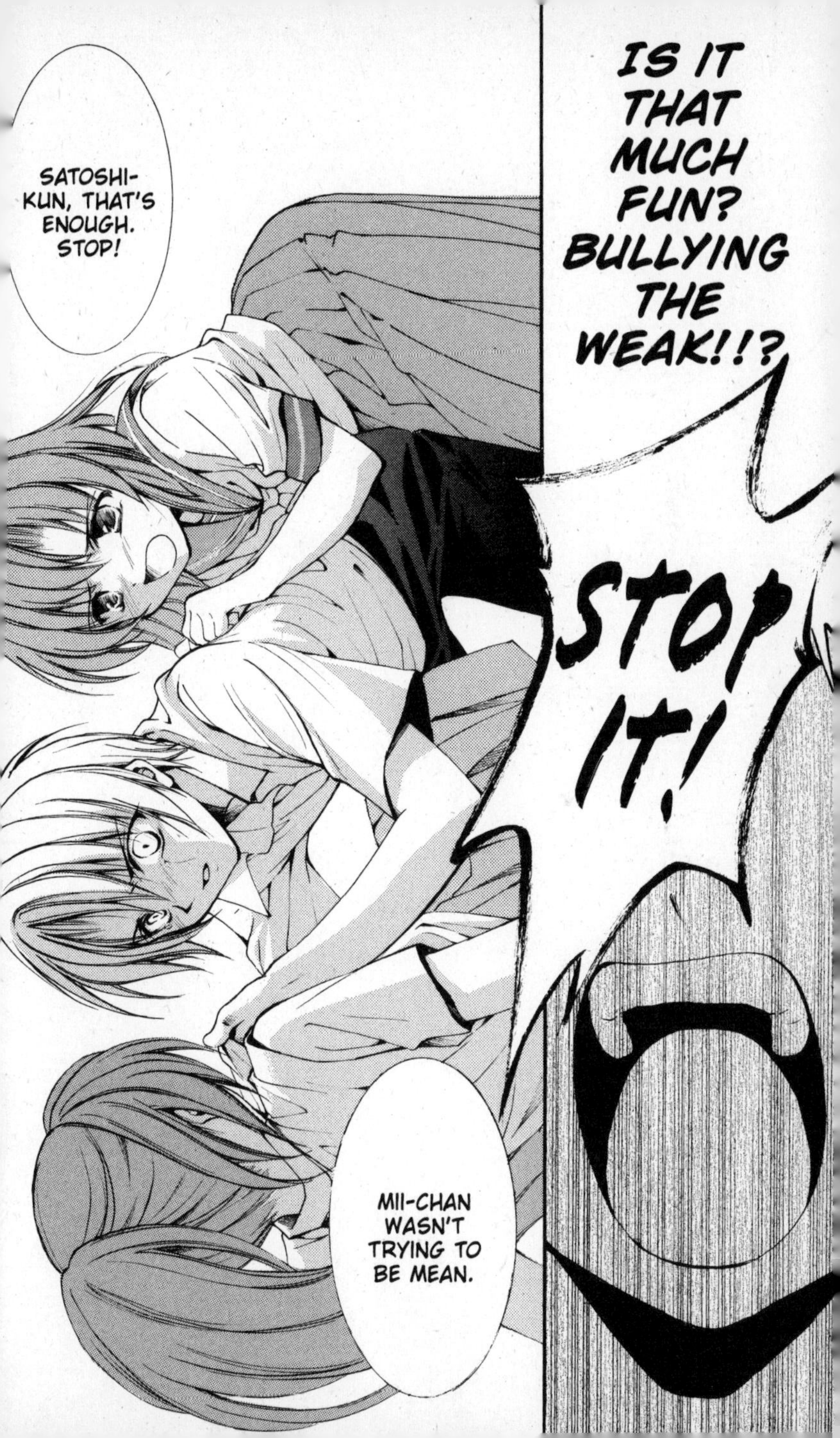
IS IT THAT MUCH FUN? BULLYING THE WEAK!!?
STOP IT!
SATOSHI-KUN, THAT'S ENOUGH. STOP!
MII-CHAN WASN'T TRYING TO BE MEAN.

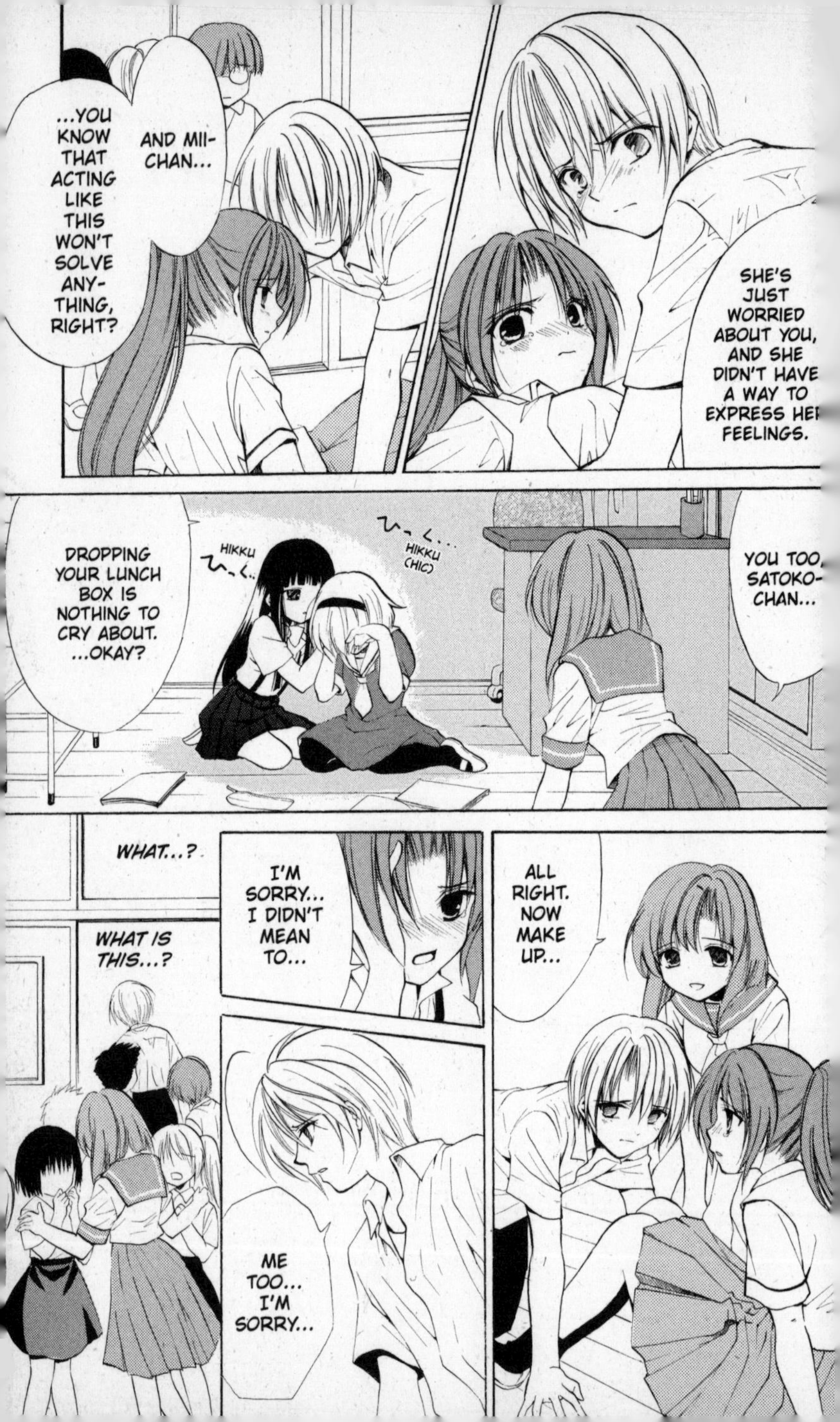
SHE'S JUST WORRIED ABOUT YOU, AND SHE DIDN'T HAVE A WAY TO EXPRESS HEF FEELINGS.
AND MII-CHAN...
...YOU KNOW THAT ACTING LIKE THIS WON'T SOLVE ANYTHING, RIGHT?
YOU TOO, SATOKO-CHAN...
ひっく...
HIKKU (HIC)
HIKKU
ひっく
DROPPING YOUR LUNCH BOX IS NOTHING TO CRY ABOUT. ...OKAY?
ALL RIGHT. NOW MAKE UP...
I'M SORRY... I DIDN'T MEAN TO...
ME TOO... I'M SORRY...
WHAT...?
WHAT IS THIS...?

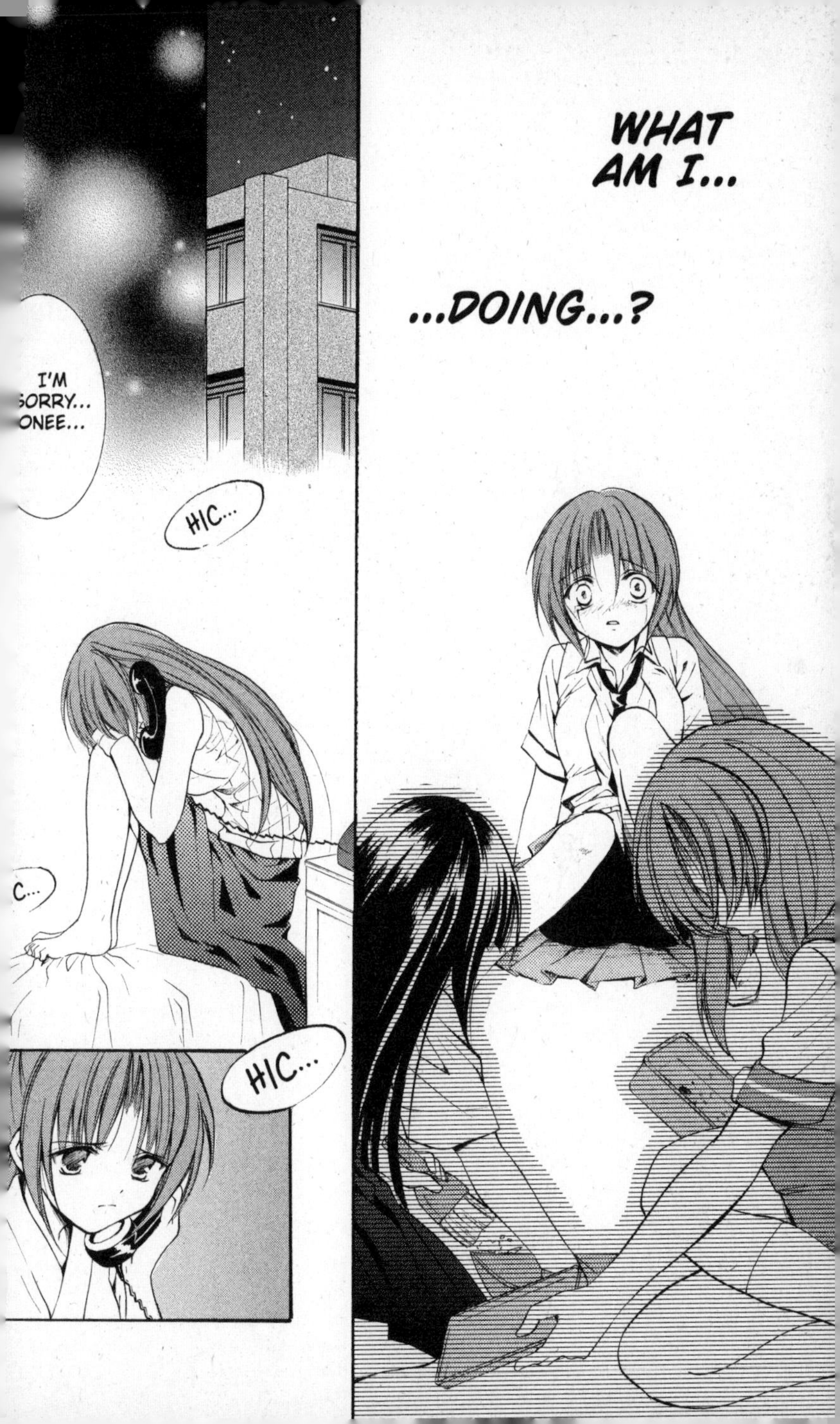
WHAT AM I...
...DOING...?
I'M SORRY... ONEE...
HIC...
C...
HIC...

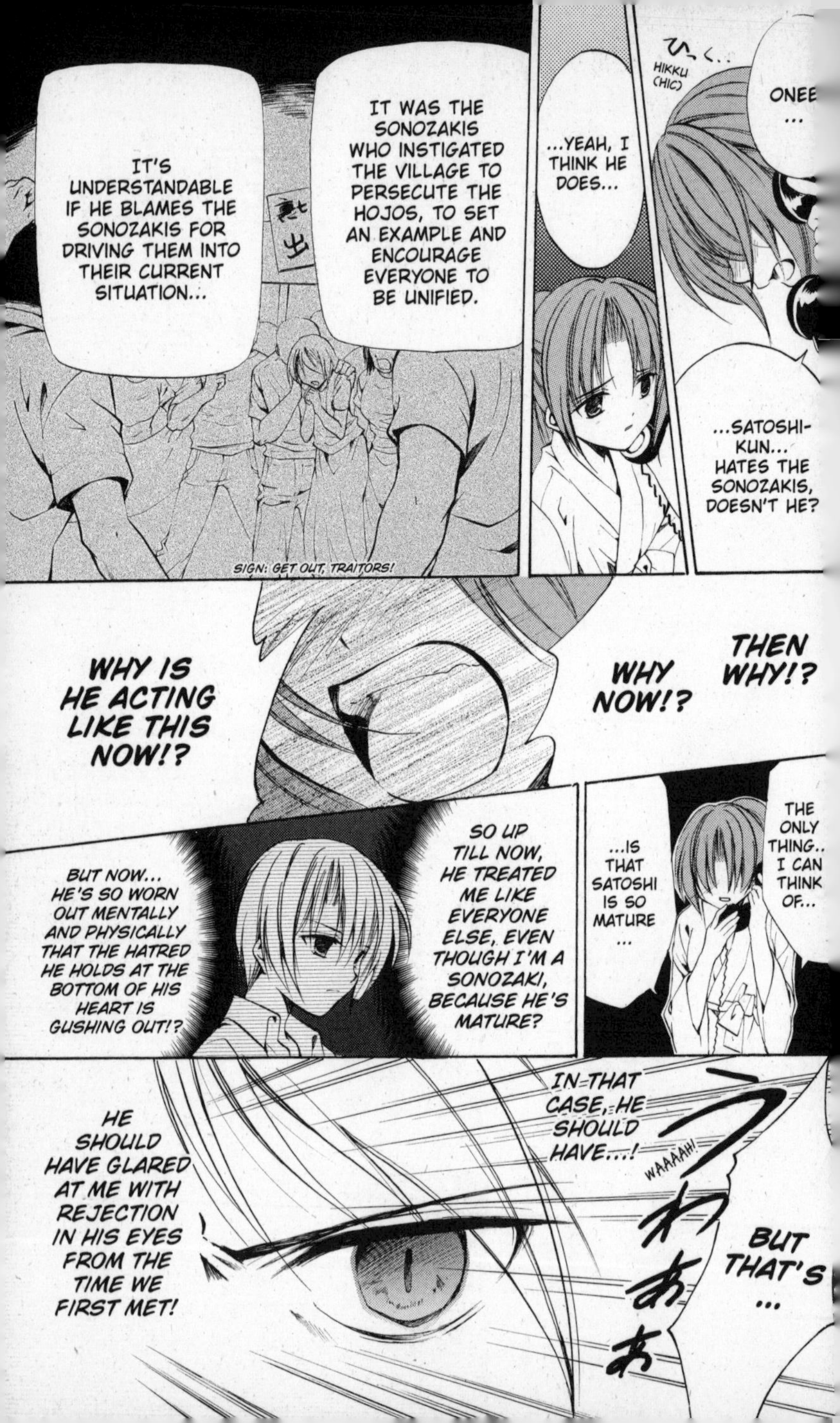
ONEE ...
ひっく..
HIKKU (HIC)
...SATOSHI-KUN... HATES THE SONOZAKIS, DOESN'T HE?
...YEAH, I THINK HE DOES...
IT WAS THE SONOZAKIS WHO INSTIGATED THE VILLAGE TO PERSECUTE THE HOJOS, TO SET AN EXAMPLE AND ENCOURAGE EVERYONE TO BE UNIFIED.
IT'S UNDERSTANDABLE IF HE BLAMES THE SONOZAKIS FOR DRIVING THEM INTO THEIR CURRENT SITUATION...
SIGN: GET OUT, TRAITORS!
THEN WHY!?
WHY NOW!?
WHY IS HE ACTING LIKE THIS NOW!?
THE ONLY THING... I CAN THINK OF...
...IS THAT SATOSHI IS SO MATURE ...
SO UP TILL NOW, HE TREATED ME LIKE EVERYONE ELSE, EVEN THOUGH I'M A SONOZAKI, BECAUSE HE'S MATURE?
BUT NOW... HE'S SO WORN OUT MENTALLY AND PHYSICALLY THAT THE HATRED HE HOLDS AT THE BOTTOM OF HIS HEART IS GUSHING OUT!?
BUT THAT'S ...
わああ
WAAAAH!
IN THAT CASE, HE SHOULD HAVE...!
HE SHOULD HAVE GLARED AT ME WITH REJECTION IN HIS EYES FROM THE TIME WE FIRST MET!

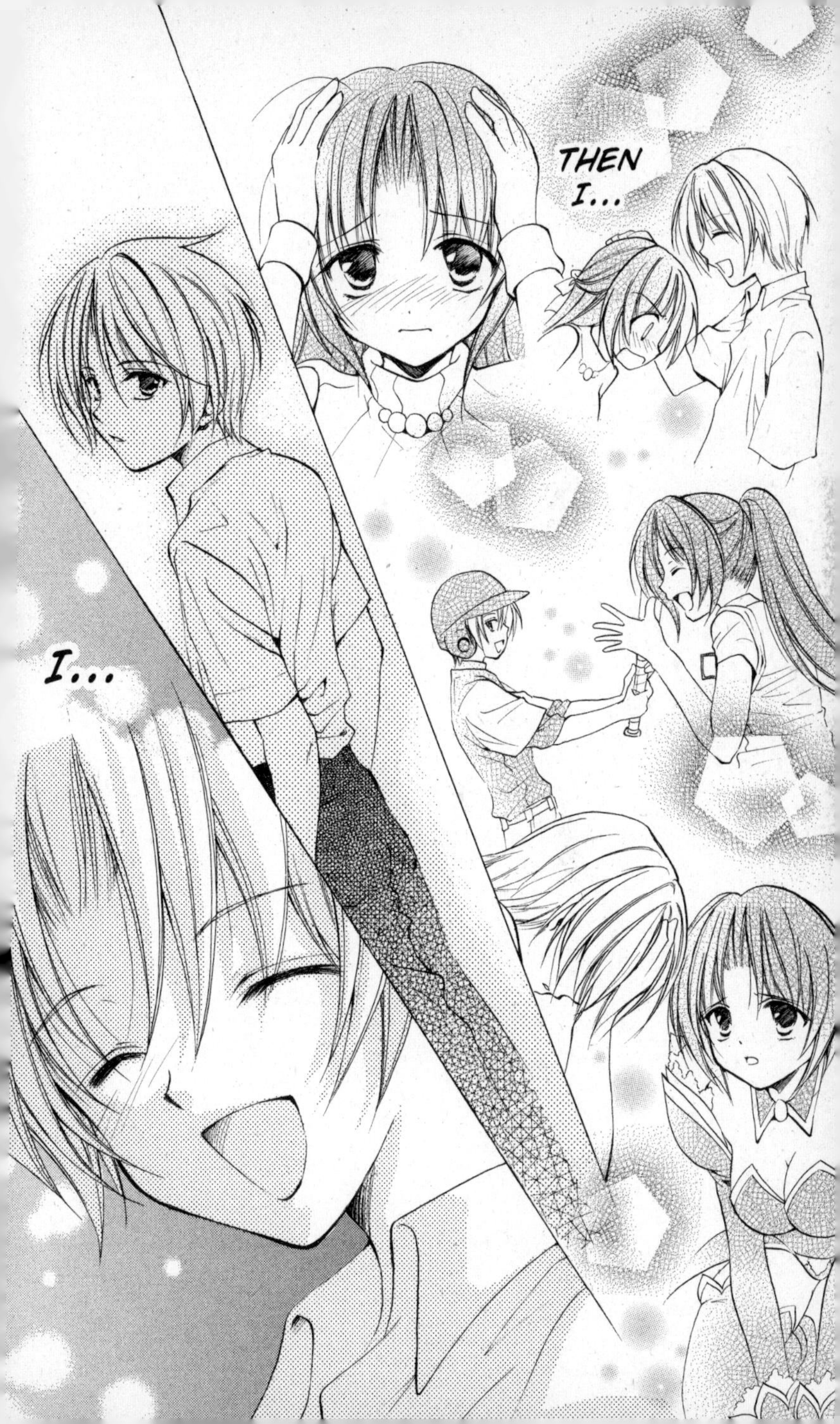
THEN I...
I...

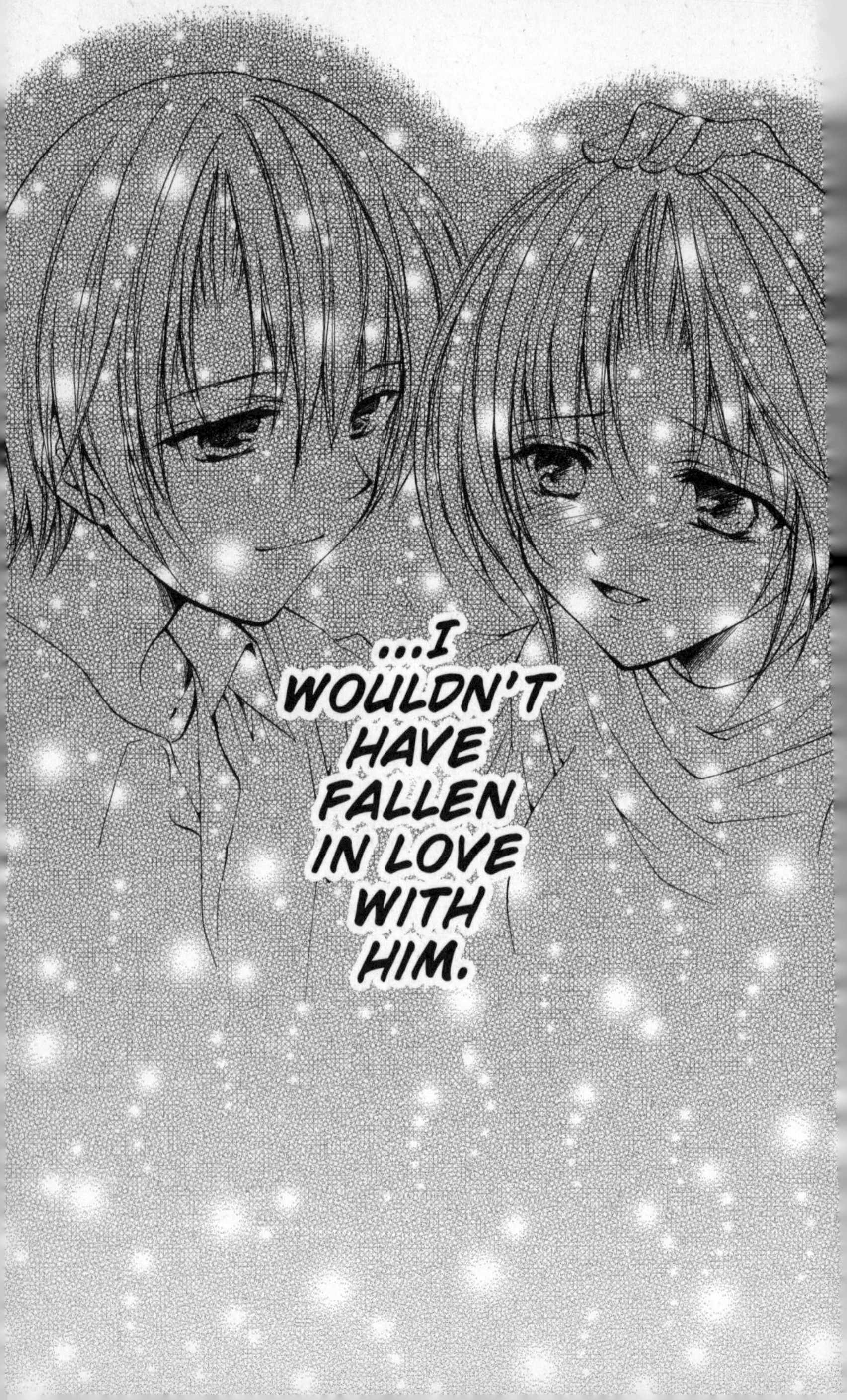
...I WOULDN'T HAVE FALLEN IN LOVE WITH HIM.

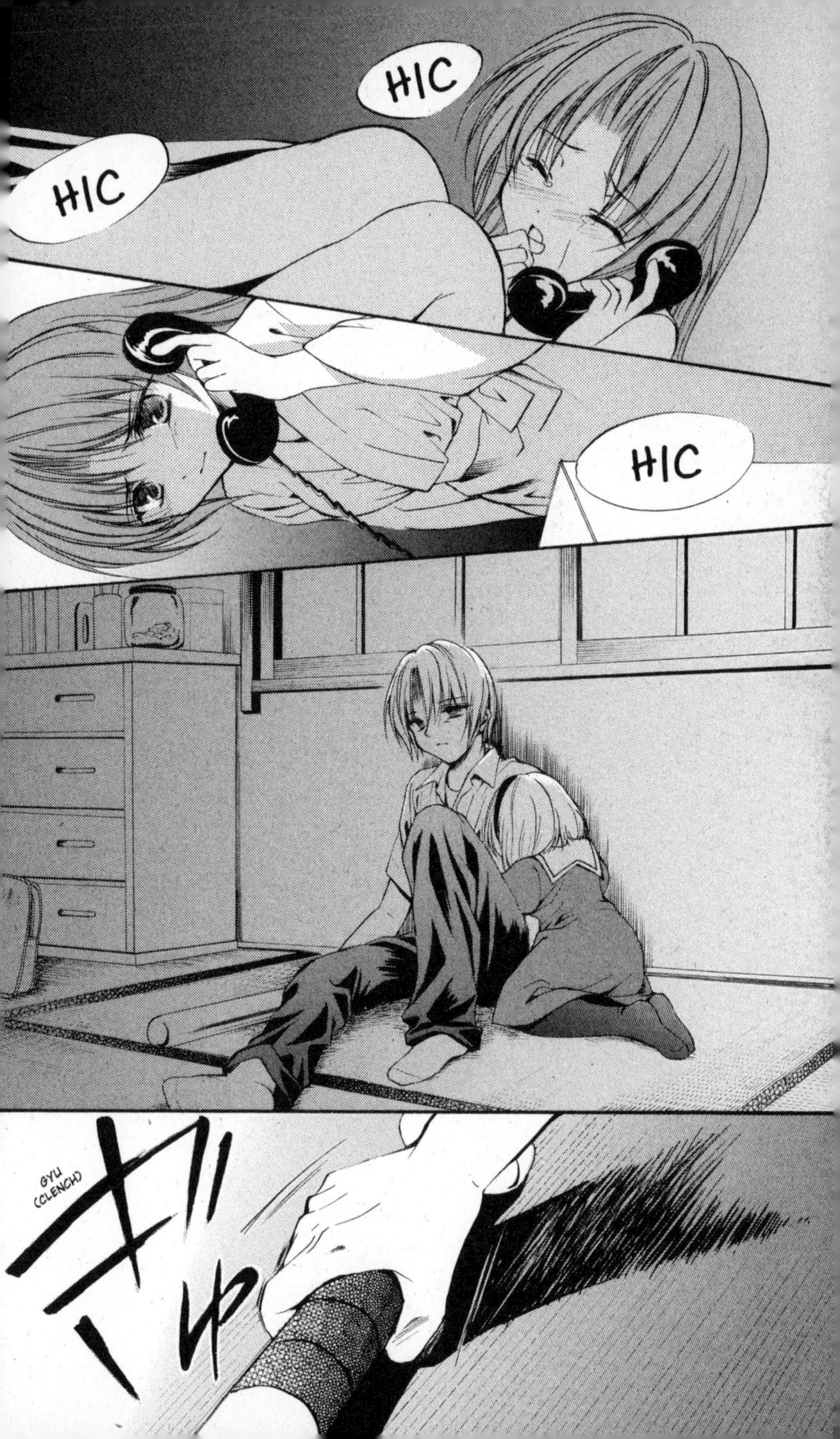
HIC
HIC
HIC
ぎゅ
GYU (CLENCH)

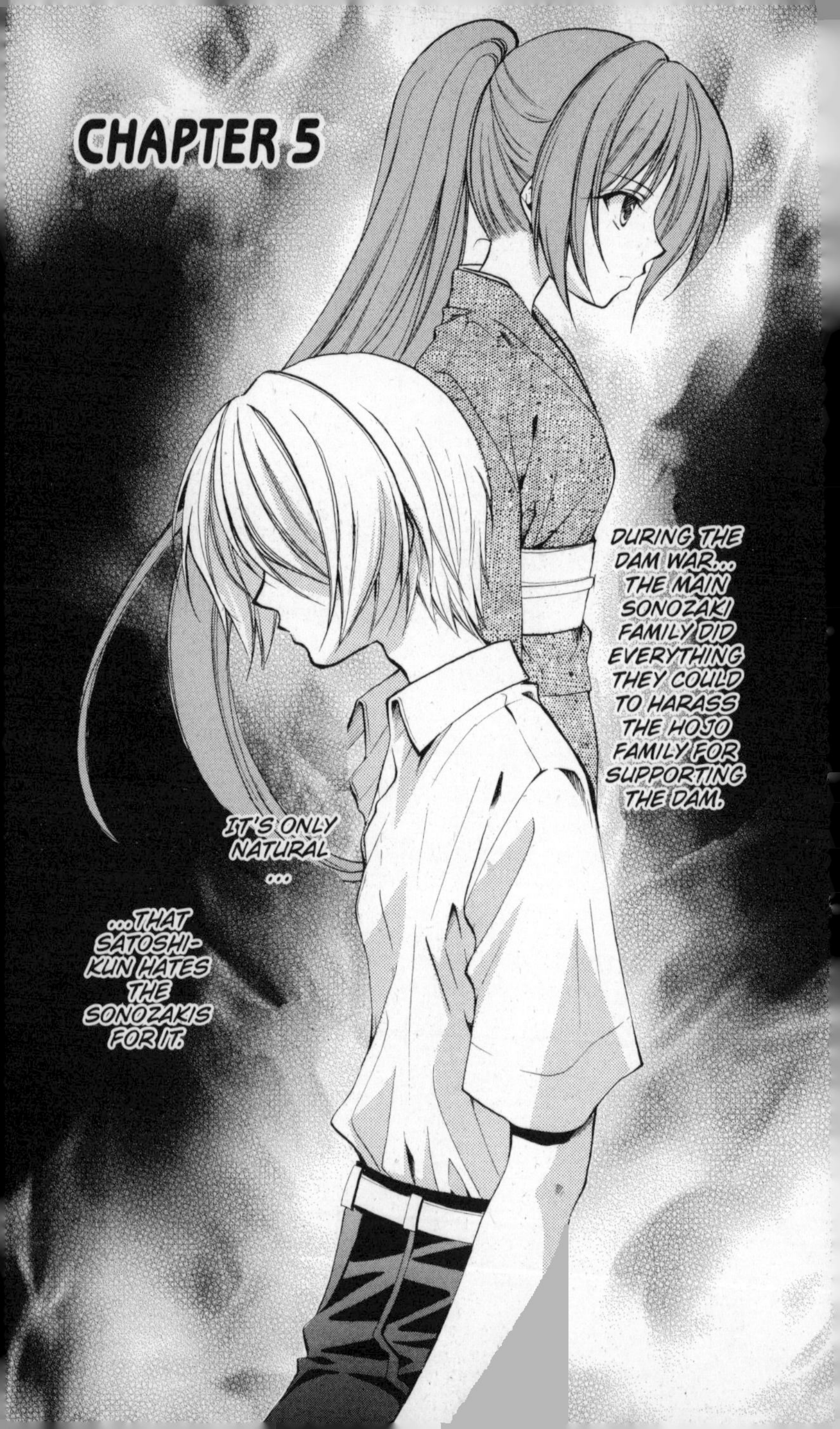
CHAPTER 5
DURING THE DAM WAR... THE MAIN SONOZAKI FAMILY DID EVERYTHING THEY COULD TO HARASS THE HOJO FAMILY FOR SUPPORTING THE DAM.
IT'S ONLY NATURAL...
...THAT SATOSHI-KUN HATES THE SONOZAKIS FOR IT.

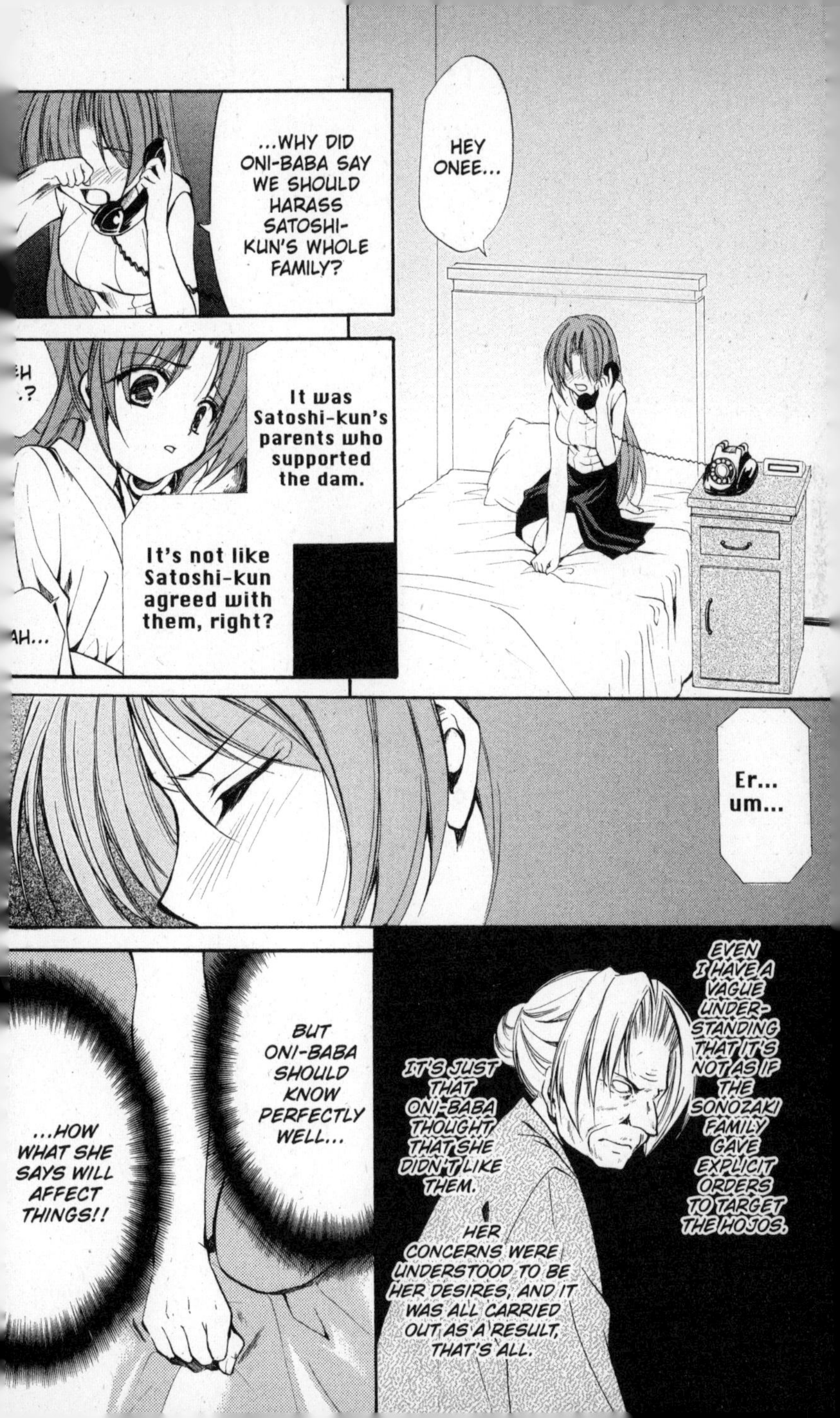
HEY ONEE...
...WHY DID ONI-BABA SAY WE SHOULD HARASS SATOSHI-KUN'S WHOLE FAMILY?
It was Satoshi-kun's parents who supported the dam.
It's not like Satoshi-kun agreed with them, right?
Er... um...
EVEN I HAVE A VAGUE UNDER-STANDING THAT IT'S NOT AS IF THE SONOZAKI FAMILY GAVE EXPLICIT ORDERS TO TARGET THE HOJOS.
IT'S JUST THAT ONI-BABA THOUGHT THAT SHE DIDN'T LIKE THEM.
HER CONCERNS WERE UNDERSTOOD TO BE HER DESIRES, AND IT WAS ALL CARRIED OUT AS A RESULT, THAT'S ALL.
BUT ONI-BABA SHOULD KNOW PERFECTLY WELL...
...HOW WHAT SHE SAYS WILL AFFECT THINGS!!

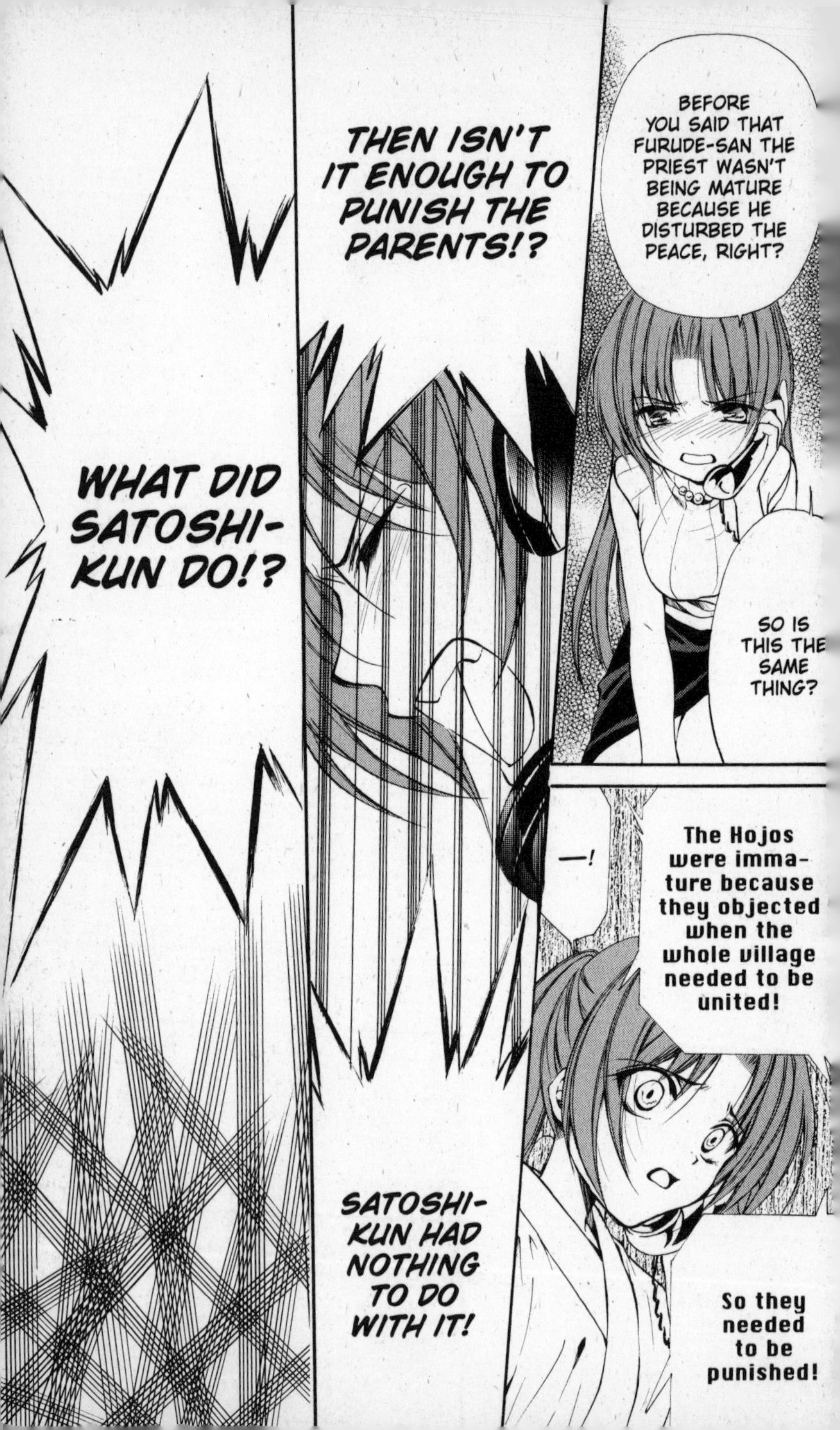
BEFORE YOU SAID THAT FURUDE-SAN THE PRIEST WASN'T BEING MATURE BECAUSE HE DISTURBED THE PEACE, RIGHT?
SO IS THIS THE SAME THING?
—!
The Hojos were immature because they objected when the whole village needed to be united!
So they needed to be punished!
THEN ISN'T IT ENOUGH TO PUNISH THE PARENTS!?
SATOSHI-KUN HAD NOTHING TO DO WITH IT!
WHAT DID SATOSHI-KUN DO!?

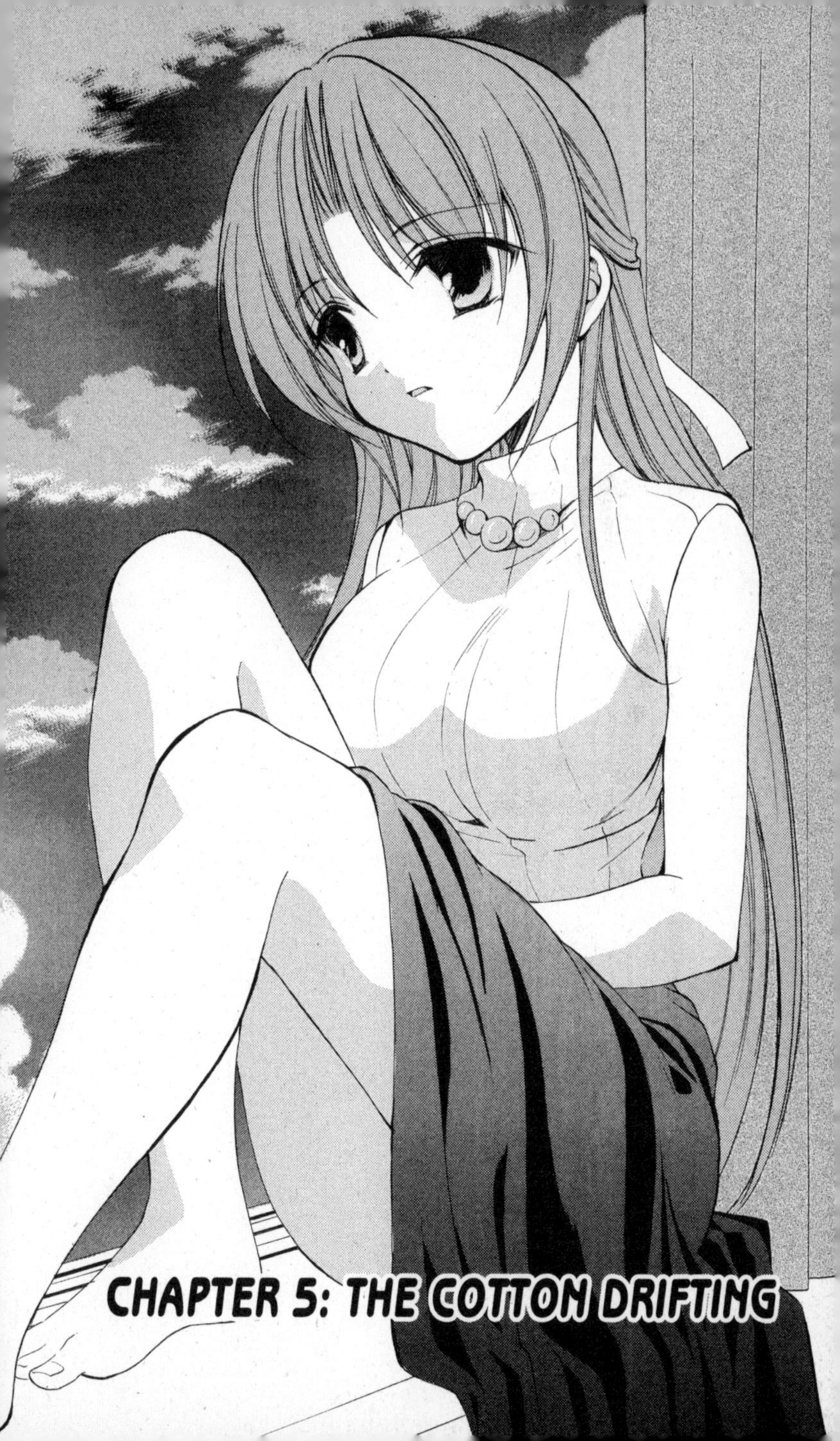
CHAPTER 5: THE COTTON DRIFTING

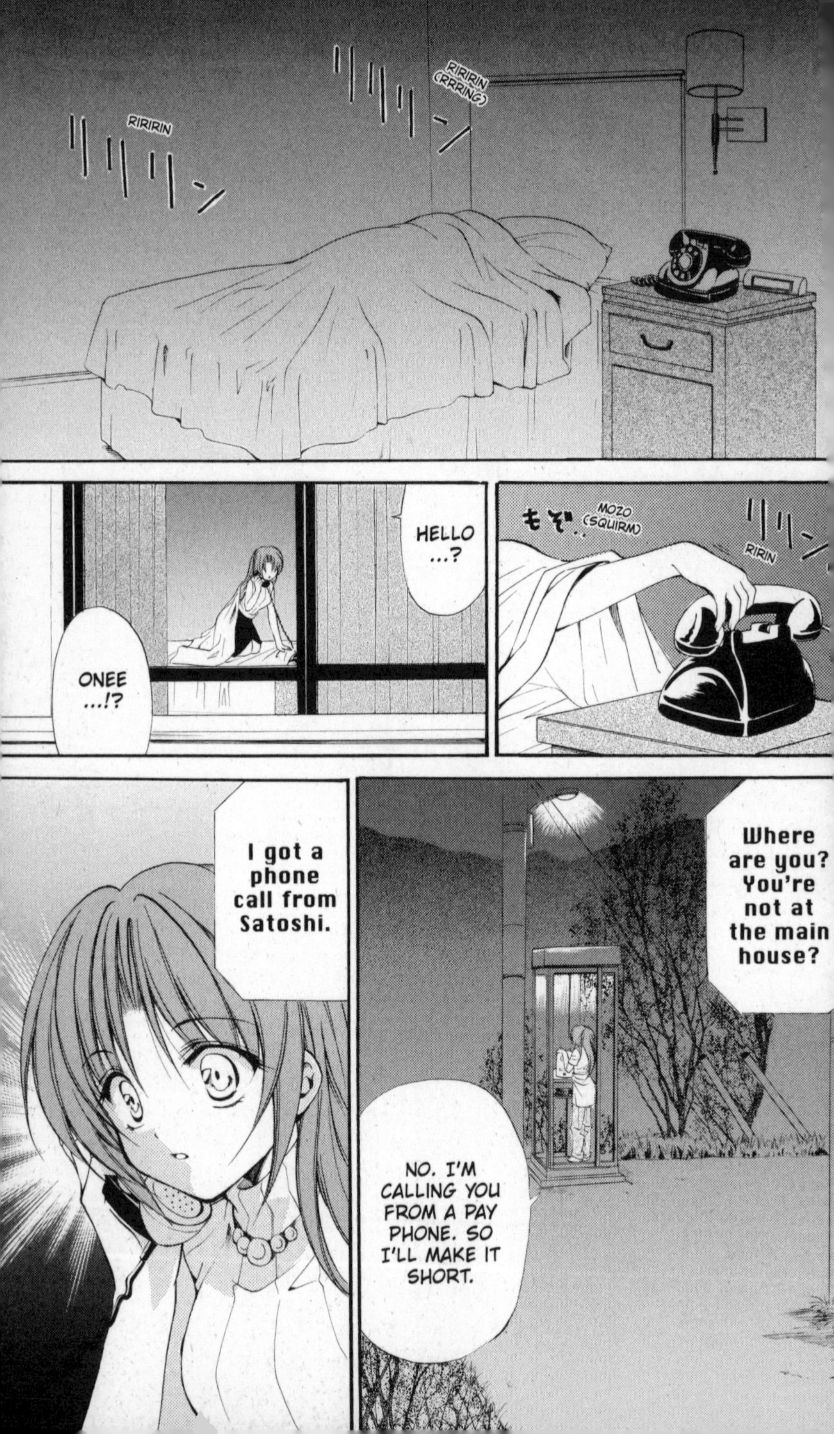
RIRIRIN (RRRING)
RIRIRIN
もぞ..
MOZO (SQUIRM)
RIRIN
HELLO ...?
ONEE ...!?
Where are you? You're not at the main house?
NO. I'M CALLING YOU FROM A PAY PHONE. SO I'LL MAKE IT SHORT.
I got a phone call from Satoshi.

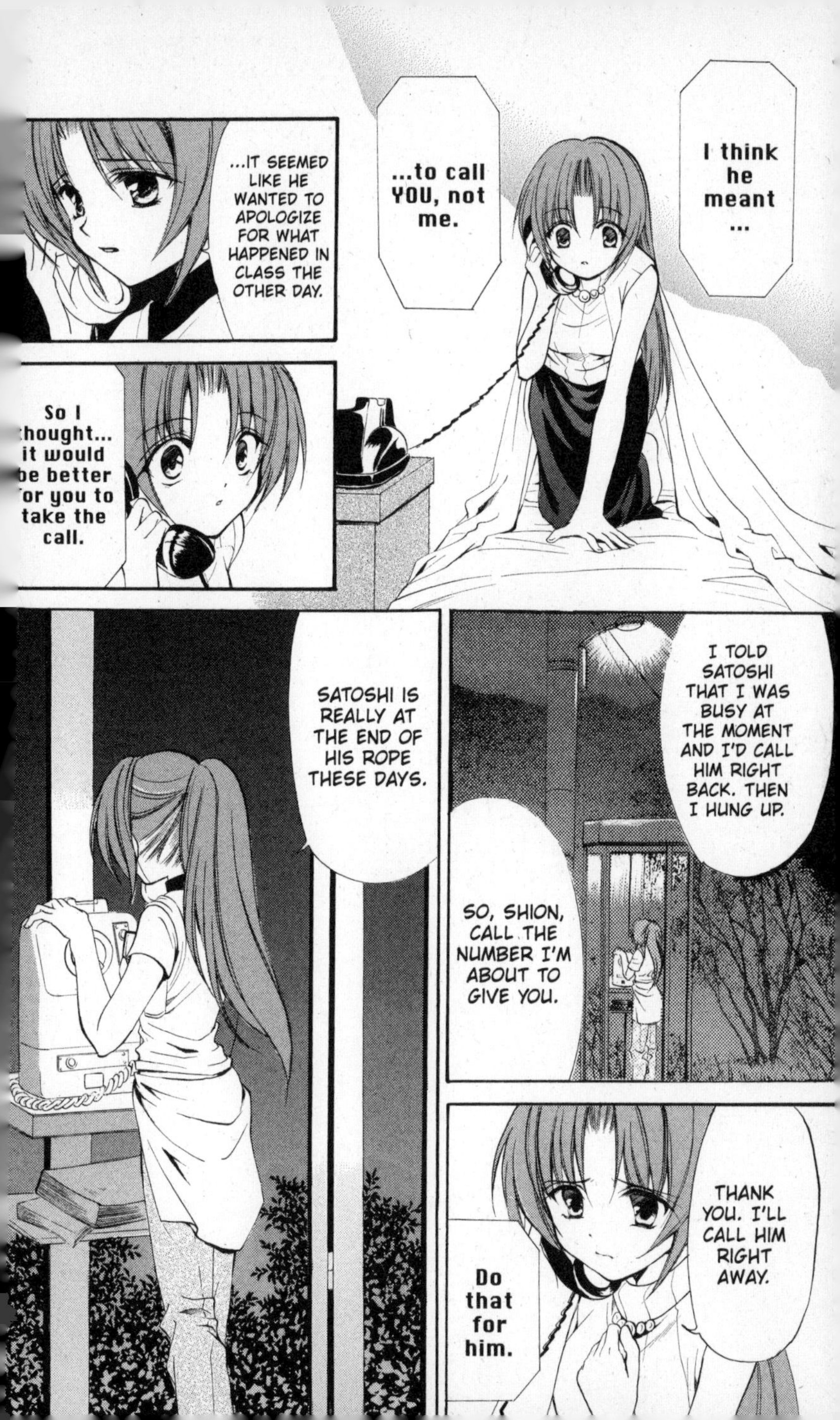

I think he meant ...
...to call YOU, not me.
...IT SEEMED LIKE HE WANTED TO APOLOGIZE FOR WHAT HAPPENED IN CLASS THE OTHER DAY.
So I thought... it would be better for you to take the call.
I TOLD SATOSHI THAT I WAS BUSY AT THE MOMENT AND I'D CALL HIM RIGHT BACK. THEN I HUNG UP.
SO, SHION, CALL THE NUMBER I'M ABOUT TO GIVE YOU.
THANK YOU. I'LL CALL HIM RIGHT AWAY.
Do that for him.
SATOSHI IS REALLY AT THE END OF HIS ROPE THESE DAYS.

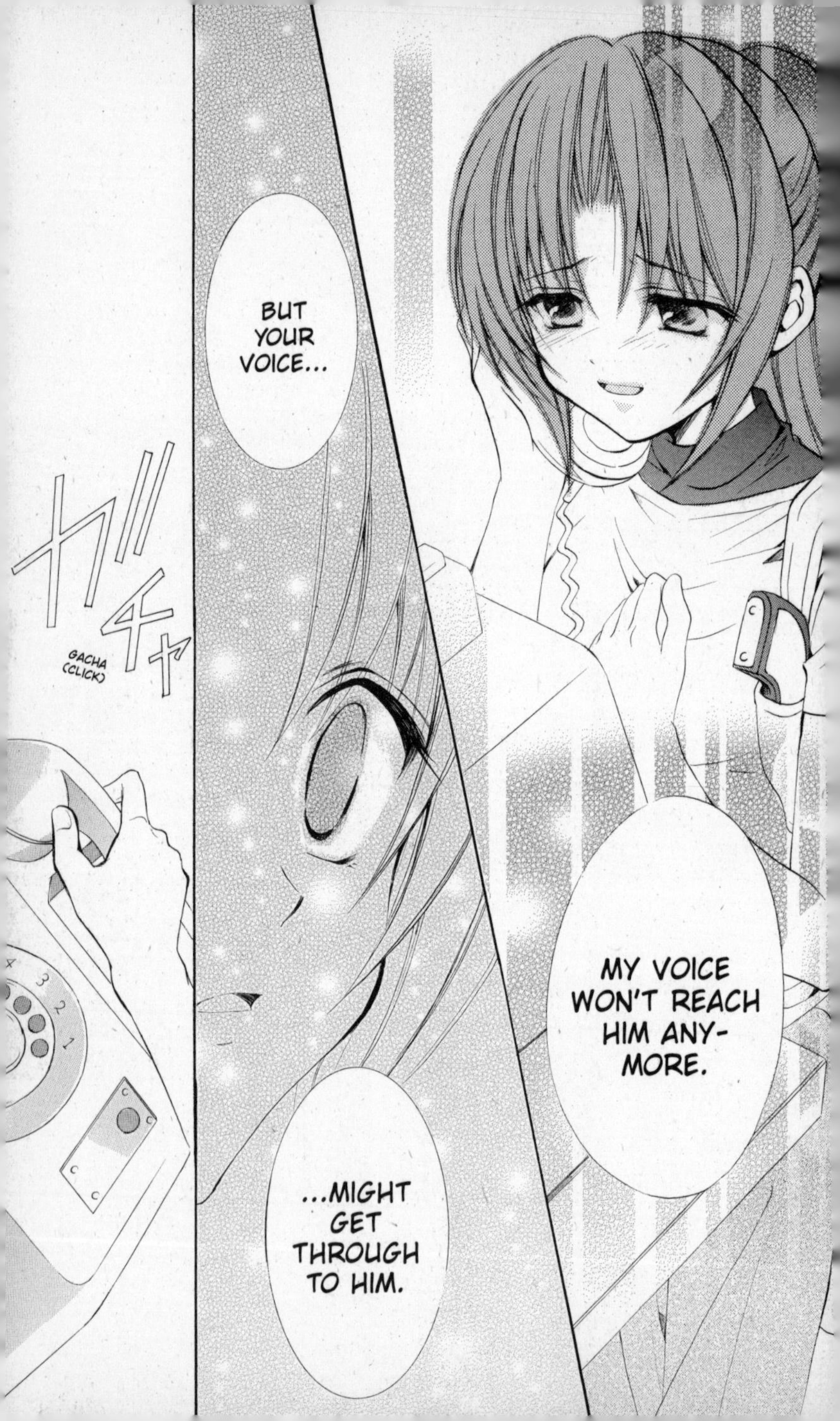
MY VOICE WON'T REACH HIM ANY-MORE.
BUT YOUR VOICE...
...MIGHT GET THROUGH TO HIM.
ガチャ
GACHA (CLICK)

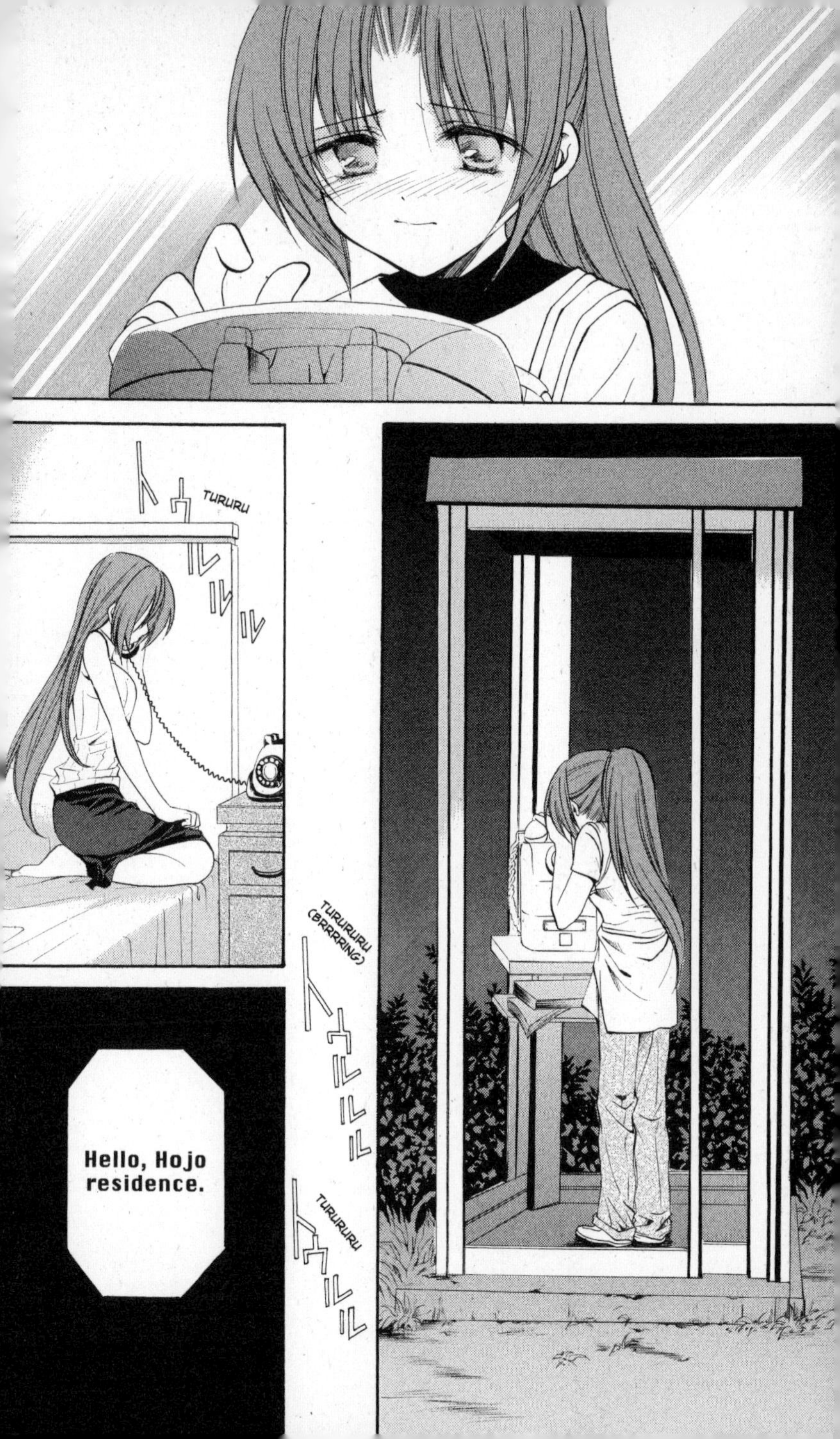
TURURURU (BRRRRING)
TURURURU
TURURU
Hello, Hojo residence.

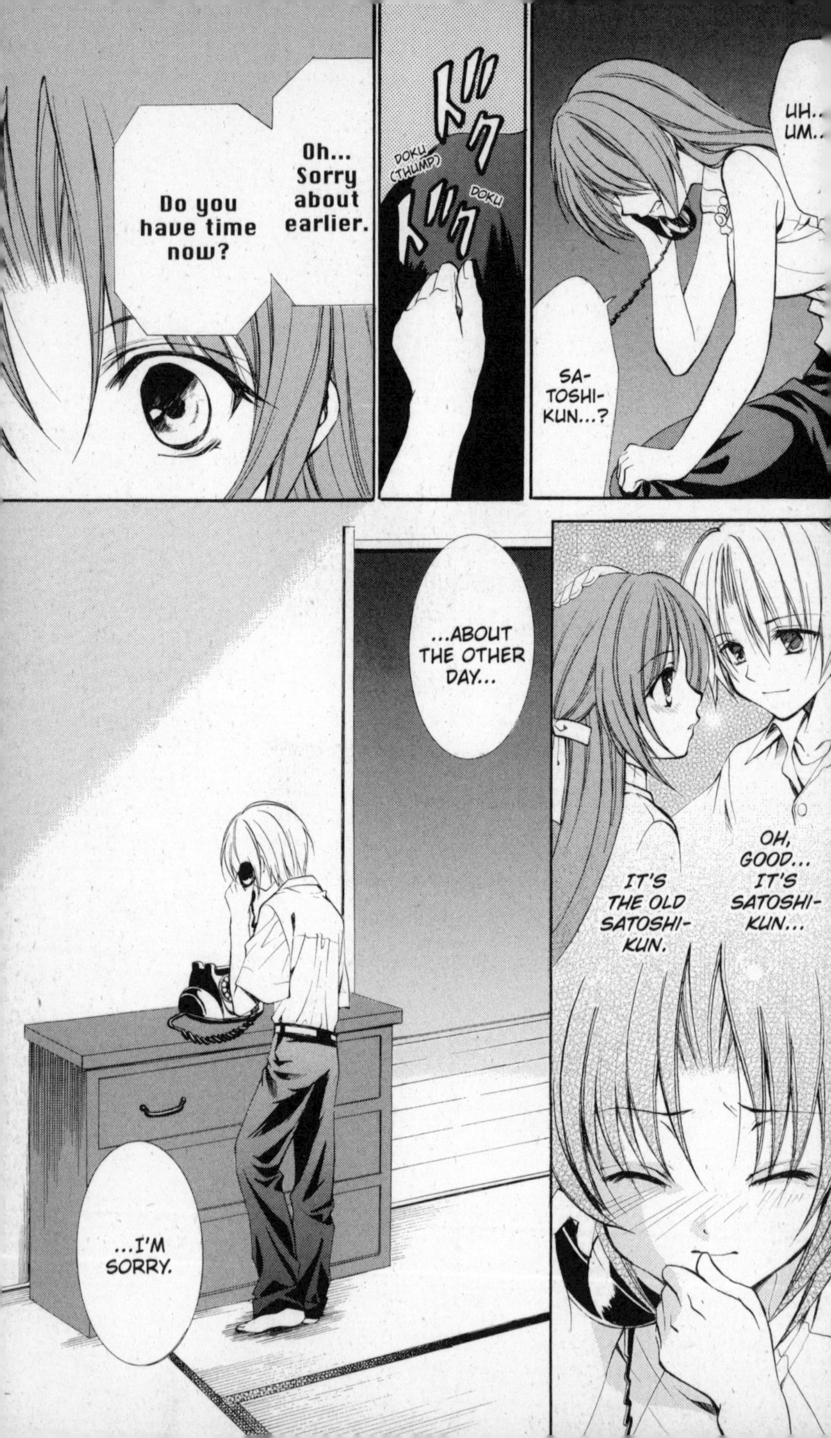
UH... UM...
SA-TOSHI-KUN...?
ドク
DOKU (THUMP)
ドク
DOKU
Oh... Sorry about earlier.
Do you have time now?
OH, GOOD... IT'S SATOSHI-KUN...
IT'S THE OLD SATOSHI-KUN.
...ABOUT THE OTHER DAY...
...I'M SORRY.

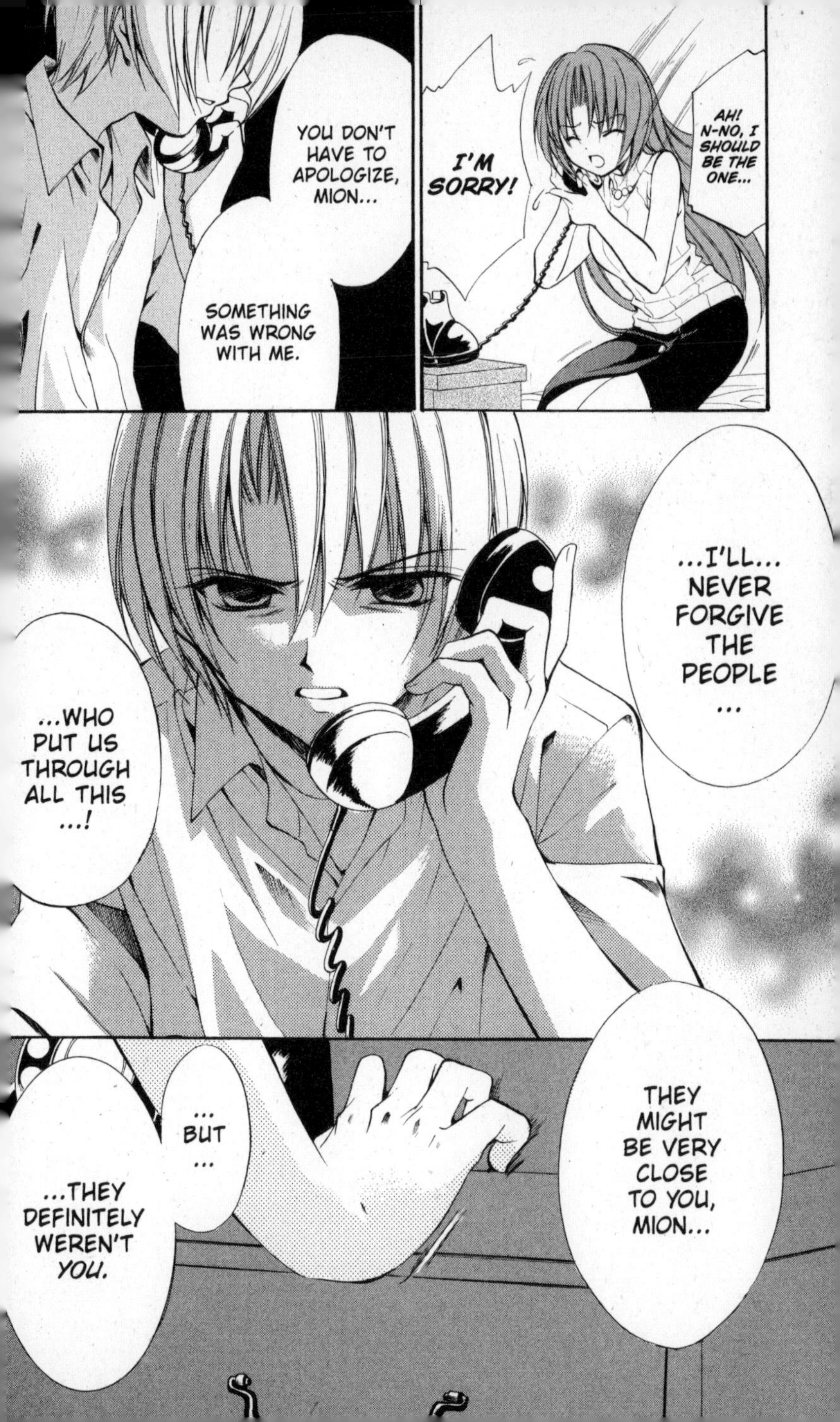
AH! N-NO, I SHOULD BE THE ONE...
I'M SORRY!
YOU DON'T HAVE TO APOLOGIZE, MION...
SOMETHING WAS WRONG WITH ME.
...I'LL... NEVER FORGIVE THE PEOPLE ...
...WHO PUT US THROUGH ALL THIS ...!
THEY MIGHT BE VERY CLOSE TO YOU, MION...
... BUT ...
...THEY DEFINITELY WEREN'T *YOU*.

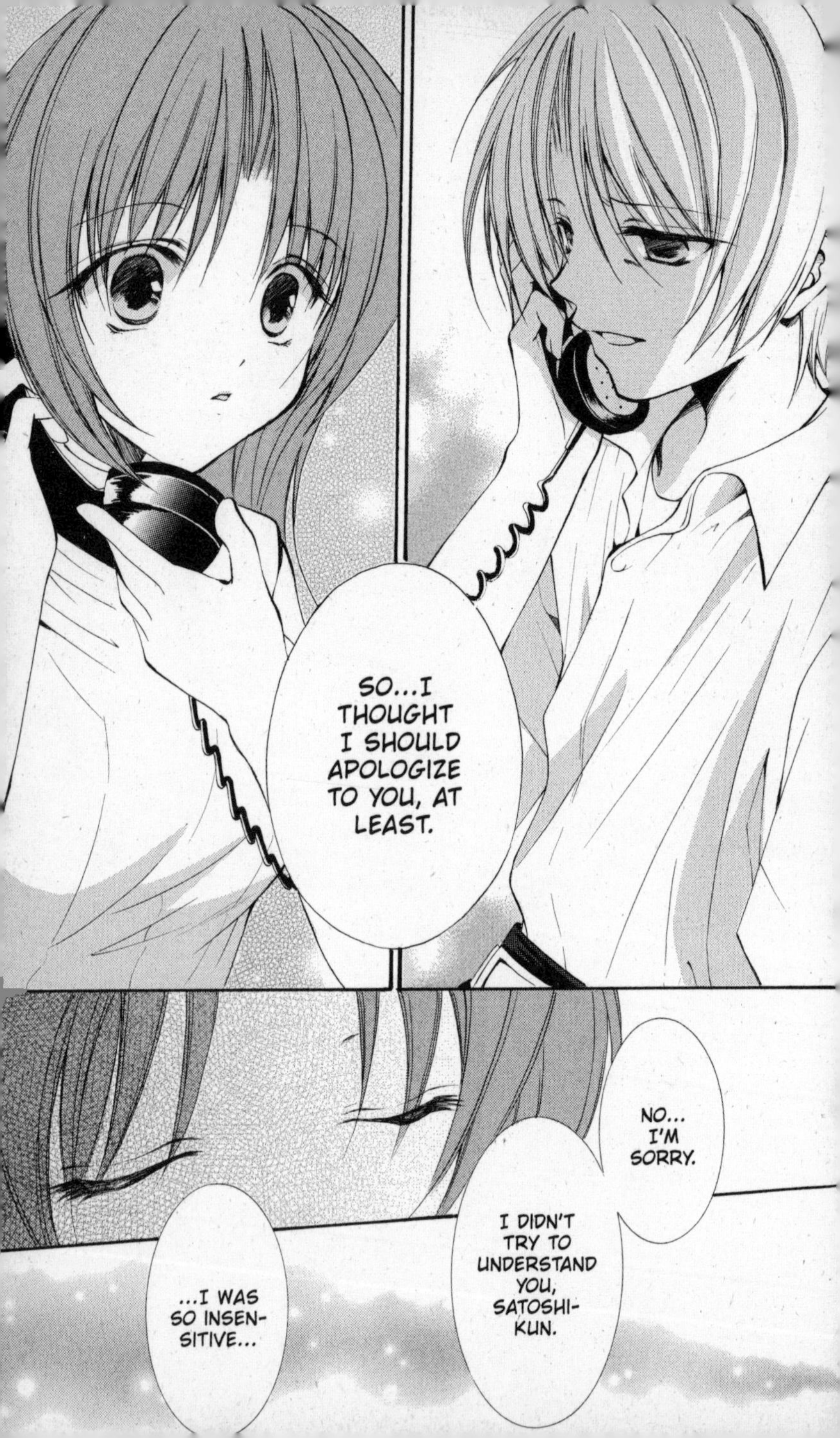
SO...I THOUGHT I SHOULD APOLOGIZE TO YOU, AT LEAST.
NO... I'M SORRY.
I DIDN'T TRY TO UNDERSTAND YOU, SATOSHI-KUN.
...I WAS SO INSENSITIVE...

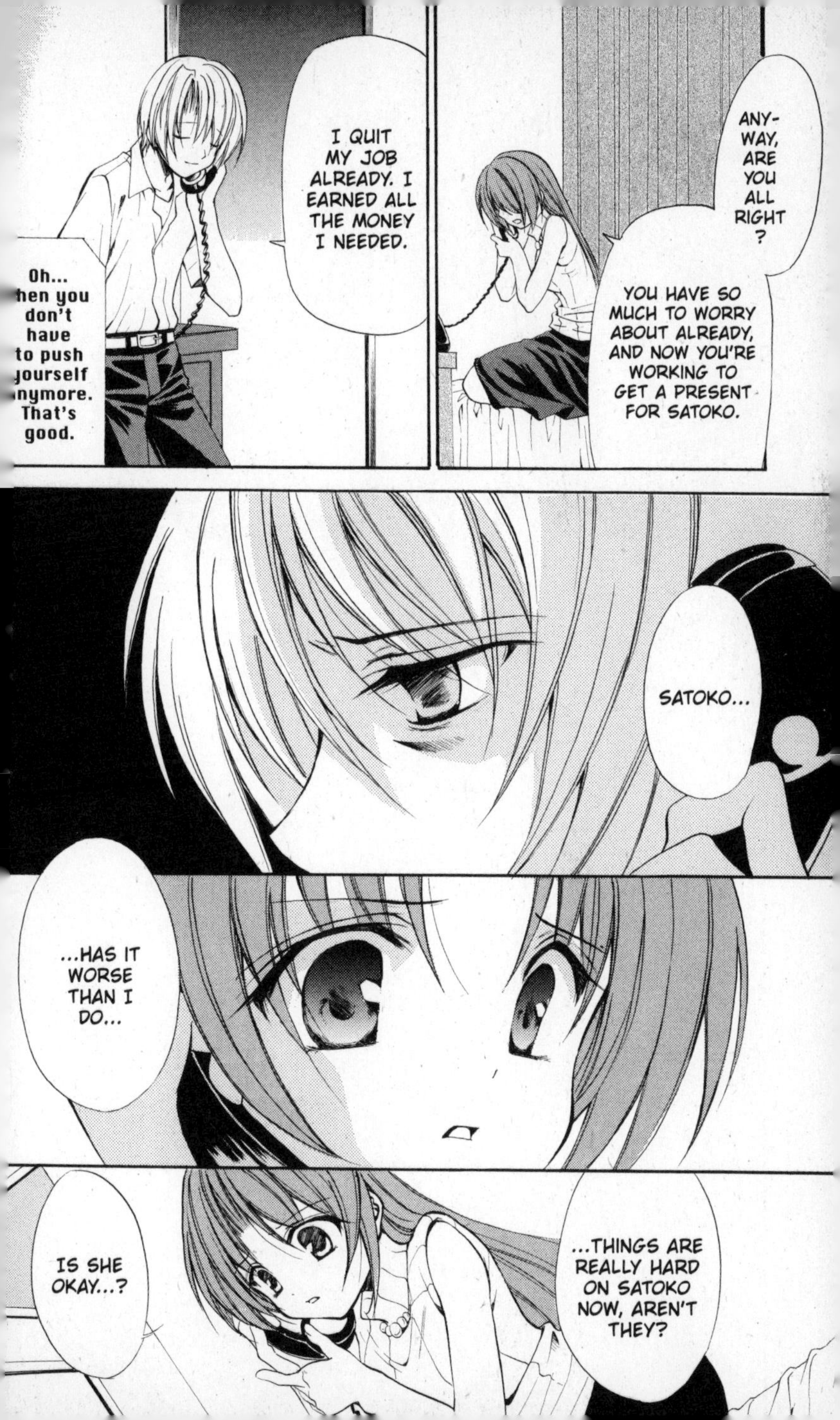
ANY-WAY, ARE YOU ALL RIGHT?
YOU HAVE SO MUCH TO WORRY ABOUT ALREADY, AND NOW YOU'RE WORKING TO GET A PRESENT FOR SATOKO.
I QUIT MY JOB ALREADY. I EARNED ALL THE MONEY I NEEDED.
Oh... hen you don't have to push yourself nymore. That's good.
SATOKO...
...HAS IT WORSE THAN I DO...
...THINGS ARE REALLY HARD ON SATOKO NOW, AREN'T THEY?
IS SHE OKAY...?

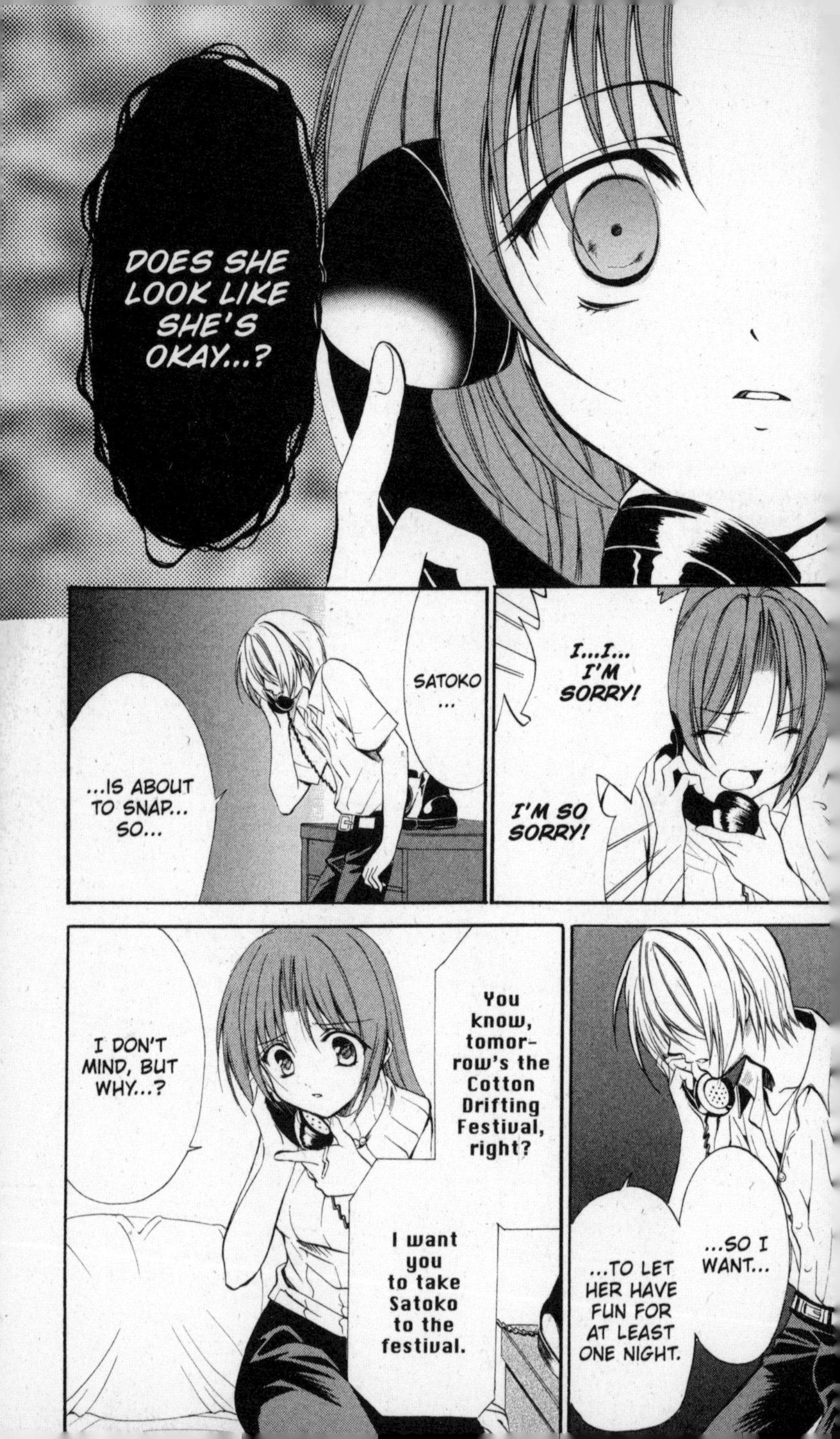
DOES SHE LOOK LIKE SHE'S OKAY...?
I...I... I'M SORRY!
I'M SO SORRY!
SATOKO...
...IS ABOUT TO SNAP... SO...
...SO I WANT...
...TO LET HER HAVE FUN FOR AT LEAST ONE NIGHT.
You know, tomorrow's the Cotton Drifting Festival, right?
I want you to take Satoko to the festival.
I DON'T MIND, BUT WHY...?

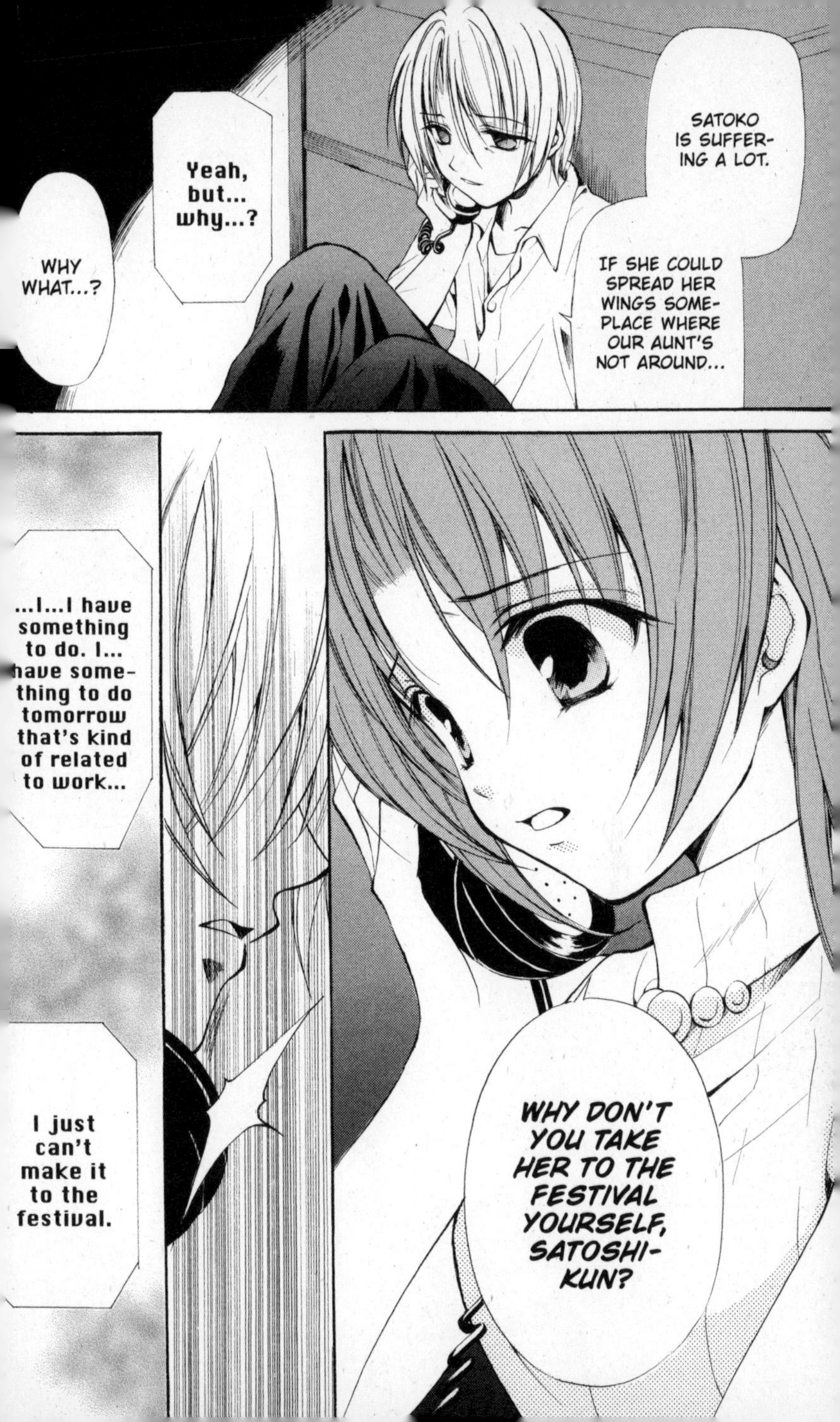

SATOKO IS SUFFERING A LOT.
IF SHE COULD SPREAD HER WINGS SOMEPLACE WHERE OUR AUNT'S NOT AROUND...
Yeah, but... why...?
WHY WHAT...?
WHY DON'T YOU TAKE HER TO THE FESTIVAL YOURSELF, SATOSHI-KUN?
...I...I have something to do. I... have something to do tomorrow that's kind of related to work...
I just can't make it to the festival.

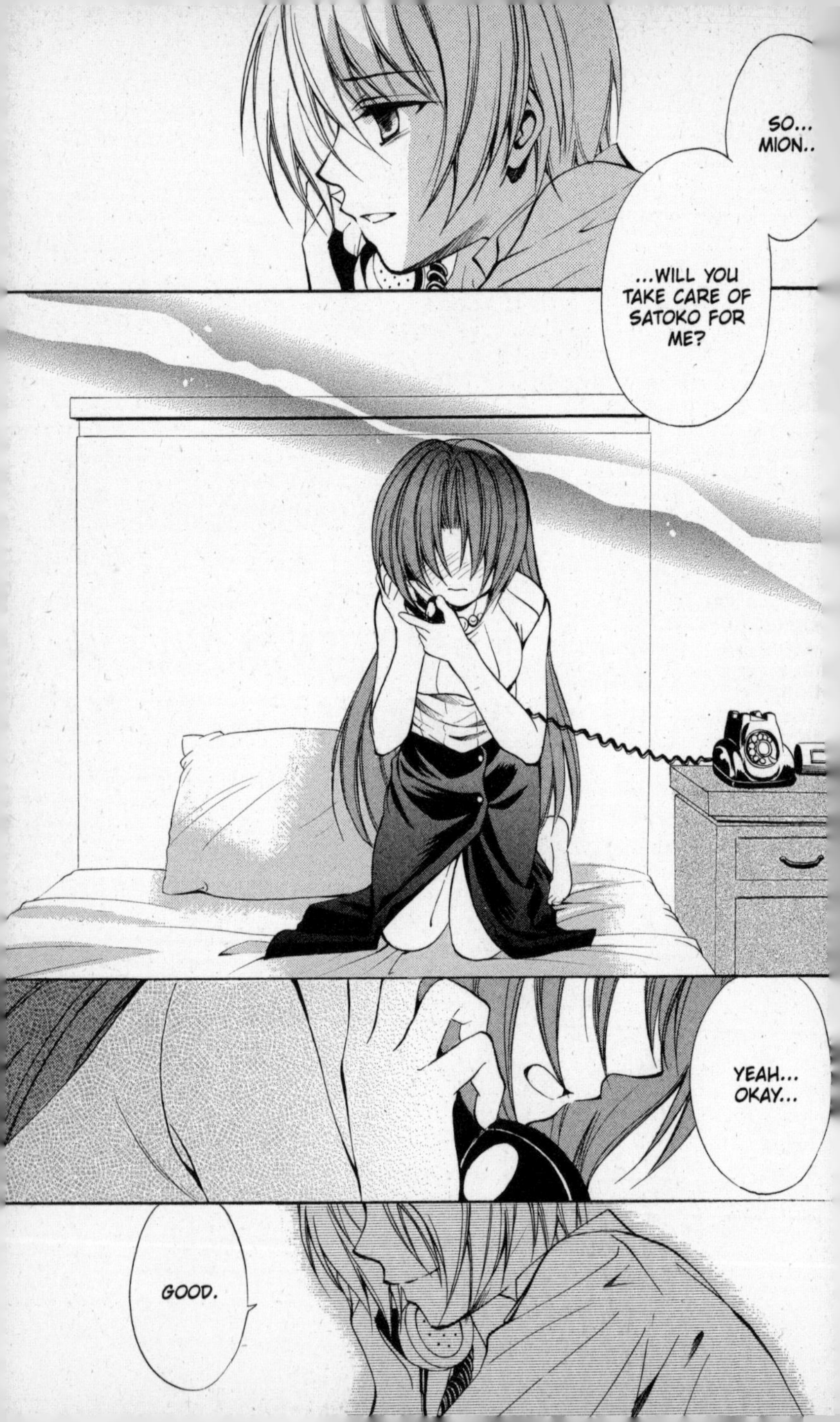
SO... MION..
...WILL YOU TAKE CARE OF SATOKO FOR ME?
YEAH... OKAY...
GOOD.

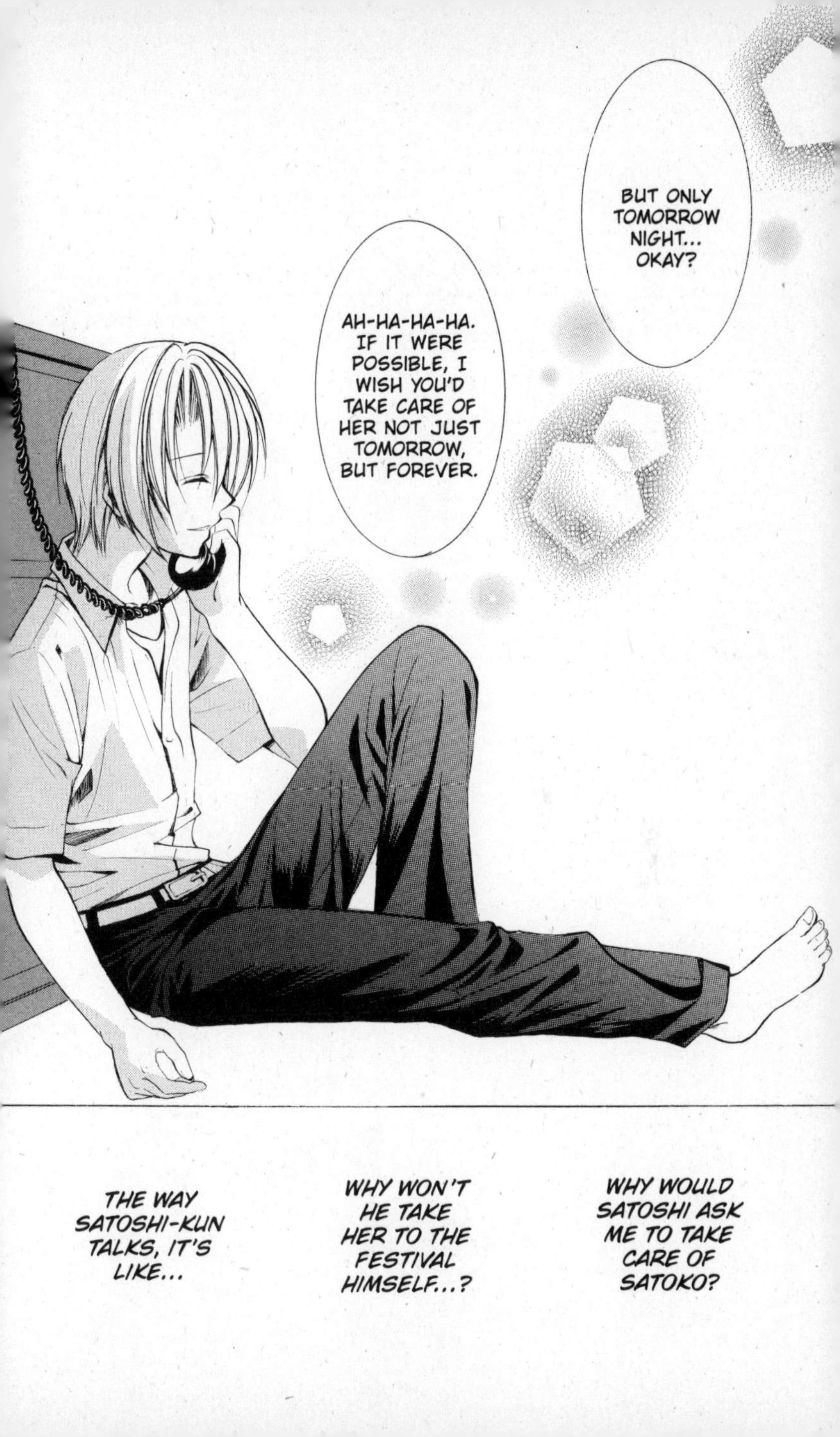
BUT ONLY TOMORROW NIGHT... OKAY?
AH-HA-HA-HA. IF IT WERE POSSIBLE, I WISH YOU'D TAKE CARE OF HER NOT JUST TOMORROW, BUT FOREVER.
WHY WOULD SATOSHI ASK ME TO TAKE CARE OF SATOKO?
WHY WON'T HE TAKE HER TO THE FESTIVAL HIMSELF...?
THE WAY SATOSHI-KUN TALKS, IT'S LIKE...

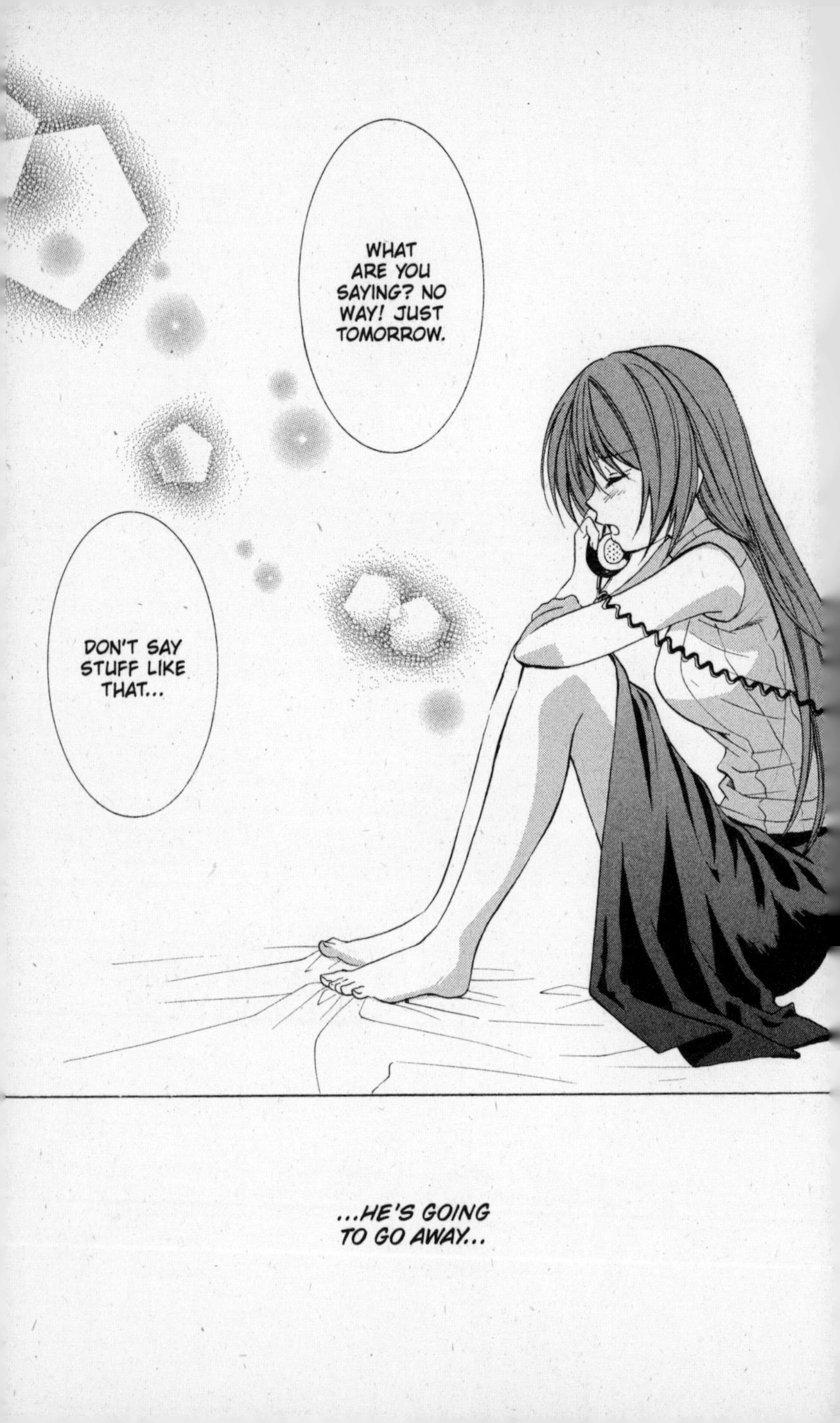
WHAT ARE YOU SAYING? NO WAY! JUST TOMORROW.
DON'T SAY STUFF LIKE THAT...
...HE'S GOING TO GO AWAY...

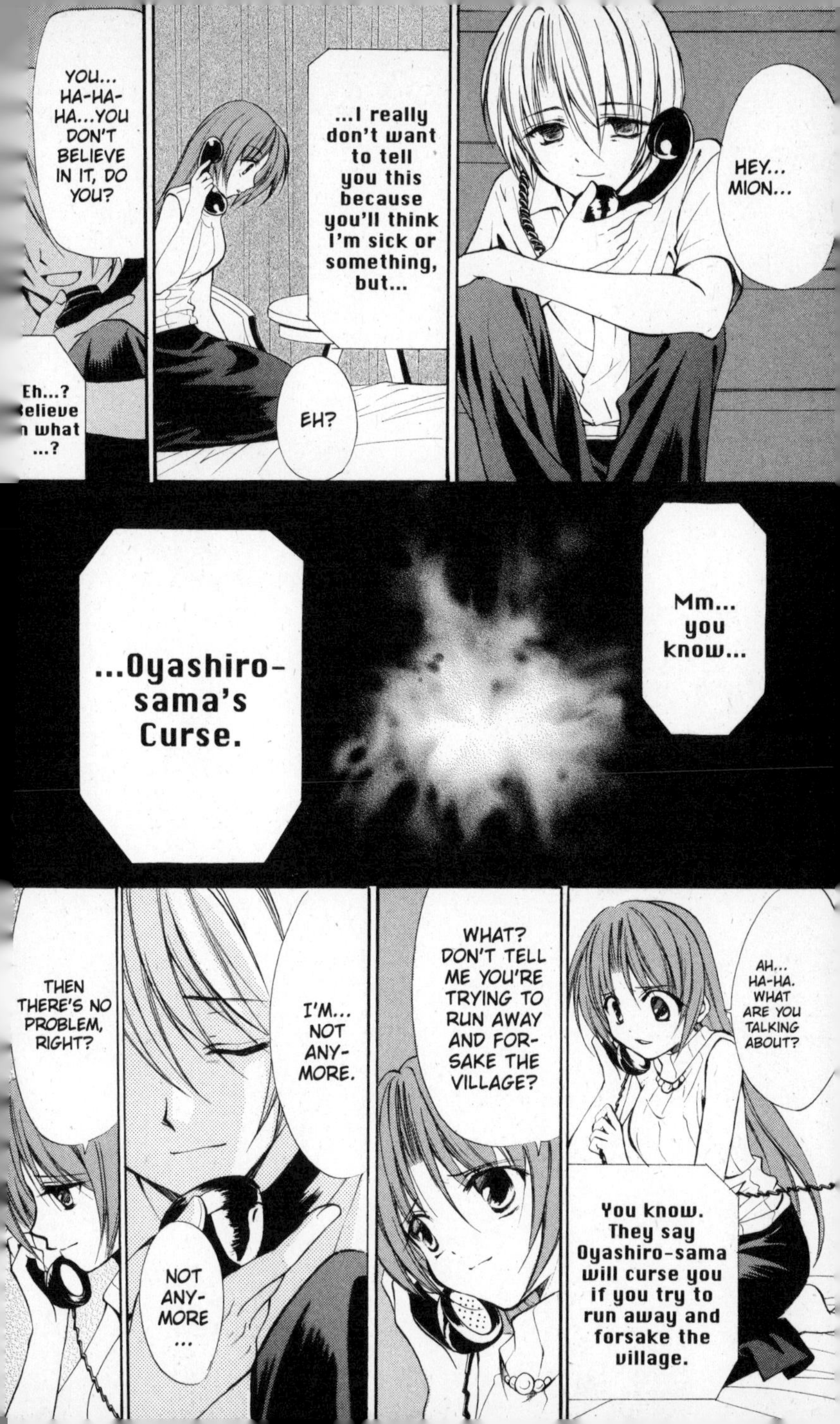
HEY... MION...
...I really don't want to tell you this because you'll think I'm sick or something, but...
EH?
YOU... HA-HA-HA...YOU DON'T BELIEVE IN IT, DO YOU?
Eh...? elieve n what ...?
Mm... you know...
...Oyashiro-sama's Curse.
AH... HA-HA. WHAT ARE YOU TALKING ABOUT?
You know. They say Oyashiro-sama will curse you if you try to run away and forsake the village.
WHAT? DON'T TELL ME YOU'RE TRYING TO RUN AWAY AND FOR-SAKE THE VILLAGE?
I'M... NOT ANY-MORE.
NOT ANY-MORE ...
THEN THERE'S NO PROBLEM, RIGHT?

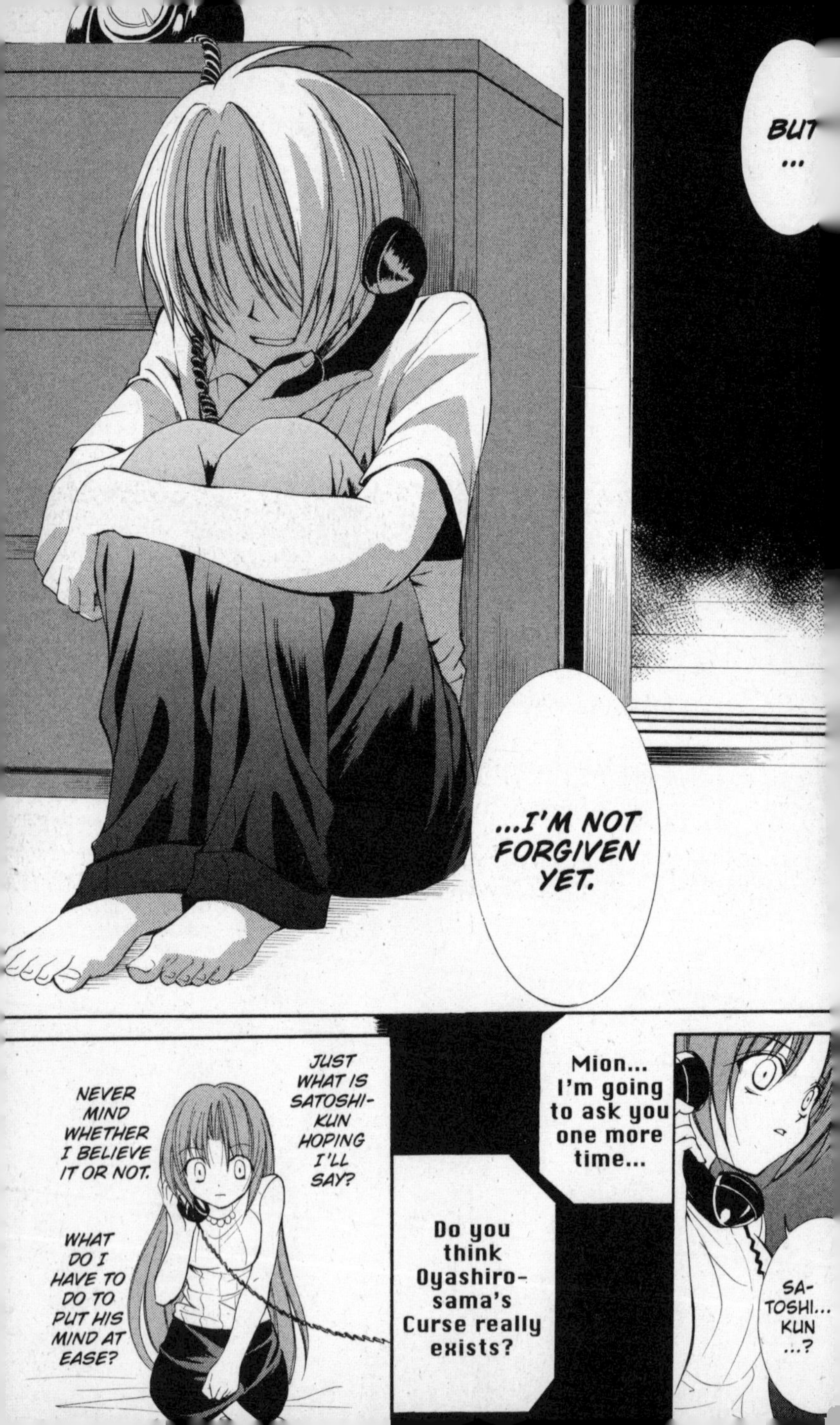
BUT...
...I'M NOT FORGIVEN YET.
SATOSHI...KUN...?
Mion... I'm going to ask you one more time...
Do you think Oyashiro-sama's Curse really exists?
JUST WHAT IS SATOSHI-KUN HOPING I'LL SAY?
NEVER MIND WHETHER I BELIEVE IT OR NOT.
WHAT DO I HAVE TO DO TO PUT HIS MIND AT EASE?

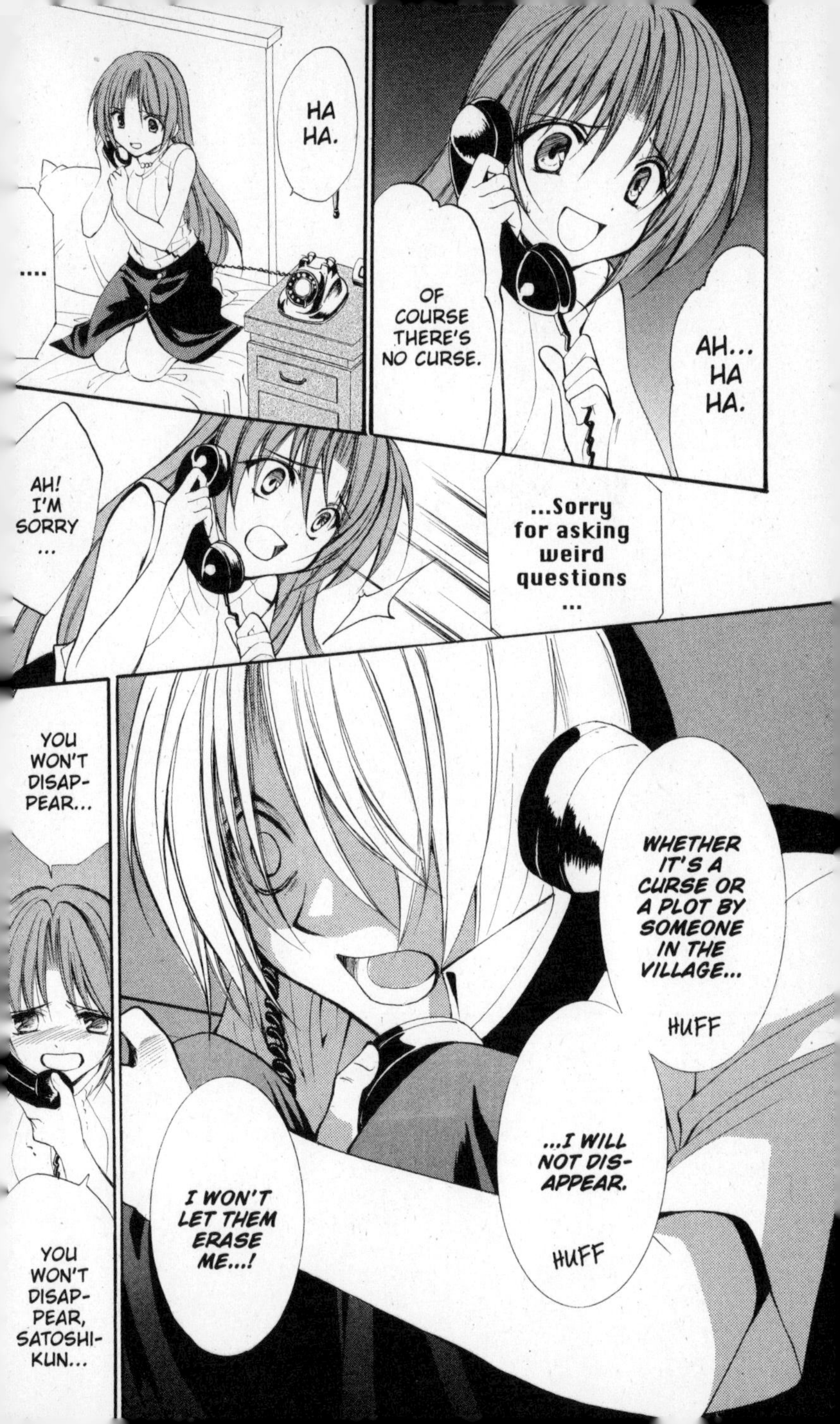
AH... HA HA.
OF COURSE THERE'S NO CURSE.
HA HA.
....
...Sorry for asking weird questions ...
AH! I'M SORRY ...
WHETHER IT'S A CURSE OR A PLOT BY SOMEONE IN THE VILLAGE...
HUFF
...I WILL NOT DIS-APPEAR.
HUFF
I WON'T LET THEM ERASE ME...!
YOU WON'T DISAP-PEAR...
YOU WON'T DISAP-PEAR, SATOSHI-KUN...

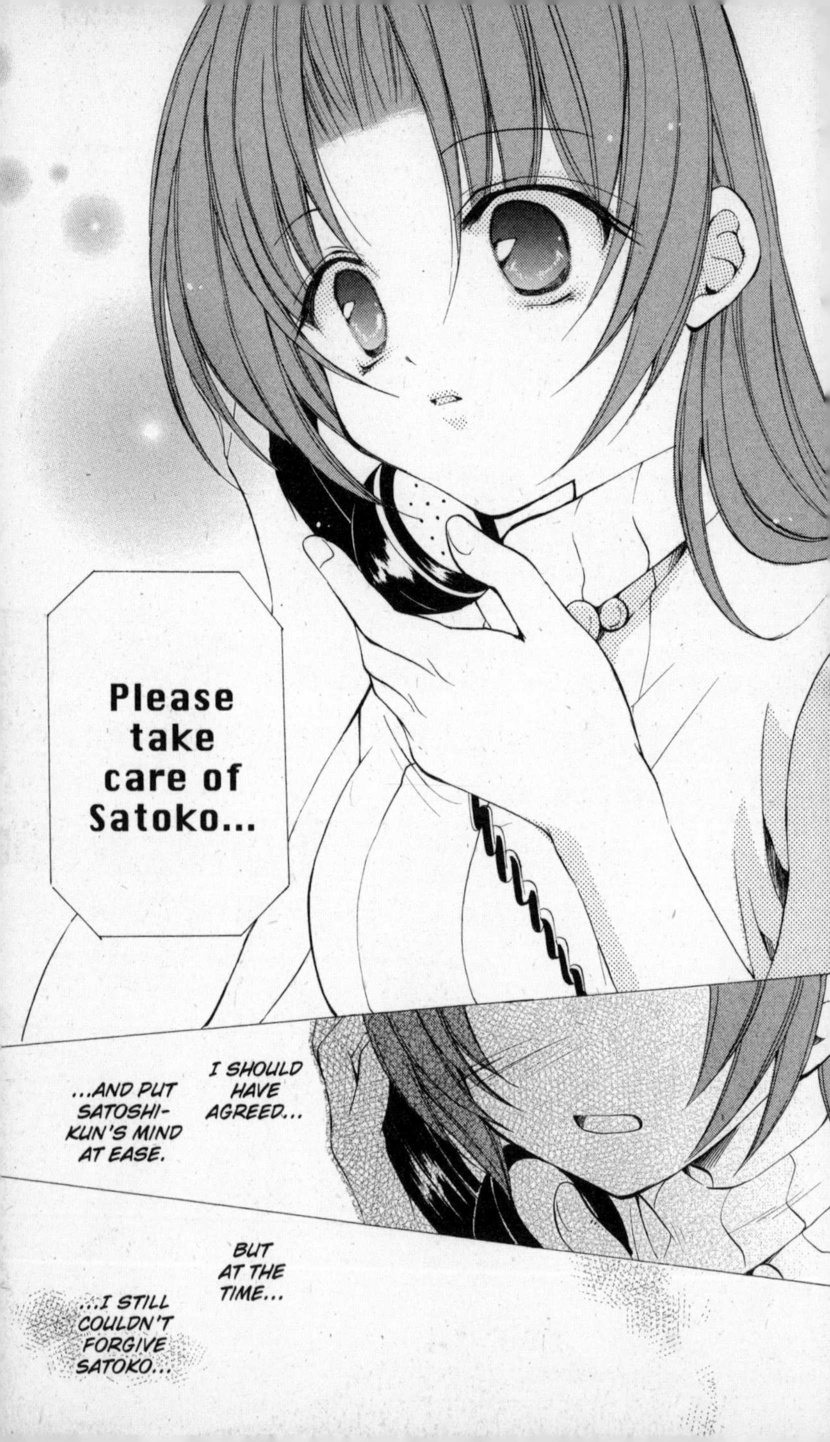
Please take care of Satoko...
I SHOULD HAVE AGREED...
...AND PUT SATOSHI-KUN'S MIND AT EASE.
BUT AT THE TIME...
...I STILL COULDN'T FORGIVE SATOKO...

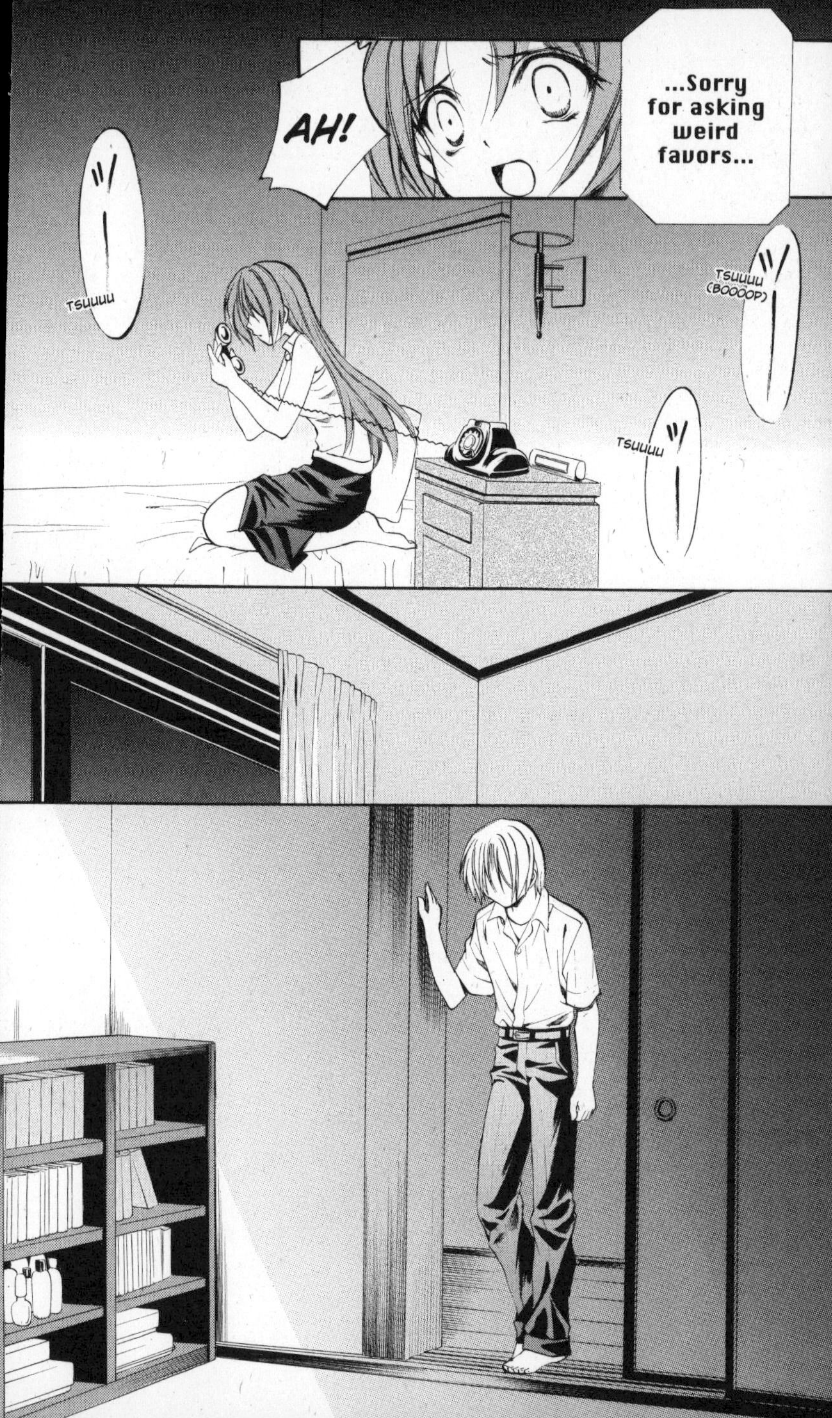
...Sorry for asking weird favors...
AH!
Tsuuuu (BOOOOP)
Tsuuuu
Tsuuuu

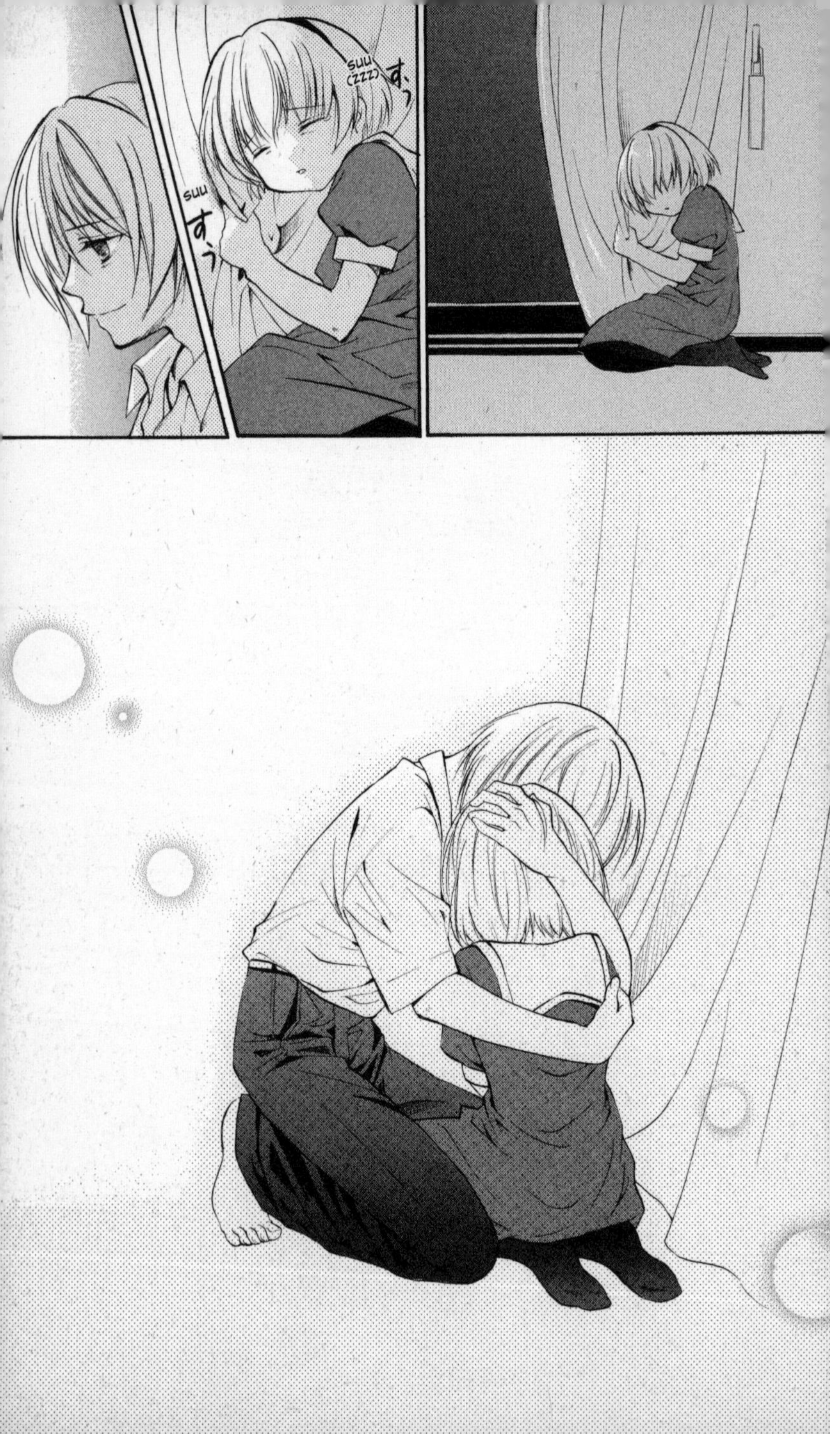
SUU (ZZZ) す
SUU す

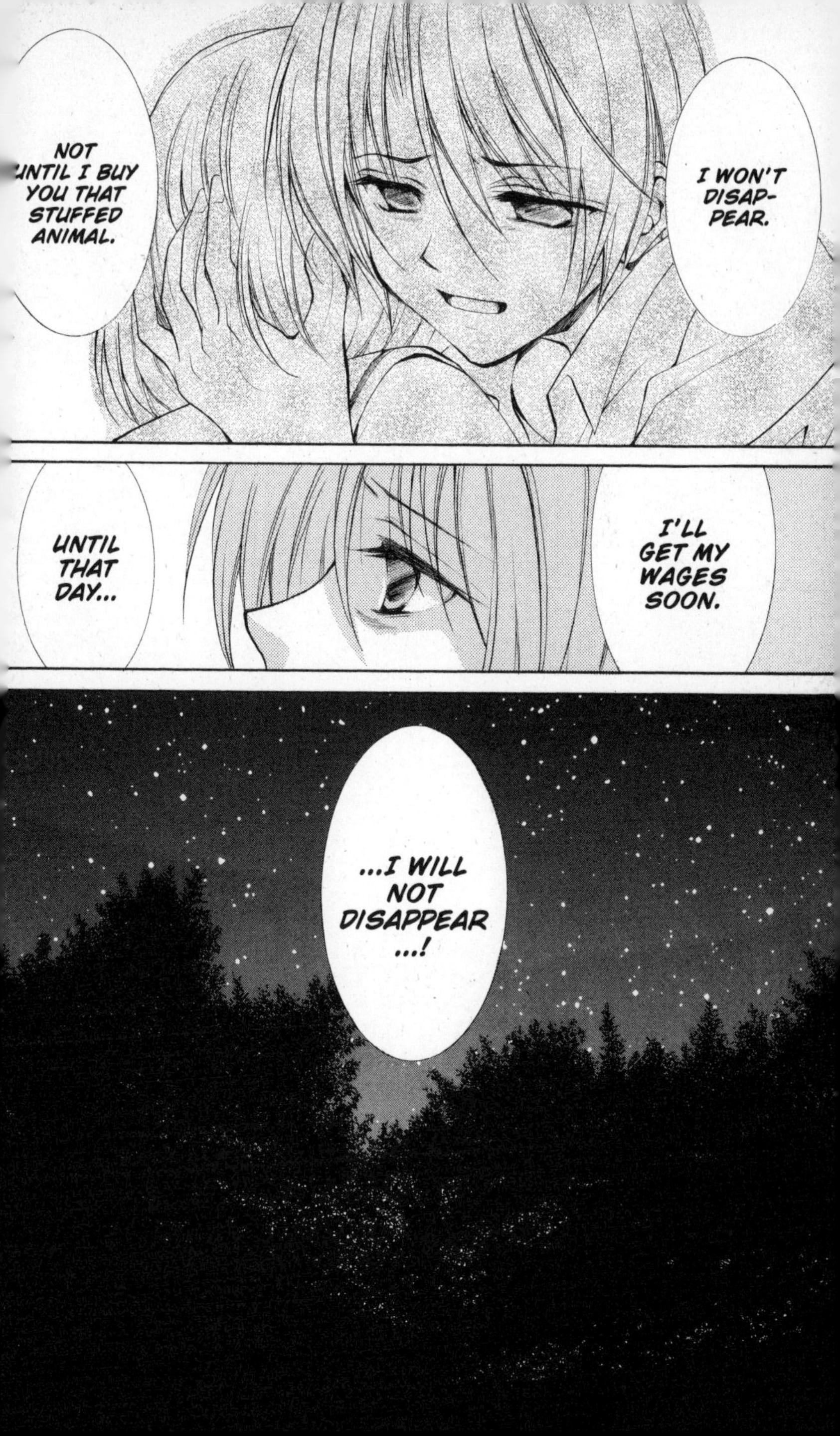
I WON'T DISAP-PEAR.
NOT UNTIL I BUY YOU THAT STUFFED ANIMAL.
I'LL GET MY WAGES SOON.
UNTIL THAT DAY...
...I WILL NOT DISAPPEAR ...!

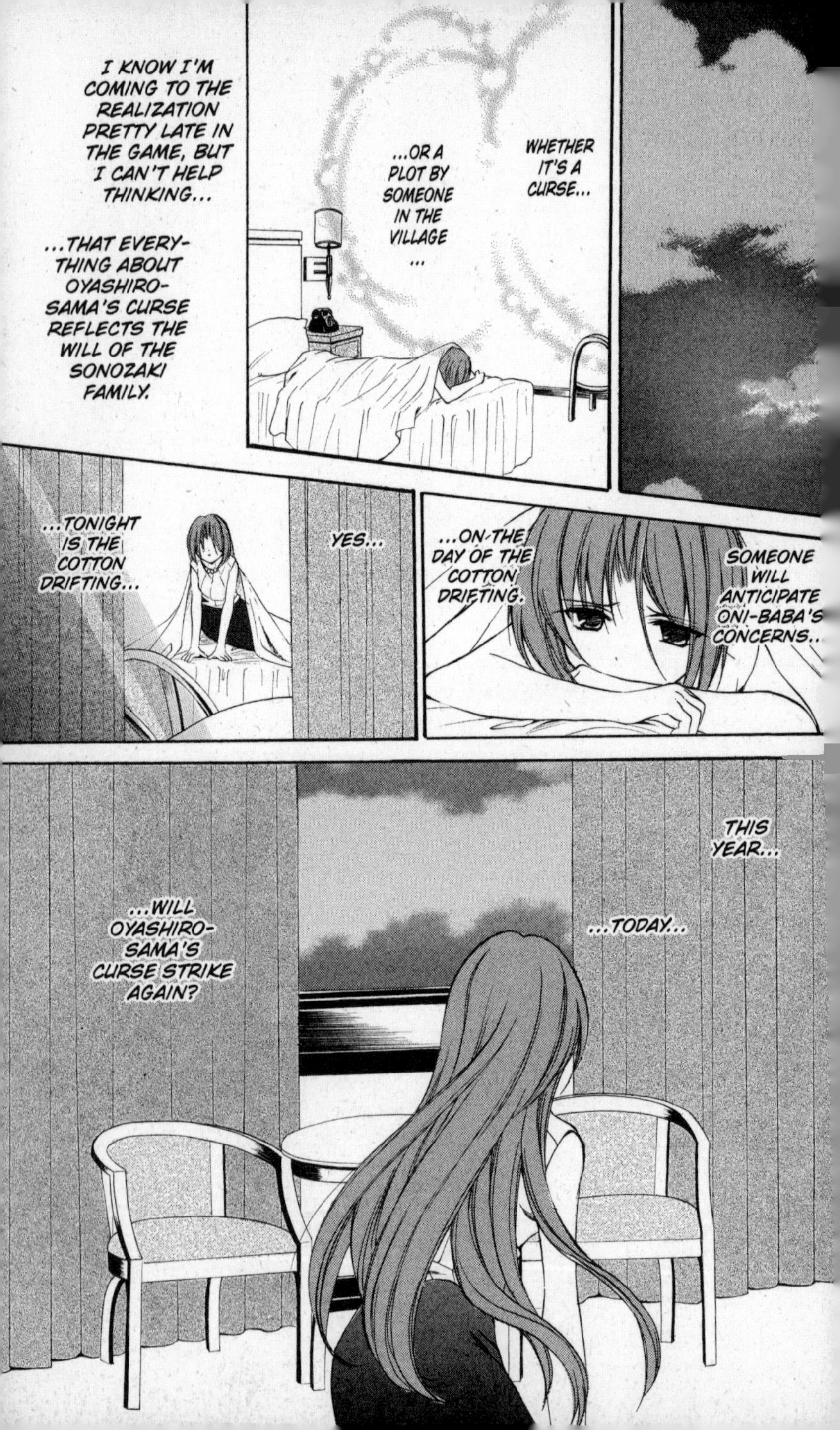
WHETHER IT'S A CURSE...
...OR A PLOT BY SOMEONE IN THE VILLAGE...
I KNOW I'M COMING TO THE REALIZATION PRETTY LATE IN THE GAME, BUT I CAN'T HELP THINKING...
...THAT EVERYTHING ABOUT OYASHIRO-SAMA'S CURSE REFLECTS THE WILL OF THE SONOZAKI FAMILY.
SOMEONE WILL ANTICIPATE ONI-BABA'S CONCERNS..
...ON THE DAY OF THE COTTON DRIFTING.
YES...
...TONIGHT IS THE COTTON DRIFTING...
THIS YEAR...
...TODAY...
...WILL OYASHIRO-SAMA'S CURSE STRIKE AGAIN?

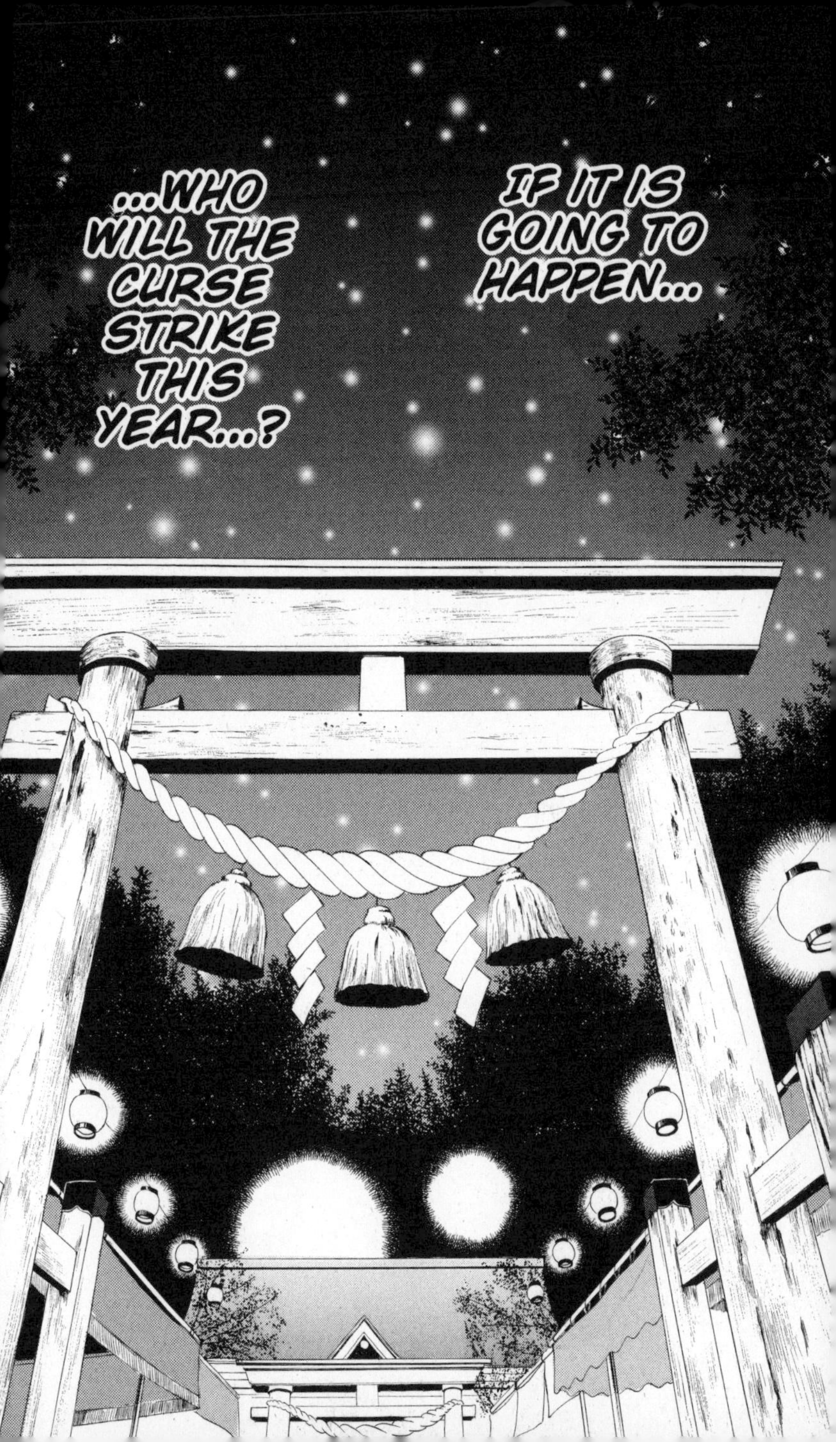
IF IT IS GOING TO HAPPEN...
...WHO WILL THE CURSE STRIKE THIS YEAR...?

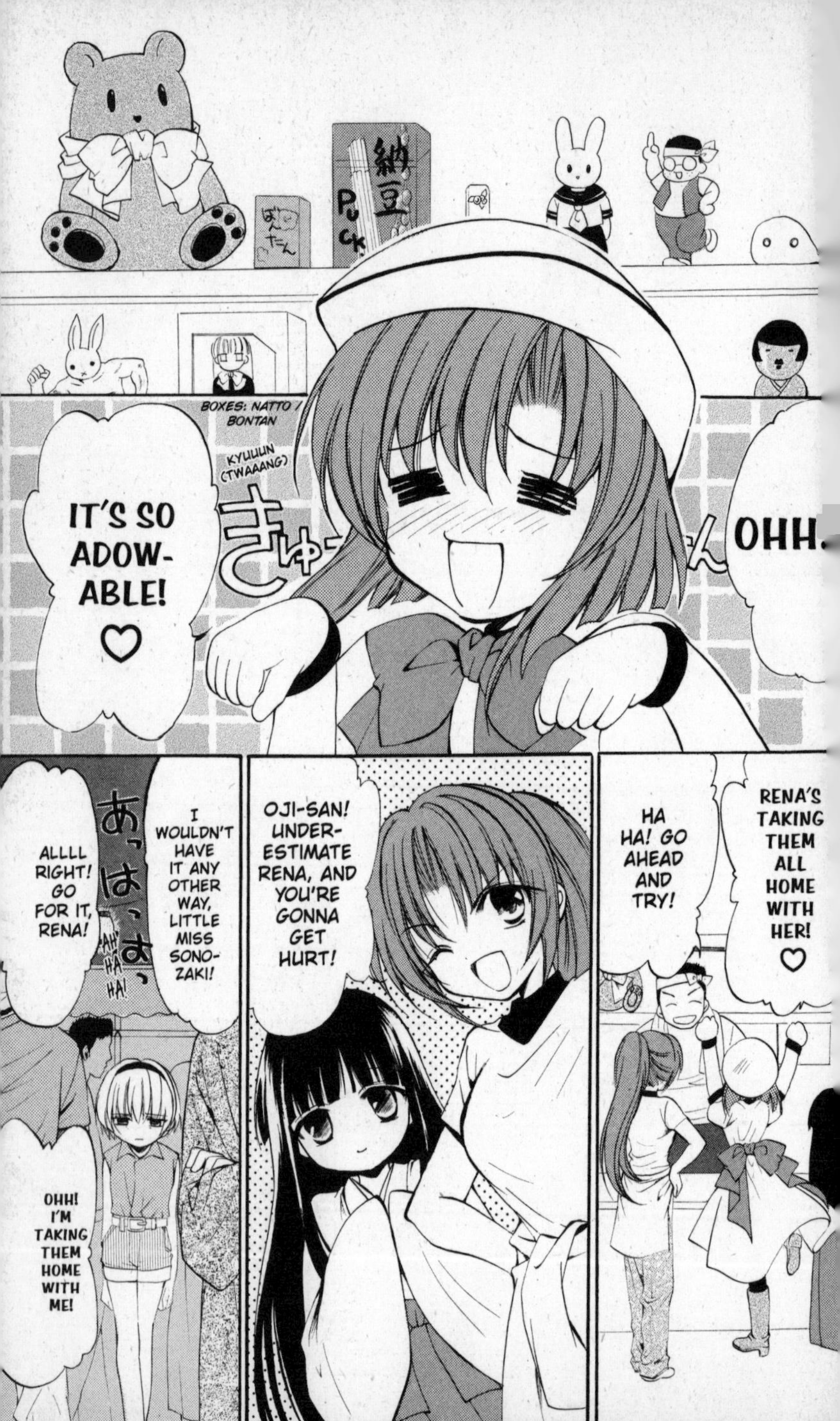
OHH.
BOXES: NATTO / BONTAN
KYUUUN (TWAAANG)
IT'S SO ADOW-ABLE! ♡
RENA'S TAKING THEM ALL HOME WITH HER! ♡
HA HA! GO AHEAD AND TRY!
OJI-SAN! UNDER-ESTIMATE RENA, AND YOU'RE GONNA GET HURT!
I WOULDN'T HAVE IT ANY OTHER WAY, LITTLE MISS SONO-ZAKI!
AH HA HA!
ALLLL RIGHT! GO FOR IT, RENA!
OHH! I'M TAKING THEM HOME WITH ME!

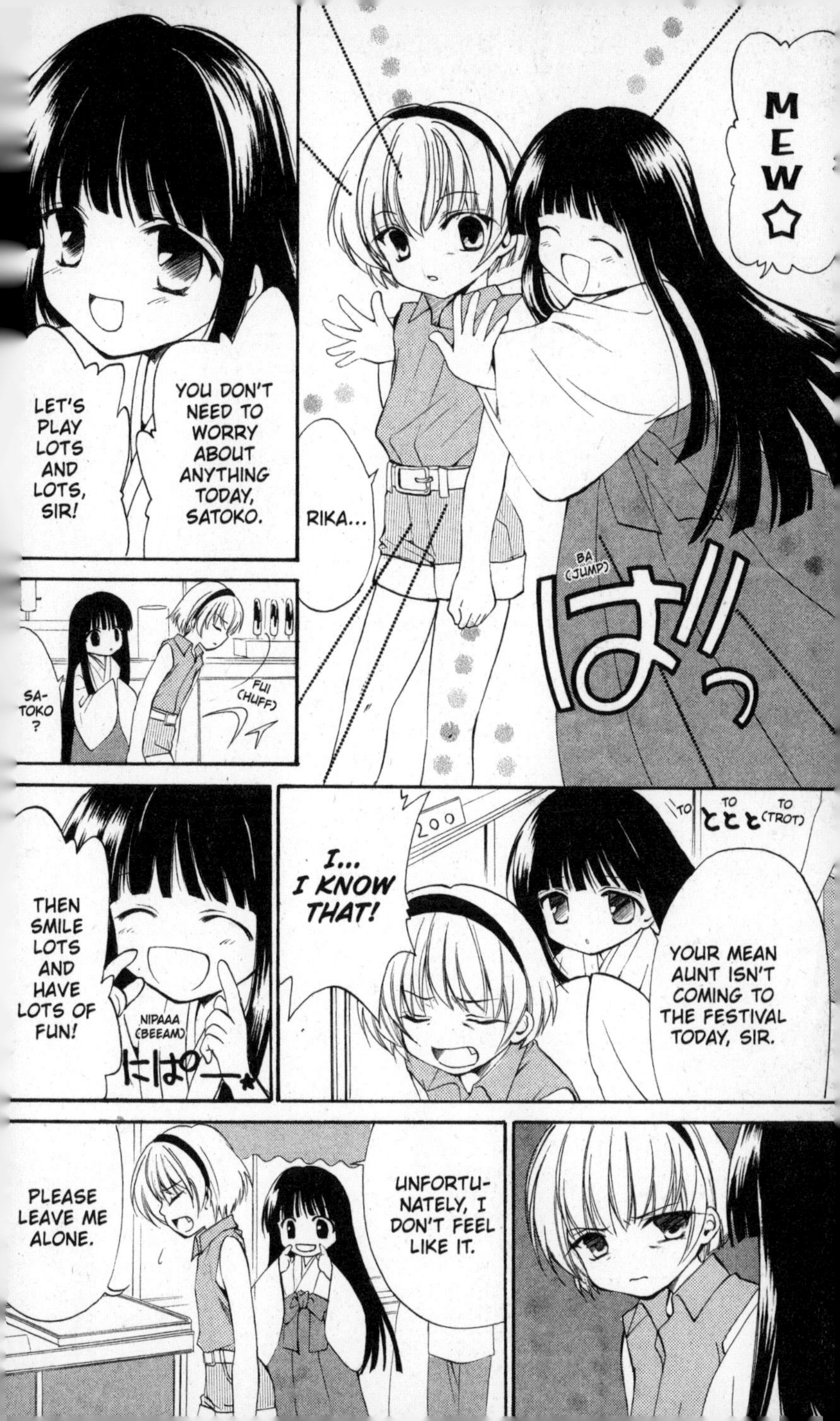
MEW☆
RIKA...
BA (JUMP)
はっ
YOU DON'T NEED TO WORRY ABOUT ANYTHING TODAY, SATOKO.
LET'S PLAY LOTS AND LOTS, SIR!
FUI (HUFF)
SA-TOKO?
TO TO TO (TROT)
ととと
200
YOUR MEAN AUNT ISN'T COMING TO THE FESTIVAL TODAY, SIR.
I... I KNOW THAT!
THEN SMILE LOTS AND HAVE LOTS OF FUN!
NIPAAA (BEEAM)
にぱー☆
UNFORTU-NATELY, I DON'T FEEL LIKE IT.
PLEASE LEAVE ME ALONE.

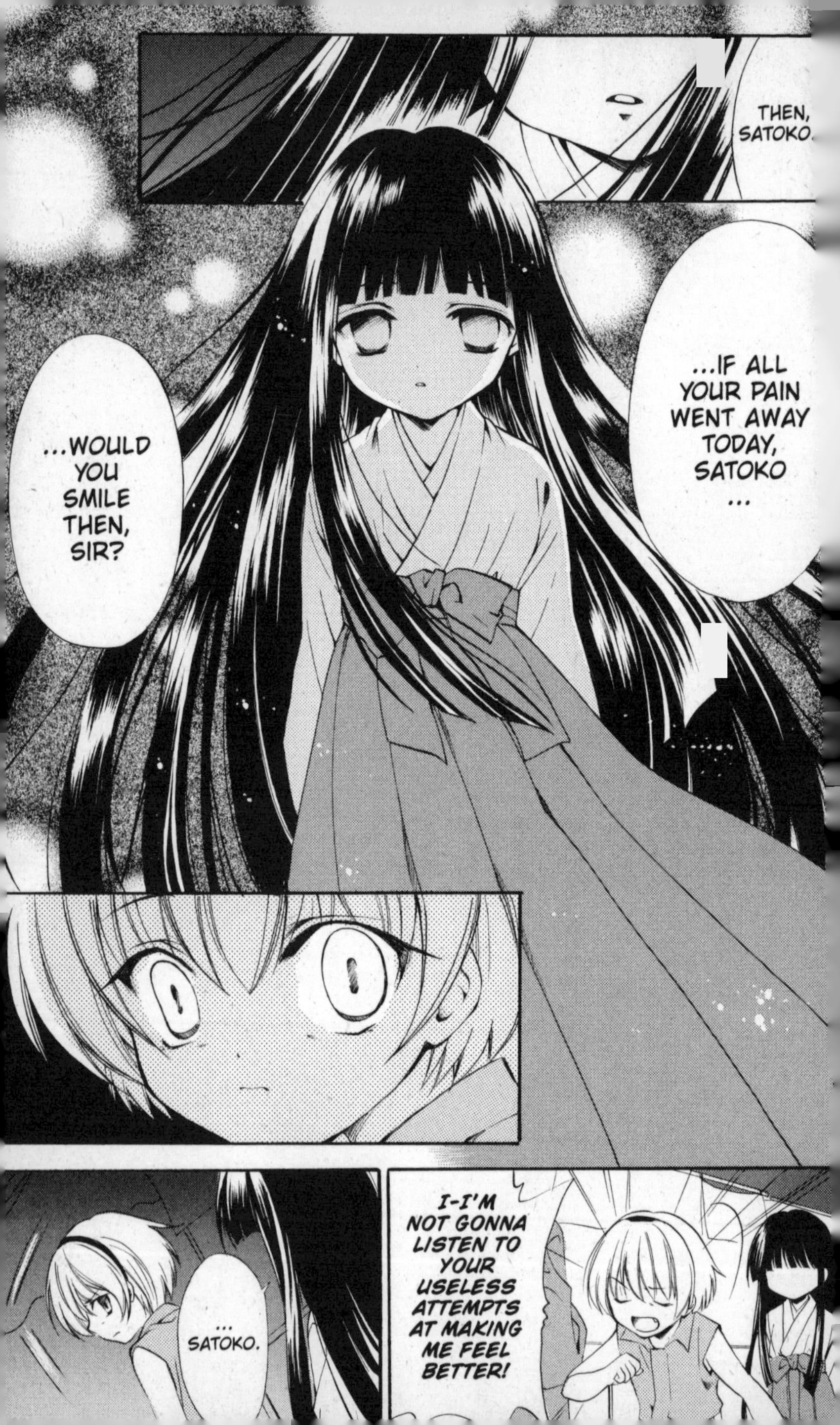
THEN, SATOKO.
...IF ALL YOUR PAIN WENT AWAY TODAY, SATOKO ...
...WOULD YOU SMILE THEN, SIR?
I-I'M NOT GONNA LISTEN TO YOUR USELESS ATTEMPTS AT MAKING ME FEEL BETTER!
... SATOKO.

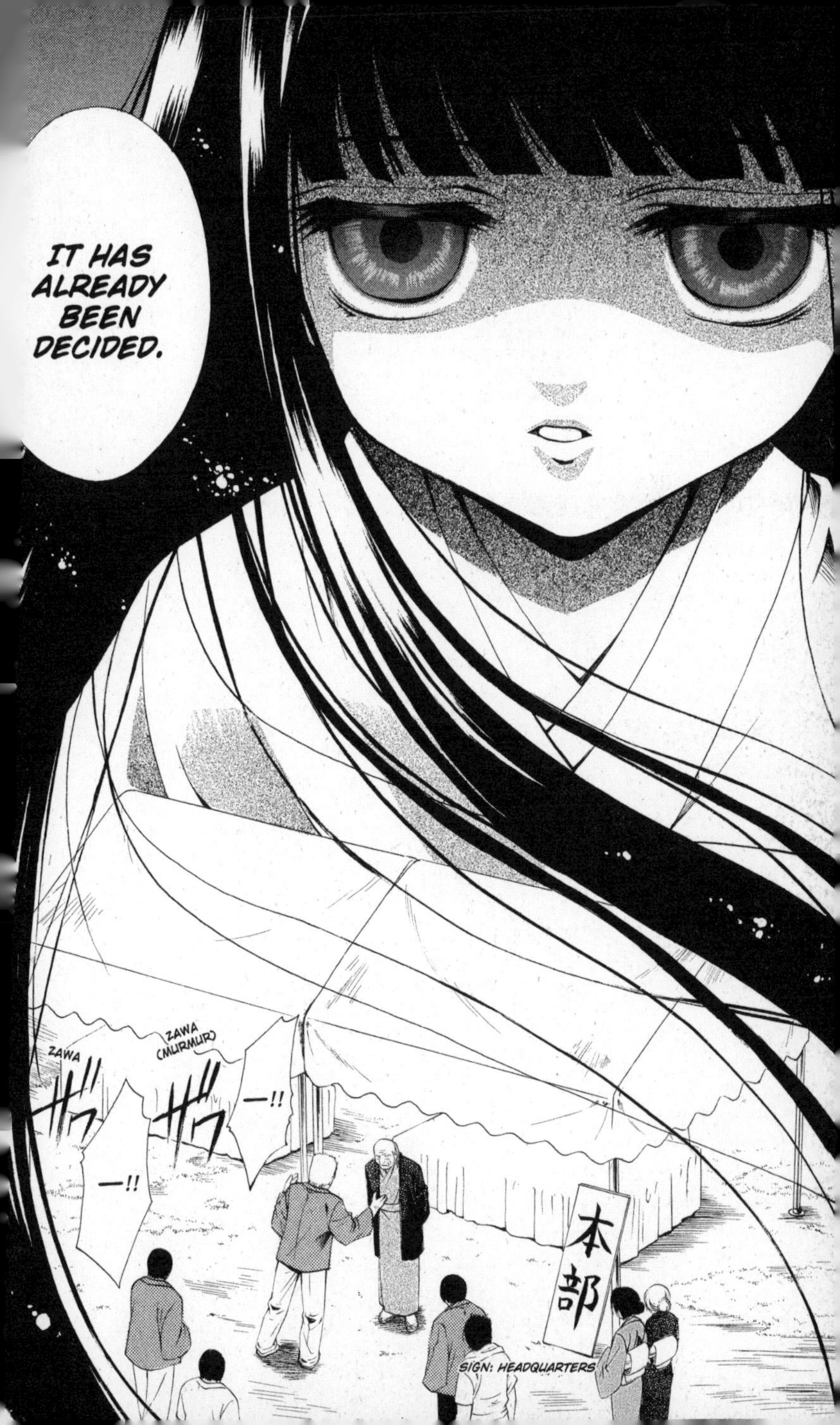
IT HAS ALREADY BEEN DECIDED.
ZAWA
ザワ
ザワ
ZAWA (MURMUR)
ー!!
ー!!
本部
SIGN: HEADQUARTERS

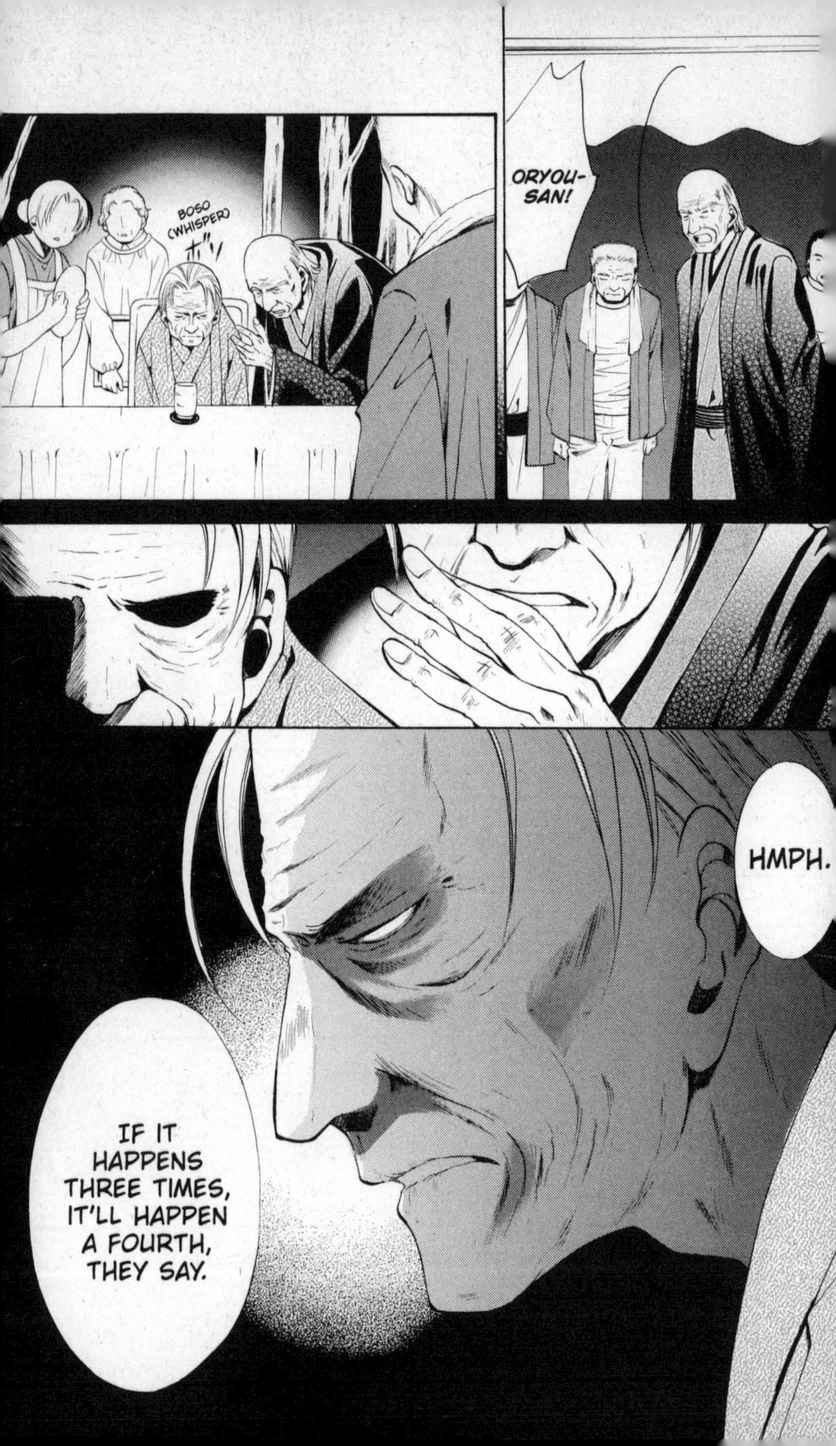
ORYOU-SAN!
BOSO (WHISPER)
ボソ
HMPH.
IF IT HAPPENS THREE TIMES, IT'LL HAPPEN A FOURTH, THEY SAY.

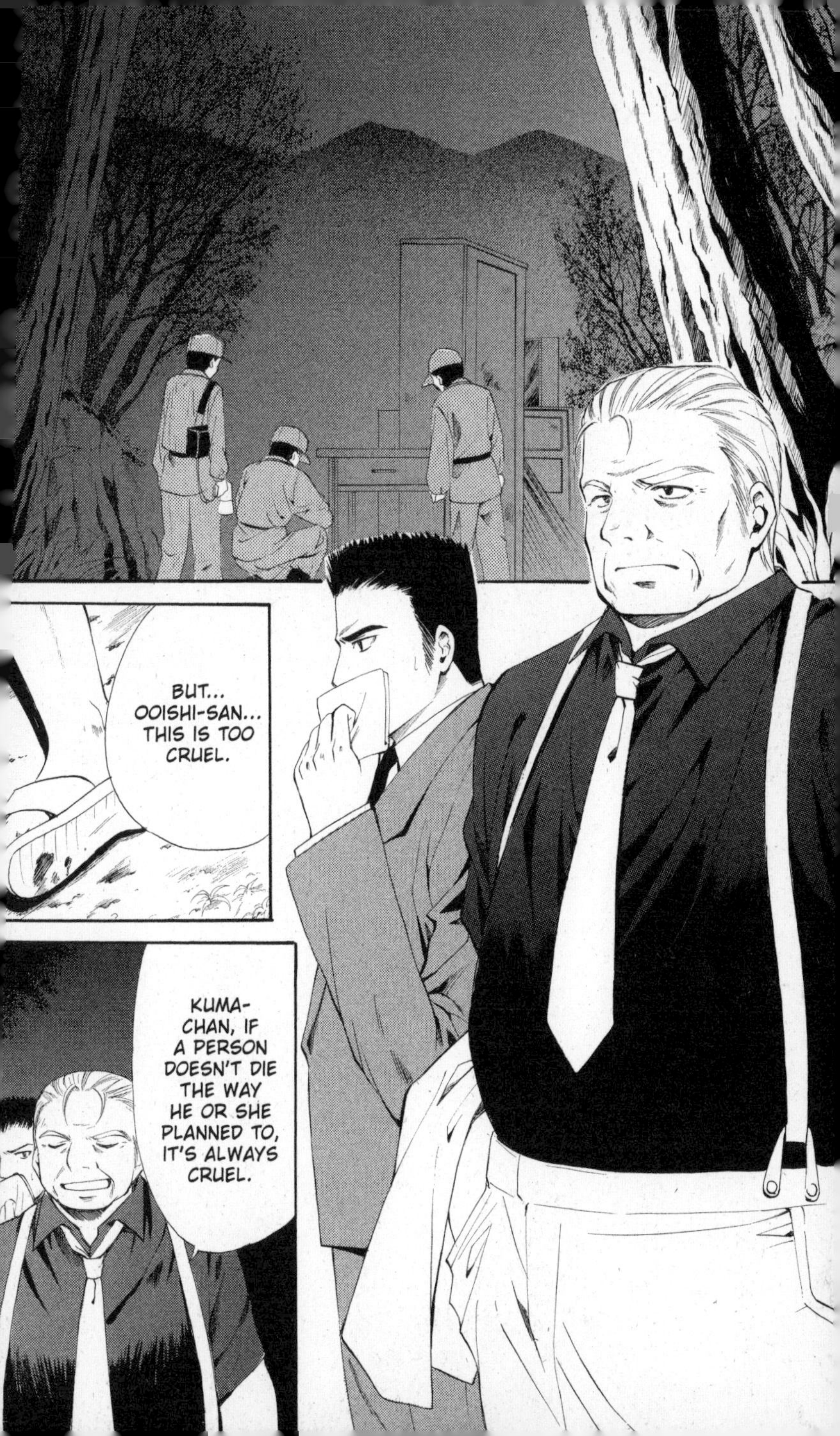
BUT... OOISHI-SAN... THIS IS TOO CRUEL.
KUMA-CHAN, IF A PERSON DOESN'T DIE THE WAY HE OR SHE PLANNED TO, IT'S ALWAYS CRUEL.

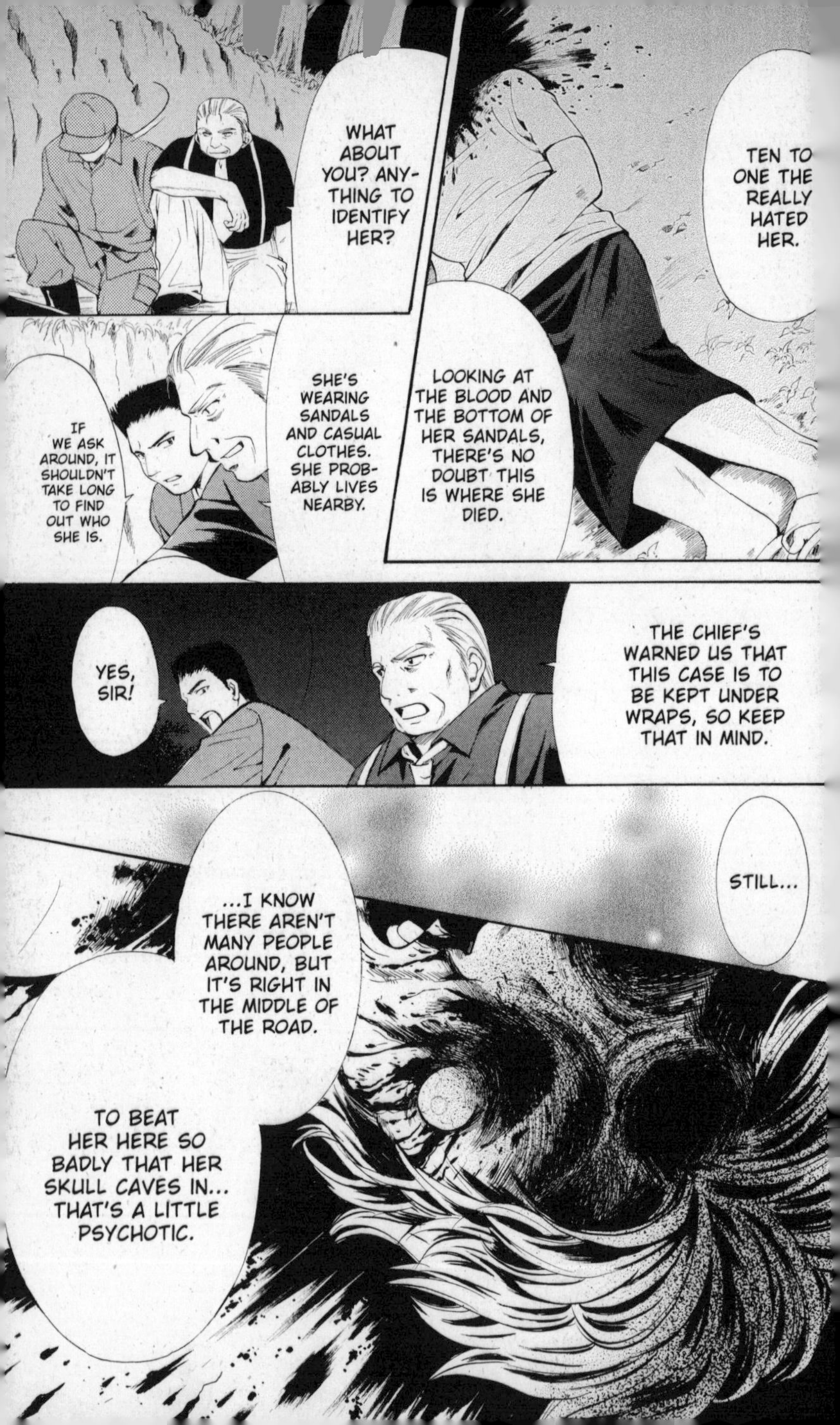

TEN TO ONE THE REALLY HATED HER.
LOOKING AT THE BLOOD AND THE BOTTOM OF HER SANDALS, THERE'S NO DOUBT THIS IS WHERE SHE DIED.
WHAT ABOUT YOU? ANY-THING TO IDENTIFY HER?
SHE'S WEARING SANDALS AND CASUAL CLOTHES. SHE PROB-ABLY LIVES NEARBY.
IF WE ASK AROUND, IT SHOULDN'T TAKE LONG TO FIND OUT WHO SHE IS.
THE CHIEF'S WARNED US THAT THIS CASE IS TO BE KEPT UNDER WRAPS, SO KEEP THAT IN MIND.
YES, SIR!
STILL...
...I KNOW THERE AREN'T MANY PEOPLE AROUND, BUT IT'S RIGHT IN THE MIDDLE OF THE ROAD.
TO BEAT HER HERE SO BADLY THAT HER SKULL CAVES IN... THAT'S A LITTLE PSYCHOTIC.

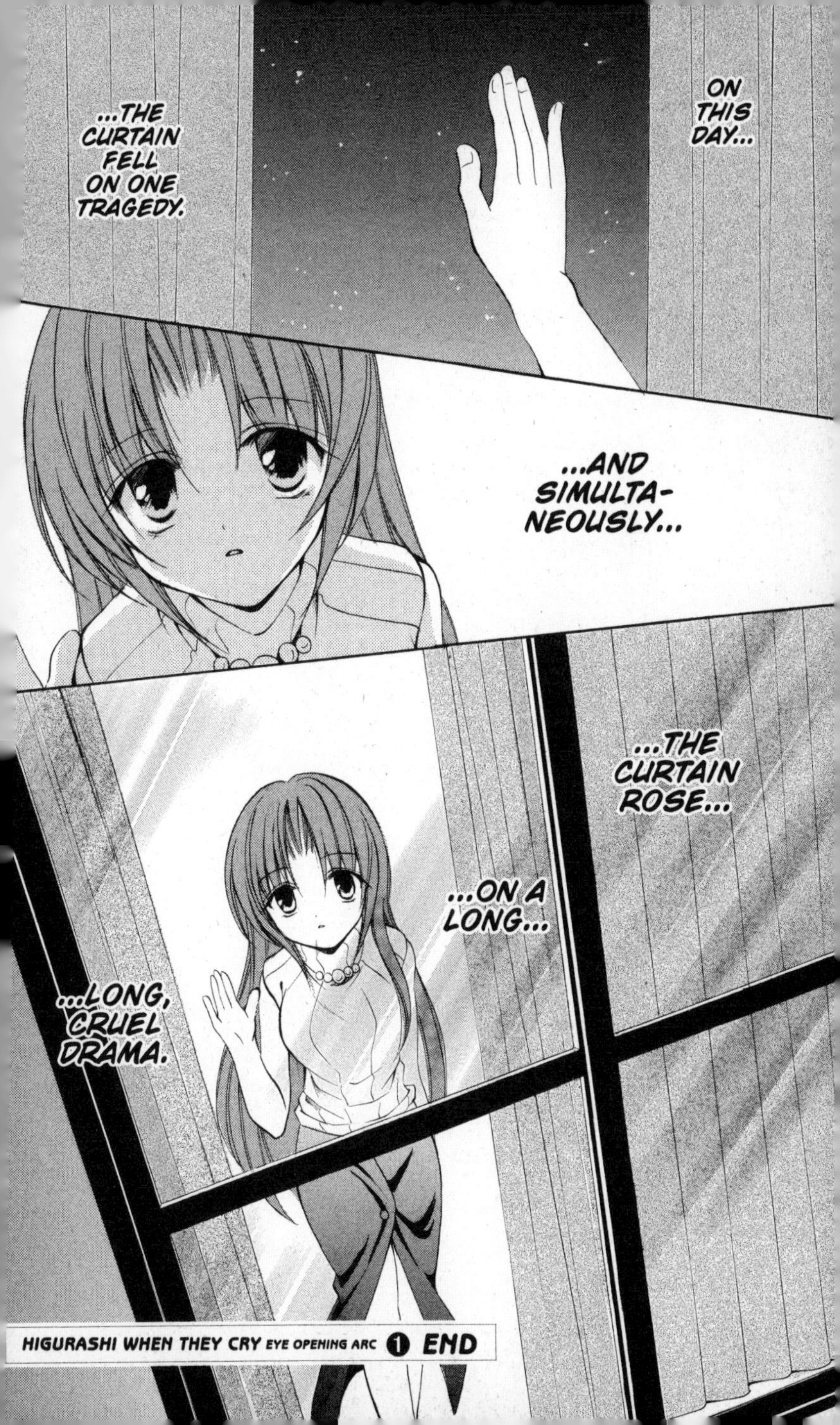
ON THIS DAY...
...THE CURTAIN FELL ON ONE TRAGEDY.
...AND SIMULTA-NEOUSLY...
...THE CURTAIN ROSE...
...ON A LONG...
...LONG, CRUEL DRAMA.
HIGURASHI WHEN THEY CRY EYE OPENING ARC 1 END

HIGURASHI WHEN THEY CRY

07th Expansion presents Welcome to Hinamizawa.
WHEN THEY CRY

ABOUT THE "EYE OPENING ARC," THAT WHICH EXPOSES "THE UNDERSIDE"

ORIGINAL STORY, SUPERVISOR: RYUKISHI07

BASED ON THE CONTENTS OF THE "EYE OPENING ARC," YOU COULD EASILY CALL IT THE "SHION ARC."

SHION SONOZAKI IS MION'S YOUNGER TWIN. AT THE SAME TIME, SHE IS THE OTHER SIDE OF MION— OR RATHER, SHE IS A CHARACTER POSITIONED ON THE OTHER SIDE OF THE STORY. SHE IS THE ONLY ONE OF ALL THE HEROINES WHO DOESN'T LIVE IN HINAMIZAWA; SHE'S NOT EVEN ALLOWED TO LIVE IN HINAMIZAWA. WHILE SHE IS THE SPITTING IMAGE OF MION, HER EXISTENCE IS THE EXACT OPPOSITE. SO I THINK YOU'LL UNDERSTAND THAT WRITING SHION'S STORY IS BASICALLY THE SAME AS DEPICTING THE UNDERSIDE OF THE WORLD OF "HIGURASHI WHEN THEY CRY."

THE "EYE OPENING ARC" STARTS IN 1982, ONE YEAR BEFORE THE MAIN STORY'S SETTING IN 1983. WHAT UNDERSIDE WILL THIS ARC EXPOSE? ...I SINCERELY HOPE YOU WILL CONTINUE TO ENJOY IT.

WHEN EVERYTHING IN THE "EYE OPENING ARC" IS REVEALED...MAYBE IT WILL SPECTACULARLY BETRAY SOME OF YOUR SPECULATION OR YOUR DEDUCTIVE REASONINGS OR YOUR EXPECTATIONS. BUT PLEASE, DON'T BE AFRAID OF THAT. BECAUSE THOSE OF YOU WHO EXPERIENCE THAT FEELING ARE THE ONES WHO WILL HAVE ENJOYED THE "EYE OPENING ARC" MOST OF ALL.

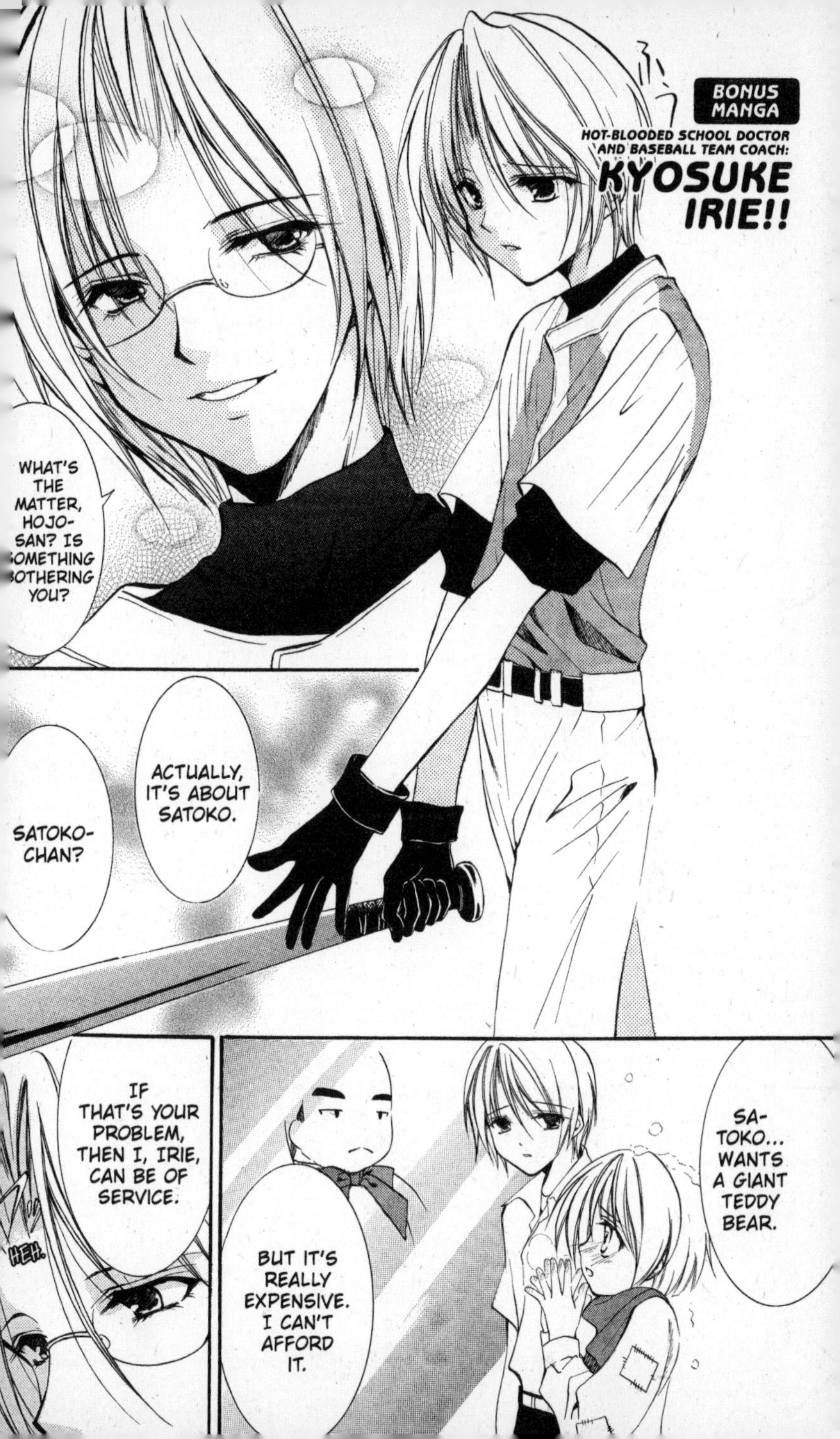
BONUS MANGA
HOT-BLOODED SCHOOL DOCTOR AND BASEBALL TEAM COACH:
KYOSUKE IRIE!!
WHAT'S THE MATTER, HOJO-SAN? IS SOMETHING BOTHERING YOU?
ACTUALLY, IT'S ABOUT SATOKO.
SATOKO-CHAN?
SA-TOKO... WANTS A GIANT TEDDY BEAR.
BUT IT'S REALLY EXPENSIVE. I CAN'T AFFORD IT.
IF THAT'S YOUR PROBLEM, THEN I, IRIE, CAN BE OF SERVICE.
HEH.

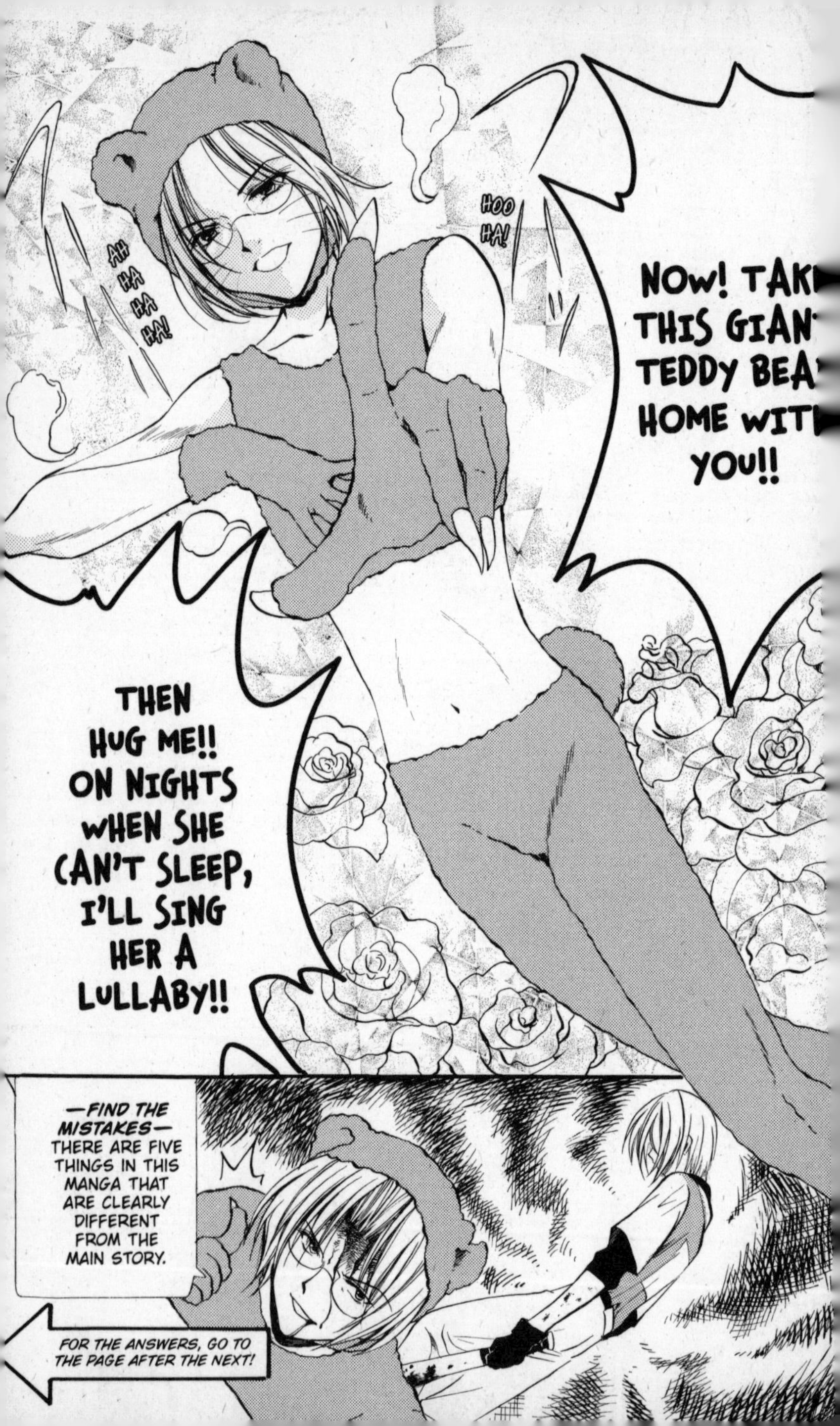
NOW! TAK THIS GIAN TEDDY BEA HOME WIT YOU!!
HOO HA!
AH HA HA HA HA!
THEN HUG ME!! ON NIGHTS WHEN SHE CAN'T SLEEP, I'LL SING HER A LULLABY!!
—FIND THE MISTAKES— THERE ARE FIVE THINGS IN THIS MANGA THAT ARE CLEARLY DIFFERENT FROM THE MAIN STORY.
FOR THE ANSWERS, GO TO THE PAGE AFTER THE NEXT!

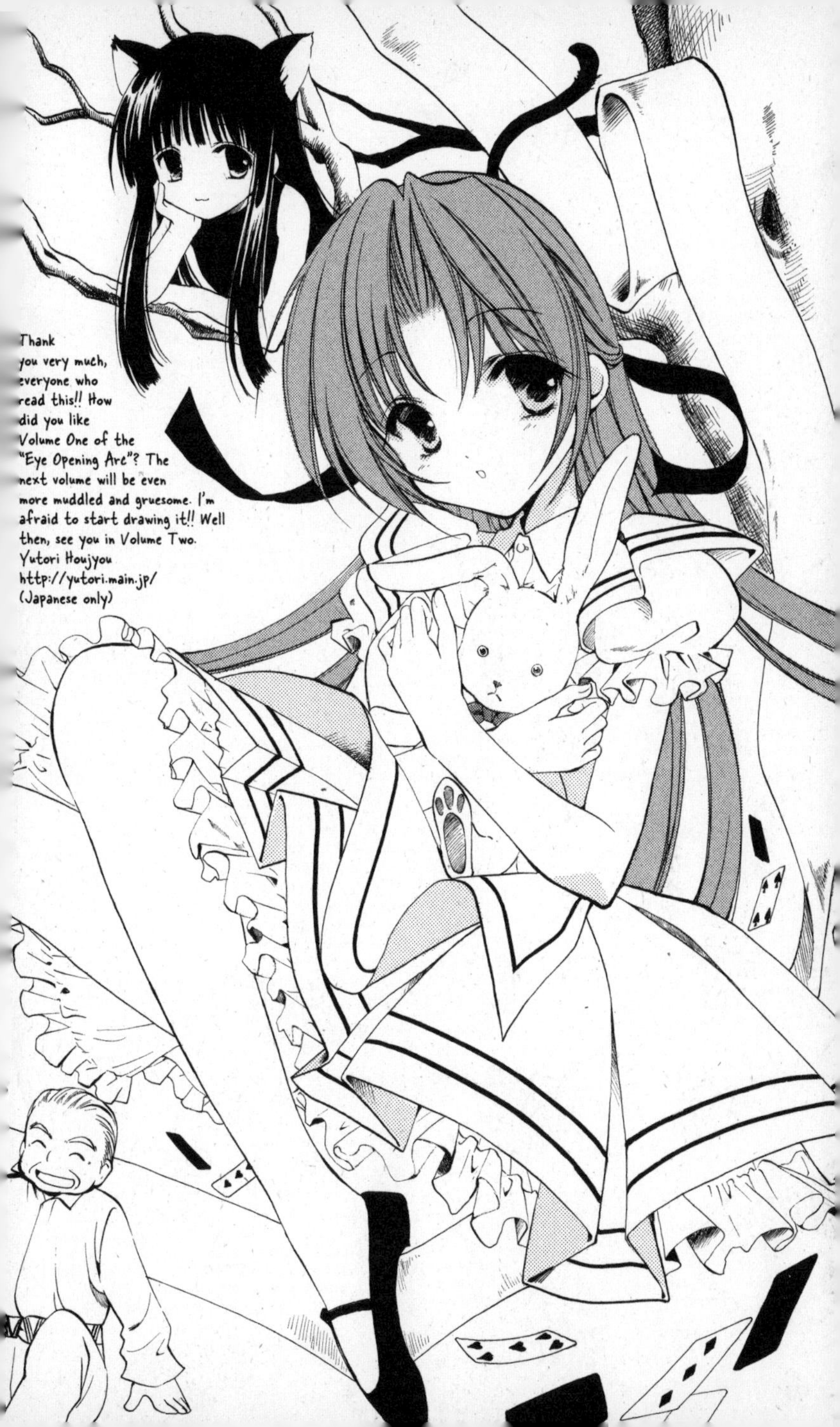
Thank you very much, everyone who read this!! How did you like Volume One of the "Eye Opening Arc"? The next volume will be even more muddled and gruesome. I'm afraid to start drawing it!! Well then, see you in Volume Two.
Yutori Houjyou
http://yutori.main.jp/
(Japanese only)

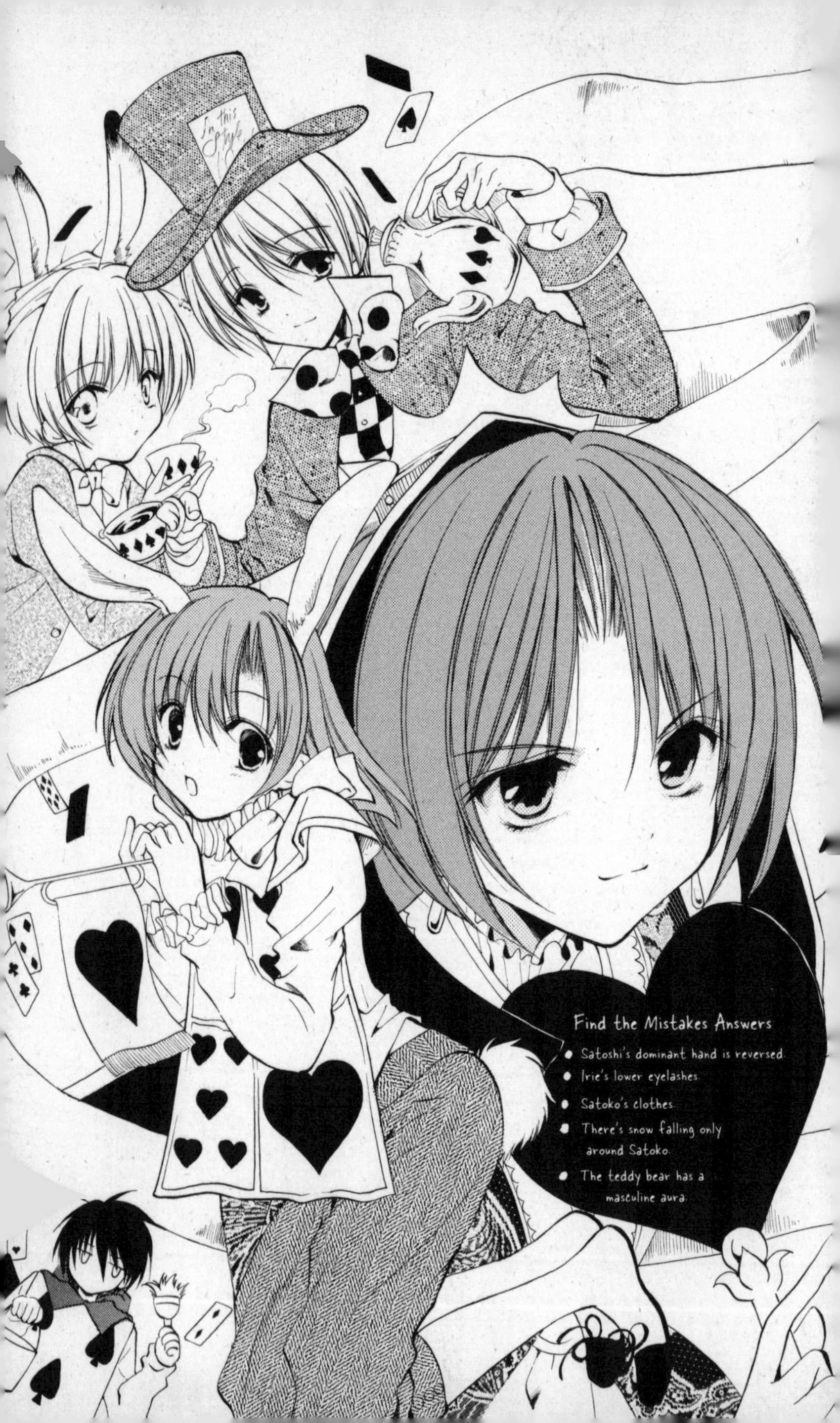
In this Style
Find the Mistakes Answers
Satoshi's dominant hand is reversed.
Irie's lower eyelashes.
Satoko's clothes.
There's snow falling only around Satoko.
The teddy bear has a masculine aura.

NEXT VOLUME, THE

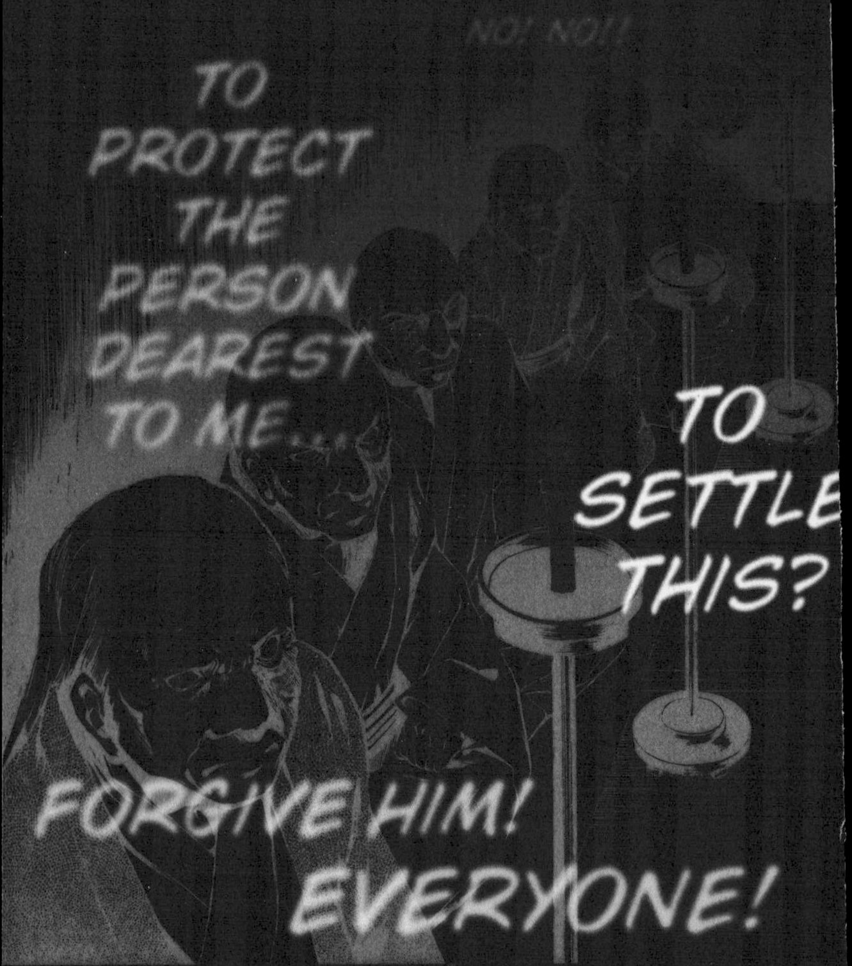
NO! NO!!
TO SETTLE THIS?
TO PROTECT THE PERSON DEAREST TO ME...
FORGIVE HIM! EVERYONE!

VOLUME TWO GOES ON SALE

HIGURASHI
WHEN THEY CRY
EYE OPENING ARC ①

RYUKISHI07
YUTORI HOUJYOU

Translation: Alethea Nibley and Athena Nibley

Lettering: AndWorld Design

Higurashi WHEN THEY CRY Eye Opening Arc, Vol. 1 © RYUKISHI07 / 07th Expansion © 2007 Yutori Houjyou / SQUARE ENIX CO., LTD. All rights reserved. First published in Japan in 2007 by SQUARE ENIX CO., LTD. English translation rights arranged with SQUARE ENIX CO., LTD. and Hachette Book Group through Tuttle-Mori Agency, Inc. Translation © 2011 by SQUARE ENIX CO., LTD.

Yen Press
Hachette Book Group
237 Park Avenue, New York, NY 10017

www.HachetteBookGroup.com
www.YenPress.com

Yen Press is an imprint of Hachette Book Group, Inc. The Yen Press name and logo are trademarks of Hachette Book Group, Inc.

First Yen Press Edition: February 2011

ISBN: 978-0-316-12376-1

10 9 8 7 6 5 4 3 2 1

BVG

Printed in the United States of America

D0920731